In gods we trust

In Gods We Trust

In Gods We Trust

New Patterns of Religious Pluralism in America

Edited by

Thomas Robbins and Dick Anthony

Transaction Books
New Brunswick (U.S.A.) and London (U.K.)

Copyright © 1981 by Transaction, Inc.
New Brunswick, New Jersey 08903

Second printing 1982

Library of Congress Catalog Number: 79-66441
ISBN: 0-87855-746-6
Printed in the United States of America

Library of Congress Cataloging in Publication Data

Main entry under title:

In gods we trust.

Consists chiefly of articles from Society magazine,
v. 15, May-June 1978.
Includes bibliography.
CONTENTS: Robbins, T. and Anthony, D. Contemporary religious patterns. — Bellah, R. Religion and legitimation in the American Republic. — Glock, C. and Piazza, T. Exploring reality structures. — [etc.]
1. United States — Religion — 1945-　 — Addresses, essays, lectures. 2. Cults — United States — Addresses, essays, lectures. I. Robbins, Thomas, 1943-
II. Anthony, Dick, 1939-　　III. Society.
BL2530.U6I48　　　301.5'8　　　79-66441
ISBN 0-87855-746-6

This book is dedicated to
Kitty Davy
and
Elly Robbins

Contents

1

DISENCHANTMENT AND RENEWAL IN MAINLINE TRADITIONS

"CIVIL RELIGION SECTS," ORIENTAL MYSTICISM AND THERAPY GROUPS

THE BRAINWASHING EXPLANATION

NEW RELIGIONS AND THE DECLINE OF COMMUNITY

List of Tables and Figures

Table

Figure

ACKNOWLEDGMENTS

The following papers appeared originally in *Society* 15, 4 (May/June 1978) —
"Religion and Legitimation in the American Republic," by Robert Bellah; "Freedom,
Love, and Community: An Outline of A Theory," by George A. Hillery, Jr.; "Con-
structing Orthodoxy," by Samuel C. Heilman; "Alienation and Apostasy," by Wade
Clark Roof; "Conversion to Fundamentalism," by James T. Richardson, Mary White
Stewart, and Robert B. Simmonds; "Religious Musical Chairs," by Andrew M.
Greeley; "Exploring Reality Structures," by Charles Y. Glock and Thomas Piazza;
"Social Consciousness and the Human Potential Movement," by Donald Stone; "Kids
in Cults," by Irvin Doress and Jack Nusan Porter; "Witches, Moonies, and Accusations
of Evil," by Anson D. Shupe, Jr. and David G. Bromley; and "New Religions,
Families, and Brainwashing," by Dick Anthony and Thomas Robbins. Some of these
papers were published originally in *Society* in an abridged form or without tables,
diagrams, and the bibliographic references that appear in the present volume.

"A Sociological Perspective on the New Religions," by Benton Johnson, was
prepared as a paper for presentation at the "Symposium on Religious Minorities in a
Secular Society" at the annual meeting of the American Association for the Advancement of Science, Denver, Colorado, February 22, 1977.

"Conversion to Fundamentalism," by James T. Richardson, Mary White Stewart,
and Robert B. Simmonds, is excerpted from *Organized Miracles: A Study of a
Contemporary, Youth, Communal, Fundamentalist Organization*, by James T.
Richardson, Mary White Stewart, and Robert B. Simmonds (Transaction Books, 1979).

"The Politics of New Cults: Non-Prophetic Observations on Science, Sin and
Scholarship," by Irving Louis Horowitz appeared originally in *Soundings* LXII, 2
(Summer 1979); an abridged version was published also in *The Nation* 228, 13, April 1,
1979.

"The Apocalypse at Jonestown," by John R. Hall, originally appeared in *Society* 16,
6 (September/October 1979).

"Getting Straight with Meher Baba" was first published in *The Journal for the
Scientific Study of Religion* 11, 2 (June 1972).

"Integrating the 'Moonie' Experience," by Trudy Solomon, was researched through
funding from an award from The Chancellor's Patent Fund of the University of
California at Berkeley.

"Freedom, Love, and Community: An Outline of a Theory," by George A. Hillery,
Jr., was first presented as a lecture at King College, Bristol, Tennessee, on February 24,
1976. A revised version will appear in *Sociology and Christian Believing*, forthcoming.

The editors wish to thank Mary Samokar for her indispensable help in compiling and
typing the bibliography and in preparing the tables and figures. We are grateful also to
our editor, Robert Chadwick, for his painstaking efforts on this book.

In Gods We Trust

INTRODUCTION

Culture Crisis and Contemporary Religion

Dick Anthony and Thomas Robbins

Religious Ferment and the Decline
of American Civil Religion

The period from 1964 through the present has been characterized by normative flux and institutional breakdown in American society. Visible indicators of this crisis include rising crime rates, falling rates of voter participation, rising indices of family disorganization, and various survey results revealing a loss of confidence in American political and economic institutions. More overt manifestations of dissidence include the campus/ghetto eruptions of the late 1960s and early 1970s and the "taxpayers' revolt" of the late 1970s. A final indicator of the normative ambiguity and dissensus of the present period is the remarkable spiritual ferment of the past 15 years. This development includes a luxuriant growth of unconventional "new religions" and quasi-religious psychotherapies, a powerful resurgence of "conservative" evangelical Christianity and neoorthodox Judaism, and dissensions and defections within Roman Catholicism and the major "liberal" denominations of Protestantism.

A linkage between the contemporary religious ferment and a broader crisis of values in American culture has been widely noted. In particular, several writers have related the current upsurge of unconventional spiritual movements to discontinuities in American "civil religion." American civil religion, according to Robert Bellah and others, involves a complex of shared religiopolitical meanings that articulate a sense of common national purpose and that rationalize the needs and purposes of the broader community.[1] However, as one sociologist has noted, in the aftermath of the Vietnam War and the Watergate episode, "It is now less possible to seek transcendence through the state."[2] Or, as Bellah argues in *The Broken Covenant*: "Today the American civil religion is an empty and broken shell."[3] In Bellah's view, the present spiritual ferment attempts a "birth of new American myths" as a reponse to the decay of civil religion.[4] Currently innovative religious groups can be viewed as evolving functional alternatives to a civil-religious tradition that is perceived increasingly as either invalid or irrelevant.

In his important essay in the present volume on "Religion and Legitimation in the American Republic," Professor Bellah reformulates his controversial civil-religion concept. He has now restricted his notion to formal symbols and statements of nationalist theism—for example, "In God We Trust." Beyond the civil religion, however, is American *public theology* that includes American "civil millenialism" and messianic conceptions of America as "God's new Israel." Different persons and groups have championed differing versions of American public theology. "Every movement to make America more fully realize its professed values has grown out of some form of public theology, from the abolitionists to the social gospel and the early socialist party, to the civil rights movement under Martin Luther King. . . . But so has every expansionist war and every form of oppression of racial minorities and immigrant groups." Contemporary new religions and resurgent traditionalist perspectives can also be viewed as putative public theologies attempting to formulate new approaches to civil religion and the meaning of America.

Particularly striking in Bellah's essay is his discussion of the role of church religion in American political culture. He implies therein that the nation has had an ominous potential for normative breakdown from the beginning because of the "uneasy compromise" between republicanism and a liberal regime embodied by the Constitution. According to Bellah, American political experience has been grounded in a fundamental ambiguity concerning the role of the state in the consolidation of public morality. The founding fathers were simultaneously attracted to two incompatible ideals: the ideal of the *virtuous republic* in which the state actively regulates and molds the moral character of the citizenry; and the ideal of the *liberal constitutional state* that restricts itself to maintaining a minimal framework of public order. The liberal constitutional state, unlike the virtuous republic, would encourage citizens to pursue their own interests without conscious attention to civic priorities. Its central governing assumption would be that each citizen's pursuit of private gain would somehow be harmonized by the "invisible hand" to produce the good society.

Bellah argues that the inherent conflict between the ideal of the virtuous republic and that of the liberal state was evaded through an assumption that *the churches would effectively maintain a disciplined moral consensus*. Given such a normative matrix, the formal constitutional structure could safely be patterned in the unrestrictive terms of laissez faire liberalism. We have in effect sought to have our cake and eat it too, and, therefore, "We artfully used religion as a way of evading the incompatibilities in our political life." Yet this evasion could only remain viable so long as the churches remained powerful social forces upholding moral solidarity. But, "Today when religion, more even than our other institutions, is uncertain about itself, the evasion is no longer tenable. Our institutionalized religious bodies," notes Bellah, "seem less and less capable of providing us with a national sense of ethical purpose." Indeed, "The balance of American religious life is slipping away from those denominations that have a historic concern for the common good, toward religious groups so privatistic and self-centered that they begin to approximate the consumer cafeteria model. . . ."

According to Benton Johnson, in his essay in this volume, long-range social trends underlie the decline of civil religion and the rise in popularity of more privatistic groups. From Johnson's perspective, Vietnam and Watergate have merely been local causes that have exacerbated an underlying long-range "contradiction" between traditional civil-religious attitudes and contemporary managerial capitalism.

Johnson argues that the essence of American civil religion has been its stress upon social altruism in work and government. Such an emphasis long compensated for the competitive individualism that is also an American tendency. By investing economic and political activity with altruistic meaning, civil religion softened the competitive rigor of the marketplace, and provided a synthesis of emotion and purpose that served as a motivational matrix for entrepreneurial capitalism.

For Johnson, then, civil religion involves a complex of widely shared religious motifs that "have linked together the private and public spheres." However, such a synthesis was possible only when the economic life of the nation was conducted largely in small family-owned businesses. In the past 50 years entrepreneurial capitalism has evolved into managerial capitalism, and most Americans now work in large impersonal corporations. Thus, the public sector is now governed by an unrestricted interplay of impersonal economic forces that are impervious to altruistic individual motives. Success in the crassest materialistic sense has become the only motive for involvement in the public sector that has widespread plausibility; softer and more generous feelings can legitimately be expressed only in private moments.

The increasing structural differentiation of American society has produced an increasing disjunction between public and private sectors of social interaction. Traditional civil religion has become increasingly implausible, and, consequently, "individual personality has become increasingly differentiated from the social system in which it participates."

The Decline of Civil Religion and the Shift in Values

According to Bellah, the decline of consensual civil religiosity and the resultant national identity crisis ultimately impinge upon local institutions that are responsible for conveying moral ideologies. Dr. Bellah believes that the "soft structures" that deal with human motivation—such as the churches, the schools, and the family—have been undermined more than other institutions in our recent upheavals. They have been particularly weakened with regard to "their capacity to transmit patterns of conscience and ethical values."

Bellah's views are borne out by the analysis prepared for this volume by Wade Clark Roof, who summarized survey data on religious defection in the early and middle 1970s. According to Roof, the figures for defection from established churches are of "staggering proportions." They suggest that the recent upsurge of unconventional new religions is merely "a small part of a larger climate of unrest taking place in the religious realm," which involves vast numbers of Americans dropping out of conventional churches and synagogues and "breaking with many of their institutional commitments."

Roof's findings indicate that defectors from established faiths tend to be young, well-educated, and middle-class. They are likely to lack confidence in dominant political, economic, and communications structures; and they are much more likely than nondefectors to be committed to the permissive "new morality" and to have liberal attitudes on such issues as homosexuality and abortion. Roof argues that the large defections from established churches are clearly related to the diffusion of values formerly encapsulated as "hippie," "radical," or "countercultural." Moreover, he points out, Protestant and Catholic faiths are "internally split over such issues as homosexuality, abortion, and women's ordination." The religious overtones of recent crusades against abortion and homosexuality "reveal the depths of conservative reaction and the close affinity to religious symbols and values."

Extrapolating from Roof's analysis, it can be argued that the Catholic church and the liberal Protestant denominations are caught between the spread of permissive countercultural morality on the one hand and the strident evangelical revival on the other.[5] If the churches opt for evangelical absolutism, they will continue to lose members among the well-educated and affluent; but if they embrace the new morality, they are in effect embracing a modern secular ethos that is hostile to theism. In the latter case they are, in a sense, repudiating their own raison d'être. The dilemma appears to be insoluble and illustrates the degree to which the churches no longer uphold a moral consensus and embody a national convenant.

Like Roof, Andrew M. Greeley is also concerned with patterns of "disidentification" from established churches. However, Greeley's analysis partly conflicts with Roof's. Father Greeley criticizes the secularization model as an explanation for apostasy. According to the secularization model, the decline of religion is a continuous process linked with modernization. Thus, better educated, more sophisticated, and more cosmopolitan persons will be more likely to drop traditional religious affiliations. In general, Greeley finds that "exogamy" (marriage outside the faith) is a better predictor of disidentification from one's traditional affiliation than variables plausibly associated with secularization. He finds that the majority of ex-Catholics, for example, have disidentified in their association with marriages to Protestants whose affiliation they have accepted. "They are happily married, devoutly practicing, believing members of Protestant denominations." Moreover, although persons under 30 are more likely to disidentify than older respondents: "When one holds religious intermarriage constant, all statistically significant differences among age groups disappear." Thus, Greeley maintains, there appears to be no trend towards irreligion as an aspect of the modernization process.

Interestingly, although Roof and Greeley are both using data from the National Opinion Research Center's general surveys, they are working with different operational definitions for religious disaffiliation. For Roof, "defectors from the American religious establishment" are defined as persons who have not only departed from an original institutional religious identification, but who also identify their present religious affiliation as "none." For Greeley, however, religious "disidentifiers" are merely persons who abandon their initial affiliation usually for the purpose of embracing another faith. Thus, Roof's contention that apostasy, in the clearcut sense in which he defines it, is caused by acculturation in modernized values is not really contradicted by Greeley's analysis.

The article by Charles Y. Glock and Thomas Piazza on "Exploring Reality Structures" also argues that a fundamental shift of values is taking place in American culture. The authors have utilized survey data to tap into the assumptions people make regarding the locus of causation for social outcomes. There are some indications that supernaturalistic or *theistic* orientations — which see God as the causal agent directly controlling events — and *individualistic* orientations — which see individual moral qualities and will power as imposing themselves on events — are waning. Such orientations appeal particularly to older persons, relatively uneducated people, and individuals from Catholic and conservative Protestant backgrounds. They are also correlated with conservative sociopolitical attitudes. On the other hand, *environmentalist* orientations — which see impersonal social forces as controlling events — and *conspiratorial* orientations — which see social relations being manipulated behind the scenes by sinister elites — appeal to younger people, the college educated, and to individuals who are liberal Protestants, atheists, agnostics, or religiously noncommitted. The latter orientations appear to be related to liberal and radical sociopolitical attitudes. Glock and Piazza suggest that "The distribution of different modes of reality structuring is changing in American society," and that "modes more supportive of traditional social arrangements are being replaced by the modes in greater opposition to social arrangements."[6]

Glock and Piazza's findings are compatible with Roof's and with the secularization model criticized by Greeley. There are also interesting convergences with Robert Bellah's analysis. The idea of a "virtuous republic," which has sources in classical antiquity and in Enlightenment thought, is, nevertheless, associated in American traditions with the puritan notion of a *covenant* and with biblical theistic symbolism. The laissez faire liberal constitutionalist idea clearly presupposes some assumptions about individual autonomy and mastery. The decline of individualistic and theistic modes of reality-structuring has undermined laissez faire liberal constitutionalism as well as the older notion of a covenant embodied in a godly republic. The decay of traditional assumptions about social causality is also undermining public theology as a vital force around which persons and groups can form movements and on which personal identities can be grounded. The transformation of values in contemporary American culture thus feeds into the civil religion crisis, which we view as the key factor underlying the current spiritual ferment and upsurge of nontraditional religiosity.

Mainstream Religious Responses to Structural Differentiation

As we mentioned earlier, Benton Johnson believes that the decline of civil religion has been caused by the extreme differentiation of public from private spheres under managerial capitalism. Johnson criticizes the views of Richard Fenn and other end-of-ideology theorists who imply that this degree of structural differentiation can be tolerated without vast difficulties.[7] Fenn has argued that under managerial capitalism, the frustration resulting from personal lack of autonomy in the public sphere will be compensated for by the expansion of opportunities for expressive gratification in private life. The decline of the Protestant ethic form of American civil religion *has* been accompanied by the loosening of cultural controls upon libidinal expression and upon other consumption activities as well. As Johnson puts it: "With the decline of family-based enterprise, there has been a growing tendency to question, and in some cases, abandon, moral norms associated with strong family ties." Rather than increasing the gratification available in the private sector, however, such desublimation has made private satisfactions more precarious: ". . . . people have tended to make demands on others for higher levels of the gratifications traditionally associated with family life and interfamily relations," and are thus more easily dissatisfied with the quality of affectivity actually available. The insulation and autonomy of nonbureaucratic expressive "enclaves" becomes problematic as competitive, achievement-oriented, and commercial values overflow into the "private" realm. "The anarchy of work is reflected in intimate relationships. The logic of the workplace invades the bedroom."

Johnson here rehearses the narcissistic jeremiads of such commenators on contemporary culture as Christopher Lasch and Richard Sennett.[8] They argue that the optimal development of normal personality requires a good deal of deferral of gratification out of a commitment to the needs of others. Too casual an indulgence in expressive impulses that are not orchestrated by reference to an underlying philosophy or religious attitude results in a chronic felt lack of meaning — or, in modern psychoanalytic terms, in narcissitic character disorder. The increasing differentiation of public and private spheres has led not only to a decline in the quality of public life, but also to a change in the nature of private sorrow. The separation of the realm of feeling from the realm of discipline and purpose has impoverished both. As Richard Sennett has argued, under managerial capitalism narcissim has become the common cold of private life, as alienation has of the public worlds of work and government.

In Johnson's view, this situation has been developing for some time, and religious change for several generations has reflected strategies for coping with it. Church religion during this period has divided into two broad tendencies, with conservatives being most concerned with ills of the private sector and liberal churches with those of the public. Conservative churches have made fewer concessions to the cognitive and moral relativities characteristic of modern culture. Consequently, they have given greater support to patterns of sublimation supportive of family life, and narcissism is less of a problem for them.

Liberal churches, on the other hand, have attempted to remain relevant to developing mainstream culture, and they have maintained the traditional civil-religious emphasis upon the reform of public life. However, in order to maintain cultural relevance, they have had to dilute supernaturalistic elements and the emphasis upon conversion that are also characteristic of traditional civil religion. Consequently, they lack resources for mobilizing and organizing the psychic resources of individuals. Thus, members of liberal denominations tend to have a less secure theological and motivational basis for making commitments in the private realm. In this respect, liberals are more prone to the existential nausea that Lasch, Sennett, and others identify as an element of the narcissistic tenor of modern culture. As a result, liberal churches are declining, as their members abandon them for new therapies and mystical religions that specialize in "the therapeutic reconstruction of the self." Conservative churches, on the other hand, are growing.

It seems likely that conservative churches are growing at least partly because they offer doctrinal support for familial and communal bonds.[9] In so doing they repudiate an expressive antinomianism that has proved problematic for many people. Such antinomian trends reached an apogee in the counterculture of the late 1960s. The Jesus movement probably became the largest of the so-called new religions because it offered a morally conservative refuge from the excesses of the youth culture's emphasis upon untrammeled self-expression. As Johnson emphasizes: "The Jesus Movement is a 'new religion' only in an equivocal sense. Its 'protest' and its countercultural themes are more stylistic than real. It is not a symptom of the erosion of tradition, but a token of the efforts to restore it."

The paper by Richardson, Stewart, and Simmonds in this volume, which is concerned with testing interactionist models of religious conversion, supports this interpretation of the growth of the Jesus movement. According to their analysis, an important element in conversion to youth culture Christianity is the convert's eventual perception that the religious movement "may furnish a way to resolve perceived difficulties." Such a realization is generally subsequent to the convert's prior unsatisfactory involvement with alternative, individualistic (e.g., psychiatric) problem-solving perspectives and/or a collectivistic (i.e., political) perspective.

The growth of the Jesus movement in the late 1960s and early 1970s, was the opening wedge of a renaissance of interest in morally conservative religion. The recent growth of conservative Protestant denominations, the Catholic charismatic movement, and the surge of neoorthodoxy within American Judaism are all evidence of a widespread repudiation of cultural modernism. The paper by Samuel C. Heilman in this volume deals with the social construction of normative and doctrinal interpretations within modern Orthodox Judaism. The "new American religious revival" has operated to render "conspicuous ethnic religion" respectable, and "as American as Jimmy Carter." The modern Jew thus finds that "he can be far more blatantly Orthodox and parochial than before without losing his share in the contemporary world." The result has been a trend toward stricter orthodoxy.

However, the "great influx of spiritual newcomers" into Orthodox Judaism has created some problems; it has filled Orthodox groups with troublesome "volitional" Jews who have actively chosen rather than inherited their religion, and who now "demand transcendence in everyday life." Such orientations pose a challenge to the "reinterpretive" traditions of American orthodoxy that have operated to reconcile the norms of Jewish orthodoxy with elements of secular modernism.

According to Johnson, conservative religious congregations "provide communities in which people who share a common consciousness can find intimacy and solace within the framework of a moral code." However, "despite their rejection of many aspects of secular society, they naively accept the institutional structure of the workaday world." Thus, traditional religionists "are no less immune than others to the distresses of work." They must work within the impersonal bureaucracies of managerial capitalism, and they remain subject to the alienation intrinsic to such settings. In fact, conservative religion may exacerbate the experience of a lack of autonomy in modern work.

Conservative religion has been tied to a model of society that emphasizes laissez faire economics and limited government as jointly composing the desirable institutional infrastructure for civil religion. Thus, according to Johnson, "cultural resources available to Americans have emphasized the autonomy of the individual and the individualistic and voluntaristic character of social relations." In the nineteenth century, when the economic life of the nation was carried on primarily through small businesses and farms, such a limited governmental laissez faire form of the civil religion seemed plausible to most people, and it did not lead too glaringly to social experiences that were inconsistent with it. With the growth of both government and large corporations in the current era of managerial capitalism, emphasis upon individual autonomy and civic virtue — as the wellsprings of vocational motivation — probably exacerbates the frustration intrinsic to contemporary public life. Thus, other more innovative religious groups have arisen that attempt to cure such frustration by creating utopian communal enclaves as examples for the revolutionary transformation of the larger society.

Civil-Religious Sects, Oriental Mysticism, and Psychotherapy Groups

As emphasized above, the Jesus movement and other neoorthodox developments in American religion are part of the new-religions phenomenon only in a rather equivocal sense. Apart from such conservative developments, the new religions that initially emerged from the counterculture of the 1960s can be seen as dividing into two tendencies that embody opposed strategies for coping with the decline of civil religion and public theology. On the other hand, there are such groups as the Unification church of Reverend Moon that promise a revitalized synthesis of political and religious themes as the basis for crystallizing personal identities. Such groups, which look toward the restoration of a national covenant and the recreation of a virtuous republic, might be termed new civil-religious sects. Jim Jones' ill-fated People's Temple also approximated this pattern, as does Synanon, and, to a lesser degree, some conservative Protestant and youth culture Christian groups emerging from the Jesus movement. On the other hand, privatistic mystical religions — Yoga Bhajan and Tibetan Buddhism — and quasi-mystical therapeutic movements — est and Scientology—implicitly reject the insertion of nationalistic or political themes in spiritual life. In part, because of their lack of overt political emphasis, such groups are frequently labeled "narcissistic."

Both eastern mystical movements (Zen Buddhism, Meher Baba) and human potential groups (est, Scientology) are monistic in the sense that they emphasize a metaphysical unity hidden behind the apparent chaos of worldly experience. They thus differ from conservative churches and civil-religious sects that might both be termed dualistic in that they both emphasize that the world is fundamentally divided between good and evil. Traditional American civil religion also has been dualistic, insofar as it has emphasized the redemption of the nation through the imposition of a homogenous set of moral rules that definitively distinguish good from evil people and good from evil nations.

Dualistic civil religion originates in the biblical notion of a covenant between God and a chosen people. Thus, the United States can achieve its "chosenness," its status as the "New Israel" only if its citizens predominantly accept the obligations of the covenant and the moral rules that are identified with God's will. As Johnson has argued, the increasing structural differentiation of the private and public sectors of American society has made unlikely the acceptance of a uniform sacred cosmos and moral order. Our society is becoming increasingly pluralistic—with ethnic, cultural, and religious diversity increasing at a rapid pace. America, therefore, has been increasingly cut off from its dualistic religious and political heritage.

Conservative churches and civil-religious sects that reemphasize a homogenous political and spiritual sacred cosmos offer one sort of solution to the resulting anomie. Members of conservative churches, however, pay the price of increasing alienation from the probably incurable pluralistic public world. Civil-religious sects, on the other hand, construct their own homogenously integrated miniature societies in microcosm, and their members thus escape the strain of routine day-to-day involvement with the morally chaotic modern society. This has costs also, not the least of which is the almost total dependency upon religious organizations that may themselves not be worthy of such total sacrifice in the final analysis. Part of the exhilaration of membership in a religious movement that is serious about its utopianism may come from the converts' sense of betting everything upon a worthy ideal. But it is a very high risk game. A great deal depends upon the correct choice of an organization intended to exemplify such ideals.

Such civil-religious sects as the Unification church, the People's Temple and Synanon provisionally heal the split between private feelings and public purpose by encouraging their members to withdraw from normal vocational involvements. Members of these types of movements are encouraged to expand all their energies in developing self-sufficient utopian communities that are to serve as models for the reform of America. However, they manage to create the experience of civilly legitimate social integration only by encouraging a uniformity of opinion and degree of obedience to authority among converts that some observers contend are appropriate to an earlier level of social evolution.

In Durkheimian terms, the best known civil-religious sects create "mechanical" rather than "organic" social solidarity, and they provoke charges of authoritarianism and brainwashing from outsiders. In addition, the high level of submission to authority, coupled with the relative social isolation of members, make the destiny of these groups highly dependent upon the mental health of their leaders. Thus, the emotional states of Jim Jones of the People's Temple, or Chuck Dedrich of Synanon appear to have had a greater influence over the destinies of their movements than would the mental health conditions of the leaders of more democratically organized or less reclusive groups.

Finally, the civil and religious character of these groups commits them to the attempted transformation of the nation as a whole. This commitment encourages confrontations with the larger society. Depending upon ther outcome, such conflicts often undermine the internal plausibility of the symbolic systems of these groups and thus make them somewhat volatile.

The currently well-known civil-religious sects seem to have the aforementioned features in common. However, the differences among them may be as important as the similarities in predicting the courses of development of specific movements and their effects upon members.

The Unification church of Reverend Sun Myung Moon is nearly unique in the systematic quality of its extrapolation of public theology. Traditionally, American civil religion has been closely linked to liberal constitutional ideals. It has thus sacrilized the separation of church and state and accepted a degree of cultural and normative diversity. The decline of civil religiosity has set the stage for a sectarian reassertion of the ideal of the virtuous republic transformed into an explicitly theocratic version of itself. The religiopolitical synthesis advocated by the Unification church entails what Irving Louis Horowitz rightly identifies as a fundamental denial of the Lockean-Jeffersonian principle of the separation of church and state. The Unification church seeks for the unity rather than the separation of the theological and the political. Unification church members regard their efforts to breach the wall of separation between church and state as not so much an attack on civil liberties as a search for new foundations for the social order. In an attempt to heal the extreme separation of public and private realms and the fragmentation of personal identity in a highly differentiated society, the Moon movement, with its implicit corporatism, articulates a reponse to the decline of civil religion that some authors have criticized as authoritarian.

The People's Temple community at Jonestown can be viewed also as a civil-religious sect putatively embodying a virtuous republic. However, John R. Hall, in his essay in this volume, identifies the uniqueness of the People's Temple as inhering in its "neither-fish-nor-fowl" quality. The People's Temple was situated on the conceptual boundaries between a "warring sect"— which defines itself as locked in a total struggle with a social environment defined as corrupt and demonically evil—and an "other-worldly sect." The latter has a "timeless" quality that insulates it from extreme conflict with an environment that it radically devalues also.

Other-worldly utopians "exist beyond time" in the sense that they feel assured of their status as a postmillenial elite. They thus lack the felt urgency of being personally responsible for bringing about the new dispensation—which will be created by divine agency. Unfortunately, the plausibility of the People's Temple as an other-worldly sect was undermined by the intensity of the Marxist and antiracist themes in the sectarian subculture. Moreover, Reverend Jones exploited conspiratorial mystiques to enhance solidarity within the community.

In emphasizing the persecution of his group by the larger society, Jones undermined the sense of insulation essential to stabilizing its identity. Yet the movement's situation as a warring sect was also hopeless. There was no way to prevail over a vast capitalist-racist "conspiracy," the omnipotence of which was emphasized continually by Jones. In this situation, mass suicide became a means of actualizing a kind of "immortality" that is not a possibility for political revolutionaries. "They could abandon apocalyptic hell by the act of mass suicide. . . . Mass suicide bridged the divergent public threads of meaningful existence at Jonestown — those of political revolution and religious salvation."

The example of Jonestown as well as the allegations against Synanon have lent a sense of urgency to the analysis of civil-religious sects. Can the proclivities of the People's Temple be generalized to other such sects, particularly the highly controversial Unification church, against which allegations of "suicide training" have been made?[10] In this connection, it appears that there are significant differences between the Unification church and the People's Temple.

Reverend Moon and his devotees do not view the noncommunist world as totally evil; it is corrupt and in danger of losing its linkage with God's grace, but it is also capable of redemption and spiritual revitalization.[11] The Moonies share with Jim Jones a departure from those other-worldly millenarian traditions that envision a divine agency as wholly responsible for the apocalypse and for the subsequent redemption of a sacred remnant of true believers. Within such traditions, the role of believers is primarily passive—to purify themselves and wait. To the contrary, the Moonies see *themselves* as shouldering the responsibility for creating the New Kingdom by winning over the masses, political lobbying, and so on. Yet it is precisely this optimistic activism that differentiates the Moon movement from the followers of Jones. The latter could neither envision divine intervention in their behalf nor victory through their own efforts, and they were thus rendered increasingly volatile and susceptible to despair.[12]

Like conservative churches and civil-religious sects, monistic movements are growing as a result of the decline in the symbolic integration of American society. The appeal of oriental mysticism (Zen and Guru MaharaJi) and quasi-mystical therapy groups (*est* and Scientology) can best be understood in relation to the needs created by this decline. Monistic groups assert a social unity hidden in the depths of the self. They posit a universal Self immanent in particular selves, by which individuals are harmoniously related to each other and to nature. Such hidden interconnections between people are not dependent upon consciously shared religious or political values. Belief in such an implicit universal order can provide a value framework that supports participation in even such a society as ours, in which consciously shared values are disintegrating.

Within most monistic systems, consciously shared value frameworks are considered intrinsically illusory. According to such perspectives, rational theologies and political ideologies are based upon distinctions between logically opposed categories of experience. Such discursive ordering of experience is seen as intrinsically illusory in that it is arbitrary and culturally relative. An indefinite number of such orderings is possible, and, therefore, no one system is more correct than any other. According to monists, belief in a particular rational ordering of experience is the essence of Maya — the illusory world of opposities. Real knowledge involves the faculty of perception, not that of reason.

From the monistic perspective, progress towards enlightenment involves glimpses of the Self or oversoul that is hidden behind the apparent chaos of experience. Culturally fragmented societies such as ours are intrinsically no different from other societies, because all societies are built upon illusory myths. Relative cultural fragmentation, moreover, can provide real opportunities for spiritual aspirants. A greater degree of cultural fragmentation makes the culturally relative or arbitrary quality of particularistic social myths—such as American civil religion—more apparent; and it therefore provides opportunities for individuals to glimpse the hidden unity in life.

Although monistic mystiques provide value frameworks that can motivate social participation, such mystiques, almost by definition, repudiate American civil religion. Traditional civil religion in the United States is dualistic and exalts the value of American political, economic, and religious institutions vis-à-vis those of other nations. Monism regards all particularistic theologies and ideologies as arbitrary, and attachment to them as that which is to be overcome by the religious quest.

Such a repudiation of the traditional American civil religion has some advantages relative to conservative churches or civil-religious sects. The latter groups reaffirm rationally constructed civil-religious theologies. Such theologies lead to an experience of social integration for their adherents, only if they are consciously accepted by an overwhelming majority of the people in a society. Dualistic civil religion defines the nation in terms of the majority's conscious acceptance of a particular rational ideology. It cannot, by definition, be a minority orientation without causing great psychic strain in its devotees. In the increasingly pluralistic society associated with managerial capitalism, monistic religion, which affirms a hidden social unity beneath the apparent diversity of competing value perspectives, offers obvious attractions.

Nevertheless, such social critics as Christopher Lasch and Thomas Wolfe have straightforwardly interpreted pluralistically tolerant monistic groups as narcissistic. They have argued that mystical movements merely supply religious rationalizations for the self-indulgent consumer ethos associated with contemporary capitalism. Benton Johnson argues, however, that at least some Eastern mystical movements, such as Meher Baba, effectively counteract such narcissistic trends. Such groups can supply moral perspectives that are supportive of family life and communal identity. In addition, by emphasizing detachment as a vocational attitude, they can soften the alienation intrinsic to involvement in bureaucratic institutions. (It might also be pointed out that the doctrine of karmic determinism taught by many such groups is more compatible with participation in large corporations than is the emphasis on free will associated with traditional civil religion.)

The Meher Baba movement, as described by Robbins and Anthony, confirms most of these general points about monistic movements. According to them, followers of Meher Baba were originally motivated to search for an alternative meaning system because of the radical disjunction between private and public realms in modern America. As part of their search, many Baba-lovers had prior involvements in bohemian countercultural milieux that emphasized untrammeled emotional expression. Such youth culture scenes would seem to encourage narcissism in that they emphasize the expression of impulses rather than the delay of gratification on behalf of long-term emotional commitments. Conversion to the Baba movement, however, typically involves repudiation of such a hang-loose ethic. Baba-lovers are generally sexually monogamous, and they tend to restrain impulses that would interfere with the development of communal life. Followers of Meher Baba, therefore, like conservative Christians and civil-religious sectarians, manage to transcend the shallow impulsivity characteristic of modern life. They do so, moreover, without becoming further alienated from the morally pluralistic public sector.

Followers of Meher Baba perceive him as the visible personification of the oversoul — the ground of being linking superficially separate individuals. Meher Baba is the secret Self of everyone, whether they consciously accept him or not. Therefore, Meher Baba-lovers feel a basis for identification with the pluralistically diverse larger society that is independent of that society's attitude towards them or their spiritual feelings.

Most Baba-lovers' capacity for involvement in bureaucratic vocational institutions goes beyond mere detachment. It includes positive or altruistic motives for vocational achievement as well. According to Robbins and Anthony, Meher Baba's personality is seen as a perfectly harmonious synthesis of the often contradictory attributes of feeling and purpose. In the terms of Parsonian sociology, Meher Baba represents an integration of the expressive role orientations characteristic of the private sector with the instrumental role orientations characteristic of the public sector. By enthusiastically participating in the public sector, then, Baba-lovers hope to actualize in their own lives the disciplined spirit of service that is characteristic of Meher Baba and, therefore, of their own true nature.

In this fashion, the Meher Baba movement (and presumably some other mystical movements as well) symbolically reintegrate public and private worlds, and compensate for the decline of civil religion. Such newly popular movements base civic virtue upon a monistic rather than a dualistic foundation, and are therefore compatible with a pluralistically diverse society.

Various academic commentators — Jacob Needleman, Robert Ornstein, Steve Tipton, and the present writers — have distinguished between ascetic mystical groups, such as the Meher Baba movement, that emphasize voluntary deprivation on behalf of prosocial goals, and egoistic mystical groups that supposedly supply shallow mystical rationalizations for self-interest and thus encourage narcissism.[13] Benton Johnson's contribution to this book implies this distinction, and it argues further that ascetic mystical movements usually are transplants of traditional oriental religions, whereas egoistic mysticism is found predominantly in such human-potential therapy groups as *est* or Scientology.[14]

est is the best known and most controversial of the new human-potential therapeutic movements. Scholarly and journalistic comment about it has tended to be highly critical and to interpret its meaning system as a reconstruction of competitive individualism that is free of the moral constraints imposed by traditional civil religion. An important theme of *est* is the injunction that "you are responsible for all your experience; you create it."[15] As Donald Stone notes in his essay in this volume: "Critics predict that this ethic of individual responsibility will legitimize the status of the wealthy, reinforce the self-doubt and self-blame of the disadvantaged, and discourage collective organization needed to redistribute power and wealth."

Stone's analysis, however, casts some doubt on these expectations. In general, the data collected by Stone challenges the conventional wisdom that narcissistic human-potential devotees lose touch with social responsibilities. Werner Erhard and his colleagues would probably expect such findings and might explain them as follows: The language of civil religion or civic virtue usually encourages mystifications that rationalize unenlightened self-interest rather than transforming it into social altruism. According to Erhard, the traditional puritanical language of moral obligation should be supplanted by a new language of *self-realization* or of enlightened self-interest. When people become free to acknowledge their real needs at a deeper level of awareness, Erhard has argued, their apparent self-interest becomes transformed into concern for others as well.

As Stone points out, *est* uses the concept of *responsibility* in a way that diverges significantly from conventional usage. Responsibility, for *est* devotees, "is not fault, blame, shame or guilt." Evaluative moral judgments are eschewed as arbitrary and dysfunctional. As a consequence, Stone reports, there is "no pronounced tendency for the advantaged *est* participants to blame the disadvantaged" for their own difficulties. There *is* some tendency, however, for participants to believe that meaningful transformation of economic and political structures requires prior widespread consciousness raising: "If everyone took *est* training the world would be transformed."

Erhard and his colleagues may or may not be mistaken in their approach to the creation of civic virtue. However, Stone's data is more supportive of Erhard's position than that of his critics. Indeed, critics, who say that *est* and other human-potential groups are narcissistic, have usually developed their arguments by way of linguistically based assumptions that appear somewhat tautological—since human potential enthusiasts are concerned with "self," they must therefore be "selfish," and so forth. In general, such critics have not put their notions—that human-potential groups lead to a reduction in social altruism—to any sort of empirical test. Unlike their critiques, Donald Stone's analysis is based upon systematically collected data. It raises important issues, and it clearly must be taken into account in evaluating the widespread current allegations that *est* and other consciousness groups operating in America socialize in privatistic social irresponsibility.

While recognizing that certain new religions are less involved in encouraging personal or psychological narcissism than some of today's therapies, Benton Johnson has nevertheless argued that both nouveau therapies and new religions have further undermined the effective reconstitution of civil religion because they have inhibited the constructive political participation of devotees. This thesis is partly repudiated by Stone's data on the social attitudes of *est* devotees. More to the point, however, is Robert Wuthnow's important paper on the "Political Aspects of the Quietistic Revival."

Wuthnow challenges what he regards as the conventional hydrodynamic assumption that energy directed into one channel (e.g., mysticism) must inevitably drain off energy from another channel (e.g., politics). Wuthnow's data indicate that persons attracted to new mystical religions are *more* likely than other persons to display the attitudes and behaviors associated with political protest and activism in the early 1970s. He argues that the relativism and antinomianism inherent in mystical orientations towards the world can operate to detach mystics from mystifications that legitimate the status quo. They can thus provide a basis for social criticism and protest. Wuthnow's analysis casts further doubt on the image of the apolitical, socially passive mystic, although it does not completely repudiate the argument that neomysticism is antithetical to the refurbished consensual civil religiosity. Perhaps the relativistic antinomianism of mystics will inevitably range them against any new putative civil religion.

The Reaction Against the New Religions

Charles Y. Glock and Thomas Piazza believe that the spread of deterministic social science perspectives is largely responsible for the undermining of supernaturalistic-theistic and individualistic perspectives regarding causal agency in human events. Elsewhere, Glock has argued that the undermining of voluntaristic assumptions regarding personal mastery and autonomy has generated a cultural crisis that underlies the upsurge of exotic religious and therapeutic orientations.[16] In this connection, Anthony and Robbins argue in their essay —''New Religions, Families and 'Brainwashing' ''—that ''many movements such as Scientology, est, Hare Krishna, or Nicheren Shoshu responded to the pervasive sense of powerlessness which afflicts many Americans. These groups offer techniques which will enable the individual to 'take power in his life' or 'make his life work.' '' Although such slogans emphasize mastery and self-management, ''the latent premise is that in today's milieu no one is spontaneously masterful; only the person who meditates, chants, or is 'trained' really has free will. Everyone outside of the movement is enmeshed in Karma or ensnared by Satan, etc.'' The widespread assumption that individuals are not automatically in control of things enhances the appeal of movements offering techniques aimed at putting the individual in charge of his life.

The spread of deterministic scientific perspectives and the undermining of assumptions of individual autonomy has produced a shift in attitudes toward deviants. Americans are more hesitant to impute responsibility to persons whose actions or beliefs depart markedly from norms. An example of this tendency is the view that converts to such utopian communal sects as Hare Krishna, the Children of God, and the Unification church have been brainwashed. As Anthony and Robbins point out, ''the application of brainwashing and mind-control metaphors to members of a social movement implies that they are not acting or thinking voluntarily and are not therefore entitled to the freedom of religion and freedom from physical restraint which applies to rational individuals.'' More specifically, the ''present use of the brainwashing concept involves an application of the medical model to religion. Certain religious beliefs are consigned to the realm of involuntary pathological symptoms.''

The medical model of social deviance has become widespread and important ''in a society of moral flux in which authorities are hesitant to acknowledge punitive intent and thus increasingly rely on social scientists to provide therapeutic legitimations for social control.'' In a sense, then, allegations that ruthless gurus and cult leaders are using techniques of mind control to seduce youthful converts represent a sort of ''secularization of evil.'' The brainwashing explanation for cult membership provides a scientific conceptualization that embellishes what is really the old-fashioned supernaturalistic imputation of satanic evil, as expressed for instance in the traditional notion of demonic spirit possession. This is the provocative argument of Anson D. Shupe, Jr. and David G. Bromley in their article—"Witches, Moonies and Accusations of Evil." This essay attempts to provide a framework for analyzing the social construction of the typifications of the evil social attitudes that are often imputed to marginal religions. The authors note that the movement in support of controversial religious deprogramming evokes "early Christian traditions of exorcism" in its concern for liberating individuals from demonic religious influence and restoring their autonomy.

The research and formulations of a number of scholars have interpreted the present agitation against cults as a genuine social movement. Typifications of mind-control processes in cults can be viewed as ideological constructions legitimating social-movement actions.[17] Recently, the present authors have formulated a theory of countersubversive movements that recur in American history and seek to mobilize opposition to such unconventional sects as the Mormons, Communists, or Moonies. Countersubversive movements respond to discontinuities and ambiguities in civil religion, and they seek to reconstitute moral boundaries by stigmatizing putatively subversive and un-American ideological groups.[18]

The paper by Trudy Solomon is particularly important in this context. Interviewing ex-Moonies, Solomon finds that respondents who had been forcefully removed from the Unification church and who had the most contact with deprogrammers and therapists tend to have the strongest negative attitudes toward the Moon church and to be more likely to interpret their prior commitment to Moonism as a product of brainwashing. Solomon's findings can be interpreted as pointing to a process of indoctrination into anticult perspectives that are systematically inculcated by deprogrammers and therapists.

Religious Ferment and the Erosion of Community

The erosion of civil religion undermines the viability of tangible, local institutions—families and churches—whose legitimacy is ultimately linked to the assumptive virtue of the broader society, nation, and American way of life. Conversely, problems impinging on churches, families, schools, and other mediating institutions from other sources ultimately enhance a climate of normative ambiguity that erodes the plausibility structure for civil religion. The present religious ferment—and the normative breakdown and cultural confusion that it reflects — is thus intertwined with structural shifts in American society arising from increasing structural differentiation and bureaucratization.

A number of writers have related the present spiritual ferment and upsurge of unconventional movements to structural changes in American society that have undermined the fabric of community in American life. The nuclear family is becoming increasingly isolated and segregated from other social processes. It cannot therefore fulfill all of the communal and affiliative needs of its members, especially adolescent and postadolescent progeny who have left their original families but have not settled down to form their own families. Traditional mediating collectivities, such as extended families, homogenous neighborhoods, or personalistic vocational and educational settings, at one time provided contexts for acculturation and communal gratification that were broader than the immediate family unit. Increasingly, however, these secondary associations have been undermined by a number of trends, including increasing geographical and vocational mobility, shifting residential patterns, and the bureaucratization of work and study settings. The nuclear family itself has been weakened by the loss of its productive functions, the transfer of much of its authority to mental-health and child-welfare professionals, the entrance of women into the labor market as career professionals, and the spread of permissive and countercultural values.

In the light of these trends, it has been argued frequently that such new social innovations as communes, encounter groups, and cults are emerging because they serve as surrogate extended families or even surrogate nuclear families.[19] In their article on "Kids in Cults" in the present volume, Irvin Doress and Jack Nusan Porter note that "Family life in America is beset by conflicts and problems." Perceiving this, older children "may look to surrogate families to meet their needs." Such persons may remain indefinitely in a cult because the latter appears to them to be a locus of loving interpersonal relations as well as a pure physical and moral environment—free of the violence, promiscuity, drug abuse, and moral ambiguity that pervades the "outer darkness" beyond the movement. The appeals developed by the new movements stress these factors. "The Unification Church constantly emphasizes the breakdown of the American family, corruption and immorality in American life (divorce, pornography, suicide, drugs and scandal) and, by contrast the work of the church toward the 'perfect family' in a 'perfect world.' "

Of course it is precisely the tendency for some communal spiritual movements to *replace* families that enrages and embitters many parents and clergymen. These critics see cults as seducing young persons away from their ascribed kinship and religious bonds. Anthony and Robbins argue that "cults, like gay militants, are being used as scapegoats for the decline of American familism. 'Brainwashing' is a convenient stick with which to beat totalistic sects which 'break up families' and remove converts from conventional social processes." In adhering to a social scientific style of explanation (use of brainwashing and mind-control concepts) for their children's defection to alien milieux, parents are beseeching the assistance of "those institutions to which they have ceded their authority, e.g., courts and psychiatrists, in subduing their children's desertion from themselves and their world."

Ultimately, the upsurge of new forms of communal and spiritual collectivity is a reaction to the dominance of impersonal bureaucratic formal structures in our society. As George A. Hillery, Jr. points out in his paper, formal organizations oriented to highly specific goal-attainment necessarily exclude familial and communal forms of interaction and their properties of love, freedom, and commitment. The primacy of formal organizations in the worlds of work and power tends to create a "need" for complementary contexts for diffuse affectivity. Such spiritual organizations specializing in affectivity can create a sense of autonomy and wholeness, and they provide communal gratifications unavailable in more formal organizations. Established institutionalized churches cannot fulfill these functions because they are themselves bureaucratically organized and somewhat depersonalized. "Formal organizations, for all their seductive utility, can have the power to cause us to act impersonally toward one another, and impersonal behavior is not in the best interest of humanity."

Conclusion

The growth of nontraditional new religions and quasi-religious therapies is taking place in the context of a broader challenge to American society. Various factors — Vietnam, Watergate, increasing structural differentiation of the public from the private sector—have undermined traditional civil religion and created a legitimation crisis for the nation. New religions minister to that crisis by providing novel mystiques that confer meaning on social processes that are no longer adequately legitimated. In doing so, cults may appear to threaten such institutions as churches, families, and neighborhoods, which have normally provided plausibility structures for civil religiosity.

These orientational institutions, however, have been undermined already by a variety of trends, and they are increasingly ineffective as loci for instilling commitment to social ideals. Moreover, commitment to families, churches, and neighborhoods has normally been supported by that synthesis of religious and political sentiment that is itself now waning. Thus the decline of civil religion is both an effect and a cause of the decline of these orientational structures.

Many new religions claim to be providing renewed support to such traditional institutions as the family, while their critics blame them for causing their disintegration. The issue of the ultimate effect of the new religions upon these institutions is presently unclear; probably they differ at least as greatly among themselves in these respects as they do from traditional religion. What *is* clear, however, is that they are not the *primary* cause either of the decline of civil religion or of the orientational institutions that normally support it. The intensity of the alarm over the new religions appears to result at least partially from a scapegoating mechanism. Attacking new religions allows people to neutralize the anxiety resulting from the waning of civil religion and its supporting institutions, without consciously acknowledging the real cause of their alarm.

Allegations of insidious brainwashing are the most obvious manifestation of their scapegoating tendency. Such allegations reinforce the perceived legitimacy of conventional meaning orientations as opposed to the supposedly programmed orientations characterizing pseudoreligions. Thus, anticult demonology, as well as some of the new cultism, strives to reconstitute civil religion and reformulate Americanism.

In his essay on Jewish orthodoxy, Samuel C. Heilman raises the possibility that the new styles of religiosity may turn out to be short-lived. Recently, observers have cited trends in this direction, including a decline of strongly authoritarian cults, a growth of evangelical Christianity on the campus at the expense of waning Oriental mystiques, and a shift of the constitution of the Jesus movement from bohemian street Christians to respectable evangelical trends within established churches. A resurgence of conventional church religiosity may even be in the offing. Trends and fads come and go, and any discussion of contemporary patterns has a built-in obsolescence factor. Whatever the religious developments that prevail in the 1980s, they are likely to respond in some measure to the following conditions: (1) a hunger for community, related to rapid social change and the erosion of traditional communal forms, (2) an erosion of Protestant ethic assumptions of automatic individual autonomy and free will, and (3) a further dissolution of moral consensus and national identity. It is conceivable, however, that these conditions may be overshadowed by unpredictable contingencies, such as war, economic collapse, or the Second Coming.

Notes

1. See particularly, Robert Bellah, "Civil Religion in American," in *Beyond Belief,* Robert Bellah, ed. (New York: Harper and Row, 1970), pp. 168–92; and John Coleman, "Civil Religion," *Sociological Analysis* 31, 2 (1970): 67–77.
2. Edward Heenan, *Mystery, Magic and Miracle* (Englewood Cliffs, N.J.: Prentice-Hall, 1973), p. 11.
3. Robert Bellah, *The Broken Covenant* (New York: Seabury, 1975), p. 145.
4. Bellah, *The Broken Covenant,* pp. 139–63.
5. See also, W. C. Roof, *Community and Commitment* (New York: Elsevier, 1977).
6. Glock and Piazza's analysis might lead one to predict a radicalizing or leftward trend in American politics. At the present writing, however, a conservative or rightward shift seems to be in progress. It is possible that the linkage between general perspectives on reality structuring and specific sociopolitical attitudes is actually rather problematic, i.e., feelings of individual helplessness can lead to a pessimistic negative evaluation of collective action for social betterment and thus to conservative opinions.
7. Johnson explicitly criticizes Richard Fenn's influential essay, "Toward a New Sociology of Religion," *Journal for the Scientific Study of Religion* II, (1972). Dr.

Fenn's views have been elaborated and modified in his recent monograph, *Toward a Theory of Secularization* (Ellington, CT.: Society for the Scientific Study of Religion, 1978).
8. See Christopher Lasch, *The Culture of Narcissism* (New York: W.W. Norton, 1979) and Richard Sennett, *The Fall of Public Man* (New York: Knopf, 1977).
9. See Jeffrey Hadden, *The Gathering Storm in the Churches* (New York: Doubleday, 1969); Dean Kelley, *Why the Conservative Churches are Growing* (New York: Harper and Row, 1977); and W. Clark Roof, *Community and Commitment: Religious Plausibility in a Liberal Protestant Church* (New York: Elsevier, 1978).
10. Jerry Carroll and Bernard Bauer, "Suicide Training in the Moon Cult," *New West* (January 29, 1979).
11. This is notwithstanding a significant tendency to interpret opposition to the church as demonically inspired, which evokes the paranoia of Reverend Jones. On the Moonist view of the world and society, see Thomas Robbins, Dick Anthony et al., "The Last Civil Religion: The Unification Church of Rev. Sun Myung Moon," *Sociological Analysis* 37, 2 (1976): 111–25.
12. Some additional differences might be noted. The Moon movement has a rather elaborate and systematic theology, called the *Divine Principle*. Moreover, the charisma of Reverend Moon is somewhat abstract and symbolic. Most disciples have little face-to-face interaction with the leader. In contrast, the People's Temple involved a vague and ambiguous doctrinal base combined with an extreme dependence upon a leader who inspired by his immediate presence. This latter pattern, which also seems to have characterized Synanon under Chuck Dederich, is obviously more volatile than the pattern of the Unification church.
13. See Jacob Needleman, *A Sense of the Cosmos* (New York: Doubleday, 1975); Steven Tipton, *Getting Saved from the Sixties* (Berkeley and Los Angeles: University of California Press, 1980); Robert Ornstein, *The Mind Field* (New York: Viking, 1976); Thomas Robbins, Dick Anthony, and James Richardson, "Theory and Research on Today's New Religions," *Sociological Analysis* 39, 2 (1978): 95–122; and Dick Anthony "The Fact Pattern: Behind the Deprogramming Controversy," *New York Review of Law and Social Change,* in press.

Needleman distinguishes between "the search for transformation" that is undertaken for its own sake and "the desire for happiness." The latter is pandered to by contemporary "spiritual pragmatism," in which "ideas which were intended as guides in the process of harmonizing the desires with the totality of human functioning became instead instruments for the satisfaction of one or another of these desires" (Needleman, 1975, p. 164). Similarly, Tipton, in analyzing American Zen devotees, distinguishes between "hard Zen," which emphasizes discipline and self-control, and popularized "soft Zen," which uses Zen symbolism to reinforce a counterculture ethic of expressive spontaneity. Ornstein makes a similar point in comparing contemporary consciousness groups (*est* and Transcendental Meditation) with traditional Sufism. Finally, Robbins, Anthony, and Richardson (1978) and Anthony (in press) divide American new religions into "one-level" religions, which emphasize the material advantages of religious conversion, and "two-level" groups, which stress the sacrifice of egoistic goals on behalf of a higher reality.
14. In distinguishing between therapies and new religions with respect to contemporary narcissism Johnson qualifies the theories developed by Christopher Lasch. Johnson cites papers by Lasch subsequently incorporated into *The Culture of Narcissism* (New York: Norton, 1979).
15. The kind of individualist perspective on a causal agency that pervades the human-potential movement may be divergent in key respects from the individualist

perspective conceptualized by Glock and Piazza. To view experiences and events as determined by an intrapsychic level of consciousnss is not quite the same as viewing events as determined by individual will power and/or innate moral qualities. (Cf. Robert Wuthnow's distinction between individualistic and mystical modes of reality structuring in his *The Consciousness Reformation* [Berkeley and Los Angles: University of California Press, 1976]).

16. Charles Glock, "Consciousness Among Contemporary Youth: An Interpretation," in *The New Religious Consciousness,* C. Glock and R. Bellah, eds. (Berkeley and Los Angeles: University of California Press, 1976), pp. 353–66.

17. See Anson D. Shupe, Jr., Spiermann, Roger, and Sam Stigall, "Deprogramming: The New Exorcism," *American Behavioral Scientists* 20, 6 (1977): 941–56, and Shupe, Roger Spielmann, and Sam Stigall, "Cults of Anti-Cultism," *Society* 17, 3 (March/April 1980): 43–46.

18. See Thomas Robbins and Dick Anthony, " 'Cults,' 'Brainwashing' and Counter-Subversion," *Annals of the American Academy of Political and Social Science* 446 (1979): 78–90.

19. See John Marx and David Ellison, "Sensitivity Training and Communes: Contemporary Quests for Community," *Pacific Sociological Review* 18, 4 (1975): 442–60. See also James Coleman, "Social Inventions," *Social Forces* 49 (1970): 163–73.

References

Anthony, Dick, in press
Bellah, Robert N., 1970, 1975
Carroll, Jerry, and Bernard Bauer, 1979
Coleman, John, 1970
Fenn, Richard K., 1972, 1978
Glock, Charles Y., 1976
Glock, Charles Y., and Robert N. Bellah, 1976
Hadden, Jeffrey, 1969
Heenan, Edward, 1973
Kelley, Dean, 1977
Lasch, Christopher, 1979
Marx, John, and David Ellison, 1975
Needleman, Jacob, 1970, 1975
Ornstein, Robert, 1976
Robbins, Thomas et al., 1976
Robbins, Thomas, and Dick Anthony, 1979
Robbins, Thomas, Dick Anthony, and James Richardson, 1978
Roof, W. Clark, 1977, 1978
Sennett, Richard, 1977
Shupe, Anson D., Jr., Roger Spielmann, and Sam Stigall, 1977, 1980
Tipton, Steven, 1979
Wuthnow, Robert, 1976

Religious Ferment and Cultural Transformation

Religion and Legitimation in the American Republic

Robert N. Bellah

Just over a decade ago I published an essay (1970) that I have never subsequently been allowed to forget. In that essay I suggested that there is such a thing as civil religion in America. My suggestion has roused passionate opposition as well as widespread acceptance. Opposition to the idea has shown little unity. Some of my opponents say there is no such thing, that I have invented something which does not exist; others say there is such a thing but there ought not to be; still others say there is such a thing but it should be called by another name, "public piety," for example, rather than civil religion. Unfortunately for me my supporters are in even greater disarray. The term *civil religion* has spread far beyond any coherent concept, or at least beyond anything I ever meant by it. Perhaps the commonest reaction is a puzzled, "Yes, there seems to be something there, but what exactly is it?" Among professional specialists in American studies there is another reaction: "We knew it all the time. What Bellah says is nothing new." And then there is perhaps a vague reference to Tocqueville. But with one or two exceptions, little in the way of conceptual clarity has been forthcoming from specialists. I would like to try once again to clarify this most troublesome problem.

I am partly to blame for the confusion by the choice of the term *civil religion*, which turned out to be far more tendentious and provocative than I at first realized. Yet the choice of the term was fortunate in that the controversies it generated are fruitful. More neutral terms such as *political religion, religion of the republic,* or *public piety* would not have generated the profound empirical ambiguities that the term *civil religion* with its two thousand years of historical resonance inevitably did.

What would be more natural than to speak about civil religion, a subject which has preoccupied theorists of republican government from Plato to Rousseau? The founders of this republic had read most of those theorists and were consciously concerned with the problem, even though they did not use the term. The difficulty comes from the fact that for most of those two thousand years there has been a profound antipathy, indeed an utter incompatibility between civil religion and Christianity. There is even a question, which we cannot explore here, whether there has not been a historic antipathy between republican government and Christianity. Most Christian political theorists down through the ages have preferred monarchy as the best form of government (Christian religious symbolism is much more monarchical than republican), and the great republican theorists—Machiavelli, Rousseau, even Tocqueville—have wondered whether Christianity could ever create good citizens. Augustine in the opening books of the *City of God* denounced Roman "civil theology" as the worship of false gods and the Roman Republic as based on false ideals and therefore as finally no commonwealth at all. Rousseau, in arguing for the necessity in a republic of a civil religion other than Christianity, wrote:

> Christianity as a religion is entirely spiritual, occupied solely with heavenly things; the country of the Christian is not of this world. ...imagine your Christian republic face to face with Sparta or Rome: the pious Christians will be beaten, crushed, and destroyed.... But I am mistaken in speaking of a Christian republic; the terms are mutually exclusive. Christianity preaches only servitude and dependence. Its spirit is so favorable to tyranny that it always profits by such a regime. True Christians are made to be slaves, and they know it and do not much mind: this short life counts for too little in their eyes.

Yet at the beginning of our history we were that contradictory thing, a Christian republic. (Samuel Adams even called us a Christian Sparta.) Or were we? Christianity was never our state religion, nor did we have in Rousseau's strict sense a civil religion, a simple set of religious dogmas to which every citizen must subscribe on pain of exile. So what did we have? What do we have now?

Tension between church and state lies deep in Christian history. The idea of a nonreligious state is a very modern and doubtful one. Through most of Western history some form of Christianity has been the established religion and has provided "religious legitimation" to the state. But under that simple formula lie faction, intrigue, anguish, tension, and on occasion massacre, rebellion, and religious war. Through much of history the state has dominated a restless church, exploited it, but never removed its refusal of final allegiance. On occasion the church has mastered the state, used it for its own ends, temporalized its spiritual loyalties into a kind of religious nationalism. In all this Christianity is no different from other religions that I have characterized as being at the historic stage. Even religions that are much more intrinsically political, such as Islam or Confucianism, have for most of their histories been involved in uneasy and unhappy alliances with state power. Relative to the first four caliphs all Muslim rulers have been viewed as at least faintly illegitimate by the religious community. Relative to the ancient sage kings all Chinese emperors have lacked fundamental legitimacy in the eyes of Confucian scholars.

The very spirituality and otherworldliness of Christianity has provided a certain avenue for reducing the tension not always open to other historic religions: the differentiation of functions, the division of spheres. Yet no solution has ever dissolved the underlying tensions described by Augustine and Rousseau. The tendency has been for every solution to break down into religion as the servant of the state or vice versa.

There have been great periodic yearnings in Western history to overcome the dichotomy, to create a society that would indeed be a Christian republic, where there would be no split in the soul between Christian and citizen. Savonarola had such a dream in fifteenth-century Florence, as did the Anabaptists in sixteenth-century Germany and some of the sectarians during the Civil War in seventeenth-century England. Most of these experiments were highly unstable and illustrated rather than refuted Rousseau's argument for mutual exclusiveness. Yet John Calvin in sixteenth-century Geneva created a city that was Christian and republican in an organic way that had few precedents (and that stood curiously behind Rousseau's own republican theorizing). Church and state were not fused; formal distinctions were sharply maintained. Yet Christian and citizen were finally two ways of saying the same thing. The New England Colonies in the seventeenth century were Christian republics in a comparable sense. In Massachusetts, for example, only Christians could be citizens, though the church did not control the state and both were governed by their members. Even though the reality of this experiment had evaporated by the early eighteenth century, the memory was still strong in the minds of the founders of the republic.

The civil theology of the youthful Hegel in Germany during the decades after the French Revolution shows that the yearning for the union of Christian and citizen was still vigorous at the end of the eighteenth century. These youthful speculations stand behind Hegel's mature political theory as well as Marx's thought about man and citizen.

Could there be a sense in which the American republic which has neither an established church nor a classic civil religion is, after all, a Christian republic, or should we say a biblical republic, in which biblical religion is indeed the civil religion? Is that what Sidney Mead (1975) means by saying that we are "a nation with the soul of a church"? The answer, as before, is yes and no. The American solution to the problem of church and state is unprecedented, unique, and confused. Let us turn from external speculation and from the introduction of tendentious terms like *civil religion* to the way in which the tradition has understood itself.

Today the almost Pavlovian response which provides a solution to all problems in this area is *the separation of church and state*. That phrase, especially when it is intensified with the unfortunate Jeffersonian image of the "wall of separation," seems to offer a clear solution when in fact it creates more difficulties than it eliminates. The phrase *separation of church and state* has no constitutional standing. The first clause of the first amendment states that "Congress shall make no law respecting an establishment of religion." That clause has a long history of interpretation which I do not intend to review here, but it certainly does not mean nor has ever meant that the American state has no interest in religion, and it certainly does not mean that religion and politics have nothing to do with each other. To the extent that the "wall of separation" image leads to those conclusions it distorts the entire history of the American understanding of religion and leads to such absurd conclusions as that religious congregations should have no tax exemption and legislative bodies should not be opened with prayer. To attribute such intentions to the founders of the republic is not only a historical error but a political error about the nature of the republic. Inspection of the second clause of the first amendment, "or prohibiting the free exercise thereof," should begin to dispel the distortions of the extreme separationist position.

The Constitution, while prohibiting a religious establishment, protects the free exercise of religion. It is this second clause to which that other common phrase *religious freedom* refers, a phrase that has often been used to sum up American teaching about religion. This phrase too has a significant Jeffersonian source, for Jefferson pointed to his authorship of a bill for "establishing religious freedom" in Virginia as one of the three things he most wanted to be remembered for. The phrase *establishing religious freedom*, which is not constitutional but which explicates the free exercise clause, suggests positive institutionalization in this area. It is religious freedom or free exercise which is the controlling idea. Prohibition of the establishment of a particular religion is required because it would be an infringement on religious freedom. Even so, today it is not uncommon for the religious freedom concept to be swallowed up in the separation concept because freedom here as elsewhere is interpreted in purely negative terms, as the liberal philosophical tradition tends to treat it. Religious freedom becomes merely the right to worship any God you please or none at all, with the implication that religion is a purely private matter of no interest or concern to political society. I will argue that "establishing religious freedom" means much more than that—that it has a powerful positive political significance. But the difficulty of interpretation is not entirely in the mind of the analyst. It is not just a question of reading late twentieth-century ideas about religion into the minds of the founders, though there is much of that. The difficulty is rooted in certain fundamental unclarities about the American political experience and the nature of the American regime, unclarities that go right back to the formative period of the republic itself.

The basic unclarity rests on whether we are a republic in recognizable relation to the republics of classical and modern times and dependent on that inner spirit of republican character and mores that makes for republican citizenship—or whether we are a liberal constitutional regime governed through artificial contrivance and the balancing of conflicting interests. What we wanted was to have our cake and eat it too, to retain the rhetoric and spirit of a republic in the political structure of a liberal constitutional state. In so doing we blurred every essential political consideration including the place of religion in public life. We artfully used religion as a way of evading the incompatibilities in our political life. For as long as the religious bodies remained vital and central in our public life the evasion was (at least partially) successful. Today when religion, more even than our other institutions, is uncertain about itself, the evasion is no longer tenable. But I am getting ahead of myself.

The great political philosophers from Aristotle to Machiavelli to Montesquieu (who had such an influence on the founders of the republic), all believed that a political regime is an expression of the total way of life of a people—its economics, its customs, its religion. The way of life correlates with the type of person the society produces and the political capacities inherent in that person. As Montesquieu said, a despotic society will have despotic customs—the arbitrary use of power, dependence of inferiors on superiors, slavery—that will produce a person primarily motivated by fear, just the right kind of subject for a despotic polity. But a republic will have republican customs—public participation in the exercise of power, political equality of citizens, a wide distribution of small and medium property with few very rich or very poor—customs that will lead to a public spiritedness, a willingness of the citizen to sacrifice his own interests for the common good, in a word a citizen motivated by republican virtue. It would be as absurd to expect a people long inured to despotism to create a successful republic as for a republican people to tolerate a despotic regime. And yet these patterns are not fixed. There is constant flux and a tendency toward degeneration—good customs become corrupted and republican regimes become despotic. Since republics go against "gravity," it is essential if a republic is to survive that it actively concern itself with the nurturing of its citizens, that it root out corruption and encourage virtue. The republican state has an ethical, educational, even spiritual role, and it will survive only so long as it reproduces republican customs and republican citizens.

The much newer form of political organization we are calling "liberal constitutionalism," though it grew in the very seedbeds of modern republicanism, developed a markedly different idea of political life, partly in response to a newly emerging economic order. Though formulated by some of the toughest minds in the history of modern philosophy—Hobbes, Locke, Hume, Adam Smith—this tradition gave rise to the most wildly utopian idea in the history of political thought, namely that a good society can result from the actions of citizens motivated by self-interest alone when those actions are organized through the proper mechanisms. A caretaker state, with proper legal restraints so that it does not interfere with the freedom of citizens, needs do little more than maintain public order and allow the economic market mechanisms and the free market in ideas to produce wealth and wisdom.

Not only are these political ideas—republicanism and liberalism—different, they are profoundly antithetical. Exclusive concern for self-interest is the very definition of the corruption of republican virtue. The tendency to emphasize the private, particularly the economic side of life in the liberal state, undermines the public participation essential to a republic. The wealth that the liberal society generates is fatal to the basic political equality of a republic. And yet the American regime has been from the beginning a mixture of republican and liberal concepts. However, the republican moment emerged first, out of the revolutionary struggle itself, and crystalized in a document, the Declaration of Independence. The liberal moment emerged second, during the complex working out of interests in the new nation, and crystalized in the Constitution. Even that division is too simple, for there are liberal elements in the Declaration and republican elements in the Constitution, but it does suggest that from the very beginning the balance has never been easy or even. For our purposes it is interesting to note that the Declaration has several central references to God and the Constitution none at all. It is time to turn to religion as a means of mediating the tensions within the American regime.

Superstructural Role

In the early republic religion had two vital locations: the superstructure and the infrastructure of the new political regime. It is to the superstructural location of religion that the Declaration points. By superstructural I mean a locus of sovereignty taken to be above the sovereignty of the state. Perhaps the most striking recognition of this superordinate sovereignty comes from the hand of Madison in 1785 during the debate on the bill establishing religious freedom in Virginia:

> It is the duty of every man to render to the Creator such homage, and such only, as he believes to be acceptable to him. This duty is precedent both in order of time and degree of obligation, to the claims of Civil Society.

Before any man can be considered as a member of Civil Society, he must be considered as a subject of the Governor of the Universe: And if a member of Civil Society, who enters into any subordinate Association, must always do it with a reservation of his duty to the general authority; much more must every man who becomes a member of any particular Civil Society, do it with a saving of his allegiance to the Universal Sovereign.

Here Madison confines himself to the superordinate sovereignty of God over the individual citizen which precedes the sovereignty of political society over him.

The Declaration of Independence points to the sovereignty of God over the collective political society itself when it refers in its opening lines to "the laws of nature and of nature's God" that stand above and judge the laws of men. It is often asserted that the God of nature is specifically not the God of the Bible. That raises problems of the relation of natural religion to biblical religion in eighteenth-century thought that I do not want to get into here, but Jefferson then goes on to say: "We hold these truths to be self evident, that all Men are created equal, that they are endowed by their Creator with certain unalienable Rights, that among these are Life, Liberty and the pursuit of Happiness. That to secure these rights, Governments are instituted among Men, deriving their just Powers from the consent of the governed. That whenever any Form of Government becomes destructive of these ends, it is the Right of the People to alter or abolish it." Here we have a distinctly biblical God, who is much more than a first principle of nature, who creates individual human beings and endows them with equality and fundamental rights.

It is significant that the reference to a suprapolitical sovereignty, to a God who stands above the nation and whose ends are standards by which to judge the nation and indeed only in terms of which the nation's existence is justified, becomes a permanent feature of American political life ever after. Washington and Jefferson reiterate, though they do not move much beyond, the language of the Declaration in their most solemn public addresses such as their inaugural addresses or Washington's Farewell Address. This highest level of religious symbolism in the political life of the republic justifies the assertion that there is a civil religion in America. Having said that, we must also say that American civil religion is formal and in a sense marginal, though very securely institutionalized. It is formal in the sparsity and abstraction of its tenets, though in this it is very close to Rousseau's civil religion. It is marginal in that it has no official support in the legal and constitutional order. It is in this connection that we must again point out the absence of any reference to God, and thus of any civil religion, in the Constitution of the United States. Belief in the tenets of the civil religion are legally incumbent on no one and there are no official interpreters of civil theology.

The marginality of American civil religion is closely connected with the liberal side of our heritage and its most important expression, the Constitution. This side has led many to deny that there is a civil religion or that there ought to be in America. And indeed from the point of view of liberal political ideology there need not and perhaps ought not to be. The state is a purely neutral legal mechanism without purposes or values. Its sole function is to protect the rights of individuals, that is to protect freedom. And yet freedom, which would seem to be an irreducible implication of liberalism on etymological grounds alone, no matter how negatively and individualistically defined, does imply a purpose and a value. Pure liberalism is a reductio ad absurdum and a pragmatic impossibility—one reason why a pure liberal state has never existed and why in America the rhetoric and to some extent the substance of republicanism have always existed in uneasy tandem with liberalism.

From the point of view of republicanism civil religion is indispensable. A republic as an active political community of participating citizens must have a purpose and a set of values. Freedom in the republican tradition is a positive value which asserts the worth and dignity of political equality and popular government. A republic must attempt to be ethical in a positive sense and to elicit the ethical commitment of its citizens. For this reason it inevitably pushes toward the symbolization of an ultimate order of existence in which republican values and virtues make sense. Such symbolization may be nothing more than the worship of the republic itself as the highest good, or it may be, as in the American case, the worship of a higher reality which upholds the standards that the republic attempts to embody.

And yet the religious needs of a genuine republic would hardly be met by the formal and marginal civil religion that has been institutionalized in the American republic. The religious superstructure of the American republic has been provided only partially by civil religion. It has been provided mainly by the religious community itself entirely outside of any formal political structures. It is here that the genius and uniqueness of the American solution is to be found. At the 1976 Democratic Convention Barbara Jordan called for the creation of a national community that would be ethical and even spiritual in content. It is in a sense prepolitical, but without it the state would be little more than a mechanism of coercion.

The first creation of a national community in America preceded the revolution by a generation or two. It was the result of the Great Awakening of the 1740s, a wave of religious revivalism that swept across the colonies and first gave them a sense of general solidarity. As the work of Nathan Hatch has shown, this religious solidarity was gradually given a more political interpretation from within the religious community itself in the 1750s and 1760s with the emergence of what he has called "civil millennialism," namely the providential religious meaning of the American colonies in world history. It is the national community with its religious inspiration that made the American

Revolution and created the new nation. The national community was, in our sense of the term, the real republic, not the liberal constitutional regime that emerged in 1789.

The liberal regime never repudiated the civil religion that was already inherent in the Declaration of Independence and indeed kept it alive in our political life even though the Constitution was silent about it. From the point of view of the legal regime, however, any further elaboration of religious symbolism beyond that of the formal and marginal civil religion was purely private. Form the point of view of the national community, still largely religious in its self-consciousness, such elaboration was public, even though lacking in any legal status. Here we can speak of public theology, as Martin Marty has called it, in distinction to civil religion. The civil millennialism of the revolutionary period was such a public theology and we have never lacked one since.

The problems of creating a national community in America did not decrease with the establishment of the constitutional regime but in a sense became more severe. With the formation of the new nation centrifugal forces that were restrained during the revolutionary struggle came to the fore and a sense of national community declined. To some extent a national community in the new nation was not fully actualized until after the trauma of the Civil War, though that event set in motion new problems that would later create even greater difficulties in maintaining a genuine national community. But, as Perry Miller has pointed out, to the extent that we did begin to create a national community in the early national period it was again religious revivalism that played an important role. I would not want to minimize the role of Enlightenment thought in complicated relation with the churches that Sidney Mead has so brilliantly emphasized. Enlightenment religion and ethics were also a form of public theology and played a significant role. Yet Jefferson's hope for a national turn to Unitarianism as the dominant religion, a turn that would have integrated public theology and formal civil religion much more intimately than was the case, was disappointed and public theology was carried out predominantly in terms of biblical symbolism.

Even though I have argued that the public theology that came out of the national community represented the real republic, I do not want to idealize it. As with all vigorous young republics it had an element of self-intoxication that has had ominous consequences for us ever after. The "chosen people" or "God's new Israel" symbolism that was eliminated from the formal civil religion was common in the public theology though it also had its critics. Public theology provided a sense of value and purpose without which the national community and ultimately even the liberal state could not have survived, but what that value and purpose were was never entirely clear. On the one hand they seemed to imply the full realization of the values laid down in the Declaration of Independence, but certainly not fully implemented in a nation that among other things still legalized slavery. On the other hand it could imply a messianic mission of manifest destiny with respect to the rest of the continent. It may be a sobering thought that most of what is both good and bad in our history is rooted in our public theology. Every movement to make America more fully realize its professed values has grown out of some form of public theology, from the abolitionists, to the social gospel and the early Socialist party, to the civil rights movement under Martin Luther King, and the farmworkers movement under Caesar Chávez. But so has every expansionist war and every form of oppression of racial minorities and immigrant groups.

The clearest and purest expression of the ethical dynamism that I have located in the realm of public theology broke through at one crucial moment in our history into civil religion itself in the person of our greatest, perhaps our only, civil theologian, Abraham Lincoln. Basing himself above all on the opening lines of the Declaration of Independence, in the Gettysburg Address he called us to complete "the great task remaining before us," the task of seeing that there is a "new birth of freedom" and that we make real for all our citizens the beliefs upon which the republic is based. In the Second Inaugural Address Lincoln incorporated biblical symbolism more centrally into the civil religion than had ever been done before or would ever be done again in his great, somber, tragic vision of an unfaithful nation in need above all of charity and justice.

It has not been my purpose here to evaluate the whole checkered story of civil religion and public theology in our national history but only to point out that they have been absolutely integral to one aspect of our national existence, namely our existence as a republican people. So far I have spoken only of the superstructural role of religion in the republic. Now I would like to turn to the infrastructural role.

Infrastructural Role

In the classical notion of a republic there is a necessity not only for the assertion of high ethical and spiritual commitments, but also for molding, socializing, educating the citizens into those ethical and spiritual beliefs so that they are internalized as republican virtue. Once again, when we look at the liberal constitutional regime we find a complete lacuna in this area. The state as a school of virtue is the last thing a liberal regime conceives itself to be. And yet here too what the liberal regime could not do the national community as the real republic could.

Partly the problem was handled through federalism. What would not be appropriate on the part of the federal government could be done at lower jurisdictional levels. Just as religion was much more open and pervasive at local and even state levels through most of our history than it ever was at the federal level, so the state as educator, and educator in the sphere of values, was widely accepted at lower jurisdictional levels. Robert Lynn (1973) has brilliantly shown how the McGuffy readers purveyed a religious and republican ideology, including a powerful stress on the common good and the joys of participation in public life, during much of the nineteenth century.

And yet, as important as public schools have been, the real school of republican virtue in America, as Alexis de Tocqueville saw with such masterful clarity, was the church. Tocqueville said religion is the first of our political institutions. It was a republican and a democratic religion that not only inculcated republican values but gave the first lessons in participation in public life. More than the laws or physical circumstances of the country, said Tocqueville, it was the mores that contributed to the success of American democracy, and the mores were rooted in religion. As a classic theorist of republican government would, Tocqueville saw that naked self-interest is the surest solvent of a republican regime, and he saw the commercial tendencies of the American people as unleashing the possibility of the unrestrained pursuit of self-interest. He also saw religion as the great restraining element that could turn naked self-interest into what he called ''self-interest rightly understood,'' that is, a self-interest that was public spirited and capable of self-sacrifice. In this way Tocqueville showed how religion mitigated the full implications of American liberalism and allowed republican institutions to survive. Late in his life he began to doubt that such a compromise would work in the long run, and his doubts have been all too fully confirmed by our recent history. Yet for its time and place Tocqueville's analysis was undoubtedly right. It gives us an essential clue to understand this strange, unique, and perhaps finally incoherent society in which we live.

What Tocqueville saw about the role of religion in such a society as ours was understood by the founders of the republic. It is significant, for example, that John Adams, during his first year as our first vice-president under the new liberal constitutional regime said: ''We have no government armed with power capable of contending with human passions unbridled by morality and religion. Our constitution was made only for a moral and a religious people. It is wholly inadequate to the government of any other.'' And Washington in his Farewell Address wrote: ''Of all the suppositions and habits which lead to political prosperity Religion and morality are indispensable supports. In vain would that man claim the tribute of Patriotism, who should labour to subvert these great Pillars of human happiness, these firmest props of the duties of Men and citizens. The mere Politician, equally with the pious man ought to respect and cherish them.'' Perhaps the recognition by our first and second presidents of the necessity of religion and morality, of the basis in the mores and religious beliefs of a people, for a successful republic, in the rather negative, circuitous, and almost apologetic terms of the above quotations, expresses the uneasy compromise between republicanism and a liberal regime that I am describing as characteristic of the new nation. But it also suggests that the relation between the way of life of a people and their form of political organization was fully understood by the founders of the republic.

It is inevitable having recently celebrated the two-hundredth anniversary of our republic that we should look around us to see how well our heritage is understood and how much of it is still operative in our public life. We might have hoped that a political campaign in that bicentennial year would have been educative in the high republican sense of the term. We have had such campaigns in the past. In the Lincoln-Douglas debates the deepest philosophical meaning of our republic and history was plumbed by two men of enormous intelligence and sensitivity to the crucial issues. Alas, we did not get that in 1976. Perhaps the Illinois farmers who drove into the towns from miles around to hear the Lincoln-Douglas debates were a different kind of people from the millions in their living rooms in front of the television screen. Perhaps there were other reasons. But in 1976 what we got was vague and listless allusions to a largely misunderstood and forgotten past, and an attitude toward the present that seems to be determined, above everything else, not to probe beneath the thinnest of surfaces. And yet the great themes I have been probing here were present in that campaign, present not in any articulate form but present in the uncertainty, the groping, the yearning for something that has so slipped out of memory as to be almost without a name. It is the ethical purpose of our republic and the republican virtue of our citizens, or rather the loss of them, that haunted that campaign.

Our rhetoric speaks in the terms of another day, another age. It does not seem to express our present reality. Yet our politicians and their constituencies are surprised and troubled by the lack of fit, less concerned to find a new rhetoric than to find an easy formula to make the old rhetoric apt again. Such an easy formula is the assertion that we must restrain, control, and diminish government, as though the enormous growth of our government were some fortuitous thing and not a sign and symptom of the kind of society in which we live.

To ask the questions the 1976 campaign did not ask is to ask whether under the social conditions of late twentieth-century America it is possible for us to survive as a republic in any sense continuous with the historic meaning of that term. If we discover that the republican element in our national polity has been corroded beyond repair, then we must consider whether a liberal constitutional regime can survive without it. Finally we must ask, if both our republic and our liberal constitutional regime lack the social conditions for survival, what kind of authoritarian regime is likely to replace them, remembering that republican and liberal regimes have been in the history of the planet few and brief. Perhaps we can even discern, beneath the battered surface of our republican polity, the form of despotism that awaits us. Of course it would be my hope to discover how to do what Machiavelli says is that most difficult of all political things, reform and refound a corrupt republic. But we must not flinch from whatever reality is to be discovered.

Corruption

I have mentioned corruption. Corruption is a great word, a political word with a precise meaning in eighteenth-century discourse even though its use has become narrowed and debased with us. Corruption is, in the language of the founders of the republic, the opposite of republican virtue. It is the thing that destroys republics. It might be well for us to remember what Franklin said on the last day of the Constitutional Convention, on September 17, 1787. Old, sick, tired, he had sat through that long hot Philadelphia summer because his presence was crucial to the acceptance of the new document. He was the very symbol of America. He rose on that last day to call for unanimous consent in hopes that that too might help the document be accepted, and he said:

> In these sentiments, Sir, I agree to this Constitution with all its faults, if they are such; because I think a general government necessary for us, and there is no form of Government but what may be a blessing to the people if well administered, and believe further that this is likely to be well administered for a course of years, and can only end in Despotism, as other forms have done before it, when the people shall have become so corrupted as to need despotic Government, being incapable of any other.

We see in those words the sentiments of an old republican, aware of the compromises contained in the new Constitution, but hoping almost against hope that the republican virtue of the people would offset them, at least for a time.

Corruption, again using eighteenth-century vocabulary, is to be found in luxury, dependence, and ignorance. Luxury is that pursuit of material things that diverts us from concern for the public good, that leads us to exclusive concern for our own good, or what we would today call "consumerism." Dependence naturally follows from luxury, for it consists in accepting the dominance of whatever person or group, or, we might say today, governmental or private corporate structure, that promises us it will take care of our material desires. The welfare state—and here I refer to the welfare that goes to the great corporations, to most of us above the median income through special tax breaks, and the workers whose livelihood depends on an enormous military budget, as much as to the "welfare" that goes to the desperately poor to keep them from starving—the welfare state, then, in all its prolixity, is the very type of what the eighteenth century meant by dependence. And finally political ignorance is the result of luxury and dependence. It is a lack of interest in public affairs, a concern only for the private, a willingness to be governed by those who promise to take care of us even without our knowledgeable consent. We would need to explore throughout our society the degree and extent to which corruption in these forms has gone in order to assess whether there is strength enough in our republic for its survival.

We would also need to look at religion, following the brilliant sociological analysis that Tocqueville made of the role of religion in our public life, a role that all the founders of the republic discerned. To what extent do our religious bodies today provide us with a national sense of ethical purpose? Certainly here there are some notable recent examples. Religious opposition to the Vietnam War was certainly more effective than the opposition of those who spelled America with a *k*. And if we have made some significant progress with respect to the place of racial minorities in our society in the last twenty years it is due in major part to religious leadership. Yet is the balance of American religious life slipping away from those denominations that have a historic concern for the common good, toward religious groups so privatistic and self-centered that they begin to approach the consumer cafeteria model of Thomas Luckmann's invisible religion? And to what extent is the local congregation any longer able to serve as a school for the creation of a self-disciplined, independent, public-spirited, in a word, virtuous, citizen? Have not the churches along with the schools and the family—what I have called the soft structures that deal primarily with human motivation—suffered more in the great upheavals through which our society has recently gone than any other of our institutions, suffered so much that their capacity to transmit patterns of conscience and ethical values has been seriously impaired? I am not prepared to say that religious communities, among which I include humanist communities, are not capable even today of providing the religious superstructure and infrastructure that would renew our republic. Indeed it is to them that I would look as always before in our history for the renewing impulse, the rebirth that any ethical institution so frequently needs. But the empirical question as to whether the moral capacity is still there on a sufficient scale seems to be open.

If we look to the scholarly community, there is not a great deal to be proud of. We have left the understanding of our basic institutions as we have left everything else, to the specialists and with notable exceptions they have not done a very good job of it. We have never established a strong academic tradition of self-reflection about the meaning of our institutions, and as our institutions changed and our republican mores corroded even what knowledge we had began to slip away. On the whole it has been the politicians more than the scholars who have carried the burden of self-interpretation. The founders were all political thinkers of distinction. Lincoln's political thought has moments of imaginative genius—his collected works are still the best initiation into a genuine understanding of the regime under which we live. Even as late as Woodrow Wilson and Calvin Coolidge we had presidents who knew our history in intricate detail and understood the theoretical basis of our institutions. In contrast we have never produced a political philosopher of the first rank. The only profound work of political philosophy on the nature of the American polity was written by a Frenchman. Still we have produced works of the second rank that are not without distinction, though they are usually somewhat isolated and eccentric and do not add up to a cumulative tradition. Such works are Orestes Brownson's *The American Republic* and Raymond Croly's *The Promise of American Life*. But in a barren time we must be grateful for such works as we have. If we turn to these works we will be referred once again to the great tradition with which I began this paper. For example on the last page of Croly's book he quotes the European-American philosopher George Santayana as saying: "If a noble and civilized democracy is to subsist, the common citizen must be something of a saint and something of a hero. We see, therefore, how justly flattering and profound, and at the same time how ominous, was Montesquieu's saying that the principle of democracy is virtue." How ominous indeed! It is in that context that we can understand the bicentennial epigram written by Harry Jaffa, one of the few political scientists who continues the great tradition today: "In 1776 the United States was so to speak nothing; but it promised to become everything. In 1976, the United States, having in a sense become everything, promises to become nothing."

One would almost think the Lord has intended to chastise us before each of our centennial celebrations so that we would not rise up too high in our pride. Before the centennial he sent us Grant. Before the bicentennial, Nixon (in whom we can perhaps discern the dim face of the despotism that awaits us—not a despotism of swastikas and brownshirts but of gameplans and administrative efficiency). It is not a moment for self-congratulation, but for sober reflection about where we have come from and where we may be going.

References

Bellah, Robert N., 1970
Hatch, Nathan O., 1977
Lynn, Robert Wood, 1973
Mead, Sidney E., 1975
Miller, Perry, 1965

A Sociological Perspective on the New Religions

Benton Johnson

Introduction

The dramatic emergence and growth of new religions in the past decade and their special appeal to youth have been widely reported in the mass media and extensively investigated by journalists, religionists, and social scientists. Although the earliest reports were largely descriptive in character and uneven in quality, studies of a more substantial nature soon got under way. The result is that we now have a considerable literature of good quality on which to draw in trying to understand these religions. As the studies of the new religions accumulated, some social scientists turned their attention to interpreting their origins, their general characteristics, and their probable consequences.

I would like to address several aspects of these issues. I will argue that these new religious manifestations, despite their many novelties and differences, share one important feature with most of the previous religious movements that achieved popularity in the United States during the past century—namely, a focus on the therapeutic transformation of the self. They overlook, however, the structural and cultural sources of much of the distress to which they respond. I will suggest what some of these sources are, and why so many people define the source of their distress in psychological or spiritual terms. Finally, I will propose some probable consequences of the new religions for American life.

The Trend in Popular Religion

It is a striking fact, not often noted by sociologists of religion, that almost all the new religious movements or themes that have attracted widespread popular support among the white population of the United States during the past century have focused on the problems of personal life. Pentecostalism promised, and still does, the peace and strength that comes from an experience of the indwelling of the Holy Spirit. The New Thought movement, including Christian Science, was and is preoccupied with health and personal effectiveness. The tone of much of this century's enormously popular literature on religious inspiration was set in 1897 by Ralph Waldo Trine in the Preface to his best seller, *In Tune With the Infinite,* in which he wrote that his book was addressed to "all who today, in this busy work-a-day world of ours, would exchange impotence for power, weakness and suffering for abounding health and strength, pain and unrest for perfect peace, poverty of whatever nature for fullness and plenty." As the century wore on, interest in various Oriental philosophies and regimens of personal enlightenment and personal development grew. In the 1950s, Alan Watts popularized a convenient form of Zen, and in the late 1960s almost all the new religions promised a change of individual consciousness and a transformation of motives. Viewed in the context of the general character of twentieth-century trends in popular religion, the themes of the new religions are only new in content — they are not new in focus.

But the emphasis on personal life is not confined to religion. It is also evident in the popularity of new therapeutic theories and regimens, of which psychoanalysis is only the most prominent intellectually. In the 1920s Couéism flourished; in the 1930s Dale Carnegie helped people win friends and influence people. More recently one may choose from among a vast assortment of therapies ranging from behavior modification and Scientology to Primal Therapy and Rolfing. Moreover, by any conventional definitions, the line between the secular and the religious has become increasingly blurred in the therapeutic enterprise. Carl Jung, a disciple of Freud, drew heavily on mythology for analytical insights, and he was highly regarded by certain Christians. Maharishi Mahesh Yogi, whose philosophy is essentially Hindu, legitimates his techniques of meditation in the name of physical science; John Lilly, a life scientist himself, turns mystic and writes books on the higher stages of consciousness; and Carlos Castaneda, an anthropologist, writes "science fiction" on the world view and powers of Yaqui shamans. The new religions are only the tip of the iceberg; they are merely the most colorful and most organized expressions of a trend toward the therapeutic reconstruction of the self that has been developing for several generations.

The new therapies and religions are all different from each other in numerous ways. Some are tightly organized, while others are as inchoate as the readership of Baba Ram Dass' books. Some enforce a strict morality; others condemn morality itself; some prescribe an arduous discipline; and still others provide easy formulas. Some engage the intellect, and others disparage it. Yet despite the bewildering and intriguing variety, all are directed toward the improvement or transformation of the self. They have one other feature in common—the vast majority of them interpret the sources of human distress in psychological or spiritual terms, and they screen out the sociological dimension of human existence. They either take the current social order for granted, or they merely insulate themselves from it in various ways, or they attempt to change it by inappropriate means. It is these features of the new movements that I would like to reflect on as a sociologist.

Structural Sources of Modern Distress

There is a school of sociological thought, most forcefully presented in the field of sociology of religion in such studies as Richard K. Fenn's 1972 essay, which argues that modern industrial societies are undergoing a process of differentiation between the public sector— where large-scale corporate "actors" make decisions concerning the production and allocation of resources— and the private sector— where individuals make decisions about their own lives. This school goes on to argue that the logic of the successful operation of the various processes in the two areas has thereby become so different that they cannot be governed by a common value system, whether that value system is articulated in religious or secular terms. The public arena requires that expert, presumably responsible decision-makers be free to manage the system without the restrictions or compulsions of value systems to which large numbers of private individuals are committed. In the private sector, concerns for the ultimate meaning of life, the determining of personal goals and personal life styles, and the pursuit of significations retain their importance. In fact, these questions become even more salient because the process of differentiation has freed individuals from the burden of having to reflect on both their private concerns and the character of the larger social systems in which they participate. This school of thought would regard the proliferation of the religious and secular cults of self-development as a simple by-product of this process of differentiation.

My own interpretation of the trend toward preoccupation with the self is based on a different theoretical orientation.[1] I do believe that complex societies have undergone processes of structural differentiation in many spheres. In some respects the individual personality has become increasingly separated from the social systems in which it participates, by virtue of the fact that more and more people have been freed from traditionally ascribed sex and kinship roles. People participate in a wider variety of activities, and they have a greater number of options open to them, especially if they belong to the middle or upper classes. This opening up of more choices to people places new demands on the personality for the development of choice-making criteria. In short, commitments that were once made routinely on the basis of tradition now become problematical, and critical reflection tends to replace blind obedience. Resources to guide this process have become widely available in recent decades, and among these are the new religions and therapies. It is also true that, just as the personality has become increasingly individuated, the organization of economic, political, and other large-scale enterprises has become enormously more complex. Few sociologists would dispute that these trends have been taking place, and that they are mutually interrelated.

My disagreement with Fenn and his colleagues concerns the nature of the relationships between the corporate or public sector and the individual or private sector in modern societies. This disagreement leads me to a different interpretation of the preoccupation with the self that is characteristic of the new therapies and religions. The key to my difference of opinion with Fenn is the simple sociological observation that individual personalities participate in both the private *and* the corporate sectors, and that although the distinction between these two arenas is an important one, it is only an analytical one. The differentiation between individual and large-scale organizations has not freed people from the necessity to participate in the latter. Quite to the contrary. It is my thesis that the current preoccupation with the self has its structural sources in the character of modern work. This preoccupation reflects a widespread distress that is produced by an inability to achieve and sustain heightened demands for satisfactions in the areas of work and intimate relations.

The development of modern economies has opened up a great many new opportunities and has encouraged people to expect increasing levels of material and psychological rewards for occupational achievement. Success in the workplace for many people has become the single most important test of personal worth. But the proliferation of new opportunities for occupational achievement is largely the result of the growth of large-scale organizations. Self-employment has declined steadily for over a century, with the result being that most of us today are dependent on the wages and salaries paid to us by employers. The character of our jobs, including our prospects for success, is increasingly governed by considerations that are systemic in character and therefore are beyond our personal control. Work takes place in formal organizations that are hierarchical in structure and are primarily responsive, through their top-level control centers, to the requirements of the market and government. Work relations are therefore highly inequalitarian. Workers tend to be evaluated individually and competitively on the basis of their contribution to the goals of the enterprise. In the world of work there are winners and losers, and those who are winning today may be losing tomorrow. The sense of achievement, and hence the feeling of self-worth, is placed in constant jeopardy because of the uncertainty of the outcome of our efforts. The search for a secure sense of self-worth based on work is made difficult by the structure of work itself—a structure that Americans by and large do not understand and that they do not control.

With the decline of the family-based enterprise, there has been a growing tendency to question and in some cases to abandon moral norms that have been associated traditionally with strong family ties. Because many of these norms facilitated the subordination of women, this questioning has affected them more dramatically than men, but the outcome of the process equally affects both sexes. People have tended to make demands on others for higher levels of the gratifications that usually have been connected with family life and interfamily relations — emotional support, love, and sexual satisfaction, for example. Women in particular have come to insist on the same rights to these satisfactions that men have. Moreover, they have increasingly demanded equal access to work opportunities.

The insistence on higher levels of gratification has brought with it a higher potential for dissatisfaction with one's personal relationships. Whereas our ability to control the conditions of work has progressively shrunk, our ability to control the conditions of love has expanded. It is now possible to abandon intimate relationships that are not satisfactory. But this freedom has its costs. It is exhilarating to find fulfillment in a new love, but it is not exhilarating to be abandoned by an old love. To the risks of work are now added the risks of love. Moreover, the risks of the latter are exacerbated by the increasing economic independence of women. For years men have intuitively understood that it is safer to act-out the frustrations of work at home than it is to act-out the frustrations of home life at work. Women's participation in work has not changed the structures of work. It is still risky to act-out home-life frustrations at work, and it now becomes unsafe for either sex to do much acting-out at home. Finally, the perils of love are also made more difficult by the competitive character of the workplace and by the tendency to make invidious comparisons in an effort to assess personal worth. Just as the success of competitors can make people envious, the success of loved ones can make people question their own worth. The anarchy of work is reflected in intimate relationships. The logic of the workplace has invaded the bedroom.

Cultural Resources for Responding to Distress

If it is true that much of the distress of our time has its structural sources in the processes I have just described, then we must ask why so many Americans have defined this distress in personal terms and have welcomed solutions that have treated it as spiritual or psychological or as a simple problem of interpersonal relations. I believe the basic reason why this is so is because it actually *seems* personal to many individuals. Persons in middle-class occupations do in fact have a measure of control over their occupational success, and they are evaluated at work in terms of their individual performance. Moreover, most people have an increasing amount of real freedom and thus real control in their intimate relationships. To this extent there is some basis in social reality for diagnosing distress as a psychological or spiritual problem.

But I think there is an additional reason for the tendency to diagnose distress in this way. By and large, the cultural resources available to Americans have emphasized the autonomy of the individual and the individualistic and voluntaristic character of social relations. The ethos of utilitarian individualism is deeply embedded in our culture. It has provided a canopy of legitimation for the pursuit of private interests. Indeed, it has defined capitalism and democratic government as the appropriate institutional forms for the successful pursuit of these interests. And its emphasis on material success and personal happiness has heightened the very sensitivity to failure that is one of the sources of discomfort itself. This culturally induced preoccupation with the self is perhaps the principal reason why psychological and spiritual approaches to certain problems, rather than social or political ones, have been so popular in the United States. When things go wrong, people feel bad. What is more important, they feel bad about themselves.

To a certain extent, the preoccupation with the self has been reinforced by the religious traditions of American culture. We must not underestimate the degree to which religion has shaped both our culture and our character. Despite evidences of secularization, religion is still a formidable influence on the American scene. By almost any measure chosen, Americans are far more religious than are the citizens of other industrial societies, a fact that should give pause to those who assume that modernization inevitably implies secularization. The extraordinary complexity of American religion makes generalizations difficult, but I believe it is safe to say that most religious movements throughout our history have placed a great deal of importance on the formation of individual character and primary relationships of people. Certainly, this emphasis typically has centered on the family and interfamily relationships, and it has just as typically reinforced traditional family morality. Even today, those who are strongly comitted to conservative Christianity may be among the least inclined to question traditional family norms. But they are no less immune than others to the distresses of work, for very few religious bodies in this country place restrictions on the full participation of their members—or at least their male members—in the structures of work.

Most religions, moreover, have made peace with the ethos of utilitarian individualism as well as with the larger institutional structures of American society. They have, of course, offered varying degrees of resistance to the more radical implications of utilitarian thought. They continue to emphasize works of charity, and they have often insisted that a person's character is as important as his success. Some of them have even seen the hand of God in political events and institutional structure. But by and large American religions have not opposed the cult of personal success, nor have they developed a coherent or realistic theory of modern society as a complex system. It is probably safe to say that the majority of Americans have a more developed theoretical understanding of the divine economy than they do of their own political economy. The churches have therefore played an important role in fostering the spirit of individualism, particularly of the economic variety, as well as a naivete concerning the structural contours of modern society. In fact, this role may be more important than sociologists realize, for religious socialization has been associated intimately with the processes of primary socialization, through which cultural motifs are mediated in the earliest years of life.

There is an important qualification that must be added. Robert Bellah has reminded us that the Puritan tradition contained a strongly developed conception of community—one that informed the private impulses of individuals with a sense of public purpose and common destiny. This not only reinforced the traditional obligations of family and church, but it also supplied a general rationale for choosing and pursuing one's "calling"—one that placed more emphasis on service to others than it did on the mere pursuit of self-interest. Above all, society itself was conceived as a community of moral purpose, indeed as a nation to which God had entrusted a sacred task in the unfolding of his plan for mankind. The private and the public therefore were not morally separated. They were moments of a divine drama in which everyone participated, and both work and love were infused with a common meaning and purpose that transcended the particular tasks and sorrows of everyday life.

Jurgen Habermas has remarked that "bourgeois ideologies"—of which utilitarianism is perhaps the most striking example—have not been able to supply the motivational resources needed for modern life. Consequently, complex societies have been "dependent on motivationally effective implementation from traditional world-views" (Habermas, 1973: 77). In this country the civil religion in general and the ethos of Protestantism in particular have been the most influential of these world views. They have helped mitigate the demoralizing effects of a calculating and atomistic utilitarianism, and they have provided a continuing source of hope for one's own future and that of the country.

There is a widespread agreement among observers of American life that the credibility of these religious resources has been seriously eroded. Religions of various kinds prosper, but the religious motifs that have been most influential and widely shared in the past, that have linked together the private and the public sectors, have lost their motivational power, if not their general appeal. And they have not been replaced with world views that can motivate the nation to transform itself in a way that will reduce the privations and distresses of modern life. There are numerous sources of the breakdown of the old religious traditions, but I would like to call attention to one in particular because I feel it has contributed much to the current preoccupation with the self and to the naivete concerning the systemic aspects of American society. I refer to the disjuncture within mainline Protestantism between what used to be called the cure of souls and the concern with constructing the good society.

Within traditional Protestantism, personal conversion preceded full initiation into the community of the faithful. Conversion involved a transformation of consciousness and desire that was at once intensely private and necessarily public in its consequences. For by an act of conversion the individual gained the hope of personal salvation and subscribed to the world view and the moral code of an organized community with a sense of historical purpose. At conversion, the believer joined a company of fellow believers on whom he could rely for consolidation and admonition. It inducted him into a company that not only cared for him, but that shared a practice of life that transcended the cares of life and formed the basis of their fellowship.

There are to this day certain Protestant bodies in which the cure of souls is still carried on within a moral community that shares a transcendent world view. But these bodies are thoroughly conservative in doctrine. What is more important is that they are thoroughly conservative in social outlook. They have no resources for the general transformation of social relationships, nor do they provide communities in which people who share a common consciousness can find intimacy and solace within the framework of a moral code. Despite their rejection of many aspects of secular society, however, they naively accept the institutional structures of the work-a-day world. It is well known, nevertheless, that a large and influential sector of American Protestantism has been developing along different lines. Protestantism is now roughly divided into two broad camps—one relatively conservative; the other relatively modern or liberal. It is largely within the liberal camp that this disjuncture has taken place. To a great extent, this disjuncture was one of the unanticipated consequences of the confrontation with the physical sciences and the secular philosophies of the nineteenth and twentieth centuries. Those who faced them most directly were urban and well-educated, by and large. Consequently, to this day the liberal denominations have a substantial constituency of such people. The intellectual leaders of the liberal movement have tried in many different ways to salvage the credibility of Christianity by making concessions to the new currents of secular thought. But in so doing, they have undercut the supernatural foundations of Christianity and thereby the transcendent basis of the need for salvation. With conversion no longer a meaningful act, the inspirations and consolations of Christian fellowship began to lose their power. At the heart of Protestantism itself, among its leading strata, the motivational resources of the traditional world view were depleted.

With the rise of liberalism, the focus of Christian interest shifted away from the next world onto this world. But the liberating possibilities of this change have not been realized fully. To be sure, liberal Christians were freed from the sense of sin and guilt that had fed the need for conversion and had been the source of continuing anxiety for many, even after conversion. But having been released from this burden, they were left with no distinctive regimen and world view to confront the burdens of ordinary living. I have already suggested what these burdens are. The new therapies, whether secular or couched in religious language, are the successors to the traditional, soul-curing therapies. They have supplied for millions the motivational resources for living that are no longer given by traditional world views.

With the shift to liberalism, Protestantism did not lose its long-standing interest in public life or its conviction that it was necessary and possible to construct the good society. Quite to the contrary. Before the turn of the century, many liberal leaders began criticizing capitalism for the miseries and injustices it had created. They advocated a redistribution of wealth, and they reiterated the traditional principle that service, not private gain, must govern the relations of work. These individuals supported the rights of labor, racial, and ethnic minorities, and the social ethos of liberal Protestantism pervaded the leadership of several prestigious denominations. Its development opened up the possibility that the Protestant community might come to understand society in a more thoroughly systemic way, and that collective action might be taken to remove the inequities of modern life through structural change. But this possibility did not become reality. With a few exceptions, liberal Protestants did not develop a coherent theory of society. The main thrust of Protestant liberalism was closely allied with that of political liberalism—a movement that did alleviate certain injustices but left the structures of work untouched, and in fact contributed to the further centralization of economic and political power.

Social Christianity was never genuinely popular among the laity. It was, and is, the project of a small but influential group of metropolitan leaders. Their proposals to make Christian practice virtually synonymous with liberal politics were not well received by the laity, and surely one reason was that so many of the Protestants were of middle-class status. Perhaps a deeper reason was that the leadership could no longer rely on the motivational resources of traditional Protestantism. To put it bluntly, it was not possible to make salvation depend on a life of political activism. The liberal leadership could not link the new public issues with the personal interests of their own constitutency, but could rely only on disinterested appeals to altruism and on the guilt and shame that a resistance to these appeals might conjure up. Now and then, they might rely on the energies produced by a displacement of personal anger. The disjunction between the new soul-curing therapies and the social concerns of the liberal Protestant leadership was now complete. It became transparent in the 1950s when many religious leaders began attacking the Christian self-help cults of Norman Vincent Peale and others. Invariably the attacks condemned the laity for a preoccupation with their own lives and for complacency in the face of the suffering of others. The attack was no doubt motivated by a genuine alarm at the heterodoxy of many of the self-help regimens as well as by a desire for social change, but it betrayed the desperation and the weakness of the leaders themselves. They did not understand the real distress of their own people, and they had no way of interpreting it to connect with the distress of others in a manner that would mobilize them to remove its real sources.[2]

How the New Religions Differ from the New Therapies

Until recently, the most popular therapeutic regimens shared the general optimism of American culture. In fact, many of them are still distinctly upbeat in tone. To be sure, their strident individualism contributed to the erosion of conventional morality, but they took the obligations of work and family for granted. They did, of course, help raise the level of personal expectations, and thereby exposed people to greater risks of disappointment. But they provided resources for coping with disappointment without becoming demoralized. As cultural traditions weakened, as the spirit of optimism faded from American life, and as the structural logic of modern work and love unfolded without check, therapies with different motifs began to appear. In the newer therapies, personal satisfaction was still the main objective, but the sense of social roots, moral obligations, and hope for the future has faded. There has been a retreat into the self and a concern for immediate experience that betrays a desperation about the quality of life.

Christopher Lasch, in a recent commentary on the newest therapies, has suggested that many of them offer prescriptions for happiness that may have the effect of accentuating the very conditions of "social welfare" that help produce unhappiness in the first place. People are advised, he notes, "not to make too large an investment in love and friendship, to avoid excessive dependence on others, and to live for the moment." They are urged to give up their inhibitions and to engage in "the nonstop celebration of the self" (Lasch, 1976: 5, 10). The result is a "collective narcissism" that further erodes the older notion that friendship and love entail reciprocal duties and restraints, and that happiness is a by-product of participating with intimates in a common enterprise that is freely undertaken. But it is precisely this kind of arrangement that is becoming increasingly difficult for people to achieve. Modern work is certainly not such an arrangement, and the process of seeking happiness by liberation from the compulsions of traditional familism has now gone so far as to threaten the very conditions of happiness itself. This process is a major source of the frustrations of personal life that underlie the popularity of the new therapies and the new religions. It is one basis for the widespread romanticization of youth and sexuality as well as the terror of aging and dying.

Lasch is right, I think, to argue that the new therapies offer no cures for the desperations of modern life. The same cannot be said, however, about most of the new religions. Though they vary greatly in doctrine, practice, and organization, almost all of them avoid the kind of narcissistic and atomizing regimens recommended by the new therapies. Some of them, such as Transcendental Meditation, Nicheren Shoshu, and even segments of the Jesus movement, make concrete benefits of a strictly personal sort available, like gifts of money from the Lord or success in hitch-hiking, but they do not legitimate these benefits in the name of an ethic of self-preoccupation. For these are by-products of the practice of regimens that are legitimated by reference to a transcendental order. Even where, in the interest of a wide appeal, such legitimations are artfully concealed from the novice, as is the case with Transcendental Meditation, they are nonetheless available to those who show a sustained interest in the regimen. Among the most highly prized of all these benefits, though not always the most easily achieved, is the total transformation of consciousness—a transformation that is produced by a subjective contact with the transcendent itself, which changes completely the very core of personal motives. No one who has observed and spoken with those who have touched the transcendent can doubt the genuineness of the experience or the reality of the personal transformation it can bring. Of course, we have no direct knowledge of the subjectivity of others, but we do have entrée to the ways they externalize it. In fact, we often have better access to these signals than the individuals do themselves. In most cases I have seen, the signals suggest that the transformation has been both tranquilizing and energizing. Contact with the transcendent, as interpreted through the teachings of one's religious tradition, provides an intuitive grasp of the ultimate unities and polarities of existence that sweeps away the confusions of ordinary life and forms the basis for the reordering of personal priorities.

Most of the new religions provide a reliable community of fellow adherents who are bound by a common regimen, including a common moral code. Most of the new therapies do not. Many of them do, of course, operate workshops, training institutes, and retreats, but by and large the treatments these afford are expected to have long-run payoffs that do not require periodic reinforcement by a community of fellow practitioners. The focus remains on the benefits that accrue to the participants in the regular conduct of their private lives within the ordinary structures of society. Usually little effort is made to hold the practitioners to a common moral code or to insist that motivations be transformed in accordance with a single framework of ultimate meaning. The ethos of utilitarian individualism is therefore deeply embedded in the assumptions and practices of the new therapies. In the human-potential movement, for example, which incorporates some motifs appropriated from Eastern religions, one is free to pick and choose a variety of regimens and points of view within the movement itself, and one is often able to try out a number of them simultaneously (Stone, 1976: 99). One sets one's own goals and discovers one's own meanings by whatever criteria seem privately appropriate.

The new religions, on the other hand, do supply such criteria, and therefore they provide the basis for the commonness of purpose that undergirds their fellowship. Even when they do not specify what work their members shall do, the general conduct of their lives is guided by a single purpose and a single moral code. Whether they live and work together communally, or whether the religious community is a kind of support group or spiritual home base after the model of most Christian congregations, the whole of life takes on a meaning marked by warmth and love for the serious devotee. Just as typically, however, sexual intimacy is governed by a strict moral code that would strike most modern Americans as repressive. It may be that these new believers have rediscovered, albeit in exaggerated form, that impulsive sexuality is just as destructive to solidary relationships as is impulsive hostility.

In general, then, the new religions do not prescribe cures for modern distress that exacerbate the distress itself. The experience of transcendence, the commonness of purpose and motive, and the support group of intimates bound by a moral code safeguard the believer in varying degrees from the anxieties of modern living.

The Impact of the New Religions

Neither the new therapies nor the new religions have any real sources for transforming the structures of work and government, for they share the American naivete concerning the character of modern social systems. For the most part, the new therapies simply ignore questions of social organization altogether. On the other hand, many of the new religions do criticize the quality of life in modern society, and they conceive their consciousness and practice as instrumental in the general transformation of human relations. But however genuine their protest may be, their means of realizing this objective are simply insufficient. I am certain that most social scientists would agree that a new world order will not be created by chanting to the *gohonzon,* or by loving Meher Baba, or by saying one's mantra forty minutes a day, or by raising one's consciousness through the practice of yoga, or by accepting Jesus as one's personal savior, or even by selfless acts of charity and social service. Nor will it be brought about by substituting monistic for dualistic thinking or replacing linear thought with intuitive awareness. I do not deny that a change of consciousnss is a precondition for any collective effort to change the world. But the content of this consciousness is also important. For unless it includes an adequate theory of society, the practice that it inspires will not produce the ends it seeks.

The protest of the new religions against the quality of modern life is therefore largely passive. This does, however, not mean that their witness can have no effect on the structures of society. I believe it can have an effect, and that to some extent it already does. Those groups that will have the least impact are the ones that isolate themselves from society in economically self-sufficient communes. A mass back-to-the-land movement would, of course, have serious social consequences, but such a movement is out of the question as long as productive land remains expensive. A more widely adoptable but less isolated arrangement is a form of communal capitalism in which the members offer such services as tree planting and house repairing that they organize and sell as a group. Although they retain control over the conditions of their work, their dependence on an outside market may tempt them to deprive others of work by underselling them. In fact, they may be able to do this quite profitably, if their own material needs are modest and they can cut expenses by living together. Such groups may, incidentally, offer models for survival that may be widely emulated if we should experience an economic collapse, though they are probably not suitable models for the organization of an industrial economy. By far, the most common arrangement seems to be that the members live apart and hold regular jobs, gathering periodically for fellowship and spiritual nourishment, and giving some of their earnings to the community for its upkeep and its various projects. This, of course, is the model of the Christian community. Most members who conform to this model participate in work on the same terms as everyone else. Even so, they may be able to insulate themselves from the stresses of work by redefining its meaning. Work can be defined in many ways: a form of yoga, a perpetual prayer, a spiritual offering, service to God, or simply as a means of earning money for one's movement. But ironically, the consequence of such redefinitions of work may be a conscientiousness and serenity of spirit that employers appreciate. Inwardly the workers dissent, but outwardly they cheerfully reproduce the existing relations of work.

It is therefore conceivable that the new religious consciousness might actually make the machinery of business and government operate more smoothly by removing some of the sources of friction caused by personal stress. There are, however, strict limits to such an arrangement. So long as mere compliance with existing institutions is sufficient to earn a living, and so long as there remains a large measure of politically guaranteed privacy, the new religions indeed may make the system run more efficiently. But in an economic or military crisis or in a crisis of political legitimacy, they might not prove responsive to either the powers that be or to those who are struggling for power. To be sure, here and there a guru or other religious leader may try to deliver support to one or another faction, and I suspect that even now some of these leaders have purposes that they conceal from their followers. The new religions do not, however, share a common perspective for the making of politically effective commitments. They lack a unified language for the mobilization of energies for public purposes. They have broken decisively with the cultural tradition, and they have little of consequence to offer in its place.

There is an important exception to what I have just said — the Jesus movement, or at least its largest sector. This movement indeed does have links to the cultural traditions of American society, which are mediated by evangelical Protestantism, the tradition that contributed most heavily to the construction of the civil religion and that even now has a sizable constituency in most sections of the country. Despite the recent emergence of an evangelical left, the political orientations of this community are largely conservative, nor are many of its leaders complacent in their conservatism. They are well aware of the long-term erosion of public enthusiasm for traditional Christianity and for the institutions of American society. For years they have launched one project after another in an effort to restore the spiritual foundations of American life. "Key 73" and the recent "I-found-it" movement are only two of the more spectacular examples. Others, such as Young Life and Campus Crusade for Christ, are less well known. Although there has been little research on the subject, I am certain that the Jesus movement has enjoyed access to the considerable resources of the evangelical community. The success of this movement owes something to the "seed money" invested by laymen, local churches, and such interdenominational alliances as the Full Gospel Businessmen's Fellowship. The Lord has indeed provided, as many Jesus People will testify. The Jesus movement is a new religion only in an equivocal sense. Its protest and its countercultural themes are more stylistic than real. It is not a symptom of the erosion of tradition, but a token of the efforts to restore it. It is a political movement in the fullest sense of the term.

Postscript: Counterculture and Aftermath

The counterculture of the 1960s, aided by the mass media, burst upon the scene as a radical protest to the quality of American life. Whatever else may be said of it, the counterculture did combine a demand for the transformation of personal life with one for the transformation of the structures of work, education, and government. It spoke of love, sexuality, and personal freedom, but it also talked about brotherhood, community, and an end to militarism, bureaucracy, and the exploitation of man and nature. It was both a symptom of the erosion of tradition and a call for its renewal in a transfigured version. It was both negation and affirmation. The fact that it was made by youth is important. But perhaps the most important fact is that it was made by an element of the population that was temporarily free from the burdens of family and work and therefore was able to reflect collectively on both its past and its future.

The counterculture, nevertheless, was never a coherent movement. It had no stable leadership, no coherent theory of self and society, and virtually no organization. Within a short time its inner tensions became transparent. In some quarters love turned to hate. Hope for the future gave way to nostalgia for the rural past. The joy of bright clothes and incense was succeeded by a sadness and guilt that was unmistakably signaled by the drab and penitential costumes that finally became a standard uniform. Even rock music, so playful in its earliest days, slipped into a minor key.

Before long it became evident that the disjunction in American culture between the personal and the political was being reproduced in the countercul- ture itself. The fusion of the two that was so marked a feature of the early counterculture began to disintegrate when two broad tendencies began to emerge. One emphasized the reconstruction of personal life. It led in various directions, such as toward a "hip capitalism" of crafts like weaving and jewelry making. It resulted in rural communes, natural foods, and experimenta- tion with new forms of consciousness. It led toward religion. The other tendency moved to political action of various kinds, student protests, bomb- ings, electoral politics, and careers in service occupations. It also led to Marxism.

Though these tendencies became increasingly clear cut and even mutually antagonistic, the hope for the good life at both the personal and the societal levels did not disappear. Many individuals participated in both, sometimes alternating between them without attaching themselves permanently to either. Even today, serious Marxists complain about the presence of "touchy-feely" people at some of their conferences. It is likely that the hope for a better society was one of the appeals of the new religions. This hope was obviously exploited by the Unification church, despite the sinister politics of its leader (Robbins et al. 1976). It was also exploited by some wings of the Jesus Movement despite the political conservatism of some of its backers and the fact that recent research suggests that the members of Jesus groups tend to be more politically conserva- tive than the members of the other new religions (Wuthnow, 1976: 275–78).[3]

I am inclined to agree with Robert Bellah that a profound disaffection with American society still characterizes most of those who participated in the counterculture or who were influenced by it. Nevertheless, the organized movements that recruited from the counterculture reflect in increasingly polarized form its own tendency to separate interest in the self from interest in social reconstruction. The new religions mirror the concern with self. The new Marxist movements, on the other hand, reflect the counterculture's political tendencies. I know much less about those groups than I do about the new religions, but I am aware that many of them have devoted serious efforts to an analysis of the systematic sources of injustice in our society and to the devising of strategies for change. Whatever its limitations, Marxism does have a sophisticated theory about society—a theory, moreover, that posits a future free from unnecessary suffering. Marxists have traditionally paid little attention to the conditions under which human motivations are generated and sustained, nor have they shown much interest in the self or in structures of intimate relations. There are indications that some Marxist intellectuals are becoming concerned with these fundamental questions at last, but it is my impression that the new Marxist movements themselves have yet to take them seriously. I suspect they will have little impact on American society until they do.

Notes

1. My basic theoretical perspective has been influenced by both Emile Durkheim and Talcott Parsons. Recently it has been very much influenced by he works of Jurgen Habermas, especially his *Legitimation Crisis*. My treatment of the new therapies as well as my conceptualization of the sources of the distress to which they address themselves has been influenced by Christopher Lasch (1976). Robert Bellah's essay on the new religions (1976) has been very useful to me, as have the theoretical chapters in Jacob Needleman's *The New Religions* (1970).
2. For a fuller treatment of my views on liberal Protestantism, see Johnson, 1976. For a discussion of the role played by religious elites in the formation of American Protestantism, see Johnson, 1975. Unfortunately, neither of these papers is currently available in print in English. They are available from the author on request.
3. The very name of the Christian World Liberation Front, a Berkeley-based Jesus group, and of its newspaper, *Right On,* are cases in point. In its early years of publication, *Right On* made extensive use of countercultural motifs such as funky cartoons and the general format of underground newspapers. More to the point, it also used a good bit of the rhetoric of revolution. In all fairness, I must add that the paper has now become a periodical of solid intellectual substance. In the mid-1970s it changed its name to *Radix*.

References

Bellah, Robert N., 1976
Fenn, Richard K., 1972
Habermas, Jurgen, 1973
Johnson, Benton, 1975, 1976
Lasch, Christopher, 1976
Needleman, Jacob, 1970
Robbins, Thomas; Dick Anthony; Madeline Doucas, and Thomas Curtis, 1976
Stone, Donald, 1976
Trine, Ralph Waldo, 1897
Wuthnow, Robert, 1976

Exploring Reality Structures

Charles Y. Glock and Thomas Piazza

All of us are confronted with the need to make sense of the world. This need reveals itself when confronting such questions as: How did the world come into being? What is the origin of life? What is the purpose of life? Is there a God? Is there an afterlife? It is also present in an everyday way as we seek to understand the things that happen to us and the events taking place in the world around us.

Over our lifetimes most of us have developed ways of understanding life which enable us to accept our world and our routine experiences. To a great extent, life goes on without everyone experiencing a constant need to make sense of it by conscious and deliberate reflection. There are times, however, when "built in" modes of understanding are not adequate to deal with particular events. At such times we experience a new need to make sense of what is taking place. The sudden and unexpected death of a loved one, for example, triggers thoughts about why this event had to happen.

Our knowledge of how people make sense of their worlds—how they structure reality—is not very great. There is no research tradition in this area. The concept of reality structuring or the construction of reality is known to us because it has been dealt with theoretically (by Berger and Luckman, for example, 1966). This theoretical work, however, has been carried out at a high level of generality, and it has not informed empirical research on contemporary social life.

In the past there has been little or no work designed to operationalize different possible ways of structuring reality and to explore what those different ways imply for the kind of lives people live and the kind of society they advocate and create. Fortunately that situation is changing, and publications on this subject are beginning to appear (see, for instance, the McCready and Greeley reference, 1976). This article is a first report on exploratory work on reality structuring being pursued as part of the Research Program in Religion and Society, Survey Research Center, University of California at Berkeley.

Our starting point was the question: How do people deal with experiences and events which call for a judgment about how the world works? We had in mind experiences in which people are personally involved and which call for an answer to the question of why they occur: experiences, for example, such as failing to get an expected promotion, or having a loved one die unexpectedly in an airplane crash, or being held up and robbed. We also had in mind conditions to which people are exposed through the mass media or other sources and which call for an explanation of how they came about: for example social inequality, suffering in the world, and discrimination against minorities.

People deal with such experiences and conditions, we postulated, by drawing on assumptions they hold about the forces which govern what happens in the world. They adopt a mode of explanation which interprets such experiences and conditions as having been produced by one or another control agent. It was not our expectation that we should find the average person to hold and be able to articulate a highly refined theory of cause and effect. Explicitly or implicitly, however, we anticipated that the ordinary person would be found to structure reality in terms of cause and effect when confronted with events and experiences such as have been described.

The assumptions people hold about the structure of reality, as defined in these terms, we considered an empirical question, to be answered by the type of research we began to envision. It required no new research, however, to specify at least some of the assumptions we would encounter. Philosophers, theologians, scientists, and pseudoscientists have been speculating for centuries about forces which influence human events and shape social life. From among these forces we chose the following as probably among those to which ordinary citizens might refer when trying to account for events which happen to them or to which they are exposed.

One assumption about the structuring of reality which we expected to find flourishing among Americans is that which conceives of reality as being structured essentially by the individual. In this conception what happens to oneself is a result of one's own will power; what happens in the world is the cumulative result of how all individuals choose to play out their destinies.

A second assumption, or set of assumptions, conceives of the causal agent in supernatural terms. Most often, in America, that agent is personified as God. We also took fate and luck into consideration as suprahuman forces which, at least in some circumstances, are assumed by people to be agents determining what happens to them and what happens in the world.

A third set of assumptions conceives of causal agents in natural, but not individualistic, terms. This set includes two forces: heredity and environment. Often these forces are seen as subject to the control of a supernatural force—when God, for example, is considered the source of the talents with which people are born. However, these forces can also be conceived as operating independently of any supernatural influence—as having a modus operandi of their own. It is when they are so conceived that we propose to consider them basic assumptions helping to structure reality.

We saw no need in our initial conceptualization to distinguish among various possible ways that heredity and environment can be invoked as control agents. Some further specification of environmental forces proved necessary, however, when we entered upon the empirical phase of our explorations, and it is appropriate to anticipate that further specification.

We discovered, in open-ended interviews undertaken to test the conceptualization of control agents here being discussed, that some respondents, when they talk about environment, have culture in mind. According to this view, for example, blacks are less well off relative to whites because they have a different cultural background. Or poor people remain poor because they grew up in poverty and it is a way of life for them. For others, environment denotes the influence exercised by social forces. This social awareness takes two forms. One form, which we shall call "conspiratorial," conceives of social relations as being consciously manipulated by those in power in order to maintain their position of power. The other form, which warrants the label "environmental" as it is ordinarily conceived, views social forces as operating independently of conscious human control. In the former sense, for example, the poor are poor because the wealthy and powerful keep them poor. In the latter sense, poverty is the result of social arrangements created by historical social forces which have not been manipulated by anyone living today.

At the beginning of our project, we had no firm expectations about the relative frequency or the circumstances under which these alternative ways of structuring reality would be invoked. We also considered it problematic what combinations of assumptions we would find. At the one extreme, it seemed possible that we might find some people who conceive of all of life as being determined by a single control agent—God for example. At the other extreme, we could conceive of people acknowledging all of the causal agents as operative, but in a varying way in different contexts.

The vehicle available to us to explore these issues was an attitude survey of the San Francisco Bay Area, being conducted for other purposes, to which we were given access. The survey was executed by the field staff of the Survey Research Center, University of California at Berkeley. The sampled population was the noninstitutionalized adult population of the five Bay Area counties: San

Francisco, San Mateo, Alameda, Contra Costa, and Marin. The data were gathered in 1973 through a mailback questionnaire. The proportion of respondents designated by the sample from whom questionnaires were received was 65 percent. The total number of completed questionnaires was 646.

We were able to ask respondents to this survey to reflect on a number of problematic situations and to tell us how they understood these things to have come about. On a social level we asked them to reflect on such conditions as poverty and racial inequality. We also asked them about things that happen to individuals rather than to social groups, such as being killed in an airplane accident, being in poor health, having success or failure in life, and becoming an alcoholic. In addition, we asked respondents to think about their own lives and to tell us how much they personally had been influenced by the control agents mentioned.

It will not be possible within the brief compass of the present article to report and comment on respondents' answers to all of the questions we asked them. It is not necessary to be so comprehensive, however, to convey something of the character of the questions and of the results.

Table 4.1 reports the distribution of responses to a question asking respondents, "To what extent do you think your life is influenced by the way you were brought up (environment), God or some other supernatural force (supernatural), luck, the characteristics you were born with (heredity), what people in power decide (conspiratorial), and your own will power (individual)?" and to the additional question, "Which of these things has had the greatest influence on the course of your life?" The answer categories to the first question were: "Determines my life almost entirely, has a strong influence, has a small influence, has no influence at all." Looking at the proportion who chose to say that a particular causal agent "determines my life almost entirely," we see that very few people—1 and 2 percent respectively—invoke luck or people in power as "determining" control agents. The other causal agents, however, all get more than a modicum of support—18 percent say will power "determines my life almost entirely," 15 percent acknowledge God in this fashion, 13 percent how they were brought up, and 12 percent heredity.

A glance at the proportion checking that a given control agent has a strong influence on their lives, suggests that many people did not interpret "almost entirely" to mean "exclusively." Rather substantial numbers are able to say that their lives are "determined almost entirely" by one causal agent while at the same time acknowledging others to have a strong influence. They were able to do so, insofar as we can discover from analysis, because they frequently interpreted "determines almost entirely" to mean "primary" rather than "virtually exclusively" as we had intended.

Answers to the question asking respondents to choose which of these influences is most important affords some support of this interpretation. With the exception of "the way you were brought up," there are relatively few addi-

TABLE 4.1

Degree of Acceptance of the Influence of Alternative Causal Agents of Life[a]

Causal Agent	Determines Almost Entirely	Strong Influence	Small Influence	No Influence	(Number)[b]	Most Important Influence
Will power	18%	66	13	3	(631)	24%
God or some other supernatural force	15%	38	26	21	(691)	20
Luck	1%	16	53	30	(611)	1
Characteristics you were born with	12%	63	19	6	(623)	17
The way you were brought up	13%	78	7	2	(534)	36
People in power	2%	26	47	25	(617)	2
						(607)

[a] The influence of culture was not included among the answer categories.

[b] N's exclude those not answering each question.

tional respondents who chose a causal agent as most important than who chose it as "determining my life almost entirely." That the pattern does not hold for the environmental response is due to a lesser tendency for it than other agents to be seen as acting independently. In any case, "the way you were brought up" is most frequently chosen as the most important control agent (36 percent), followed by will power (24 percent), God (20 percent), and heredity (17 percent). Once again, luck and people in power scarcely gain any responses.

Another situation about which respondents were asked read as follows: "Twin brothers grow up—one to become a successful lawyer, the other to become a criminal and to spend most of his life in jail. As you think about this and similar stories you've heard, how do you explain them?" The causal agents most often selected to account for the twin brothers growing up so differently are environment (45 percent) and will power (35 percent). These were also the most frequently chosen, it will be recalled, as being most influential in shaping one's own life. There were substantially fewer who conceived of what happened to the twin brothers to be a result of heredity (5 percent) than who acknowledged the importance of heredity in their own lives (17 percent)—an understandable difference since the fact that the brothers are twins reduces the possibility of a genetic factor. Comparatively, respondents were also less likely to attribute the experiences of the twin brothers to supernatural causes (7 percent "God" plus 8 percent "fate") than they were to recognize the importance of supernatural influences in their own lives (20 percent).

Another tack we pursued was to ask respondents to reflect on such social conditions as suffering, poverty, and racial inequality, and to report how they accounted for these conditions. The question on poverty asked respondents to choose from among six explanations of poverty the one they judged most important. The explanation which gained the strongest support—37 percent of the sample—is the environmental one—"The poor are poor because social arrangements in America don't give all people an equal chance." There is very little support—2 percent—for the idea that poverty is the result of heredity— "Poor people are born without the talent to get ahead." The other four explanations gained about equal allegiance: 15 percent chose an individualistic explanation—"The poor simply aren't willing to work hard; they wouldn't be poor if they tried not to be"; 16 percent chose a supernatural explanation— "God gave people different abilities so that the work of the world will get done"; 17 percent chose a conspiratorial explanation—"The poor are poor because the wealthy and powerful keep them poor"; and 13 percent chose a cultural explanation—"Poor people are used to being poor because they grew up with it and it's a way of life for them."

Respondents vary considerably in the consistency of their responses to different questions. For some respondents all of life appears to be governed by a single control agent. Environment or God or heredity or one of the other control agents is conceived as determining virtually everything that happens to people and the world.

Other respondents are more discriminating in the control agents they invoke to explain different experiences and events. Their mode of explanation is multicausal rather than unicausal. They may conceive of particular events as being multiply caused, referring, for example, to both environment and heredity as contributing to how a person fares in life. Or they may see one agent as being responsible for some events and another as the cause of others. A person dying unexpectedly in an airplane accident, for example, might be accounted for as God's will, whereas someone's becoming an alcoholic will be explained as a result of individual choice. It is beyond the scope of the present article to deal with the different modes of structuring reality in all of their complexity. Simply by virtue of space, we are unable to deal with those whose modes are essentially multicausal.

We are in a position, however, to say something more about respondents who conceive reality to be determined primarily by a single control agent. Adopting the criteria that to be so identified requires, first, that a respondent opt for the same control agent in more than 50 percent of the times he or she had an opportunity to do so and second, that this requirement be satisfied for only one control agent—it turned out that 300, or 46 percent of the 646 respondents are characterized as unicausal in reality structuring, whereas the balance of 54 percent are multicausal. Of the 300 scoring as unicausal, 125 are environmentalists, meaning that they explain most or all the things they were asked about to be the result of environment, 65 are individualists, 46 culturalists, 35 supernaturalists, 24 conspiratorialists, and 5 hereditarians.

The balance of this report is based on these "pure types," omitting the hereditarians because of the paucity of cases. The number of cases available for analyzing the other types also leaves something to be desired, but the purpose of our inquiry is exploratory. We see our effort as possibly opening up new avenues of inquiry, not as settling the issues addressed in any final way.

Our inquiries were undertaken only in part out of curiosity about the character of the explanatory systems to which people refer when they are confronted with situations calling for a structuring of reality. We were also interested to discover what structuring reality in a particular way implies for political outlook, for support of different kinds of social arrangements in society, and for personal moral standards.

We harbored some suspicions about what we would find the politics of those in the different mode types to be. Generally speaking, we anticipated finding the individualists and the supernaturalists to be more conservative on the average than the environmentalists. The individualists, we reasoned, would lean to be conservative and perhaps reactionary, because it would follow from their orientation that individuals ought to be responsible for themselves and not rely on the government for help. Supernatural views would lean towards conservatism, we believed, because persons in this mode would not be inclined to want human beings to interfere in God's design.

We expected those in the environmental and conspiratorial modes to lean toward the liberal side of the political spectrum because criticism of existing social arrangements is implicit in them. As between the two, it seemed self-evident from the way the modes have been operationalized that the conspiratorialists ought to be found more disposed to radical positions and the environmentalists more reformist in their political orientation.

We were not sure what to expect of the cultural mode. In one sense, the mode is akin to the environmental and conspiratorial modes in giving recognition to environmental influences in the structuring of reality. At the same time, it seemed plausible that taking a cultural view of things might be associated with the belief that culture is a given about which not very much can be done. It also seemed plausible that to adopt a cultural explanation of social inequality, for example, might be a way of saying indirectly that cultural differences are genetic differences and of asserting the superiority of one culture over others.

The questionnaire offered many opportunities to put these speculations to test. For this report, we have selected from the various possibilities a few to convey the general tenor of the findings. Perhaps the most direct test of the speculations is to see how well they fare with respondents' self-description of their politics. Respondents were asked, ''How would you describe your politics now—would you say you are a radical, a liberal, a conservative, a strong conservative, or are you middle-of-the-road?''

Table 4.2 shows that the environmentalists and conspiratorialists are more likely than the individualists and supernaturalists to identify as radical or liberal, with those in the conspiratorial mode being the most inclined in this direction. In turn, the individualists and supernaturalists are more likely to be conservative than the environmentalists and conspiratorialists. The culturalists resemble most closely the individualists in their distribution of responses; they are overwhelmingly middle-of-the-road or conservative. Noteworthy is the different shape of distributions of individualists and supernaturalists. The modal response for individualists is middle of the road whereas it is conservative for the supernaturalists. But there are almost twice as many supernaturalists as individualists who chose the radical and liberal identification. Being in the supernatural mode seems to allow for countenancing rather different political postures.

These results conform to our expectations in a relative way. Those in the conspiratorial mode are more given to a radical stance than those in the other modes, but not everyone in the mode is a radical. In turn, compared to the environmentalists and conspiratorialists, those in the other three modes are more likely to be conservative, but they are not all conservative. Nevertheless, mode and political posture have considerable connections with each other.

TABLE 4.2
Political Self-Identification by Mode of Structuring Reality

Political Self-Identification	Individu-alistic	Super-natural	Cultural	Enviorn-mental	Conspira-torial	Total Respondents[a]
Radical	4%	7%	4%	2%	15%	5%
Liberal	18	32	14	41	64	34
Middle-of-the-road	41	5	40	40	14	33
Conservative	37	56	40	16	7	26
Strong Conservative	0	0	2	1	0	2
(100%=)[b]	(53)	(31)	(41)	(112)	(23)	(551)

[a]The total column includes those not classified in the typology.

[b]N's exclude those not answering this question.

A more instructive test of our speculations, because a wider range of the political spectrum is tapped and in a more concrete way, was provided by the responses to a question asking respondents, "Which of the following statements comes closest to expressing your view about how much government should be doing to help black people in the United States?" The answer categories provided for several responses which may be judged reactionary: "The government shouldn't be doing anything at all; it should be left up to individuals"; and "Nothing more; government has done too much already"; two additional responses indicating more or less of support for the status quo: "Nothing more; what government is doing now is enough"; and "No new laws are necessary, but the present laws against discrimination should be strictly enforced"; a mildly reformist response: "New and tougher laws against racial discrimination should be passed and strictly enforced"; a strongly reformist response: "The government needs to do more than fight discrimination, it should use tax money to insure better jobs, housing, and education for black people even if this means discrimination in reverse"; and a radical response: "I think the federal and state governments in the United States are racist and it is unrealistic to expect them to help black people."

The upper part of Table 4.3 reports the percentage of those in each mode category who chose each of these responses. The lower part of the table reports a different kind of statistic—one designed to assess the extent to which being in a particular mode predisposes respondents to overselect or underselect the alternative answers to the government action question in comparison to the average of all respondents. A score of zero or close to zero means that those achieving this score are responding as the average respondent does. The higher the score, the greater the over or underselection, except that underselection scores range from zero to minus 1.00 while overselection scores have no fixed upper limit. This over-under statistic aids in the interpretation of tables such as this one where, because of the many response categories, it is difficult to judge from the percentage table alone all that is going on.

Looking first at the upper part of the table, we see, once again, that the individualists and the supernaturalists choose the reactionary responses more often than the environmentalists and the conspiratorialists, with the individualists being especially prone to say "leave it up to individuals." At the opposite extreme, the individualists and supernaturalists offer no support for the radical response. Its support comes overwhelmingly from conspiratorialists.

By way of introduction to the lower table, it may be read in either direction. Reading across the table provides a comparative picture of the relative degree each of the five mode types over or underselect reactionary, status quo, reformist, and radical responses to the government action question. Reading down the columns of the table reveals the extent to which each response category on the government action question attracted or repelled those in each of the modes.

Compared to the average respondent, those in the individualistic mode are the most prone of the five types to overselect the *reactionary* response—across the first row of figures. Of the alternative responses, the individualists—now read down the first column—were the most attracted relatively by the *reactionary* response and most repelled by the *radical* response.

The supernaturalists divided their responses as on the political question. The tended to avoid the status quo response as they did the middle-of-the-road response previously. They also have no stomach for the radical response but show an almost equal disposition to overselect a reactionary and a reformist response. It would appear that seeing God as control agent produces on the part of some the kind of conservative reaction we anticipated. Others who conceive God to be in control are stimulated to sympathy for those in some distress.

The culturalists are the most likely to overselect the status quo responses and these are the only responses they overselect. Of the other alternatives, they are most repelled by the radical response and least by the reactionary response. Their modal posture, as in the previous question, is essentially conservative. The environmentalists overselect the reformist response, but reject relatively the radical response. The conspiratorialists are disposed relatively both to the reformist and the radical responses, but most especially to the latter.

Our speculations about the political consequences of the different modes extended also to moral consequences. We expected that the modes conducive to a conservative political stance would also be conducive to a conservative moral posture and vice versa. Results are generally concordant with these expectations. That is to say, the supernaturalists, the individualists, and the culturalists are always more conservative than those in the environmental and conspiratorial modes. However, which of the first three modes is the most conservative and which of the latter the more liberal differs somewhat according to the kind of moral issue being addressed.

On any issue which touches on individual responsibilities and rights—the efficacy of hard work, for example, or the individual's right to sell private property to anyone he chooses, the individualists will be the most prone to uphold such responsibilities and rights. On issues having to do with what has come to be called "conventional morality"—being honest, not giving in to sexual impulses, for example—the supernaturalists are the most prone to conservatism. The culturalists are virtually always less conservative than the supernaturalists and individualists, but especially so on issues in which a cultural element is present. For example on a question asking white respondents about their attitudes toward racial intermarriage, the culturalists show a moderate tendency to underselect $(-.19)$ the most conservative response cate-

TABLE 4.3
Government Action to Help Black People by Mode of Structuring Reality (White Respondents Only)

Government Action	Reality Structuring Mode					Total Respondents
	Individualistic	Supernatural	Cultural	Environmental	Conspiratorial	
Reactionary						
Leave to individuals	33%	11%	12%	8%	0%	11%
Gov't done too much	13	13	7	9	0	7
Status Quo						
Gov't doing enough	14	21	26	9	0	15
Enforce present laws	25	15	44	37	43	36
Reformist						
Pass tougher laws	9	16	3	23	27	15

TABLE 4.3 (Continued)

Reverse discrimination	6	24	8	13	19	14
Radical						
Gov't is racist	0	0	0	1	11	3
(100% =)	(51)	(21)	(38)	(97)	(12)	(478)

Over-Under Scores[a]

	Individu-alistic	Super-natural	Cultural	Environ-mental	Conspira-torial	Total Percentage
Reactionary	1.62	.33	.03	-.03	-1.00	18%
Status quo	-.23	-.29	.38	-.10	-.15	51
Reformist	-.49	.41	-.60	.26	.61	29
Radical	-1.00	-1.00	-1.00	-.63	2.96	3

[a]Score equals (observed frequency)/(expected frequency) - 1.

gory ("Blacks and whites should marry their own kind"). The individualists and supernaturalists, on the other hand, overselect that response; their respective over/under scores are .92 and 1.42. As for the environmentalists and conspiratorialists, the latter show the greater tendency to liberal responses both on issues having to do with the rights and responsibilities of the individual and on those bearing on conventional morality.

Given the exploratory nature of our inquiry, we cannot draw any firm conclusions from these results, although we feel we are onto something promising. It may occur to some readers, as it has occurred to us, that we may be involved in a tautology; demonstrating merely that liberal responses tend to go together, as do conservative ones. We believe that it is not being tautological if we are getting at underlying processes leading to conservatism and liberalism, which we think we are. We have also been uneasy, given the general tendency for three of the modes to lean conservatively and two liberally, that we may have been overly elaborate in constructing a typology where a dichotomy or scale might do as well. Our conviction that we are in fact dealing with a typology stems from the theoretical points already made. The conviction is reinforced by evidence, to be presented shortly, that the types are drawn from different parts of the social structure. We also recognize the additional possibility that our interpretation—that the modes of reality structuring are the "causes" of the consequences we have found them to be associated with—may be spurious. For example, the supernaturalists may be more disposed to be more helpful to individuals in distress not because of their convictions that God is omnipresent in the world, but because they are more likely to be women. Testing for spuriousness, given the number of cases we are dealing with, is difficult. Insofar as testing is possible, however, they reveal the modes to be related independently to political and social attitudes when differences in background characteristics are controlled.

Finally, we want to report some findings on the background characteristics of the persons in the different mode categories. We want to do this in the context of another speculation, namely that the distribution of different modes of reality structuring is changing in American society and, more specifically, that the modes more supportive of traditional social arrangements are being replaced by the modes in greater opposition to such arrangements. The reasoning behind the speculation is that scientific and social scientific perspectives are being diffused increasingly throughout society, in a popularized way through the mass media, especially television, and in a more sophisticated way through higher education. This means, we suspect, that more people are structuring reality from the perspective of the environmental and conspiratorial modes and fewer are doing so according to the individualistic and supernaturalistic modes. The social sciences do not deny that human beings possess free choice, but they raise serious doubts that the freedom is as extensive as those who subscribe to individualistic ways of structuring reality believe. In turn, the social sciences do

TABLE 4.4

Relative Attraction of Different Reality Structuring Modes to Respondents of Different Ages and Educational Backgrounds (Over-Under Scores)

	Reality Structuring Mode					
Age, Education	Individu-alistic	Super-natural	Cultural	Environ-mental	Conspira-torial	Total Percentage
Young (under 30)						
High School	-.04	-.32	-.64	.10	.28	19%
College (1+ yrs)	-.93	-.93	-.78	.78	-.18	12
Middle Age (30-49)						
High School	.84	.06	.21	-.39	-.17	18
College	-.28	-.86	.20	.69	.47	13
Older (50+)						
High School	.30	1.29	-.08	-.40	-.04	25
College	-.53	-.36	1.33	-.26	-.40	13
(Number =)	(65)	(35)	(46)	(125)	(24)	(646)

not deny the existence of God, but they do make suspect the anthropomorphic view dominant in America's past. By demonstrating other factors to be at work in shaping individual lives and social arrangements, the social sciences raise doubts about ideas which conceive of God or other supernatural agents as playing a decisive role in these realms.

It is not possible with cross-sectional data such as ours to test these speculations in a conclusive way. Moreover, data from the Bay Area cannot speak for American society as a whole. Circumstantial evidence for the changes envisioned, however, would be a finding that the environmental and conspiratorial modes are more prevalent among younger people and the more educated.

Table 4.4 presents the attractiveness of the different modes to respondents of different ages and levels of education. Pretty much as expected, the supernaturalist mode attracts those with less than college education and especially older, relatively uneducated persons. The individualistic mode is also oversubscribed to by the less than college educated, but its appeal is relatively more to the middle-aged than the old. The culturalist mode, and this may help to account for some of the earlier findings about it, tends to recruit among older persons, but from the more educated among them. It is the mode of choice of persons over 50 who have gone to college. The environmentalist mode is especially subscribed to by the college educated who are young or middle-aged.

It tends to be rejected by older respondents whatever their level of education. The conspiratorial mode attracts younger persons of less education and middle-aged persons of college education; the latter perhaps because they were young and at college during the turmoil of the sixties.

These results suggest that a shift in the distribution of modes is taking place and in the direction postulated. As we cautioned earlier, however, with cross-sectional data we cannot be sure, since what we may be observing is a life cycle phenomenon rather than a sign of generational change.

We have also looked at the religious background of respondents in the different modes on the assumption that if, as is widely accepted, there is a general trend toward secularization and if the distribution of modes is changing in the direction postulated, we should find those in the environmental and conspiratorial modes to be recruited relatively more from outside than inside the churches and those in conservative churches to be especially disposed to the supernaturalist mode.

TABLE 4.5
Religious Identification of Respondents in Each Mode
(Over-Under Scores)

	Reality Structuring Mode					
	Individu- alistic	Super- natural	Cultural	Environ- mental	Conspira- torial	Total Percentage
Religious Identification						
Liberal Protestant[a]	-1.00	-1.00	-.18	.63	-.27	8%
Moderate Protestant[b]	.62	.95	-.12	.04	.25	15
Conservative Protestant[c]	.84	1.31	-.16	-.25	-.59	14
Roman Catholic	.03	.23	-.67	-.27	.40	29
No Religious Beliefs	-.32	-1.00	.43	.24	-.82	19
Agnostic/Atheist	-.70	-.68	.64	.34	1.38	10
Humanist	-.18	-1.00	1.82	-.44	-.60	5
(Number =)	(57)	(27)	(41)	(94)	(18)	(518)

[a]Episcopalians, United Presbyterians, United Church of Christ, Unitarians

[b]American Baptists, American Lutherans, Lutheran Church in America, Methodists

[c]Southern Baptists, Missouri Lutherans, Presbyterian-U.S., Conservative Sects

(Religions other than Protestant and Roman Catholic were omitted because of the small number of cases in each.)

By and large the results conform to expectations. The supernatural mode is overselected by conservative Protestants especially, and also by Roman Catholics and moderate Protestants. It is strongly underselected by liberal Protestants and by those outside the churches. The environmentalist is the mode of choice of liberal Protestants and of those who say they have no religious beliefs. In turn, the conspiratorial is the mode of choice of those who say they are agnostics or atheists rather than the blander, "no religious beliefs"; Roman Catholics also show a tendency to overselect this mode.

Conservative Protestants are the most prone to overselect the individualistic mode, but to a lesser degree it is also overselected by moderate Protestants. We might also note that a majority of individualists acknowledge a belief in God—76 percent. Like the supernaturalists, the individualists apparently acknowledge God as creator but disagree about whom he has left in charge of his creation.

The culturalist mode is overselected only by those outside the churches and in this respect the mode is similar to the environmental mode. This may reflect a generational change in the reality structuring of the areligious. Recall that while the two modes recruit especially from the college educated, the culturalists tend to be older and those in the environmental mode younger.

These data on religion, like the earlier data on age and education, afford no conclusive demonstration of a generational shift in the distribution of the different modes. Taken together, however, the two sets of data are suggestive of such change and in the expected direction. Juxtaposing these findings with the earlier ones on the political and moral correlates of the different modes, the possibility is raised that shifts in the structuring of reality may be a significant input into the more general changes taking place in American society.

Although we plan on further examination of the present data set to engage in more refined testing of this hypothesis than we have presented here, it will require new research involving improvement in the conceptualization and operationalization of reality structuring and data on the national population and at more than one point in time to afford a wholly rigorous test.

References

Berger, Peter, and Thomas Luckman, 1966
McCready, William C., with Andrew M. Greeley, 1976

Disenchantment and Renewal in Mainline Traditions

Alienation and Apostasy

Wade Clark Roof

In the past decade this country has seen the striking rise of many new religious and quasi-religious groups attracting thousands of Americans seeking to experiment with novel, and at times bizarre, spiritual phenomena. Such groups—for example, Eastern mystical cults, Jesus followers, "Moonies," Transcendental Meditation, "Born Again" Christians, and the various human potential movements—have become highly visible since the mid-sixties, emerging during a time of widespread cultural unrest and turmoil. Exactly how many groups and how many people are involved is unknown, but their impact on American life cannot be judged simply in terms of numbers. For while there may be relatively few serious, highly committed followers of the new faiths, many as a result of religious experimentation have been led to a greater awareness of spiritual alternatives, and are more inclined today to question, and if necessary to reject, conventional religious values and identities. Even Americans not likely to become ardent enthusiasts of the new movements, easily find themselves dissatisfied with established religion; and many have chosen to abandon the churches and synagogues in favor of no organized religious affiliation.

Just how widespread this malaise is at present, and the extent to which people are defecting from traditional Protestant, Catholic, and Jewish loyalties—either in search of new religious alternatives or simply out of disenchantment—are matters attracting a good deal of speculation but very little research. The most extensive investigation to date of the religious aspects of the youth counterculture is the Berkeley Religious Consciousness Project, directed by Charles Y. Glock and Robert N. Bellah, which shows that the magnitude of change is enormous indeed. In the San Francisco Bay Area, one out of every four persons interviewed was attracted to the new faiths. Though far fewer were actually devotees, the fact that so many were attracted is itself a measure of their influence. But even more striking were the figures for defection from established churches: almost a fourth of the sample did not associate themselves with organized religion, and fully half had abandoned institutional religious ties since growing up. These are staggering proportions, suggesting that the turn to new religions is but a small part of the larger climate of unrest and ferment taking place in the religious realm. While relatively few people may have joined these movements, large numbers of Americans appear to be dropping out of churches and synagogues, or at the very least breaking with many of their institutional commitments.

But San Francisco is hardly a microcosm of American society, and considering its distinctive history as a seedbed for new cultural styles and social movements of all kinds, there is probably less religious change almost anywhere else in the country. Yet the changes foreshadowed raise important questions for society at large. Are many Americans abandoning their conventional religious identities in the seventies? Who are the defectors, in terms of their social and cultural characteristics? Is defection limited to the young, or is it spreading across other sectors of society?

In Search of Answers

In seeking answers to these questions, we rely on data from the General Social Surveys of the National Opinion Research Center. These annual surveys beginning in 1972, asking virtually identical questions from year to year, provide a barometer of American values and sentiments in the seventies. By merging the surveys for the past five years (1972-76), information is available on approximately 7,500 representative Americans. Given the large sample it is possible to explore many issues—such as switching away from an institutional religious identity—which otherwise could not be done.

For our purposes the surveys are useful because in addition to asking about people's current religious preferences, they included a question on the religion in which the respondent was raised. Juxtaposing these two, we are able to sort out those who though brought up as Protestant, Catholic, or Jew, no longer choose to identify in these terms. Having abandoned an institutional religious identification in favor of "none," such individuals may be thought of as defectors from the American religious establishment. This does not tell us whether the people involved have turned to other religious groups, but it is helpful for looking at the symbolic meanings associated with traditional religion and reactions to these in a time of cultural unrest and spiritual ferment. More than anything else, it tells us something about the depths of alienation in contemporary America, and extent to which this alienation is manifesting itself in apostasy from established faiths.

Extent of Religious Defection

Religious defection is occurring primarily among the young. Among those 18-25 years of age, the proportions for liberal Protestants and Catholics average about 15 percent (see Table 5.1). Similar if not stronger age breakdowns appear to hold for Jews, but because of too few cases the percentages are unreliable. For conservative Protestants defection generally is about half that for the other groups. Yet even here age differences are no less apparent than in the other traditions.

TABLE 5.1
Defection Among Protestants, Catholics, and Jews by Age (Percentages)

Percentage Switching to "None"

Age	Liberal Protestants (969)	Moderate Protestants (808)	Conservative Protestants (1175)	Catholics (1564)	Jews* (149)
18 - 25	16	17	8	14	---
26 - 35	6	10	6	9	---
36 - 50	5	6	2	7	---
51 - 65	5	1	4	2	---
66 up	3	3	1	3	---
TOTAL	6	6	4	7	11

*Too few cases for age breakdown

Such patterns for Protestants are understandable, considering that liberal Protestant bodies are known to have greater difficulties in inspiring strong commitment to the institution than more conservative churches and sects. Liberal theology, less rigid membership standards, and the thrust generally at accommodating modern secular culture within these faiths results in less of a hold on their members. Among youth in these churches particularly, there are serious problems of institutional loyalty and religious identity. More surprising perhaps, are the Catholic trends and changes. Defection among Catholics in the seventies is equal to, if not greater than, that for liberal Protestants. This is probably a relatively recent phenomenon owing to the changed circumstances of Catholicism in the modern world. Events of the last decade and a half, including the liturgical changes following Vatican Council II and the papal encyclical on birth control, have done much to undermine the traditional authority of the church and to bring about a climate of apathy among younger Catholics. Whatever the sources of these changes, the interesting point is that the gap between Protestants and Catholics in dropping out has closed considerably in recent years.

Some of this decline can be attributed to the normal developmental process, since many studies have shown that college students especially tend to lose interest in religion. But this is hardly a full explanation. Not just youth but Americans of all ages appear to be less inclined today to identify in religious group terms. Twenty years ago when as Will Herberg observed, "not to identify oneself and be identified as either a Protestant, a Catholic, or a Jew was somehow not to be an American," social pressures were much stronger to belong to one of the major religious communities. In 1957, for example, the special census on religion showed that only 2.7 percent of Americans reported themselves as "none." By contrast the NORC data for the seventies show that 6.7 percent now define themselves this way. Especially telling in this respect are the net increases among those who have switched from the religion in which raised: "nones" have increased by 144 percent in the intervening years, roughly three or four times as much as any of the mainline denominations. Most of the major religious groups have lost in the shifting of religious preferences in the seventies, with gains mainly for the religious fringe and "nones."

Also there have been marked cultural shifts among youth in recent years, especially with regard to the meaning systems used for interpreting their lives. Traditional theistic beliefs and values have lost much of their plausibility and are being partly replaced by more mystical, personally oriented approaches to life. Religion for youth is very much a privatized matter today, with the result that many have turned away from visible group loyalties as a basis for self-identification. Consequently, many youth in the seventies have been weaned away from the established faiths and now seek their identity in either secular or contracultural settings.

Social Correlates of Defection

Who are the defectors from the religious establishment? What are their social and background characteristics? To check this, we look at a number of social correlates to see who are most likely to switch out of the established faiths see Table 5.2. For those under 35 years of age we find the following:

TABLE 5.2
Social Correlates of Religious Defection

Characteristics	Percent Switching to "None" (Age 18-35)
Sex	
Male	14%
Female	7
Region	
North East	16
North Central	9
South	9
West	18
Education	
Less than high school	9
High school graduate	7
Some college	15
College graduate	19
Post-graduate	14
Income	
Less than $6,000	12
$6,000 to $10,000	11
$10,000 to $20,000	9
More than $20,000	14
Work Status	
Employed	12
Not employed	10
Marital Status	
Single	12
Married	11
Father's SES	
Low	9
Medium	10
High	16

Sex. Males are twice more likely to defect than females as shown by 14 and 7 percentages, respectively. Even stronger sex differentials exist among those of Protestant background, simply because liberal Protestant males are among the most prone to drop out. For Catholics differences are less, probably because many young Catholic women are unwilling to accept church teachings on birth control. All things considered, sex is perhaps the best predictor of religious defection.

Region. Switching out of the established faiths is more common in the West and Northeast, less so in the South and North Central states. The proportions reach very high levels for young Protestants in the West, especially for liberal Protestants; among young Catholics the differences are similar but less striking. The patterns of defection vary much like other religious differences do by region.

Education. The higher the educational level the greater the chances of dropping out, although the generalization glosses over some interesting exceptions. High school graduates drop out less than those without a high school education, and postgraduates do so slightly less than the college educated. This latter exception holds for Protestants but not for Catholics, who defect in larger proportions at the postgraduate level.

Income. Income differences are not as strong as might be expected. Almost equal proportions drop out at opposite ends of the income scale. Among Catholics differences are somewhat sharper as a result of their greater defection at high-income levels. But income as a correlate is relatively weak and hardly a basis for arguing that affluence leads to apostasy.

Work Status. Individuals with jobs switch slightly more often than those without. But the differences are small and probably have little bearing on defection. Contrary to speculation about youth in the sixties and seventies, religious dropouts are not necessarily those without jobs or unable to support themselves economically.

Marital Status. Whether a person is married or not, has little effect on defection. Those married are about as likely to drop out as singles, suggesting that defection is hardly limited to the unattached without family responsibilities.

Father's SES. Those with higher status, middle-class background tend to defect more than those from the working class. The greater the father's occupational status, education, and income, the greater the likelihood of dropping out. For Protestants and Catholics alike the pattern holds, but is especially pronounced for the latter.

Several conclusions emerge from this social profile. One is that religious defection in recent years, not unlike in previous times, follows clearly along age, sex, educational, and regional lines. Secular influences in modern society are generally greater among the young, the educated, for men more than women, and occur more in the West and North. Historically in the American experience these have been the collectivities most exposed to changing styles and cultural trends. A second conclusion is that young defectors are prone to come from affluent, middle-class families, and are as likely to be married and hold jobs or not. This flies in the face of interpretations implying that religious dropouts are marginal persons in society—youth who are single, without work, and geographically unsettled. The profile indicates that religious defection is widespread in American society, and not simply restricted to those who in previous years were labeled as "flower children." Such a pattern suggests a generational break in cultural styles and institutional commitments, in keeping with the emergence of the so-called counterculture and its influence in the late sixties.

Cultural Alienation and the New Morality

Institutional defection does not occur in a cultural vacuum. Such shifts in institutional loyalties among youth have to be viewed in terms of the larger cultural process: the emergence of a solidified, self-conscious counterculture in response to the Vietnam War in the late sixties, and its subsequent transformation following the winding down of the war in the early seventies. Early on the counterculture directed its attention to America's involvement in the war and to the corporate economic structures supporting it; but gradually as the situation in Vietnam changed, it focused less on political and economic concerns and more on general values and lifestyles. As the focus changed, so did the institutions that were to become victims of reaction. Established religion was one in which a clash could hardly be avoided given the opposition of the mainline faiths to many countercultural values such as alternative lifestyles, homosexuality, and the "new consciousness."

Organized religion was not to be singled out for confrontation as had been the political process earlier, simply because the clash had to do with intangible yet fundamental beliefs and values. Nonetheless the clash was bound up with the widespread alienation felt by youth toward American institutions—a generalized estrangement little helped by the domestic crisis of Watergate in the early seventies. The extensiveness of this alienation is shown by the degree to which dropouts from the churches also lacked confidence in other institutions (see Table 5.3). A crisis of confidence extended broadly to many realms including government, corporations, labor, the military, and the media. Fully a third of those having abandoned their religious identity expressed "hardly any" confidence in these basic structures of American life. What occurred appears to be less a self-conscious religious response than a widespread pattern of institutional reaction and realignment. The distrust and disaffection generated in earlier years against the political process spread throughout the society, engulfing the various institutional realms.

TABLE 5.3
Confidence in American Institutions Among Religious Drop-Outs

Institution	Percent Expressing "Hardly Any" Confidence
Organized Religion	42
Major Companies	35
Executive Branch of Federal Government	46
Congress	32
Military	35
Television	33
Labor	32

By the mid-seventies political radicalism had waned and there was growing acceptance for much of what the counterculture stood for. The values and meaning systems—especially that often described as the "new morality"—set in motion in the preceding years continued to spread, often gaining acceptance in unexpected quarters. New moral norms and social values associated earlier with a small countercultural minority had by this time spread to the mainstream of college youth, and from the colleges to larger numbers of noncollege youth, including many just entering the work force, housewives, and high school students. This diffusion of values from a tiny minority to large sectors of American youth and beyond was, as Daniel Yankelovich describes, an "extraordinary pattern of change." Americans under 35 years of age especially have been highly influenced by changing values in matters of family and sexual styles, drugs and leisure, attitudes toward authority, and concern over personal self-fulfillment.

Individuals endorsing these values are more likely to be dissatisfied with conventional institutions, including established religion. Religious defection occurs far more frequently among those committed to the new morality (see

TABLE 5.4
Religious Defectors and Value Commitments by Age Groups

Item	Age Categories				
	18-25	26-35	36-50	51-65	Over 65
Taken Part in Civil Rights Demonstration					
Yes	41	24	18	--	--
No	11	7	4	2	3
Taken Part in Anti-War Demonstration					
Yes	43	42	25	4	--
No	8	6	6	2	--
Regard Homosexuality As Always Wrong					
Yes	5	3	3	2	2
No	23	19	12	6	7
Favor Legalizing Marijuana					
Yes	22	20	16	7	8
No	6	5	3	2	3
Favor Legal Abortion for Single Women					
Yes	20	14	8	5	5
No	5	4	3	1	1
Regard Extra-Marital Sex As Always Wrong					
Yes	5	4	3	2	2
No	23	15	12	5	6

Table 5.4). On all six items covering issues of marijuana, abortion, homosexuality, sexual norms, and protest activity, those committed are much more inclined to defect. Defection is most pronounced for the young, but even among those over 35 it occurs. Mainline religious institutions are identified with the established order, closely akin to the dominant cultural values of society, and thus rejection of one often entails abandonment of the other. As the counterculture has shifted more to concerns of values and meanings, this tension no doubt has increased.

Upward Diffusion of New Values?

This spread of new cultural values and styles among young Americans illustrates the pace of recent change, and their growing attraction to many Americans. Even though noncollege youth were slower in adopting the values than the college educated, the rapid spread has resulted in an astonishingly swift closing of the gap in outlook between these two. This being the case, would we not also expect some "upward" movement of the values among older Americans? And if so, perhaps greater religious defection as well? Youth having grown up in the sixties are now assuming adult roles and carrying their values with them as they marry, have children, hold jobs, and settle down in their communities. Admittedly there is a tendency to become more traditional with age and life-cycle obligations, but even so it is unlikely the cultural changes of the past decade will quickly dissipate. Moreover, many of the cultural trends originating with the young—for example, women's rights and attitudes toward marijuana—are spreading across generational lines and becoming more diffused throughout society. Much of what once passed as radical or even hippie is today accepted in many respectable sectors.

With the NORC data we cannot examine very thoroughly this possibility, but the evidence we have supports it. Table 5.5 shows the extent Americans were adopting the new morality values as well as religious changes, from 1973 to 1976. The new morality index consists of three items (marijuana, abortion, and homosexuality); and the proportions shown are for those scoring high on the index within each of the age groups. During the three-year period little change occurred within the youngest age category, reflecting perhaps a leveling off in trends among those previously most receptive to the values. But for those in the 26-35 age category there were moderate increases, from 36 percent in 1973 to 50 percent by 1976. Increases were less for older Americans but clearly evident. Gradually the new values were catching on, slowly diffusing throughout the society among those who, say even five years earlier, would not have been inclined to endorse the views.

Also evident, though less striking, were religious changes during the period. Both the switching-to-none and church attendance trends indicate shifts paralleling those of the new morality. Americans above age 25, and particularly

TABLE 5.5
The New Morality and Religious Defection, 1973 and 1976

| | Age Categories | | | | |
	18-25	26-35	36-50	51-65	66+
Percent High on New Morality					
1973	55	36	30	22	12
1976	56	50	36	28	20
	+1	+14	+6	+6	+8
Percent Switching to No Religious Preference					
1973	13	7	4	1	1
1976	13	10	8	4	2
	0	+3	+4	+3	+1
Percent Attending Church Less than Weekly					
1973	72	57	51	51	49
1976	70	65	57	53	50
	-2	+8	+6	+2	+1

those between 25 and 50 appear to have declined somewhat in institutional religious loyalties. The shifts are small and should not be overdrawn, yet interestingly they occur simultanously with the changing values and attitudes. What we observe here suggests a "percolate-up" effect: cultural values and institutional styles originating with youth and spreading more widely through society. Ironically the changes are coming at a time when commitments among youth are stabilizing or even possibly turning around. Religious defection may have bottomed out among the very young, but perhaps the trends toward greater acceptance of the new values and religious defection will continue among the successive age groups. Trends set in motion in one age group will work themselves out in other quarters, even though the pace of acceptance will likely slow down considerably.

Future Prospects

It is unlikely that the new morality will replace the old or that religious defection will increase significantly in the near future. Traditional values and styles continue to evoke strong commitments in the populace at large, placing limits on how far trends can go. However widespread the alienation and apostasy of the seventies, they must be viewed in the larger context of change and resistance to change, new culture and the old. The trends as described fit mainly for young Americans caught up in the counterculture of the sixties and seventies; it remains to be seen what the overall impact of these changes will be for America generally.

To a considerable extent the future depends on how well the mainline religious institutions can adjust to changing values and lifestyles. At present Protestant and Catholic faiths are internally split over such issues as homosexuality, abortion, and women's ordination, issues that are likely to continue to divide for a long time and polarize the population into bitter group struggles. Recent crusades as that led by Anita Bryant against homosexual rights and the Right to Life movement opposing legalized abortion reveal the depths of conservative reaction and the close affinity of these issues to religious symbols and values. Should these forces prevail there will likely be further defections from the churches, certainly among the young and maybe even among many older Americans. The new morality has spread too far and taken too strong a hold in the populace for the churches to turn their backs on these issues.

But it is also possible that out of the clash will come a more responsive and forthright religious institution. This might very well work against the trend toward defection and possibly even stem the tide in the direction of greater church loyalties. Already there is some evidence in the past year or so suggesting a turn toward greater church loyalty on the part of those who are highly committed. And as new age groups mature, not having experienced the counterculture of the sixties, the churches might regain some of their favor.

Whatever the future prospects, the defections of the seventies will likely be remembered for their positive, and not simply negative consequences. For churches and synagogues the defections called attention to how far removed these institutions had become from the world of the young. For the young the defections came about out of an intense clash over values and meanings. For both there were gains in integrity, conviction, and identity.

References

Caplovitz, David, and Fred Sherrow, 1977
Glock, Charles Y., and Robert N. Bellah, 1976
Wuthnow, Robert, 1976
Yankelovich, Daniel, 1974

Religious Musical Chairs

Andrew M. Greeley

The literature of religious disidentification generally offers three different kinds of explanations for the phenomenon of people withdrawing from the religious denomination in which they were raised.

The secularization model. In the form advanced by Charles Y. Glock and his students, *secularization* means that the more sophisticated, the better educated, the more cosmopolitan people become, the less likely they are to maintain their ties with their traditional religious affiliations or with any religious affiliation at all. Robert Wuthnow has reexamined this explanation and found it deficient in many respects. A more popularized form of the secularization model can be found in the thinking of many religious leaders. Whatever factors lead people to the fringe of a denomination will lead them out of the denomination when they become powerful. A person will drift into the low levels of religious devotion because, let us say, of dissatisfaction with the sexual ethic or racial stance of his denomination, and then when his dissatisfaction grows stronger will drift across the line separating the identifier with the disidentifier.

The family strain model. Most serious research done on religious disidentification (by John Kotre, Joseph Zelan, David Caplowitz, and Andrew M. Greeley) emphasizes the powerful influence of family background in the decision to disidentify religiously. The church, as Kotre has pointed out, is an institution which emits many stimuli. Which stimulus one chooses to focus on in determining to identify or disidentify is a function of the psychological perspective one brings from the family experience to one's encounter with the church. Living apart from one's family, coming from a broken family, a family in which there is conflict, or a family in which there is unusual strain between a person and his parents are powerful predictors of religious disidentification. Similarly, the religious disidentifiers are likely to be dissatisfied and unhappy personally and to take strong liberal stands on political and social issues. Zelan and Caplowitz suggest that an ideology of political liberalism may become a substitute religion for them.

The religious intermarriage or "musical chairs" model. This explanation, contained in one essay by the present author and much of the research literature on Jewish intermarriage, recognizes that the American population plays a game of religious musical chairs at the time of marriage. Men and women rearrange their religious affiliations to minimize the strain and conflict which might exist in a family because of different religious loyalties. In such a game of musical chairs, religious conviction, faith and unbelief, devotion and loyalty are less important than minimizing family conflict. The conversion will usually be in the direction of the more devout of the two marriage partners.

There has been relatively little research done on either religious disidentification or religious exogamy in recent years. Caplovitz's monograph on disidentification is concerned basically with young people who graduated from college in the early 1960s. The Jewish exogamy studies focus on that denomination and show mixed and conflicting findings. However, the National Opinion Research Center (NORC) General Social Survey has asked questions about present and past religious identification for four of its five annual surveys as well as a number of other questions which enable us to test each of the three explanations offered above for religious disidentification.

Questions about age and education will enable us to examine the Glock model of secularization. Questions about sexual attitudes and belief in life after death will permit us to examine the variant of the secularization model which sees disidentification as a continuous behavior logically linked with low levels of religious practice. Questions about whether the respondent lived with both parents at age 16, about trust, psychological well-being, and political disaffiliation will enable us to examine the family strain/disaffiliated personality model. Finally, questions about the religious affiliation of spouse at 16 and the present time will enable us to investigate the musical chairs model.

The most plausible explanation for the religious disidentification phenomenon is religious exogamy—an especially powerful explanation for Catholics. There is also some support for the other explanation, though virtually none for the Glock secularization thesis. It is true that both the young and the better educated are more likely to disidentify religiously, but this can be explained by increased exogamy and an increase in the level of general societal disaffiliation.

To say that disidentification is connected with exogamy does not mean that one has a clear notion of how the two relate to one another. Not all disidentifiers marry out of their denominations and not all participants in exogamous marriage disidentify. Where the two phenomena do occur, one does not know whether disidentification came before the marriage or after it, and whether if it came before it was a time immediately before the marriage, taking place with the marriage in mind, or was an earlier event which might have been accounted for by either of the other two explanatory models. In the present analysis we find that there are a substantial number of young unmarried people whose disidentification can be accounted for by an alienation/disaffiliation model. These young people are part of a special phenomenon that occurred in the late 1960s. There may have been among older generations a similar disidentification based on anger or disbelief; but if this disidentification occurred prior to a religiously mixed marriage, very little trace of it can be found among those who entered religiously mixed marriages and then disidentified. It would appear that musical chairs is one way out of a denomination—a response to the religious convictions of one's spouse—while religious alienation, for reasons either of conviction or a general tendency toward disaffiliation, is another way out with relatively little linkage between the two. Nonetheless, since we are dealing with a phenomenon that occurred sometime between the sixteenth birthdays of our respondents and the present, the most we will be able to do here is to speculate about the connections. A much more detailed study of the religious maturation process between the late teens and the late twenties would be required for more precise information and precise explanations of the complex link between religious identification and marriage. There is substantial evidence to believe that young people make up their minds about their religious affiliation at about the same time they make up their minds about their political affiliation—sometime between 17 and 30 (the generation that grew up in the 1960s tends to have suspended ultimate decision about both these affiliations).

The questions in the General Social Survey pertinent to our analysis are at least as good as items ever available for the study of disidentification and exogamy in the past. Nonetheless, they leave something to be desired. In a study explicitly designed to study disidentification better operational indicators would surely have been designed.

For the present analysis the following variables were routinely built into the mathematical models: age, sex, respondent's education, respondent's spouse's education, respondent's parents' education, geographic region, city size, personal psychological well-being, marital adjustment, whether one lived with one's mother and father at 16, belief in life after death, church attendance, approval of extramarital sex, premarital sex, the distribution of birth control information to teenagers, belief that most people can be trusted, support for prayer and bible reading in public schools, confidence in religious leadership, support for the legalization of marijuana, and certain anomie items about whether people can be trusted to be fair, whether life is exciting or dull, and marital status.

The issues explored here are extremely complicated. For purposes of simplicity of presentation, correlational analysis is used most of the time. One of the disadvantages of using correlation/multiple regression is that when the distribution of respondents is skewed (for example, only one-sixth of our respondents have disidentified religiously), the correlation coefficients are likely to be relatively small and to obscure important relationships that nonparametric statistics would reveal. The problem is even more serious when the distribution on the second variable (area of the country in which the respondent lives) is also badly skewed. Thus evidence was found to sustain the conviction that religiously mixed marriages are more likely for Catholics who live in the South and West than for those who live in the Northeast and North Central regions of the country. However, since only a relatively small proportion of the Catholic population lives outside of the Northeast and North Central regions, the regional variable is not a powerful explanation of religious disidentification (because most religious disidentification for Catholics still occurs in the North where most Catholics live). Similarly, disidentification rates are high among those who were not living in an intact family at age 16. Again, only a relatively small proportion of the population did not live in intact families; therefore, an unintact family is not an important explanation for religious disidentification. Most religious disidentification occurs among those who came from intact families. When one chooses between parametric and nonparametric statistics in an analysis like the one here, one realizes that there are costs and advantages to both techniques. The costs in a decision to use parametric statistics here are a loss of some interesting and useful information; but the benefits include a much clearer, orderly, and systematic presentation of a subject matter which is complicated enough to begin with.

Ten percent of those who were Protestants at age 16 are no longer Protestants, while 16.5 percent of Catholics and 16 percent of Jews have disidentified with their denominations. (Jews are omitted from this analysis because 150 respondents are not sufficient for generalizations in an area in which there is intensive research being carried on by other scholars. There is not sufficient numbers for most Protestant denominations to permit detailed analysis— though, as we will note later, Baptists alone have a lower mixed marriage rate than other Protestant denominations. The Baptist/non-Baptist dichotomy, however, was not statistically significant in any other of the models constructed).

Sixteen percent of those who were Protestant at age 16 contracted marriages with spouses who were not Protestant at age 16. Thirty-nine percent of Catholics contracted such exogamous marriages, as did 15 percent of Jews. However, when one looks at the present endogamy rates, one notes that they fall to 11 percent for Protestants, 23 percent for Catholics, and 10 percent for Jews. In other words, the game of religious musical chairs, by which spouses reduce exogamy rates by religious change, cuts by one-third Protestant and Jewish exogamy rates and cuts almost in half Catholic exogamy rates.

Two-fifths of those who were Catholic at 16, in other words, married people who were not Catholics; but only about one-fourth of those who are Catholics today are married to people who are not Catholics today. Some of those who were Catholic at 16, in other words, have become non-Catholic; others remain Catholic and their spouses who were non-Catholic at 16 have become Catholic. The net result of the rearrangements of religious affiliation in association with exogamous marriages is a 2 percent loss in total membership for Protestants and a 7 percent net loss for Catholics. While 9 percent of those born Protestant disidentify, 7 percentage points of that disidentification is compensated for by conversions—most in association with religiously mixed marriages—and while 16.5 percent of those who were born have disidentified, 10 percentage points of that change is compensated for by converts—again, most of them in association with religiously mixed marriages.

Disidentification is closely related to exogamy. For both Catholics and Protestants, only 6 percent who married a spouse who was the same religion as they were at 16 have disidentified, while 30 percent of those who married out of their denomination have disidentified. Disidentification, in other words, is five times higher in exogamous marriage as it is in endogamous marriages. About one-fifth of both denominations who were never married have disidentified. Whether in conjunction with marriage such respondents will reidentify with their old religion, identify with a new one, or remain disidentified is at best a matter of conjecture. However, most of the unmarried disidentifiers are young, and, as we shall suggest later, there seems to be a special dynamism at work among the disidentifying young.

TABLE 6.1
Disidentification Rates Among American Denominations*
(Percent)

Affiliation at Age 16	Current Affiliation					
	Protestant	Catholic	Jew	Other	None	Total
Protestant (3961)		3.4	0.1	0.7	5.5	9.7
Catholic (1625)	8.5		0.4	0.4	7.2	16.5
Jew (150)	2.7	0.7		1.3	11.3	16.0

*Proportion religious affiliation at the age of 16 who no longer claim that affiliation.

Exogamy accounts for 50 percent of Catholic disidentification and 34 percent of Protestant disidentification. One-fourth of Protestants married to other Protestants have disidentified, while only 13 percent of the Catholics married to other Catholics have disidentified. Approximately four-fifths of the married Catholics who have disidentified entered religiously exogamous marriages, as opposed to 56 percent of the disidentifiers among married Protestants in religiously mixed marriages. Among Protestants and Catholics, then, an absolute majority of the married disidentifiers are in religious mixed marriages— more than half the Protestants and almost four-fifths of the Catholics. The exogamy explanation of disidentification is clearly the most powerful. But the question remains as to whether there are dynamics at work which lead to both disidentification and mixed marriage. Do people enter mixed marriages because they have disidentified, or are there two separate paths out of religious denominations—one through mixed marriage and one that may lead to mixed marriage but would operate independently of mixed marriage?

TABLE 6.2
Exogamy Rates Among Americans (Percent)

Denomination	Religion at Age 16	Present Religion
Protestant	16	11(2724)
Catholic	39	23(1025)
Jew	15	10(97)

The musical chairs model works as follows: Eighty percent of those who were Protestant at 16 married others who were Protestant at 16; four percent married spouses with Protestant identification at 16 but have themselves disidentified (a disidentification independent of marriage). Five percent entered religiously mixed marriages and now disidentify; another 4 percent have entered religiously mixed marriages, but their spouse became Protestant so that now the marriage is endogamous. Finally, 7 percent of the Protestants entered marriages which then and now are religiously exogamous, in which neither the respondent nor the spouse changed religious identification. It is the third and fourth categories, then, which represent the religious musical chairs—5 percent of the Protestants marry out of the denomination and move out of it, 4 percent move out but the spouse moves into the Protestant denomination—a net loss of 1 percent.

TABLE 6.3
"Survival" Rates for Protestants and Catholics
(Net Loss—"Musical Chairs" Has Been Played)

Protestant   Catholic

2%   7%

For Catholics the mixed marriage rates are much higher—44 percent of American Catholics marry persons who were not Catholics at 16. Twelve percentage points of this group disidentify with the church, but another 8 percentage points are in marriages in which the spouse has converted to Catholicism, making it a net loss of 4 percentage points to American Catholicism because of religious intermarriage. Twenty percent of those Catholics who entered religiously mixed marriages are still in religiously mixed marriages with no change in spouse or self. Conversion as a result of mixed marriages among Catholics is more likely than disidentification, and a continuation of the marriage as mixed is most likely.

There are almost a bewildering number of possibilities: (1) Why do people disidentify if they are not in mixed marriages? (2) Why do people enter mixed marriages? (3) Why do some of the exogamously married disidentify? (4) Why do some "convert" their spouses, and why do some remain in marriages which continue to be religiously mixed? (5) What impact does "marriage conversion"

TABLE 6.4
Disidentification Rates for Marital Groups
(Percent Disidentifying)

	Protestant	Catholic
Never married	18	21
Married in	6	6
Married out	30	30
Widowed	7	12
Separated	20	21
Divorced	13	12

TABLE 6.5
Disidentification and Marriage (Percent)

	Protestant	Catholic
Never married	21	23
Married in	27	13*
Married out	34**	50***
Separated, widowed, and divorced	18	16
Total	100 (385)	100 (257)

*Three percentage points of this group, how-
ever, have been divorced in the past, although they
are now married to Catholics. If these are added
to the marriage related disidentifiers, 84 percent
of those who were raised Catholics and are presently
married but who have disidentified have done so in
connection with a religiously mixed marriage or a
divorce.

**56 percent of the disidentifiers among the
married.

***79 percent of the disidentifiers among the
married.

have on denomination? (6) Are those who were recruited in association with
marriage as devout as the born members of the denomination? The answer to
each question assumes a different comparison, one that is logically designed to
provide an answer.

The first question has to do with that minority of disidentifiers whose
decision is not related to a religiously exogamous marriage. The analytic
variables available to us enable us to explain 14 percent of the disidentification
of Protestants and 17 percent of the disidentification of Catholics—when one
compares the unmarried respondents or endogamously married respondents
who disidentify with the unmarried respondents and the endogamously married
respondents who do not disidentify. For Protestants there are no statistically

TABLE 6.6
Religious Disidentification and Mixed Marriages (Percent)

Spouses' Religion at 16	Self-identification Now	Spouse's Identification Now	Protestant Religion at 16	Catholic Religion at 16
In	In		80	56
In	Out		4	4
Out	Out		5*	12
Out	In	In	4**	8
Out	In	Out	7***	20
Total			100(2751)	100(1066)

* Convert to other faith

** Spouse converted

*** Existing mixed marriage

TABLE 6.7
Comparisons in This Research

Question	Groups Compared	Fig. or Table
1. Why do those who are not in religiously mixed marriages disidentify?	The unmarried and endogamously* married, disidentifiers versus nondisidentifiers.	Fig. 1
2. Why do people enter religiously mixed marriages?	The endogamously married versus the exogamously** married.	Fig. 2
3. Why do some exogamous marriages correlate with disidentification?	Exogamously married who remain exogamous compared to those in which self disidentifies.	Fig. 3
4. Why do other exogamous marriages correlate with conversion of the spouse to self's religion?	Exogamously married who remain exogamous compared to those which endogamy has been achieved by conversion of spouse.	Fig. 4
5. How religious are "marriage converts" in the new denomination?	"Converts" in question 4 compared with members of "receiving" denomination in endogamous marriages.	Table 8
6. How religious are "marriage converts" compared to old denomination?	"Converts" in question 4 compared to endogamously married in "sending" denomination.	Table 9

*Endogamously married are defined as those whose religion at 16 is the same as the described religion of spouse at 16.

**Exogamously married are those whose religion at 16 is different from that of described religion of spouse at 16. Disidentification of self or conversion of spouse (as measured by present religion question) may have happened before marriage, at the time of marriage, or after it.

significant relationships in the multiple regression model between nonmarital disidentification and demographic variables, such as age, education, sex, and region. Three of the predictors of disidentification have to do with religion—confidence in religious leaders, belief in life after death, support for prayer and Bible reading in the classroom—while three have to do with "moral issues—premarital sex, extramarital sex, and legalization of marijuana. A generalized disaffiliation as measured by being a political "independent" also relates to Protestant disidentification, but only indirectly through the two "blocks" or religious and moral issues. Nonmarital disidentification for American Protestants, then, insofar as it can be explained by the tools available to us, seems to be a rather straightforward religious and moral disenchantment. There are other factors at work, but as far as our theories and analytic tools are able to be used on the question of nonmarital disidentification, it would seem that Protestants disidentify for religious and ethical reasons.

Among Catholics, the religious and ethical reasons are also at work—somethat more strongly. There is a $-.21$ relationship between confidence in religious leaders and disidentification and .17 between support for the legalization of marijuana and disidentification. There are also direct relationships between disidentification and age $(-.1)$, education $(-.11)$, general disaffiliation $(.10)$, and divorce $(.18)$. The three most powerful predictors of disidentification among Catholics whose disidentification is not related to religiously mixed marriage are a previous divorce, low confidence in the clergy, and political liberalism as represented by support for the legalization of marijuana. Our rather complex model has two separate subsystems, a religious subsystem at the bottom of the model that involves divorce, belief in life after death, and confidence in religious leadership; and a "secular" subsystem at the top of the model that involves age, education, "unaffiliation," and support for the legalization of marijuana. Younger Catholics, better educated Catholics, Catholics who are political independents, and Catholics who support the legalization of marijuana are more likely to disidentify, as are Catholics who have been divorced, who have a low level of confidence in religious leadership, and who do not believe in life after death. Among that minority of Catholic disidentifiers whose disidentification is not marriage associated, both the first and second models described in the beginning (the secularization model and the alienation model) seem to apply. The secularization model applies in two forms—age and education on the one hand and a continuation of problems with the clergy and religious conviction on the other. (Confidence in religious leadership can be taken as a rough equivalent indicator of attitudes toward clerical performance, and life after death as a rough equivalent indicator of attitudes toward doctrine. Sexual attitudes while tested, were not strong enough in their influence on Catholic disidentification to be included in this model—or any of the models presented here for Catholics, save that a previous divorce may in some indirect sense represent an indicator of sexual attitudes.)

FIGURE 6.1-A
Nonmarital Disidentifiers for Protestants*

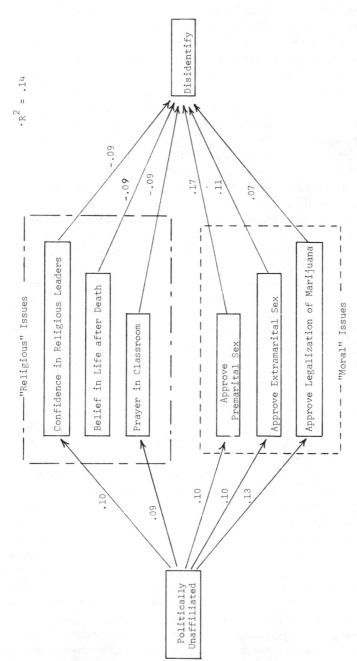

*Unmarried respondents who married within their own denomination but nonetheless disidentify compared to those who are unmarried or married within their denomination but who have not disidentified.

NOTE: In all figures only statistically significant parameters are presented. Dotted lines are occasionally added for symmetry.

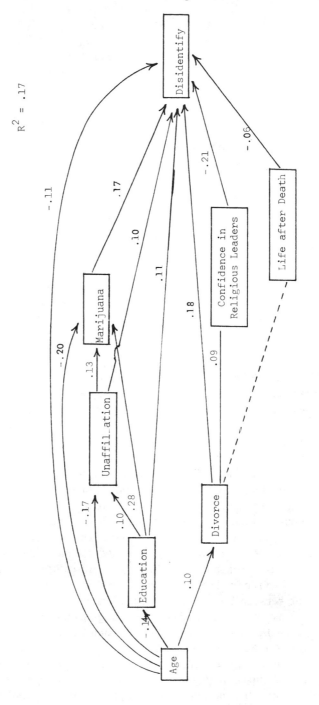

FIGURE 6.1-B
Nonmarital Disidentifiers for Catholics

TABLE 6.8
Religiousness of Converts*
(Gammas)**

	Protestant	Catholic
Church attendance	--	--
Life after death	-.32	.32
Confidence in religious leadership	--	--
Extramarital sex (approves)	--	--
Premarital sex (approves)	--	--
Birth control information for teens	--	--
Prayer in public schools	.37	--
Marriage happiness	--	.32

*Marriage converts compared to members of "receiving" denomination who are endogamously married and have not disidentified.

**Only statistically significant relationships shown.

The data available do not provide much illumination on the question of why young people choose to marry outside of their religious denomination. For Protestants intermarriage is more likely to occur among the young and in the metropolitan area of the North, and less likely among Baptists. The Catholic picture is more complicated. Polish, German, French, and English Catholics are more likely to enter religious intermarriage than Irish Catholics, Italians, and Spanish-speaking. They are also more likely to enter religiously mixed marriages if they are from the South and if there is a previous divorce in their marital experience. There is no connection between their own education and religious intermarriage, but both their mother's and spouse's education correlate positively with religious intermarriage. Thus the better educated the mother is and the more education the spouse has, the more likely one is to enter an exogamous marriage if one is Catholic. Perhaps if one has a better educated mother one is more likely to be in a social environment in which there is more mixing between Protestants and Catholics and perhaps also, better educated women as potential marriage partners. Region plays a part for both Protestants and Catholics. Denomination for Protestants and ethnicity for Catholics are roughly parallel factors for both groups.

We can only give a meager answer to the question of why people enter religiously mixed marriages, even though such marriages are in turn a substantial answer to the question of why people disidentify from the denomination in

FIGURE 6.2
Religiously Mixed Marriages*

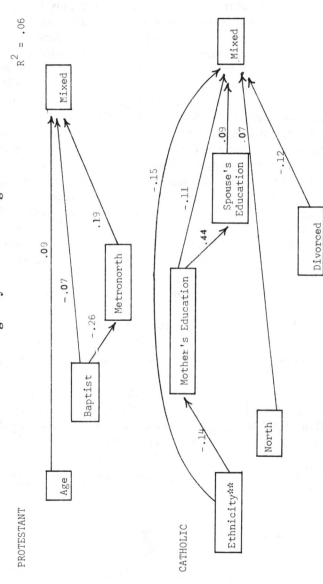

$R^2 = .06$

*Comparison between those who married spouses of the same religion at the age of 16 and those who married spouses of different religion at age 16.

**Irish, Italian, Latino

which they were raised. The data available provide virtually no information on the childhood, familial, or religious experiences of our respondents, and it ought not to be expected that we would be very successful in explaining choice of marriage partners. The critical question is not why people enter religiously mixed marriages, but rather why some of those who do, disidentify with their denomination. One must compare those who entered exogamous marriages and remained in their denomination without their spouses converting and those who enter religiously exogamous marriages and disidentify with their own religion.

For Protestants this identification correlates positively with education. The better educated a Protestant is in the exogamous situation, the more likely he is to disidentify. Also, there is a surprisingly high correlation between not living with both parents at age 16 and disidentifying (.23). Finally, those Protestants who have left their own denomination in association with a mixed marriage are much more likely to report a higher level of marital happiness than those who remain Protestant in religiously mixed marriages. Respondents who had rather unhappy and troubled childhoods seem to find happiness in the marriage they have entered. It is possible that this combination of unhappy childhood and deep satisfaction in a relationship with a spouse leads one to disidentify with one's original religion and join that of the spouse. It could also be that the sharing of values that results from religious conversion in this particular case (not in any other comparisons) leads to a higher level of marital happiness.

The model explaining Catholic disidentification in exogamous marriages is completely different. There is a large negative correlation of $-.20$ with being Irish. (Thirty-eight percent of those Catholics in religiously mixed marriages whose spouses have not converted disidentify with Catholicism. However, only 15 percent of the Irish in such marriages disidentify, the only group that is statistically different from any of the others. The Irish are less likely to enter

TABLE 6.9
Religiousness of Catholics Who Have Converted to Protestantism in Association With Marriages Compared to Endogamously Married Catholics (Percent)

	Converts to Protestantism	Catholics
Weekly church attenders	41	52
Believing life after death	72	76
Very happy	61*	40
	(88)	(609)

*Significantly different from Catholics.

TABLE 6.10
Happiness of Marriage and Conversion

	Protestant converted to Catholicism and married to Catholics	Catholic married to Catholic
Male	89*(46)	72(291)
Female	74**(58)	65(319)

	Catholic spouse of Protestant convert to Catholicism	Catholic married to Catholic
Male	65**(43)	72(291)
Female	69**(39)	65(319)

	Catholics converted to Protestantism and married to Protestant spouse	Protestant married to Protestant
Male	65**(72)	71(1053)
Female	66**(69)	67(1140)

*Significant difference

**No significant difference

mixed marriages, and once they have entered them, they are much less likely to disidentify.) There is also a − .14 relationship between belief in life after death and disidentification for Catholics, and a .12 between personal psychological well-being and disidentification. Catholic disidentifiers, in this particular set of circumstances, are no more likely to describe their marriages as happy than those who do not disidentify, but they are more likely to describe themselves as personally happy—a phenomenon which may be roughly parallel to the marital happiness described by Protestant disidentifiers.

In the introduction we raised the possibility that there may be two different systems of disidentification at work among Americans, one applying to those who entered religiously mixed marriages and the other applying either to the unmarried or those who entered endogamous marriages. We have presented, on the one hand, a picture of religious and moral crisis for Protestants and alienation and disaffiliation for Catholics. On the other hand, we have a picture of personal and marital psychological well-being, ethnicity for Catholics, and broken family for Protestants. While we still can explain only a relatively small

TABLE 6.11
Disidentification by Age and Education
(Percent Disidentifying)

A. AGE

	Protestants		Catholics	
	Under 30	Over 30	Under 30	Over 30
All	15	8*	21	15*
Endogamous	7(363)	4**(1939)	9(117)	6**(535)
Exogamous	30(109)	28***(340)	31(101)	29**(314)

*Statistically significant difference from those under 30.

**No difference.

B. EDUCATION

	Protestants		Catholics	
	College	No College	College	No College
All	15(1158)	8*(2793)	22(503)	14*(1118)
Endogamous	7(657)	3**(2642)	8(174)	6**(476)
Exogamous	36(140)	16*(309)	30(136)	30**(178)

*Statistically significant difference from college students.

**No statistically significant difference.

amount of the variance, there seems little overlap in the reasons why the exogamously married disidentify and the reasons why others disidentify. Religiously mixed marriages do not seem to produce the kind of disidentification that can be considered a religious crisis, while the disidentification of the unmarried and the endogamously married does seem to correlate with a set of variables that could be described as religious crisis. This explanation is disappointingly weak given the fact that religiously mixed marriage is the most important explanation of religious disidentification. One would still like to know more of why some people in mixed marriages disidentify and others do not. One possibility would be that the explanation for disidentification lies less with the respondent himself than in the respondent's spouse. Might it not be that the musical chairs at time of exogamous marriage is a response to the religious

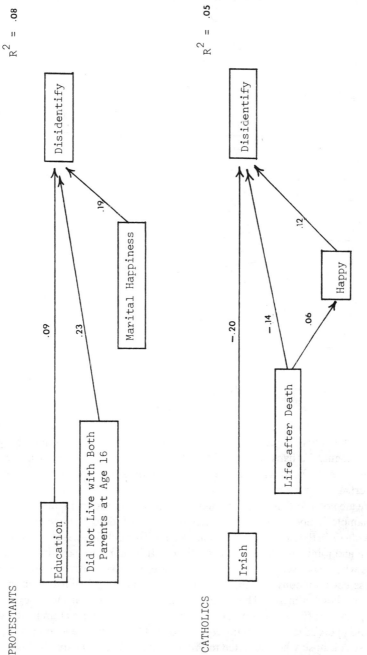

FIGURE 6.3
Disidentification as a Result of Exogamy*

PROTESTANTS

$R^2 = .08$

Education → .09 → Disidentify

Did Not Live with Both Parents at Age 16 → .23 → Disidentify

Marital Happiness → .19 → Disidentify

CATHOLICS

$R^2 = .05$

Irish → −.20 → Disidentify

Life after Death → −.14 → Disidentify

Life after Death → .06 → Happy

Happy → .12 → Disidentify

*Exogamously married who disidentify compared to exogamously married who do not.

FIGURE 6.4
"Marriage Conversion"* (Spouse Joins Self's Religion)

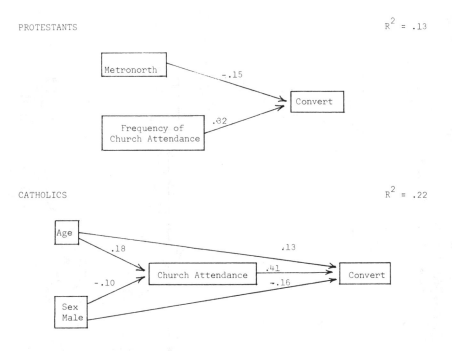

PROTESTANTS R^2 = .13

CATHOLICS R^2 = .22

*Comparison between exogamously married whose spouse does not join self's religion (and self does not disidentify) and exogamously married whose spouse does join self's religion.

needs, demands, or convictions of the spouse with the stronger religious commitment? Perhaps one should look at the matter the other way around, looking not at those who disidentify but rather at the spouses of those who convert.

We are not able to look at the spouses of the disidentifiers in our sample since the sample is not a study of families but of individuals. However, there are individuals in the sample whose spouses have disidentified with their religion of origin and joined the respondent's religion. It is therefore possible to ask how those whose spouses convert differ from those in mixed marriages in which the spouse does not convert—the two people continuing to live together with two religious commitments. The spouses of the converts are far more devout than the spouses of those who do not convert—a beta of .41 with church attendance for the spouses of those who converted to Catholicism and one of .32 for spouses of those who converted to Protestantism. Those outside the metropolitan North are more likely to have spouses who converted to Protestantism; older Catholics and female Catholics are more likely than younger Catholics and male Catholics to report their spouses have converted.

We do not know whether the high level of church attendance reported by the spouses of converts was a cause or a result of the conversion, since all we know is church attendance at the present time and not church attendance at the time of the marriage. It could be that the mutual and self-conscious reinforcement of religious values that comes from a "marriage conversion" leads the spouse to higher religious devotion than he/she would otherwise have had. However, it is certainly valid to speculate that the high level of religious practice observed among the spouses of converts reveals a deep religious commitment which existed also at the time of the marriage and which balanced the game of musical chairs in favor of the more devout partner. One may tentatively conclude that in religious disidentification associated with mixed marriage the important variables are less those to be found relating to the marriage partner who disidentified and more relating to the marriage partner with whose denomination the spouse comes to identify. One converts to the religion of the more devout spouse. The religious crisis of a mixed marriage which leads to disidentification is not so much the crisis of lack of faith or commitment in one's own denomination as it is a crisis of stronger faith and commitment of the other person to his/her denomination.

It should not be thought, however, that the conversion is unauthentic or hypocritical, that the spouse merely goes along with the religion to which he/she has converted in order to keep the more devout member of the pair happy. There are little differences between those who were born Protestant or Catholic and convert when it comes to religious behavior. Catholic converts are even more likely than born Catholics to believe in life after death (though Protestant converts are less likely to believe in it than born Protestants). In terms of confidence in the clergy, church attendance, and sexual attitudes, converts and born members of denominations do not differ from one another at a level which achieves statistical significance. Converts are no less devout and, save for the Catholic belief in life after death, no more devout than those born in a denomination. However, those who have converted to Catholicism are not only more likely to report that they are happy in their marriages than those who have remained in religiously mixed marriages, they are also more likely to report that they are more happy in their marriages than are born Catholics married to other Catholics. Marital happiness among Catholics is more strongly affected by conversion than it is by initial endogamy.

If one compares those Catholics who converted to Protestantism with those who remained Catholics, the converts are about as religious as those who remain Catholics. There is no statistically significant difference in church attendance. (Because of the small size of the number of converts, the 9 percentage point difference in weekly church attendance between converts to

Protestantism and Catholics is not statistically significant.) Nor is there any significant difference in belief in life after death, and the marriage converts to Protestantism are significantly more likely to say they are very happy than Catholics who are still practicing Catholics. Those Catholics who have converted to Protestantism and Protestants who have converted to Catholicism because of religiously mixed marriages, in other words, have not become unbelievers or undevout; they have simply shifted the locus of their religious belief to another denomination—in all likelihood because the religious convictions of their spouse were stronger. The switch means greater marital happiness for those who convert to Catholicism and greater personal happiness for those who convert to Protestantism.

The greater marital happiness for converts to Catholicism seems to be confined—at least as far as statistical significance goes—to Protestant men who have converted to the religion of their Catholic wives. Nine-tenths of such men described their marriages as "very happy." The same is not true of Catholics, men and women, who have converted to the Protestantism of their spouses.

Does this phenomenon of greater marital satisfaction among men who converted to the Catholicism of their wives correspond to a higher level of satisfaction for their wives, that is to say, for the women whose husbands have converted to Catholicism because they (the wives) are Catholic? We are not dealing with the same couples but rather with national samples—and by now with a very small number of cases—of the two different categories, that is, male converts to the Catholicism of their wives and Catholic women whose husbands have converted to Catholicism. The data show, as one might expect if the higher level of satisfaction is shared by husbands and wives, that Catholic women whose husbands have converted to Catholicism report a higher level of marital satisfaction than Catholic women married to husbands who were always Catholic. But the difference (69 percent saying "very happy" for the former and 65 percent for the latter) is not statistically significant even though it is in the hypothesized direction. One can therefore say only tentatively that religiously mixed marriages which end up as Catholic marriages because of the conversion of the male partner to Catholicism produce the highest level of satisfaction (as perceived and reported by the respondent) of any marriages in the country.

To summarize our findings we will provide tentative answers to the six questions asked earlier.

1. *Why do those who are not in religious mixed marriages disidentify?* Protestants, insofar as our data provide answers, disidentify for religious and moral reasons; Catholics for religious reasons such as divorce, belief in life after death, anger at the clergy, and also more general reasons of alienation, as measured by political nonidentification.

2. *Why do people enter religiously mixed marriages?* Baptists are less likely than other Protestants to do so; Irish, Italian, and Hispanic Catholics are less

likely than other Catholics to do so. Younger Protestants and higher status Catholics (as measured by their mother's and spouse's educational achievement), as well as divorced Catholics are more likely to enter exogamous marriages.

3. *Why do some exogamous marriages correlate with disidentification?* Marital happiness for Protestants and personal happiness for Catholics correlates with disidentification. Leaving the church of one's origin gives Protestants higher levels of marital happiness and Catholics higher levels of personal happiness. Those who grew up Irish Catholics are much less likely to disidentify in mixed marriages, and those Protestants who were raised in broken families are much more likely to disidentify as Protestants.

4. *Why do other exogamous marriages correlate with conversion of the spouse to self's religion?* The principal correlate of marrying a spouse who converts is one's own high level of church attendance—perhaps a reflection of the situation at the time of marriage in which the self was perceived as by far the more religious of the two and hence the one who determined the religious course the family would take.

5. *How religious are marriage converts in the new denomination?* Generally speaking, they are at least as religious as those who were born in the denomination.

6. *How religious are married converts compared to those in the denomination they left behind?* The answer seems to be that marriage conversion may lead to a shift in affiliation, but it does not lead to a change in religious devotion.

The last question provides an appropriate way to begin a final discussion of the various models proposed to explain religious disidentification. Quite clearly, mixed marriages are the major cause of religious disidentification. They have relatively little impact on the personal religious behavior of the people involved. Rather, they change the denominational situation in which religious behavior occurs. A mixed marriage, in other words, may lead to a crisis of religious affiliation but not to a crisis of religious conviction or devotion. However, that kind of religious disidentification which occurs in a nonmarital and nonmixed marital context seems to involve for both Protestants and Catholics a religious and moral crisis, which for Catholics, at any rate, seems to have some connection with a more general alienation.

Is disidentification, then, merely a continuation of dynamics that are already at work in leading to low levels of religious practice? Does one drift to the fringes of the church and then if the factors affecting drift grow stronger, eventually drift out? The answer seems to be that such a process is indeed one way out, but a way out for only a minority of the disidentifiers. The other way is followed by the majority of Catholics who enter religiously mixed marriages in which faith and devotion do not change but affiliation does.

Finally, let us turn to the secularization explanation. Is it true that both youthfulness and education lead to higher rates of religious disidentification, which suggests that society is tending toward a higher level of religious nonaffiliation and indifference? The data show that those with college education and those under 30, both among Protestants and Catholics, are more likely to disidentify. For Catholics under 30, the disidentification rate is 21 percent, for Catholics over 30, 15 percent. For Protestants under 30, the disidentification rate is 15 percent, and over 30, 8 percent. Virtually the same percentages apply to the difference between college attenders and nonattenders. However, when one holds religious intermarriage constant, all statistically significant differences among age groups disappear. If Protestants and Catholics under 30 are more likely to disidentify, the reason is that they are more likely to enter religiously mixed marriages. We have suggested before that since religiously mixed marriage represents a crisis of denominational affiliation and not one of religious conviction, the secularization trend, insofar as it is measured by higher youthful rates of disidentification is a trend which may affect denominational affiliation but not religious devotion.

A control for exogamy also eliminates statistically significant differences between Catholic college attenders and nonattenders, though a difference does remain among exogamous Protestants (36 percent of the college attenders disidentify, as opposed to 16 percent of those who did not attend college).

Among those who enter religiously mixed marriages there are no differences between Protestants and Catholics and between those under and over 30—about three out of 10 in all four categories of exogamous marriages disidentify.

Is the higher level of religious disidentification among the young part of a more general alienation syndrome that was the result of disturbances in American society in the late 1960s and early 1970s? It is well known that a large number of young people under 30 have not yet made a choice between the two political parties and continue to be political independents. Nie, Petrocik, and

TABLE 6.12
Age, Religious Disidentification and Party Disaffiliation
(Percent Disidentifying)

	Protestants		Catholics	
	Disaffiliate	Affiliate	Disaffiliate	Affiliate
Under 30	21*(406)	10*(432)	29*(238)	13**(224)
Over 30	12(938)	7(2157)	16(406)	13(746)

*Statistically significant differences from those over 30.

**Not statistically significant different from those over 30.

FIGURE 6.5
Political Disaffiliation, Exogamy, and Religious Disidentification Among Those Under 30

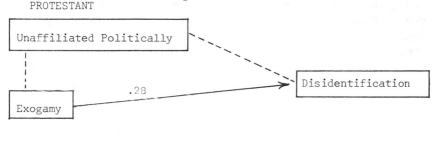

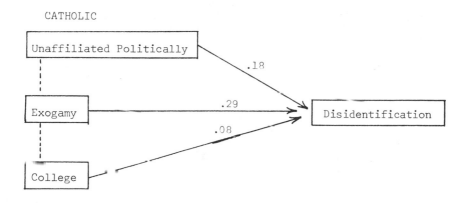

Verba have raised the question of whether this group will ever be politically mobilized. A parallel question is whether they will ever be religiously mobilized. The important question here is whether those who are unmobilized politically are also unmobilized religiously. Are the political nonidentifiers the same ones as the religious disidentifier? Our data suggest that for Catholics, at any rate, they are. The politically affiliated Catholics under 30 are no more likely than those over 30 to disidentify religiously. However, it is precisely among those Catholics who are both under 30 and politically disaffiliated that one finds a rate of religious disidentification twice that of both their affiliated age peers and their fellow disaffiliates over 30. A similar pattern appears for Protestants. The highest disidentification rate is among disaffiliates under 30. Among the affiliates, there is a statistically significant but very small (3 percentage points) difference between the younger and the older group.

Is mixed marriage or a more general nonaffiliation syndrome the more important predictor of religious disidentification for those under 30? Exogamy continues to be the strongest predictor, even for those under 30, of religious disidentification. But for Catholics there is also an independent contribution of college education (.09) and an independent contribution of societal nonaffiliation, as measured by lack of political affiliation. Alienation from societal institutions, in other words, does not seem to be a particularly pertinent factor in explaining disidentification of the young Protestants, but it does seem to be an influence on the disidentification of young Catholics—perhaps a sign of the acute institutional crisis which afflicted Roman Catholicism in the late 1960s and early 1970s.

By far the largest number of those who have disidentified from the Roman Catholic church have done so in association with religiously mixed marriages. They are happily married, devoutly practicing, believing members of Protestant denominations. They may have gone through a crisis of institutional affiliation but they do not seem to have suffered any acute crisis of religious conviction. Attempts to "reclaim" them are not likely to be very successful or even advisable.

References

Caplovitz, David, 1977
Glock, Charles Y., and Rodney Stark, 1965
Kotre, John, 1971
Greeley, Andrew M., William C. McCready, and Kathleen McCourt, 1976
Wuthnow, Robert, 1976, 1976b

Conversion to Fundamentalism

James T. Richardson, Mary White Stewart,
and Robert B. Simmonds

Some have characterized these times as an age of "true believers," or so it seems from reading and viewing popular media treatments of the Jesus movement and some related phenomena. All kinds of esoteric groups have gained a foothold in modern Western society, and in some instances that "beachhead" has been developed into a virtual "conquering" of certain social groups, ready to try something (anything?) new (or even old) in their quest for security and meaning in life. Here we will not try to chronicle all the various groups that have developed and gained followings in recent times, but rather focus on the process whereby new members are absorbed into such movements. This process is not movement specific, as very similar things are found anytime people are persuaded to affiliate with any new movement. The vehicle for our investigation of this phenomenon will be the Christ Communal Organization (CCO), and some data relevant to the idea of conversion will be presented from our study. However, our work has broader application, and the general model suggested can be used to study recruitment of new members by many different types of social groups.

Major Elements in a General Conversion Model

Any model of conversion should attend to the importance of *prior socialization*. We do not intend that this variable be treated in a simplistic and/or deterministic fashion, but instead would suggest that the operation of this important predisposing variable be both movement specific and temporally specific. Prior socialization furnishes what Lofland and Stark (1965) refer to as perspectives for defining problems and their solutions, and also contributes a basic general orientation to people.

We have developed general orientations using two cross-classified dimensions—individualistic/collectivistic and supportive/opposed—and we have suggested two additional perspectives—physiological and conventional—to complement the three presented by Lofland and Stark (religious, political, and psychiatric). Generally, we would expect conversion processes to involve individuals moving within general orientations and perspectives, unless a traumatic experience had disallowed further consideration of that orientation or perspective or there are no available alternatives. We also noted that certain general orientations and perspectives can be direct causes of perceived difficulties at times when a basic orientation and perspectives associated with it in a given culture do not "work" any longer (i.e., do not allow an individual to function effectively). General orientations and perspectives can also make individuals and groups both more and less susceptible to appeals from certain kinds of groups and movements.

Prior socialization is not a unitary concept. We must know the kind(s) of content to which a person has been socialized, the amount, timing, and intensity of exposure to that content(s), the level of personal commitment developed toward the specific content area, any previous shifts from one general perspective to another, and any previous multiple and simultaneous commitments to different general orientations and/or perspectives. We would generally expect that early, more lengthy, and intense socialization experiences that had developed strong personal commitments toward certain general orientations and perspectives would have the most lasting effects, which would generally be expected to manifest themselves in later conversion experiences.

A second major element concerns *perceived personal difficulties or problems*. Such may be the result of direct interaction between prior socialization experiences and temporal conditions. The perceived difficulties can be specific, more general or amorphous, or, in a situation suggestive of a maximum propensity toward conversion, a person (or group) may feel both general and specific tensions. Glock's work (1964) on types of deprivation furnishes some insight into types of tensions or frustrations that might result in the perception of a personal difficulty, as does Parrucci's work (1968) dealing with the relationship of societal integration and regulation vis à vis conversion. The psychological and religious concept of guilt may also be employed in explicating perceived difficulties, as demonstrated by Gordon and Richardson, Simmonds, and Hander. Particularly in modern society, there may well be a continual perception of personal difficulties and problems for many people. This aspect of modern society may aid in understanding why there seems to be such a plethora of new movements developing constantly. There is a kind of continual conversion process from one group to another operating for many individuals, as they seek a resolution to perceived general problems—which may not be soluble in the classic sense.

A third element involves *the perception that a certain movement may furnish a way to resolve perceived difficulties.* This element incorporates Lofland and Stark's notions of defining oneself as a certain type of seeker and of reaching a turning point with Gerlach and Hine's ideas (1970) of initial contact with a movement participant and focusing of needs. There is a relationship between elements one and two of the general model being presented here and this element. Prior socialization can help make one aware of certain problem-solving orientations and perspectives alternatives, while precluding other perspectives and orientations. There is a predisposition toward some movements and movement groups because of prior socialization. However, particularly in situations where the felt needs are more amorphous and little understood, simple contact with certain groups may define a problem and a solution (Gerlach and Hine seem to adopt such a view). The relationship between elements one and three of our model has been alluded to in the discussion of element one. Assuming the operation of element two and something of a trigger, we would expect most individuals to seek solutions to perceived problems within the same perspective and orientation before going to other perspectives and/or another general orientation, unless such alternatives had already been tried and disproven and unless such perspectives and orientations were consciously defined as part of the problem.

Other important aspects of this element of our general model need further delineation. Some individuals in contemporary society seem prone to move from one solution to another in a serial-like fashion (serial alternatives). This movement, which illustrates the immense ideological mobility of modern life, results from the relatively large number of alternatives available in modern pluralistic society and the inability of any one choice to definitively assert itself as *the way* to resolve personal difficulties. This serial alternative approach dictates that instead of just focusing on one movement and/or group and its converts, and on one "conversion event," we must examine the conversion careers or trajectories of participants as they move from one group to another if we are to fully understand conversion phenomena and what is happening in our society. Conversion to any given contemporary movement and/or group is but one in a series of steps, not an ultimate goal. This means that the defining of a particular movement and/or group as a way to solve perceived difficulties may be a temporary occurrence, and that such transitory events should not be reified by social scientists studying them. Such a tendency to freeze movements in and out of groups does little justice to the dynamism of contemporary society.

A fourth analytically important element of our general model concerns the *lack or loss of meaningful positive ties with society*. This element does not operate chronologically (occurring only after the first three elements have become operational), but instead is related to all the first three elements. Prior socialization can contribute to a person's feeling isolated from society, which may become manifest in terms of general or specific tensions felt by individuals. Encountering a given group that is developing in contrast to the greater society or some of its specific institutional structures can help convince individuals of their isolation. These concerns for the interrelationship of this element with the first three (and the next one) notwithstanding, we still think it valuable enough to attend to separately, a view shared by some theorists in this area.

We do not want to be accused of disallowing cognitive elements in the conversion process, and have emphasized them in the first three elements of this general model, dealing with the operation of predispositions—some of which are certainly cognitive—in the conversion process. The fourth and fifth elements are much more situational, to use Lofland and Stark's term, and also incorporate activity or behaviors. Given that individuals and groups are predisposed toward certain movements and/or groups as ways to solve perceived difficulties, the operation of the variable *affective ties* will help explain why and how conversion occurs. Let us briefly examine how affective ties work with reference to the greater society.

Generally converts have weak ties with nongroup members, which implies few ties with the greater society. Lofland and Stark's work emphasizes this view, with the explicit inclusion in their conversion model of the notion of weak affective ties with noncult members. Gerlach and Hine suggest something similar with their emphasis on the commitment event which seems to imply the relatively small importance of outgroup social, economic, kinship, and friendship ties. White's works suggests that interaction with nongroup members must lessen for conversion to occur. Thibaut and Kelly's work (1959) suggests that the ''comparison level of alternatives'' must be high in order for a change of group allegiance to occur, a position that also seems indicative of weakening nongroup ties.

The only exception we have noted to the usual operation of this variable is in the interesting case of a potential convert having a positive affective tie with someone outside a given group who holds a positive view of the group. This situation might well furnish some encouragement for a person to join who has some strong ties with nongroup members. With this one exception, we generally expect that converts will have weak ties to nongroup members, or that ties extant at the time of contact will lessen in importance.

The fifth element of the general model concerns *the pulling effect of the operation of developing affective ties between potential converts and group members*, an effect contrasted to the pushing effect of the typical operation of affective ties with nongroup members. The literature of conversion abounds with references to this variable. Both Lofland and Stark and Gerlach and Hine emphasize the importance of developing positive affective ties with group members, as do others such as White (1968) and those in the "brainwashing" tradition.

Our discussion of the fourth general element contains several points germane to the operation of this variable, but we also want to move beyond that treatment and focus on the way in which ingroup affective ties are developed. Lofland and Stark press as their last factor *intensive interaction*, and say that such usually occurs in communal situations where the potential convert moves into a living situation with some group members. Gerlach and Hine include *reeducation through intense group interaction*, and note that the individual is recruited into a given small cell, not into a movement as a whole. The entire brainwashing tradition appears to agree about the necessity of severely limiting interaction with anyone except those chosen to be a part of a group. The "revolutionary colleges" developed in China shortly after the Communist takeover amply demonstrate their appreciation of the importance of intense interaction to "conversion." And White focuses on the interaction model of religious influence, implying that this is the process whereby affective ties are developed between potential converts and group members. All this literature thus leads us to emphasize the importance of intense interaction between potential converts and group members on initial conversion, and the possibly even greater importance of interaction on maintaining a new member in a group and making that person into what Lofland and Stark refer to as a "deployable agent."

This interaction variable, which can be operationalized in many different ways, functions with the fourth element of our general model as well. If interaction is minimal (for whatever reason) between potential converts and nongroup members, this will usually mean that affective ties with nongroup members will weaken. There is no rule of human behavior that says affective ties are directly related to amount or intensity of interaction. However, especially in cases where some volitional element enters the picture, it seems that one might usually expect a positive relationship between affective ties and amount of intensity of interaction. The volitional element is important in part because of the implications for volition in the dissonance literature. Once a decision has been made by an individual to allow contact with a group, there may well be tendencies to encourage interaction and the development of ingroup affective ties, at least partially to justify (or perhaps to test) the initial decision to allow the contact.

Results of Partial Test of Model

The general model developed by combining parts of the Lofland and the Gerlach and Hine models and extending them is difficult to test fully. This difficulty arises because of the type of information that must be obtained and of methodological difficulties associated with field research on a phenomenon such as the Jesus movement. An attempt was made, however, to apply parts of the model to CCO members, in an effort to explain why members joined. Each of the five elements of our general model will be discussed in turn, not as specific hypotheses, but more as expectations.

First Expectation

The data indicate that members had experienced considerable religious socialization. The majority of CCO members attended church in their early years, and they generally attended frequently, even if the majority (60 percent) were not from strictly fundamentalist backgrounds. Data on length of time involved in this early religious socialization is not available, although other data cited (such as type of church to which they belonged and frequency of attendance) substantiate our idea that religious socialization would be important to most members. Thus many could be thought to possess an individualistically oriented religious perspective.

The fact that religious socialization is important in the background of most participants seems indisputable. However, the meaning of this involvement is subject to great debate. We know of no research other than our own that has attempted to address Berger's theory (1967) that such socialization leads to alienation, and the notion that the degree of alienation varies by type of religious socialization. We were able to gather some suggestive data from our population of study, but it cannot be treated as a conclusive test of the Berger theory, even though in general it supports the theorizing. Our tentative data support the view that most members thought of the institutional structure as sacred, implying that they were alienated, as Berger uses the term.

Although such results are subject to differing interpretations, some would say that they are in accord with Erich Fromm's theories (1950) about the debilitating effects of authoritarian religion. They also mesh with the Berger theorizing, as they give the impression of people not very adept or interested in effecting change in the institutional structure of society.

One explanation for the somewhat unexpected finding of more persons with religious socialization in "moderate" groups, is related to socioeconomic class. Most members were from middle-class or upper middle-class families using the criteria of parents' average annual income, father's occupation, and years of education. According to Stark (1964), Demerath (1965), and others, conservative denominations are largely composed of persons in the lower and working class. Thus our finding of only 40 percent conservative (including Catholics) is not so surprising, given the class-of-origin make-up of CCO.

Second Expectation

Our second expectation is that young persons who convert to CCO will report experiencing some form of major difficulty or dissatisfaction in their lives prior to joining. In addition, there may be other specific indicators of situational disruption such as divorce of parents, bad drug experience, or high mobility.

Several questions were asked for the purpose of indirectly assessing disruptions in the lives of the respondents. Such events and circumstances as parental deaths, divorces, high mobility, poor relationships with parents or siblings, and bad drug experiences, especially those occurring shortly before their contact with the group, were seen as possible indicators of stress which could be resolved through affiliation with a warm, supportive group.

At the risk of appearing to oversimplify, the data indicate some general state of frustration or tension for most members, a situation probably not dissimilar to that of many American youths in the 1960s. The data also indicate considerable disquiet by the majority of members in the six-month period prior to joining CCO. Bad drug experiences was the most prevalent problem.

Immediately before joining (the last few days before) 19 (22 percent) reported highly disruptive situations such as use of alcohol or drugs, being frightened or upset; 28 (32 percent) reported moderately disrupted lives, such as traveling, being on the streets, hitchhiking; and 22 (35 percent) reported no disruption, such as staying with family or friends, working, or going to school.

Although members did not report excessively tension-filled or disruptive relationships with parents and siblings, many reported that during the period immediately prior to contact with the group, they were depressed or upset by specific circumstances. This information provides limited support for the contention that preconverts perceived disruption or crisis in their lives prior to joining. Gordon's study also revealed a pattern of some major personal loss preceding affiliation.

Third Expectation

Our third expectation was that these young people would perceive a fundamentalist-oriented religious group (such as CCO) as offering a possible solution to their felt problems. This expectation may seem a bit nonsensical, since our data represent a post hoc test which reveals that 100 percent have adopted a religious perspective in defining and solving personal difficulties. We want to move beyond such a simple concern and examine the conversion histories of some CCO members, along with presenting data on how they may have sifted through certain other possible ways of defining and solving felt difficulties.

In terms of the latter concern, recall the several possible perspectives of Lofland and Stark, and our own formulation of two other perspectives. These perspectives, we suggested, could fruitfully be characterized in terms of either individualistic or collectivistic general orientations. Our data indicate that many CCO members had sifted through several alternatives on their way to CCO. All of the several perspectives discussed seem to have been tried by some CCO members at some time in their quest for meaning.

Lofland and Stark's psychiatric perspective (individualistic in orientation) was tried by some. Forty-one (47 percent) respondents had at some time in their lives been to a psychiatrist or psychologist, although only eight had been in the year prior to the interview. Only six respondents felt that the experience had been beneficial, while 32 of the 41 (78 percent) said it did not help them. Respondents reported that the main reason the counseling was not beneficial was that the psychiatrist was incompetent or lacking in ability. Twenty of the 32 (62 percent) gave this response. Four felt that the experience had caused them even more problems. Those who had attempted to deal with their problems in this manner were not pleased with the results. We can suggest then, that most respondents did not have a psychiatric perspective before joining (contrast this to Anthony et al. (1978), who discuss the confluence of interest in psychiatry and interest in Eastern-oriented religious groups). Quite a few had "tried it," but for most the alternative was not viable. At the time of interview, only 10 (11 percent) respondents felt that psychological counseling would be of benefit for a deeply troubled person. Fifty-nine (67 percent) members felt that such a person should "seek Christ" or ask the Lord for help.

The political perspective, which can be either individualistic or collectivistic in orientation, was tried by some, although fewer claimed to have been involved in this alternative than was the case with the psychiatric perspective. Only 28 percent claimed to have been involved in any political activities before conversion, and very few of those were very active. As a group, CCO members became even less political when they joined, with 71 of those interviewed saying they were totally uninterested in politics, and some 67 saying that nothing could be accomplished by being politically active. Thus we see a pattern of some trying this alternative and giving it up shortly, but with the majority viewing political definitions and solutions to problems not viable. Note that the one alternative perspective with a possible collectivistic general orientation attracted less than half the members who had tried the individualistic-oriented psychiatric perspective. Gordon (1974) found no Jesus movement members with a radical political background in his small population study. Such information seems to support our idea that crossing the major boundary between collectivistic and individualistic orientations is more difficult and therefore less frequent than shifts within a general perspective. And these data do not lend much support to the contention of some that Jesus movement groups converted many young people from a life of political activism.

The newly delineated physiological perspective (individualistic general orientation) was tried by many CCO members prior to joining. The data on drug use indicate that about 90 percent of CCO members interviewed had used drugs prior to joining. This drug use was in most cases taken quite seriously, involving long-term use of relatively hard drugs. Apparently this is a familiar pattern in the movement, since Adams and Fox (1972) and others also noted this kind of finding. Although our data are not as systematic as we would like concerning some other possible activities contained within the scope of the physiological perspective, we have, through our long-term contact with group members, learned that many had had considerable sexual experience before joining CCO and several had also been into other individualistically oriented activities such as health foods and "nature trips." Thus this perspective was tried by most (if not all), but was given up in favor of the latent religious perspective.

An important point has been suggested in the writings of W.H. Clark (1969), who thinks that the use of drugs has evoked a religious type of experience for many young people, who in our culture have been taught not to have such experiences. He sees some contemporary religious groups among the young as being the product of a natural evolution from unfeeling, irreligious young people, to religious-feeling people through drugs. As evidence he says that many people in new religious movements decided to stop using drugs before getting involved in a religious group. They simply became more interested in their religious experiences than in drugs that induced the experience. Our data lend some support to this analysis, as does the study of Adams and Fox, and also Austin (1977). This approach furnishes a theoretical prediction about the type of conversion trajectory followed by many participants, a prediction borne out by Adams and Fox's data on the history of participants' movements from drugs to the Jesus movement.

Our data concerning the exact pattern of movement through the several perspectives is less thorough than we need to establish the proportion of members who followed certain specific conversion trajectories. However, we can make some speculative comments. Plainly many members went from an individualistic general orientation with a religious perspective to other individualistically oriented perspectives such as the physiological one, and then "returned home" to a religious perspective similar to that of their rearing. A few took a "detour" into the collectivistic oriented political arena, but returned to more familiar turf. A considerable number included a sojourn with the psychiatric perspective in their movement through a conversion career, and we suspect that all used a conventional "muddle through" perspective at some time during their movement from one orientation to another or from one perspective within an orientation to another. Further research along these lines of thought needs to be done before we can be firm in our position, but it is safe to say that our ideas about serial alternatives, conversion careers and trajectories, and conversion opportunity structures offer some promise.

Fourth Expectation

Our fourth expectation was that persons who become converts would have tenuous ties with society which would be further loosened or broken in order for them to become members. Seventy (79 percent) persons reported that they had friends whom they felt very close to before coming to CCO. Twenty-six (37 percent) of these said they had many close friends and 28 (40 percent) said they had at least one or two. Fifty-two (74 percent) of these persons said they could go to their friends and talk about deep personal problems, nine said they sometimes could, and 12 said they could not. In all 61 (69 percent) respondents felt they had at least one close dependable friend, so it cannot be concluded that they were isolates, as Lofland and Stark found in their study. It is possible that although the respondents were not friendless, they and their friends were mutually isolated from rewarding interactive ties. Thus the member and his or her friends may both have been members of an "isolate class." Direct information concerning this question was not gathered.

Over half participated in activities at school, primarily sports or music and drama. Seventy-five (85 percent) respondents dated or went out before they joined, 36 (48 percent) of these very often (at least every weekend), and 11 (15 percent) at least twice a month. Fifty-six (64 percent) respondents reported that they had had serious romantic involvements before joining the group. These self-descriptions were for a period often not immediately prior to joining the group. Recall the data about personal disruptions just prior to affiliating.

Despite some indications that the converts were not total social isolates, their ties with others did not appear to be excessively rewarding. Forty-seven (53 percent) respondents characterized their lives before joining as unhappy or very unhappy. Of course this evaluation was retrospective and may have been influenced by the situation at the time of interview—82 (91 percent) respondents characterized their present lives as happy or very happy. One further indication that social ties on the outside may have been lacking in warmth or strength is the indication by 31 (35 percent) respondents that the warmth, closeness, and love were the factors which first attracted them to the group. Thirty-eight (43 percent) gave religious reasons such as "the Lord's will" or "people doing the Lord's work." Such reasons might be viewed as rationalizations by some.

We also investigated the question of whether outgroup ties were broken. There are several indications that ties were loosened or broken with nonmembers. Fifty-five (64 percent) members said they felt more distant from friends than they had before joining. Length of membership had little effect on whether respondents saw friends as often as they used to, with almost 100 percent in each membership category seeing friends from outside CCO less often. Feelings of distance or closeness to friends did not appear to change over time. Respondents in all categories felt more distant from friends. Eighty-six (98 percent) said they no longer saw their friends as often as they used to, which was at least partially attributable to spatial separation.

Although respondents indicated more distance from friends, their relationships with parents were described as closer than before joining for 54 (61 percent) members, a significant finding, especially when coupled with the finding that 51 reported that their parents approved more of the lives they were now leading than they had of the lives they had led prior to affiliation. Twenty-two (25 percent) said that they felt more distant from their parents. There was no difference between males and females. Feelings of distance from or closeness to friends did not appear to change significantly with time in the group, with respondents in all categories feeling more distant from friends. Those who had been members from six months to one year, however, felt slightly closer to their friends outside the group than persons who had been members for more or less time, an intriguing finding.

Most respondents felt that people in general either disapproved of the group and groups like it or were ambivalent in their feelings. Only 13 (15 percent) said that they thought most people had positive feelings toward such groups, which may indicate a break with or lack of ties to the greater society. Fifty-seven (65 percent) indicated that they felt weaker ties with American society than they had before joining. Only 12 (14 percent) felt stronger ties with American society. Length of membership did not appear to influence the respondents' reports of the ties they felt to American society.

A change in significant others from outside to within the group indicated the breaking of ties with the old. Forty-one (47 percent) persons said that before joining there had been an individual who had a great influence on them. For twenty-seven (66 percent) of these, the influential person had been a friend. Only five (12 percent) of the original 41 persons said that that individual still had a strong influence over them. Thus, sect members were not isolated from their society to the extent that Lofland and Stark found in their study. However, many members did not have especially rewarding ties and most such ties were generally weakened or broken at least for a time after a person became a member of the group.

These data are not surprising, given the physical isolation of the group, the relatively authoritarian structure, and their world view, all of which encouraged the weakening of outgroup ties. The group encouraged its members to "find fellowship among fellow Christians," to "shun things of this world," and the philosophy of the group was otherworldy in orientation, calling members to spend their energies getting "closer to the Lord" so that they may "live forever with Christ." Members reflect a disinterest in politics, social problems, and other worldly occurrences.

Fifth Expectation

Our fifth expectation was that maintenance of membership depends on the development of rewarding ingroup ties. The development of affective ties with group members is important in explaining who converts to and remains in the group. It was expected that the group must become the member's reference group if he or she was to remain a member. Strong positive interactional ties between sect members which are more rewarding than outgroup ties provide the basis for maintenance of faith.

In the group, kinship terms were used consistently and a familistic atmosphere was deliberately fostered. Members were addressed as "brother" or "sister," an indication of closeness. Members overwhelmingly reported that they were happy and satisfied with their lives as members, although most had been materially better off before they joined the sect. Only one person said that he was not happy.

Members did not report that they joined the sect in order to enter a fellowship of warmth, security, and acceptance. Sixty-four (72 percent) members said that they joined to be close to the Lord or because it was the Lord's will. Only four (6 percent) said they joined to be with the people or because of the fellowship. However, other data suggest that these reports may have been rationalizations. As reported already, 31 members (35 percent) were first attracted by the fellowship and warmth. Thirty-six (41 percent) were attracted by "the people doing the Lord's work" or by the "presence of the Lord." In addition, 74 (84 percent) persons said that if they had to leave the group, they would miss most the fellowship and the brothers and sisters.

An indication of close interactional ties within the group was the statement by 76 (86 percent) respondents that most of the persons to whom they felt closest were also members of the group. Of these, 35 (40 percent) said that all of the persons to whom they felt close were fellow members. All members felt close to some other members of the group. More new members said that most persons to whom they felt close were not group members than did older members, although most persons said all or most of the persons to whom they felt close were group members. A further indication of close ingroup ties was gained from a question about to whom they felt like talking when they were depressed or unhappy. Of the 37 persons who said they felt like talking to someone when they were depressed or unhappy, 34 (92 percent) said that person was a member of the group.

In sum, members appeared to have developed strong ingroup ties, which is not surprising, given the communal lifestyle. For most, the persons to whom they felt closest were other CCO members; the fellowship and brothers and sisters would be most missed if they had to leave; and their lives were described as very happy. These data lend support to the importance of the development of strong ingroup ties for commitment to occur. We plan to continue our research in an effort to test ideas about the importance of such ties to maintaining long-term commitment, a point stressed by Gerlach and Hine.

Conclusions

We are not suggesting that these data allow a full test of all aspects of the model of conversion or commitment that we have developed, based particularly on the work of Lofland and Stark, and Gerlach and Hine. We are missing data that would allow full confidence in our theorizing, although available data suggests that our approach is sound. One major problem is that of a possible "ecological fallacy," since what we have done is present group percentage data which can be misleading. We do hope and plan to do such a "cohort analysis" in the future. For instance we might take just the group of individuals that did not fit our initial expectations and see if they fit the model in other ways. Recall our notion of serial alternatives. We have tentatively developed a "crash pad hypothesis" involving such people. Simply stated we would expect that persons, even if they had no background of religious socialization, would, if they "crashed" with the group (which always welcomes visitors) at a time when alternatives to problematic situations seemed unavailable, be prone to affiliate.

References

Adams, Robert, and Robert Fox, 1972
Anthony, Dick, Thomas Robbins, Madeline Doucas, and Thomas Curtis, 1978
Austin, Roy, 1977
Berger, Peter, !967
Clark, W.H., 1969
Demerath, Nicholas J., 1965
Fromm, Erich, 1950
Gerlach, Luther, and Virginia Hine, 1970
Glock, Charles Y., 1964
Gordon, David, 1974
Lifton, Robert J., 1961
Lofland, John, and Rodney Stark, 1965
Parrucci, D.J., 1968
Richardson, James T., and Robert Simmonds, 1972
Stark, Rodney, 1964
Thibaut, J.W., and Harold Kelley, 1959
White, Richard, 1968

Constructing Orthodoxy

Samuel C. Heilman

"There is a certain people scattered abroad and dispersed among the peoples in all the provinces" (Esther 3:8). Often unnoticed and unexotic, calling themselves both contemporary and traditional, modern and orthodox, they live in the tension between past and present, the secular and the parochial, the particular and the universal—and accept that painful double existence. Modern Orthodox Jews, those who identify themselves through their commitment to adhere faithfully to the beliefs, principles, and traditions of Jewish law and observance without being either remote from or untouched by life in the contemporary secular world, are by no means the only but perhaps the paradigmatic practitioners of this desperate dialectic.

More operationally, these Jews may be defined as those who are affiliated with Orthodox institutions (synagogue, school, voluntary associations, etc.), who strictly observe Jewish dietary laws (keep kosher) and laws of family purity (use a *mikveh* or ritual bath), who religiously observe the holy days and the Sabbath, and who have made some active public expression of a commitment to a synthesis of Jewish and secular values and education. Because of these joint commitments (particularly their strict observance of the ban of travel other than by foot on the Sabbath) these people also necessarily live together in Orthodox Jewish communities. As such, they remain "locals," bonded to a relatively uniform and parochial home community. Insofar as they identify with the beliefs and practices of that place, they confirm and maintain one another's Orthodox expression of Jewishness. In the insider Yiddish vernacular, such a Jewish lifestyle and social circle is *heimisch*, homey, offering both a retreat from the outside world and a group feeling. Among these Orthodox Jews, the repeated patterns of religious life make for an inertial Orthodoxy operating on the strength of local community custom.

In addition to these parochial commitments, modern Orthodox Jews maintain an active and regular involvement in and attachment to the secular, pluralistic, cosmopolitan world, brought about by their extended secular educational training, business pursuits, or profession. This attachment has grown markedly in the last quarter century, a period which at once has seen an increase in Orthodox day school and yeshiva (academy of higher Jewish study) education as well as an increase in involvement in the outside world.

For example, a recent survey of students registered at Queens College, the academic jewel of the City University of New York, reveals that between 1962 and 1977 registration of students coming from Orthodox day schools and yeshivas increased tenfold. Moreover, since 1968 when enrollments at colleges began to decline, Orthodox Jewish students at Queens tripled in number to 6 percent of the total registrants in 1977 (the figures rose a full 0.5 percent between fall 1976 and spring 1977). Even taking into account the residential migration patterns in New York and such factors as "open enrollment" by which admissions requirements were eased, the figures indicate a growing involvement with secular education and the broadened perspectives it portends—perspectives which Wade Roof, in a *American Sociological Review* article, has convincingly shown to undermine the plausibility of traditional religious beliefs and practices. As Roof documents, when education levels rise, religious orthodoxy declines.

There is further demonstration of the cosmopolitanization—the move out of the ghetto—of the Orthodox parochial. For example, the number of those affiliated with the Association of Orthodox Jewish Scientists has more than doubled in the last decade. There is now a newly organized Association of Orthodox Jewish Faculty and Personnel. Kosher food is offered at such elite campuses as Amherst and Oberlin as well as the large state universities where in the past Orthodox students never appeared. Kosher restaurants are now more than ethnic delicatessens but offer as well gourmet French, Chinese, Italian, and other continental cuisine. And airlines flying to even the most obscure and remote locales carry kosher food. The Orthodox Jew has clearly plunged into the modern world.

In spite of this immersion in the contemporary secular world, those who would characterize themselves as modern Orthodox Jews have not given up their distinctive Orthodox practice and belief. For these people, "Orthodoxy," as one of my informants in the community once put it, "is the bottom line."

Modernity with its alternative outlooks, nontraditional lifestyles, and aggressive individuality, may be pursued only as long as it does not annihilate a fundamental attachment to a strict observance of Torah (the corpus of Jewish law, lore, and rabbinic commentary which is the central organizing element of Jewish religion and tradition considered by believers to be divinely inspired and revealed). Modern Orthodoxy does not consist of a coequal mix of the modern and Orthodox. Rather it recognizes the legitimacy of modernity insofar as it does not destroy Orthodoxy; it admits to a vacuum in Jewish thinking and practice that leaves room for accommodation with contemporaneity. Always, however, that modernity remains restrained. How much of an alternative lifestyle or aggressive individuality is possible, after all, if one is committed to eating only kosher food and regularly praying with a *minyan* (quorum) of other Orthodox Jews? For all of the growing availability of kosher food in far-off places and the increasing number of Orthodox Jews there (a presence admittedly abetted by the Modern Orthodox element), the ritual demands—to say nothing of social and emotional ones—of Orthodoxy constrain the rush toward modernity.

The modern Orthodox Jew implicitly tests the pluralistic tolerance of contemporary American society by demanding, first that it not question his right to oscillate between the two inconsistent worlds he inhabits, and second that it accept and adapt to his stubborn and unfashionable Orthodoxy even as he moves into the modern milieu. Thus, for example, the modern Orthodox Jew who wears his *yarmulke* on his head while smoking pot or who works as a physician in an ultramodern research hospital but takes Friday evenings and Saturdays off to observe his Sabbath does not want to be asked why he has not either given up his archaic Orthodoxies in favor of his modernity (as have his reformist brethren) or retreated completely to the ghetto (as have his more traditionalist counterparts). At first he was satisfied with the civil inattention with which America reacted to his public modern Orthodoxy—it was preferable to the exclusions of earlier Jewish history. Only recently (and this point I shall examine later) in an age of militant ethnicity and a growing national religious consciousness, the modern Orthodox Jew has begun to expect American society to accept and confirm the legitimacy, the "Americanism," of his organized dualism and distinctive Orthodoxy.

Initially, the move into the modern American world was not easy; nor was it one-way. In the process, such Jews discovered that the sectarian and traditionalist character of their Orthodoxy clashed with the pluralism and chronic change dominating American society. Committed by inertia, circumstance, and desire to being integrated in these two fundamentally antithetical worlds, modern Orthodox Jews in the past spent a great deal of their energies organizing their lives so as to minimize the conflicts inherent in their dualism. This often meant living what one insider has called "a schizoid life—full-fledged Orthodox Jew and at the same time full-fledged American." Nevertheless, these *homini duplex* evolved ways to ease their alternation between the timeless sacred orthodoxies of yesterday and the timely secular demands of today.

The purpose of this article is to examine a critical dimension of the mechanisms by which modern Orthodox Jews have carried out their cosmological oscillations: reinterpretation. The increased mobility, education, and accompanying general involvement of Orthodox Jews in contemporary America, along with what some students of this community have called a "contraacculturative" trend toward flamboyant and aggressive assertions of ethnic Orthodoxy, placed such reinterpretation of past and present and the continuity it allows among perhaps the most crucial ideological tasks for the traditionalist moderns. To be true to the old-time religion while remaining equal to the demands of the day was and is a difficult task.

Contemporization and Traditioning

The interpretive reconstruction of the past in terms of the present and vice versa may be generally said to have two components: contemporization and traditioning. Essentially cognitive in character, they are constituted by an interpretive fusion of traditional and contemporary cultural elements. In contemporization, the past is seen as framing and explaining the present, providing both its context and syntax. In the case of modern Orthodox Jews, this signifies the effort to make Torah a part of and relevant to the modern world. The dimension of reinterpretation being one in which, as Herskovits once put it, "old meanings are ascribed to new elements," this effort explains, exemplifies, and elaborates Torah and Orthodox Jewish life and observance (what insiders call "Torah-true" Judaism) in terms such that even the most archaic-sounding and obscure references are supplied with modern parallels. It injects the overriding presence of the past into the world of the present. Thus, for example, a recent rabbinic responsum applies talmudic laws regarding the ransome of captive slaves to the situation of contemporary airplane hijack victims. The point, not lost upon those who read, hear, or abide by the rabbinic decision, is that even the apparently archaic traditions of slavery offer insights into guides for the vagaries and terrors of contemporary life.

Correlative with this process of reinterpretation is its complement, traditioning. Defined originally by Philip Rieff (1970) as a recognition of the "authority of the old," it is the thinking wherein new elements are associated with old meanings, where modern realities are reconsidered in light of the cultural significance of old forms, where the present intrudes upon the past. Unlike its counterfeit, traditionalism, which leaves the past inert and operates on the principle of credulity and a reliance upon an unquestioned past, traditioning requires a reassessment of the past with a concomitant reaffirmation of its authority. It establishes rationally what faith postulates a priori, so that in place of what Durkheim referred to as "passive resignation" to tradition there is instead an "enlightened allegiance." Again, in the case of modern Orthodox Jews, this describes a situation where the Torah with its old meanings is left intact as new elements of present-day life are adapted to it. Against the backdrop of the contemporary world, the old Torah is seen as revealing new truths. Thus, for example, the ancient and sacred menstrual prohibitions and injunctions are reinterpreted as a period of psychological and physical regeneration. What, without such reinterpretation, might seem as a restrictive period, defined by archaic demands becomes—once traditioned—a symbol of the human effort to reestablish equilibrium.

Together, contemporization and traditioning, although indigenous to modern Orthodoxy, define an overlapping program of reinterpretation which is the essence of civilization. In another sense, they are part of the ever-present competition between the *authoritative* (often consecrated) official doctrine and the *interpretable*, those matters over which there are permissible differences of explanation. In the modern Orthodox Jewish milieu this process is supported by an ethos which prescribes that, as Grand Rabbi Kook once put it, "the old must be made new; the new must be made holy."

Generating Reinterpretation

Both contemporization and traditioning presume some contact between the modern and traditional worlds. Without such encounter, there can be no sensation of the need to reconcile the two; the citizens of the one world would know nothing of the other. Instead, the traditional world would remain in the eternal yesterday, with its habituated activity and unswerving attachment to age-old authorities. Such a "life for the sake of culture," as Ortega y Gasset once described it, eschews the antitraditional escape of the individual—though it does not see itself as "anti" anything for it ignorantly dismisses all other realities. For generations this has been the attitude of strict, traditional Jewish Orthodoxy, for whom tradition is a virtue and the past a cherished entity. These traditionalist Jews, espousing isolation from the non-Orthodox, modern world, have, to all extents possible, "attempted," as one insider put it recently in *Tradition*, a journal of Orthodox Jewish thought, "to fence in their members or to fence out the secular." The greater their success, the less do contemporization and traditioning remain part of the program of their lives. One such radical traditionalist, Rabbi Moshe Meiselman, who has given up an academic career in mathematics to become a dean of a major American yeshiva, expresses this isolationist point of view most explicitly when he writes in a rejoinder to a modernist article in *Tradition*: "To view Judaism within a foreign [read: secular] context is to strip Judaism of its vital force, if not completely to castrate it."

On the other hand, for moderns, dedicated to the interminable opening of possibility, "public opinion," as Park once put it, "sets itself up as an authority as over against tradition and custom," and they feel no need to reconcile past and present. Here one discovers a mentality that sets modern society in opposition both to its own history and to those societies of the present that are premodern, while it also makes the novel the source of interest and curiosity about the self and the touchstone of judgment. Such radical individualism has consistently shaped the attitudes of modern reformers of Judaism whose prime directive has been to appreciate the qualities of the times in which one lives and whose first principle is, in the words of one reformist rabbi, "Be true to yourself. . . . Be true to your own [contemporary] standards." For these moderns whose "old gods are growing old or already dead and others are not yet born"—to cite Durkheims's old slogan about the dawn of a new moral order—there are few perceived needs for bringing the Jewish past and present into any sort of mutual relationship.

There are pockets of traditional society on the modern scene and outposts of modernity in the most remote contexts, and therefore a complete isolation of one from the other is practically impossible. Among even the most modern, one discovers efforts to find some meaning in the past—even if it is little more than a contemporary nostalgia for a return to roots, for a reality and authenticity thought to be in purer, simpler lifestyles of bygone days. With Jews such efforts may, for example, take the form of inserting old Yiddishisms into contemporary speech, eating in the "kosher style" without a strict allegiance to Jewish dietary law, or lighting a Sabbath candle while one goes on with the profane business of everyday life. Although such blending of past and present borders on being dismissive of the former, making of it a museum piece to be used for ornamentation but not to be taken seriously, it nevertheless indicates at least a rudimentary consciousness of the past within the contemporary context.

Similarly among the most traditional quarters of society, modernity seeps in. For example, even among the most isolationist traditionals, there are instrumental and technological tokens of modernity, while contemporary language intrudes itself even among those who think they speak only their own ancient tongue. Among the most insulated of Orthodox Jews, the Chassidim, one hears members characterize one or another of their fold as "too modern," as well as concern about the creeping "fruits of modernism." A reporter and editor of the *New York Times* offers a description of a Chassidic commuter bus as part of the fare of the daily metropolitan column "Around New York." Even more startling, the Chassidim are pleased to be featured! While such Orthodox Jews remain primarily bound to their insular, traditional universe, they, for example, vote in national and local elections, learn English or read newspapers—all the while making compromises with modernity.

The Modern Orthodox Case

To say that those at the extremes are not immune from contemporization and traditioning is not to say that they represent the paradigms of the process. For extremist moderns, tradition remains embedded in modernity in a position of servitude and destined for annihilation while for their traditional counterparts, the opposite is the case. Those groups in the middle, by choice wedded neither to a reified, authoritative tradition nor to an eternally interpretable one, are the ones who find themselves locked into a constant process of reinterpretation.

Unlike the conservative Jews who have negotiated themselves out of the conflict through gradual but inexorable revisions and deletions of tradition, modern Orthodox Jews live with the tentativeness of reinterpretation. They are, in the words of one of their spokesmen, Immanuel Jakobivits, once rabbi of a prominent American Orthodox synagogue and now British chief rabbi, dedicated to demonstrating in their lives "the capacity of traditional Judaism to harmonize its timeless teachings with modern conditions," a harmony that accepts, as I shall later elaborate, dissonance.

The desire to confront the experiences of the twentieth century with Orthodox Judaism and vice versa is representative of the modern Orthodox ideal expressed in the maxim of Jewish emancipation: *Torah im derekh eretz*—the blending of Torah-true Judaism with the demands of the secular host culture. Such an ideal has been a Jewish aspiration since at least Moses Mendelssohn's day when Jews, in their exodus from the ghetto and the *numerus clausus*, were charged to "Comply with the customs and the civil constitutions of the countries in which you are transplanted, but, at the same time, be constant to the faith of your forefathers."

While some translated this injunction into the maxim of Jewish bifurcation—"Be a man in the street and a Jew in your own house"—others sought to fuse the two, hoping that acculturation without secularization was possible. They remained convinced, as Rabbi Leo Jung, a pioneer of American modern Orthodoxy once put it, that their way of life was "not to be identified with ghetto conditions," nor was it inconsistent with the practical and intellectual demands of the day.

Viewing themselves as interpreters of an authoritative order rather than prophets of a new one, such Jews moved cautiously out of the ghetto. Once outside, they discovered that even the most "enlightened" Gentiles required, as a prerequisite for acceptance into their society, that the "Jew free himself first of his hateful Jewish superstitions and prejudices," as Voltaire put it. The Jew would, in short, have to undergo resocialization. This was true not only for those prepared to totally excise their Jewishness from their character but even more intensely for those who sought to retain their religion and peoplehood in an atmosphere hostile to it.

America, no less than other countries—Spain, France, Poland, Germany, and others where Jews once lived in conspicuous numbers—has required the resocialization of what Bruno Bauer once called "the Sabbath Jew," the visible exemplar of a separate society. Those who did not transform themselves into the white American Protestant ideal were initially relegated to the status of outcast or oddity. As Nathan Glazer in his study of American Judaism, Marshall Sklare in his pioneering research on America's Jews, and Will Herberg in his popular essays on American religion suggested: "Jewishness," unrefined and an obtrusive ethnicity, was to be transformed into "judaism," a civil American religion, essentially indistinguishable from the other "major faiths," and Jews—*Yidn*—were to be made into "citizens."

For Reform Judaism, which stood ready to remodel both the symbols and practice of faith so as to make them appropriate to secular culture, such demands were in order. Conservative Jews "conserved" Jewish tradition by giving up all that defied the merger of "Americanism and Judaism." But while the Reform Jew threw away his *yarmulke* and the Conservative Jew carried it in his pocket—to be worn only within the boundaries of the Jewish community—the modern Orthodox Jew took to wearing it, maintaining all the trappings of his Orthodoxy, even as he moved into modern American society.

In doing so, this Jew tested not only his capacity to maintain his obtrusive Orthodoxy in the modern world but also the tolerance of that world toward him. At first America responded to the growing number of such Jews with curiosity and a measure of discomfort, expressed, for example, in the roster of court challenges of such matters as the legality of kosher butchering of meat or the right of an Orthodox Jew to build a synagogue where zoning ordinances prohibited it. Later, America learned to react to modern Orthodoxy with civil inattention, a studied ignorance toward what seemed unchangeable.

Once the Orthodox Jew stepped into that modern secular world, he found that unless he was content to be at best studiously ignored, he would have to either adapt his Orthodoxy to America or change America. The first alternative, prevalent before the very recent religious awakening of America, seemed the most plausible: to be taken seriously and embraced by secular society, this Sabbath Jew had to become resocialized.

Socialization and the Ideology of Reinterpretation

Socialization, be it primary, secondary, or repeated, denotes the process of transmitting a group's culture to newcomers. From the point of view of those newcomers—be they children, immigrants, converts, or the like—socialization represents the development of skills, knowledge, attitudes, and values useful for carrying on like a native. The development of an ideology or creed which integrates the skills, knowledge, attitudes, and values becomes as well a part of the process.

Although all socialization requires those undergoing it to periodically reevaluate their present behavior and beliefs in light of their past and vice versa, this program becomes particularly difficult when one is not only learning new patterns but also trying to hold on to what Redfield called previous and discrepant "ideas of the good life." In this case, one feels impelled to include in the socialization process an ideology which integrates the old and the new. Interpretation, or more precisely reinterpretation, becomes crucial to this effort.

Accordingly, in secondary socialization, as Berger and Luckman (1966) in their study of the *Social Construction of Reality* put it, "the present is interpreted so as to stand in a continuous relationship with the past, with a tendency to minimize such transformations as have actually taken place." The present is perceived as a continuity of the past. Similarly in resocialization, the past is reinterpreted to conform to present reality, with the tendency to retroject into the past various elements that were subjectively unavailable at the time. The past becomes understandable in terms of the present. These two complementary processes define the context in which the impulse toward the pyrotechnic interpretations of traditioning and contemporization make sense.

To close the emotional gap between things as they were and as one would have them be, the Jews who sought to retain their Jewish identity while becoming native to a Gentile (secular) world emphasized an ideology which proscribed interpretation and reinterpretation as—again to quote Rabbi Jung—"not only a privilege but a duty." For many who stood fast with the faith, the ability to demonstrate that the Torah offered a program for the modern world which in turn was not inimical to Torah became a "historical duty."

Writing recently for an audience of his modern Orthodox peers, Rabbi David Hartman nicely articulates this ideology. It requires, he suggests, training young Orthodox modernists to believe—as one learns Maimonides did (always invoking the parochial and traditional authority)—"that experiential and intellectual encounter with modern values and insights can help deepen and illuminate one's commitment to the tradition."

Such contemporization and traditioning became for many the key defense of a modern yet Orthodox Jewry to the cultured among its despisers, a defense by the intellect. Born out of *pilpul*, the dialectic of talmudic rationalization and argument whose aim was the maintenance of the time-hallowed while demonstrating the relevance of the unnoticed sentence of the tradition to a problem currently under consideration, these reinterpretations became central to the new socialization.

Life in both secular and parochial societies and such secondary socialization as it required was sustained in part by the Jewish communal reliance upon rabbinic responsa. These are Judaic legal opinions which, steeped in tradition, seek to resolve the confrontation between the fixed, normative world of sacred law and the fluid social condition. As Orthodox immersion into modern life intensifies, so responsa increase. Among the most discussed new books in modern Orthodox circles is Rabbi David Bleich's English summary (for the "modern reader") of responsa literature. And a quick survey of Jewish bookstores along New York's Lower East Side reveals as well a flourishing responsa literature.

Doubling

In the resocialization of the modern Orthodox Jew the result has often been a feeling of living in two worlds with a desire to be native to both. Put differently, the ideology of interpretation and reinterpretation has led to a kind of doubling—a bicultural situation of stabilized dualism.

As a psychological mechanism, the invention of doubling has been explained by Freud as "an [unconscious] insurance against destruction . . . a preservation against extinction." A similar survival mentality seems at work among groups which want to ensure their continued pluralist existence. Here the layering of behavior and thought becomes explicit, actual, necessary in an immediately practical way. It becomes ideology rather than unconscious impulse. Accordingly, those groups, like modern Orthodox Jews, which try to harmonize sometimes antithetical worlds, evolve a bivalent posture in which one may hedge all possibilities. What the traditional world lacks, the modern one offers and vice versa; the doubler remains nourished and sustained by both. He survives. Hardened by a realization that all social arrangements are, as anthropologist Clifford Geertz puts it, "riddled with insoluble antinomies," this doubler—although trying his best to contemporize and tradition—is often resigned to the patterned desperation of his double life. As Lawrence Kaplan, a modern Orthodox Jew writing recently in *Commentary* (1976) put it: "It is possible and necessary, to live with the dissonance and tension between halakhic [i.e., traditional Judaic legal] values and modern ones." The underlying conviction seems to be that out of such conflict growth emerges. And indeed, the ideologues of the movement—from Hirsch and Mendelssohn to Soloveitchick and his contemporaries—have stressed the inevitability of such conflict along with its inherent spiritual promise.

But the dissonances of doubling may be muted; that, in part, is the purpose of contemporization and traditioning. Generally, such muting may take two forms: synthesis or nihilation. In the former the emphasis is on blending while in the latter on blocking out contradiction. Considered analytically, contemporization and traditioning contain elements of synthesis and nihilation. That is, they refer to reinterpretations where on the one hand a reciprocal fusion between past and present dialectically generates a third path—either a traditioned modernity or a contemporized tradition. On the other hand, both imply to some extent a conceptual liquidation of that which does not fit smoothly into the reinterpretive process. Put differently, doubling consists of both interchange and division.

Synthesis

Attached to synthetic and nihilistic elements of reinterpretation are particular attitudes. With the former, the underlying attitude supports the notion that past and present have something to offer each other; relevance becomes transtemporal. Transformation seems to be a motif of all such synthesis of past and present. Three possibilities may be considered: transformation of time, symbols, and behavior.

Temporal Transformation

Contemporization and its counterpart represent a transformation wherein time becomes subservient to perceived social necessity. The past, no longer immune to change, must constantly come to terms with the present just as the present cannot ignore the past. At the very least, each becomes a prologue to the other. Each with its own particular logic and aesthetic reframes the other. This framing, as Goffman has suggested as true of all frameworks, organizes more than meaning; it also organizes involvement and defines action.

Engrossed in their reinterpretations and supporting activities, people may free themselves from sensing the competing demands of their bitemporal and bicultural existence. The social and cultural order which makes anachronism the first principle of order breaks, reconstructs, and constrains time, repressing its governance. People live now and then. (Of course they may also appear "unrealistic" or "lost in their own worlds"—an indictment often aimed at the committed modern Orthodox.)

If initiated by the solitary individual such temporal permutation would be viewed as a pathological loss of orientation. Carried on within a cultural ethos of contemporization and traditioning, this same process becomes the basic ideological structure of modern Orthodoxy. It appears, in the words of one such time traveler, "as part of the nature of things."

Among Jews such ideological transformation of time is deeply rooted in the hermeneutics of talmudic interpretation. There, among the first principles of biblical exegesis, one finds the statement: "There is no earlier or later in the Torah" (Pesachim 6b). That is, an interpretive understanding of the Torah requires a shredding of chronological order.

In its reflection in the everyday life of modern Orthodox Jews, such temporal transformation turns yesterday into today. For example in contemporization, the timelessness of the Sabbath is conceived as a timely way of regenerating oneself for the challenges of weekly life. Or in modern Orthodox traditioning, the good fortunes of today are viewed as vindications of and repayment for the strict observances of yesterday. The eternal and the ephemeral are thereby synthesized. Recent research (what little there is) on those newly embracing Orthodoxy while maintaining their links to the secular world, the so-called modern *baal t' shuva* (penitent)—"B.T." in the vernacular—reveals a deeply felt self-commitment to this sort of synthesis. More about him later.

Symbol Transformation

Contemporization and traditioning also transform symbols. In contemporization, the apparently superannuated symbols of yesterday become revitalized in the present, translated into modern terms. Similarly in traditioning, the symbols of contemporary life become analogues and emblems of a more vital past. In both cases, the original meaning of the symbols is convolved to meaning something else, and the resulting new (synthetic) meaning is held onto with intensity and conviction.

In the Jewish case, this transformation of symbols has often meant a refinement of "coarse" Old Testament symbols, an exercise first begun by biblical commentators. An eye for an eye was to mean, according to the commentators, "If one blinded the eye of his fellow, he pays him the [market] value of his eye." Or it has resulted in endowing modern devices and practices with the timeless sanctity of religion. For example the modern Orthodox Jew who chooses to employ age-old symbols in a contemporary frame of mind is exhorted, when donning the *tallit*, the time-honored fringed garment which is part of the male's prayer garb, to—in the words of the *Jewish Catalogue*, the contemporary popular guide for Jewish reinterpretation—"keep [the old] symbols in mind as you put on and wear the tallit. Other associations will probably occur to you. Nurture them." Or, such Jews look, for example, at the time clock, used to turn on otherwise prohibited lights on the Sabbath, and consider it a semireligious symbol. In the transformation of symbols, "perspective," as Ortega put it, "becomes one of the component parts of reality."

Behavioral Transformation

In contemporization, practices based upon custom and tradition are given new expression and added significance. In the case of modern Orthodoxy, an example might be the knotting of *tzitzit*, the ritual of tying of fringes on a four-cornered garment as mandated in the Old Testament (Numbers 15: 37-41). Contemporized, the practice—although not losing its traditional meaning—may become macrame, a contemporary fad. Hence one may tie *tzitzit*, remain true to the old Torah law, and still be involved in a fashionable, modern pursuit.

Correspondingly in traditioning, a new practice is invested with all the authority and character of an age-old ritual. "The new is made holy" through a perceived nexus with previous holiness. For example, among a growing number of modern Orthodox Jews, the naming of a new-born daughter, originally carried out with little or none of the ceremonial surrounding the ritual of naming a son, is becoming a rite of similar proportions, albeit of different substance. The present is reconceived in terms of the past just as with contemporization the opposite is the case.

Transformations have in the past been rewarded and thereby encouraged by the secular world since they are seen as proof of the latter's ultimate dominance. Jews who manage to successfully reframe their Orthodoxy in modern terms are celebrated as present-day "court Jews," refined and civilized specimens of the real thing. They become one of the many token outsiders that the nominally pluralist America accepts into its midst. Underlying such acceptance has of course been the unstated but clear message that transformation is a propaedeutic to Americanization.

Nihilation

Complementary to the synthesis of past and present is, as already suggested, a certain amount of conceptual liquidation or nihilation. Here one denies the reality of phenomena or interpretations of phenomena that do not fit into an otherwise balanced universe. Certain dimensions of time, symbols, behavior, or belief which seem hopelessly discrepant are either diverted from one's attention or even repudiated. Along with such an attitude comes what Goffman calls a "disinvolvement" or withdrawal from situations where the discrepancy must be confronted.

Because even the most modern of Orthodox Jews view their Judaism as an all-encompassing life form—the "bottom line"—which does not consider the world as ultimately divisible into secular and hallowed sectors, and which demands, as one modern Orthodox spokesman, Bernard Weinberger, writes, "unequivocal, unqualified, and unambiguous acceptance of the *Halakhah*" (i.e., the corpus of Jewish law and associated observance—literally "the way"), a repudiative nihilation of parochial tradition is unthinkable. Moreover, because these Jews seek also to be *of* as well as *in* the contemporary world, modern themes are not easily repudiated. Accordingly, the nihilation implicit in modern Orthodox reinterpretation becomes primarily one of the diversion of attention. Here two possibilities exist: inattention and disattention.

Inattention may be defined, after Goffman, as "a kind of dimming of lights," where there is an "appreciation" of matters outside one's immediate focus of attention but no great involvement with it. Disattention on the other hand, represents an *active* withdrawal of attention of anything outside the circle of one's concern. The boundaries of compartmentalization become far more pronounced in the latter than in the former. In both, however, one extricates oneself and finally becomes disinvolved from the unassimilatable or unpalatable.

For modern Orthodox Jews such compartmentalization makes up the nihilative aspect of their reinterpretations and associated layering of behavior. While the effort is made to bring about a harmonic blend of tradition and the contemporary world, there are nevertheless some areas of strain where no amount of reinterpretation seems able to overcome certain dissonances. In such cases, the discordant matters are either made peripheral, inattended; or they are actively repressed and forgotten, disattended. Such nihilistic correlates of reinterpretation neutralize threats to what are considered appropriate social definitions of reality by assigning, as Berger and Luckman note, ''an inferior ontological status, and thereby a not-to-be-taken-seriously cognitive status, to all definitions outside'' that social reality. Indeed, there are those who suggest that such segmentation is typical of modern life.

More specifically, in the nihilative aspect of their contemporization, modern Orthodox Jews may either ignore those laws and observances which do not fit into the modern world or actively blot them out. Such action does not presume an ideological repudiation whereby the inappropriate is wiped off the books, as it were—the approach of Conservative and Reform Judaism; it simply means that such matters are left in the background. For example, while the divine revelation of the Torah is considered to be a fundamental article of Jewish faith, reaffirmed by many in their daily prayers, in the modern world where religion is peripheral and personal rather than central and social, little if anything is ever said about this matter except in the stylized fashion of rabbinic sermons.

In a recent essay arguing for a modern approach to Orthodox life, Rabbi David Hartman suggests that the observant Jew be prepared to explain his religious practice to nonobservant outsiders, that he ''be trained to speak intelligibly without having to validate the significance of his actions solely by an appeal to faith.'' In the modern age, the struggle between faith and reason tilts in favor of the latter. Although the matter remains commonly inattended, left as a formalistic pronouncement in prayer, it may, if the believer is pressed to account for his prayers, be disattended. In this case, such questions are routinely assigned to theological vituosi while the layman disinvolves himself. The dissonant element is put out of the humdrum of everyday life. In the three years of my participant observation in a modern Orthodox synagogue, I never once witnessed the laity discussing the theology which seemed to underlie their entire religious behavior.

The compartmentalizing nihilations of contemporization may occur in Jewish observances as well. Here practices out of tune with the contemporary world simply lapse into neglect. For example, although there is a requirement to recite a benediction upon having successfully evacuated one's bowel or bladder, many modern Orthodox Jews simply fail to recite this prayer when immersed in the flow of modern secular life. The requirement is not repudiated but simply inattended for the moment. If challenged, the very same Jew will likely admit the omission as a transgression—although he is not likely to belabor the point. (There seems to be a tacit agreement among modern Orthodox Jews to leave inattended matters undiscussed.) Similarly, laws prohibiting one from having intimate physical contact (even without intercourse) with woman other than one's wife (Lev. 18:6) are simply disattended. In the cosmopolitan atmosphere of the global village, the insularity proposed in such laws is actively overlooked. The social graces of pecking kisses, embraces, and handshakes are maintained even while the law is disattended.

There is nihilation implicit in traditioning as well. Here either one mutes or obliviates the radical contemporaneity of certain actions in order to make them contiguous with tradition, or one forces meanings on the past which destroy its integrity. For example, among many modern Orthodox women a chic, modern wig is used as a *sheital*, the ritually mandated head cover for married females. No longer the unremarkable peruke originally worn to insure the modesty of the married women, the contemporary *sheital* is now closer to a public celebration of her sensuality, fashion-consciousness, and good looks. Such traditioning fits the contemporary wig into the age-old conception of the *sheital* only by disattending the antithetical character of the chic *sheital*. If one wonders how people can possibly handle the complicated orchestrations of synthesis and nihilation implicit in their contemporization and traditioning, one might simply answer: "All things are possible to him that believes" (Mark 10:27). For the contemporizing and traditioning faithful the time-honored Cartesian maxim which puts *cogito* before all else is the essence of belief. Believing requires reinterpretive thinking.

As with the previously discussed synthetic transformations by modern Orthodox Jews, America remains very much present behind their nihilations. Making up the bulk of outsiders to whom one's Orthodoxy must be made intelligible, modern America has retained an implicit power to judge the success and adequacy of such reinterpretations. Insufficient or inappropriate efforts were in the past guarantees of exclusion from the modern world; American ignorance of Orthodoxy meant not only unfamiliarity with but also neglect of these would-be moderns.

The American Religious Revival and Modern Orthodoxy

The new American religious revival portends a change both in the character of modern Orthodoxy as well as American response to it. Now that conspicuous ethnic religion has not only become respectable but as American as Jimmy Carter, reinterpretation has become far less crucial for the modern. He finds instead that he can be far more blatantly Orthodox and parochial than before without losing his share in the contemporary world. Not surprisingly, therefore, one finds a recent trend toward a stricter Orthodoxy in modern America. For example, Rabbi Steven Riskin, once the voice of reinterpretation among American modern Orthodox Jews, has now opened a day school which demands of its students a rigorous Orthodox lifestyle. And the Chassidim, notably the Lubavitch sect, are swarming with new recruits whom they aggressively pursue from Harvard Square to Scarsdale and Berkeley.

This turnabout has forced a change in American modern Orthodoxy where, after several generations, reinterpretation had become second nature. Nowhere is the strain of such change seen more clearly than in modern Orthodox reactions to the *baal t' shuva* (B.T.), the neophyte in the community. In the past, and still to a great extent in the present, academies of Jewish learning and their teachers (who have also served as ideologues and spokesmen) have handled neophytes (usually children). In recent years, however, Orthodoxy in general and modern Orthodoxy in particular have experienced the great influx of spiritual newcomers who have begun to inundate all faiths. What some have called the "resouling of Judaism" has yielded increasing numbers of volitional rather than inertial Jews; people who actively choose their religion and its way of observance rather than those who simply fall into the path. More often than not these new Orthodox Jews (the B.T.'s) come unschooled in their religion. Sending them to the yeshiva, a process advocated by many and followed by some, is not always practical or possible, especially for those who remain bonded in some way to the modern world from whence they came. Explanation and education thus occurs within the lay community. Frequently "turned on" by modern Orthodox rabbis and leaders, these B.T.'s often come finally to live in modern Orthodox communities, communities filled with people who do not require a complete renunciation of the B.T.'s' modernist past.

Once there they often strike a discordant note with the inertial modern Orthodoxy they find. In their enthusiasm for their newly found faith, the B.T.'s find it hard to take their Judaism for granted. They demand transcendence in everyday life and practice a conspicuous and aggressive Orthodoxy. They are often struck by the dualism they witness, frequently interpreting it as duplicity. They cannot abide with contradiction and demand explanation. In short, they force the everyday modern Orthodox Jew to conform to the rabbi's description or else account for the difference. They wish to know, for example, how one can separate everyday secular life from religious sensibility. If one is indeed Orthodox in observance, how can one also be a slumlord or dishonest businessman, or how can "permitted" food be eaten in otherwise nonkosher restaurants? Is not the choice all or nothing?

The questions asked defy simplistic answers. The ubiquitousness of the B.T.—hardly any modern Orthodox Jew does not know one, many have married them—makes his questions increasingly part of the everyday life of modern Orthodoxy. These questions pose a challenge to the "business as usual" approach to reinterpretation and in particular to doubling, synthesis, and nihilation. Ironically, the "success" of modern Orthodoxy in attracting large numbers of converts from less Orthodox backgrounds may bring about fundamental changes in its future character. Moreover, their conspicuousness will test America's sufferance of the Jews—something about which a people used to persecution and pogrom has doubts.

Of course the possibility remains that the newcomers will be made into reinterpreters as well, particularly if the new-found American "religion" turns out to be short lived. There are some signs of this among those in their late thirties and beyond who have established families. In most modern Orthodox communities, the older B.T 's are indistinguishable from other natives. Yet there are also signs of a move toward a stricter Orthodoxy, one that emphasizes faith over acculturation. There are greater numbers of modernist parents sending their children to traditionalist yeshivas that discourage modernism. This contraacculturative modern Orthodoxy may move the old reinterpreters back to basics or out toward Conservative Judaism. It is too early to tell exactly what will occur.

Conclusion

It is often presumed that the modern world forces upon its inhabitants a radical break with the past and that those who chose to embrace the past necessarily lose their portion in the world of the present. I have tried to suggest that while in the long run that may be the case, there are—as the situation of modern Orthodox Jews illustrates—cognitive processes of interpretation which, at least for a time, may make possible a pattern of life in both past and present.

Via reinterpretation those, like modern Orthodox Jews, who wish to live in two time-worlds are able to layer their behavior, synthesize, transform, or nihilate elements of such worlds and generally shift their attention and involvement so that the dissonances of their lives do not overpower them. That program becomes their practical ideology, their doctrine for survival. To the extent that many of us find ourselves increasingly having to reconcile ever more discrepant pasts with a concomitant rush of compelling presents, contemporization and traditioning, the current preoccupation of modern Orthodox Jews, have become part of our lives.

References

Berger, Peter, and Thomas Luckman, 1966
Heilman, Samuel C., 1976, 1977
Kaplan, Lawrence, 1976
Liebman, C., 1965
Rieff, Philip, 1970

"Civil Religion Sects," Oriental Mysticism, and Therapy Groups

The Politics of New Cults:
Non-Prophetic Observations
On Science, Sin and Scholarship

Irving Louis Horowitz

Several years ago, in an article in *The Atlantic*, entitled "Science, Sin and Scholarship" (March 1977), I explored some of the political and ethical questions raised by the participation of senior representatives of the academic community—especially from the scientific, literary and social scientific fields —in a conference wholly subsidized by the Reverend Sun Myung Moon and his Unification Church. The questions have since been hotly debated in theological circles and in university forums, and they have received intermittent attention in the popular press, in courtroom trials, and among members of the intellectual class directly affected by such participation.

The 1978 publication of *Science, Sin and Scholarship: The Politics of Reverend Moon and the Unification Church* further intensified debate on the ethics of participation. Since the anthology contained a wide range of data and discourse, covering in depth the key statements by representatives of mainline religions and offering analyses by leading journalists and social researchers, the character of the debate broadened, and my own sense of situation deepened. What started as a relatively straightforward extension of my earlier writings on social science participation in government projects soon took on unexpected dimensions. What follows is not intended as either autobiography or apologetics.[1] But it is an attempt to deepen the discussion of what the Moon phenomenon represents in the post-Jonestown era, a period in which social and religious analysis has focused on the nature of cults and the new sects generally but has not necessarily come closer to the marrow of the new religions.

The question of whether any particular grouping like the Unification Church represents a cult, as its critics claim, or an authentic religion, as the Moon personnel claim, is fundamentally irrelevant. The main feature of the Unification Church, and to a lesser extent other such groups, is their character as civil religions. Behind that pleasant phrase is a categorical denial of the Lockean-Jeffersonian principle of the separation of church and state. The writings and social behavior of this church reveal the assumption that an integration of church and state is prerequisite to any new theocratic world order. This element in the Moon theology should give civil libertarians, religious minorities, and those who advocate social and political pluralism, cause for concern. The Unification Church represents nothing short of a direct assault on the notion that there are organizational limits to religious practice. It is further a rejection of the rights of individuals to resist evangelization campaigns or similar incursions into their private lives.

The Unification Church and its stated quest for universal values of harmony, unity and tranquility, is little else than the transliteration of the discredited notion of world order through world morality writ large. Indeed, it is no coincidence that some of the people associated with such earlier cosmic political efforts have found it easy to drift into the Moon organization. The Unification Church not only represents an integration of the political and religious, but a long-range ambitious integration of non-Communist nations against Communist nations. This political framework is subsumed under generalized rhetoric calling for a moral struggle of good against evil—however that may be defined by the Unification Church at any point in time. Despite its miniscule size in the United States, the Unification Church is an international political organization, and must be so perceived. Its worldwide networks and linkages make it quite different from most local, rural and regionally based cults.[2]

The Unification Church also represents the first instance in which a religious group has shifted its emphasis from what might be called charismatics or fundamentalist proselytizing on a direct appeal basis, to a huge marketing effort synchronizing newspaper publicity, indeed newspaper ownership, with followers or acolytes who provide a mass battering ram for delivering the theocratic message. The inner organization of the Unification Church is manifestly rational-totalitarian. There is scant room for doubt, willingness to debate only fellow theological travelers, and a direct assault on any who are perceived or declared to be enemies. Once such a negative definition of an individual or a group is imputed, the Church utilizes every technique at its disposal: from legal harassment to personal confrontation and threat.

It would be a mistake to place groups such as those of the Reverend Moon and the Reverend Jones under one umbrella. There are organizational, ideological and structural differences that must be dealt with in a serious and sober way. For example, the Jones group had a Leninist ideology; the Moon group is equally forthright in its anti-Communist posture. The Jones forces retreated from the major centers of Western civilization; whereas the Moon effort is directed at precisely such centers, having maximum strength in large urban regions. Reverend Jones's appeal was directly and unambiguously charismatic; the Moon effort offers an entire hierarchical and organizational range that functions adequately and often independently of the "perfect master." Again, the issue is not cults vs. religions, but rather the function and structure of these organizations as they impact the national society and the international polity.

Reverend Moon and the Unification Church represent a serious, albeit limited, incursion into the political parameters of American life. His movement has shown a demonstrated ability to attract a small, but not inconsequential segment of the academic elite, albeit a special conservative variety of that elite; old in demographic terms, unconcerned with democratic norms. It has also been able to attract a group of serious and capable young people, who appear to be far more intellectually oriented than the conventional fundamentalist found in American Protestant evangelical movements. The main threat to it resides in the American pluralistic value system which has always posed an obstacle to religious centralism and hegemonic control.

However much one's own predilection and training constrains the need to speak within the framework of political sociology, it soon becomes apparent that conventional labels do not easily exhaust messianic movements. The Sun Myung Moon effort moves not only toward a sociology of religion but more profoundly, toward a political theology. For example, soon after the publication of *Science, Sin and Scholarship*, a volume dedicated to the defense and favorable appraisal of the Unification Church appeared, entitled: *A Time for Consideration*. Without offering invidious comparisons, apologias, or for that matter a summary review of an alternative volume, it is relevant to say that in this area we are confronted by a choice of rhetorics which are almost as diverse as C. P. Snow's designation of the two cultures of science and literature.

Positive theological appraisals of the Moon position emphasize that the Unification Church is distinctive in its quest for the unity of morals and science, unlike the conventional Protestant dualism. In this regard, the Church searches for the unity rather than the separation of the theological and the political. Its efforts to breach the wall of separatism between church and state is considered not so much an attack on civil liberties, as a search for new foundations for the social order. In this regard the Unification Church sees itself as a passionate yet realistic, release from the contraints of the inherited Christian conception of the King's two bodies: Caesar and Christ in external conflict. Even if there are those who recoil at the Reverend Moon representing himself as a synthetic figure combining the virtues of Christ with the worldly achievements of Caesar, conceptually his vision touches on a soft spot within the conventional American religious modality. But beyond strictly theological considerations, it is crucial to keep in mind that the Unification Church is a form of practice and not just a belief system. This church views itself not only as providing long-range theological resolution to large-scale macrosocial issues, but immediate sustenance and relief to the alienation of our times. It does this presumably through the bonded community, providing a sense of belongingness in the here and now and not just in the hereafter.

While this Moon rhetoric is clearly self-serving, it is so close to the marrow of theological discourse generally that it would be dangerous simply to view the Unification Church from the point of view of the social background of its members, or the political purposes of its organization, or even the cleverness of its marketing orientation. While these aspects are all in evidence, there is something here that moves beyond the reach of a strictly sociological critique. That something is powerful enough to cancel out the rational inhibitions placed before those who would enter such a special totalistic institutional life.

The theological critique of the Unification Church has a philosophical dimension which must be recognized as significant and incorporated into any useful social analysis. For example, critics of Moon view the quest for moral universals as nothing other than the dogmatic quest for certainty. The effort to get beyond the empirical is considered to be an attempt to crash the limits of knowledge in a spurious, anti-scientific manner. The organizational claims for a bonded community can just as readily be viewed as abject submission to the totalitarian temptation, an irrational response to the necessity of choice. This denial of choice in the name of security can be considered the infantilization of human experience. In short, the very notions viewed as favorable by advocates can be perceived as pernicious by critics.

Criticism from mainline religious institutions presents a serious assault on the new religions, certainly this particular new religion called the Unification Church. But one must also recognize that the choice of rhetoric partially determines the outcome. Hence the question of rhetoric itself becomes a subject for analysis by the sociology of knowledge. What are the social foundations, institutional arrangements, and ideological proclivities that lead some to use an affirmative rhetoric and others a critical rhetoric? Nor is this a lesser order of problem than defining Moon's politics. It is a prime order of concern because the Unification Church represents, after all, a special problem for Christianity. It is a Christian heresy, something that emerges in reaction to the current despair born of the Western experience. The Unification Church offers an infusion of Orientalism: not only to create a new worldwide religious movement, but to share in what was formerly a special mission of Baptists, Methodists and other Evangelical sects. In short, the Reverend Moon's announced intention is to absorb the Christian experience as part of a newer Messianic movement which he will lead to triumph.

If there is a special question of the relationship of Christianity to the Unification Church, having to do with an alternative eschatalogical position, there is another problem of relation of the Church to the Jewish people. It is not necessarily a theological problem, for this ground has been covered in numerous discussions and debates. In the final analysis, it is a philogenetic memory problem. The church of the Reverend Moon is an evangelical church. It disseminates its activities in a vigorous manner, recalling a medieval past in which Jewish children were separated from their parents by force and baptized as Christians. Even if modern Jews are remote from such experiences, they must have uneasiness at the Unification Church's insistence on separating children from parents. As pointed out earlier, many of the Church's converts are Jewish. The notion of a sealed community, of intensive conversion efforts, of the acceptance of living deities, all of these are experienced by Jews, and probably to some degree by mainline Christian churches as well, as one more form of idolatry; a form of cultism which has practical manifestations not only in terms of church membership, but in fundamental beliefs, and hence deep human structures.

Other elements that require deeper sociological study have to do with the breakdown of personal goals, intimate family life, and identification with larger collective units within civil society.[3] Privatization has become such a prevailing fact of American life, that any concept of constraints or limits is itself considered an ultimate form of illiberality. In such a climate of permissiveness, one must expect at least a portion of the younger population to seek models of authority that provide guidelines and norms for the conduct of ordinary everyday life. The agony of constant choice without resolve is not a young person's game. The Unification Church as surrogate family may still affect only a small portion of the population, but for that portion it does provide an effective therapeutic setting that offers linkage to the larger society without its turmoils. The political characteristics of the Unification Church and its intellectual vanguard can best be understood as offering an island of certainty amidst a sea of troubles.

At the risk of overgeneralization, I would say that a major problem in the mainline religious movements of our time is that they are based on a sophisticated set of theological principles and premises, a sophisticated framework hammered out over hundreds and even thousands of years. But the price of this transformation of religion into theology is a perfunctory ceremonialism. It offers rational, and partial, participation that may not reach a segment of people who need maximum participation in the actual, felt, spiritual content of religion as a personal experience. As a result, mainline religions have reacted either with hostility, or more often, mimicry of intensified evangelization of their own.[4]

Exactly this sort of void is filled by movements like the Unification Church. Its great strength is in its practice, its ability to organize psychologically as well as socially, the *Geist* as well as the *Gesellschaft*. The lives of the young take on meaning in a prescribed form that provides a sense of importance today and destiny tomorrow. Those who see only the painful vacuity of the Moon theology, its creaky propositions that have been and will continue to be subject to scathing attack by mainline religions, must therefore appreciate that the shortcomings in its theological analysis are more than compensated for by its practical capacities to reach into the immediate experience of a segment of the population otherwise bereft of a sense of purpose, history and science. The appeal of the Unification Church to those searching to overcome the fragmentation of concepts that dominate our times is precisely what unites its novices and intellectuals, its young and its old, its panhandlers and pundits.

This leaves us with the policy implications of a phenomenon such as the Unification Church. By that I mean simply: how does one respond? The solutions thus far profferred, such as deprogramming, or legislation limiting solicitation or congregation, come into conflict with constitutional guarantees. Laws against kidnapping and brainwashing work in both directions. Moreover there are fewer cases in which the Moon organization has done the kidnapping than the reverse. One response to such onerous forms of legislation is simply what might be called "nonpolicy," or a reliance upon the natural history of religious movements; as the Unification Church becomes organizationally solidified, participating almost as any other Protestant sect within a larger American pluralism, the movement may find itself secure and wealthy enough not to push too hard against established religions.

There is a great deal to commend this point of view. The Unification Church's growth in numbers has leveled off, and its great zeal has given way, even according to its many apologetics, to quiet writings and discussions between professors, clergy and others.

I would suggest that there is a third course of action worth pursuing—albeit with caution; and that is to view the present system of law as containing constraints upon any organization's efforts to engage in deceptive advertising, fraudulent marketing, prevent free movement of its members, employ physical restraint—activities which the Moon organization has, at one point or another, been accused of, often with telling effect. It might well be that these criticisms, like the assumption of the direct linkage between the Reverend Sun Myung Moon and the South Korean government or its police arm, the KCIA, will turn out to be less ominous than originally predicted. If so, any effort at punitive response must also be modulated and modified.

The unseemly way in which the Moon organization has moved to crush further hearing of its activities in the United States and its full-scale advertising blitz intended to prevent and frustrate further investigation of its secular activities would indicate that this approach should be carefully considered and not dismissed as a regulatory device.[5]

Within the framework of American life there is always the possibility not only for dialogue but for demagogery. There are no simple answers to a phenomenon such as the Unification Church, and no simple policy will suffice: certainly none that will single them out for punitive damages and treatment apart from that accorded to all minorities. But the recognition that a social movement such as the Unification Church represents a problem in political sociology no less than an issue in political theology, should itself provide some appreciation not only of the magnitude of the problem of cults and sects, but of the potential for human reason to address these problems.

If this sounds like a clarion call for a return to the century-old "warfare" in the United States between science and theology, then the meaning of my remarks will have been woefully misunderstood. I do not think that the task of science is to engage in ideological conflict with religion. Indeed, this phase in American intellectual history coincided with a science that was mechanistic and a religion that was formalistic. The present is a world in which science is imaginative, and anything but mechanical in form. At the same time, the new religions present an equally imaginative effort to cope with alienation and anomie in a post-industrial order. The conflicts are real, but they concern values not ideologies: they concern such questions as whether decision making should be based on evidence or on faith; whether decisions should be made after testing propositions or in terms of divine laws; whether a world which limps along on partial and shifting truths is to be preferred to one of perfect harmonies.

It might well be that matters will be resolved in favor of impassioned new religions over and against rationalistic sciences. This outcome would be no small tragedy, but one hardly unknown to the annals of human society. But not to be ready continually to run such risks is simply to exchange one form of fanaticism for another, to subvert a scientific view in the very act of combatting a fanatic viewpoint. The world of social science is highly risky. However, that of the new cults is only superficially risk-free. One has only to note the tragedy of Guyana to comprehend a very large shortcoming in the new religious movements which dot the American landscape today. The tragic consequences of fanaticism will remain the best argument for pluralism, partial truths and peace.

The anomaly in the current cultural condition of America is that there is an increased demand for certainty in all aspects of our existence while both the need for flexibility and the fact of fragmentation becomes greater. The mystification of astrophysics into science fiction; the psychologization of social problems by transforming public issues into private ailments; the privatization of personal life by denying the importance of the political process; the transformation of community into spectacle, and public discourse into mass marketing orgies; all of these provide the ground and source of movements such as the Unification Church and the Peoples Temple. They accurately sense the present mood and tempo of modern life. Hence, the struggle for the minds of the American people provides new expressions of old struggles: the competition between the democratic and the authoritarian in the guise of a reconsideration of cults, sects and religions.

Notes

1. A series of futile efforts by the Unification Church and its conduits were made after publication of *Science, Sin and Scholarship* to prevent its distribution, and in fact, to reclaim copies that had already been shipped. This was but one of several efforts on the part of the Unification Church to prevent scientific or critical literature about its activities from being disseminated. In each case the legal charges varied, but the purpose was always the same: preventing the dissemination of such books. This effort came to a head when a $4 million libel suit, brought against a volume written by Dusty Sklar, entitled: *Gods and Beasts: The Nazis and the Occult,* was dismissed in the New York State Supreme Court. Justice Edward J. Greenfield ruled that "the complaint is based on statements reflecting the author's opinion, with no issue of fact as to knowledge of falsity or reckless disregard for truth being shown to exist."
   It is interesting to note that when the Moon people have used the courts to extend civil liberties, such as the briefs against deprogrammers, and to permit panhandling, these suits were upheld. When the Moon effort was directed toward the curbing of constitutional rights or civil liberties, such efforts have uniformly been rebuked. Thus, inadvertently, the Unification Church has rendered a service by further delineating the limits of censorship and the rights of citizens.
2. These international dimensions notwithstanding, the demographic characteristics of the Unification Church should not be misinterpreted. In the hub-bub of controversy and special meetings—mass and elite—the actual size of the Moon church tends to be grossly overestimated. While mass rallies for a special event like the God Bless America Rally can bring forth roughly 30,000 people, and specialized meetings like those of the International Conference on the Unity of Sciences can net 500 invited guests, the actual national membership count varies in estimates from 2,000 to 30,000. This is not to say that membership uniquely determines power and influence. The history of political conspiracies indicates little such connection. Nor has the expected demise of the Unification Church come about, despite the failure of its leaders to realize 144,000 converts by its target year of 1967, or 200,000 by its Bicentennial Rally of 1976. Neither Armaggedon nor a new Garden of Eden materialized. In short, the Unification Church like so many movements before it, has been absorbed into the mainstream of American religious life. It is one more sect in the civic culture: and hence, part of the political pluralism and religious protestantism that its disciples so roundly deplore.
3. Lest there be any doubt that there have been dramatic changes in the feelings of young people in particular with respect to their capacity to integrate into today's society, a new piece of research conducted by the Survey Research Center, under

the supervision of Joseph Veroff, should put those doubts to rest. In a twenty-year panel study comparing 1957 and 1976, Veroff found the following series of propositions to be true: People are more anxious about the world and they feel less in tune with it; a greater percentage of people feel that they are not going to be happier in the future; young people more often report anxiety symptoms, such as trouble sleeping, nervousness, headaches, and loss of appetite, factors that can be separated from physical ill health. Comparing the two studies, people are now more unhappy about their communities and country (24 percent vs. 13 percent), their jobs (12 percent vs. 13 percent) and their interpersonal lives (13 percent vs. 30 percent). In short, while people in America still uphold the fundamental norms of the society and believe in long-term happiness their problems have mounted to the point where the proportion of people who feel they can handle problems by themselves has sharply declined from 44 percent to 36 percent. This is probably the most significant finding, since these new religions offer a mechanism for problem management; the other area that has most sharply declined in the past twenty years. Joseph Veroff, "Americans Seek Self-Development, Suffer Anxiety from Changing Roles," *Institute for Social Research Newsletter*, Vol. 7, No. 1 (Winter 1979), pp. 4–5.

4. The rise of the new cults has generated a sense of crisis in mainline religious denominations. Christian churches, even one so powerful as the Catholic church, have begun to turn toward evangelization as a method of building religious institutions. In his sharp critique of this mimicking pattern, Andrew M. Greeley, in his newest work entitled: *Crisis in the Church*, points out that there is little evidence that there are massive numbers of alienated on unchurched or disidentified Americans eagerly awaiting recruitment by one or another religious denomination; that religious affiliation is a complex, involved phenomenon located in family structure rather than in individual behavior; and further, that much discussion about evangelization does not seem to be either well informed or intelligent, but rather views it as a zealot activity without regard for complex and intricate aspects of American social and ethical life. While the views of Professor Greeley may be considered far from definitive, they do point out the huge gap which exists between a clerical, evangelical fervor and a secular scientific society. Andrew M. Greeley, *Crisis in the Church: A Study of Religion in America* (Chicago: The Thomas More Press, 1979), esp. pp. 243–61.

5. In a series of advertisements in the *New York Times,* the *Washington Post* and the *Los Angeles Times,* promoting the Reverend Sun Myung Moon's volume, *Our Response: Investigation of Korean-American Relations,* the Unification Church used its media skills to attack the findings of former Congressman Donald Fraser's House Subcommittee on International Organizations, claiming that $685,000 of the taxpayer's money was spent and that the committee "laid a very large and expensive egg." The advertisements noted that a CIA report stating that the Korean government and the director of the KCIA had founded the Unification Church "had no basis in fact." As might be expected, the advertisements ignored the central findings of the committee. There was strong evidence, the committee reported, "that the Unification Church systematically violated U.S. tax, immigration, banking, currency, and Foreign Agents Registration Act laws, as well as State and local laws relating to charity fraud, and that these violations were related to the organization's overall goals of gaining temporal power." The statement issued by the Reverend Moon, that "Mr. Fraser's defeat was due to more than political

fortune," that it "was an act of God," represents a warning and a threat against any further congressional hearings, especially those scheduled by Senator Dole and Representative Zablocki on the status of cults in America. Presumably, the same providential fate awaits Dole and Zablocki as befell Fraser if they continue with hearings. With such an approach, it is little wonder that lobbying by the Moon forces on Capitol Hill has been intense and unrelenting.

References

Greeley, Andrew M., 1979
Horowitz, Irving Louis, 1977, 1978, 1979
Sklar, Dusty, 1977
Veroff, Joseph, 1979

The Apocalypse at Jonestown

John R. Hall

The events of November 1978 at Jonestown, Guyana have been well documented, indeed probably better documented than most incidents in the realm of the bizarre. Beyond the wealth of "facts" that have been drawn from interviews with survivors of all stripes, there remain piles of as yet unsifted documents and tapes. If they can ever be examined, these will perhaps add something in the way of detail, but it is unlikely they will change very much the broad lines of our understanding of Jonestown. The major dimensions of the events and the outlines of various intrigues are already before us. But so far we have been caught in a flood of instant analysis. Some of this has been insightful, but much of the accompanying moral outrage has clouded our ability to comprehend the events themselves. We need a more considered look at what sort of social phenomenon Jonestown was, and why, and how the Reverend Jim Jones and his staff led the 900 people at Jonestown to die in mass murder and suicide. On the face of it, the action is unparalleled and incredible.

The news media have sought to account for Jonestown largely by looking for parallels in history. Yet we have not been terribly enlightened by the examples they have found, usually because they have searched for cases that bear the outer trappings of the event but have fundamentally different causes. Thus, at

171

Masada, in 73 A.D. the Jews who committed suicide under siege by Roman soldiers knew their fate was death, and they chose to die by their own hands rather than at those of the Romans. In World War II Japanese kamikaze pilots acted with the knowledge that direct, tangible, strategic results would stem from their altruistic suicides, if they were properly executed. And in Hitler's concentration camps, though there was occasional cooperation by Jews in their own executions, the Nazi executioners had no intentions of dying themselves.

Besides pointing to parallels that don't quite fit, the news media have portrayed Jim Jones as irrational — a madman who had perverse tendencies from early in his youth. They have labelled the Peoples Temple a "cult," perhaps in the hope that a label will suffice when an explanation is unavailable. And they have quite correctly plumbed the key issue of how Jones and his staff were able to bring the mass murder/suicide to completion, drawing largely on the explanations of psychiatrists who have suggested the concept of "brainwashing" as the answer.

But Jones was crazy like a fox! Though he may have been "possessed" or "crazed," both the organizational effectiveness of the Peoples Temple for more than fifteen years and the actual carrying out of the mass murder/suicide show that Jones and his immediate staff knew what they were doing.

Moreover, the Peoples Temple only became a cult when the media discovered the tragedy at Jonestown. As an Indiana woman whose teenager died there commented: "I can't understand why they call the Peoples Temple a cult. To the people, it was their church. . . ."[1]

It is questionable whether the term cult has any sociological utility, for as Harold Fallding has observed, it is a pejorative term most often used by members of one religion to describe a heretical or competing religion, of which they disapprove (1974, p. 27).[2] Of course, even if the use of the term "cult" in the press has been sloppy and inappropriate, some comparisons — for example, to the Unification church, the Krishna Society, and the Children of God — have been quite apt. But these comparisons have triggered a sort of guilt by association. In this view, Jonestown is not such an aberrant case among numerous exotic and bizarre religious cults. The only thing stopping some people from "cleaning up" the cult situation is the constitutional guarantee of freedom of religion.[3]

Finally, the brainwashing concept is an important but nevertheless incomplete basis for understanding the mass murder/suicide. There can be no way to determine how many people at Jonestown freely chose to drink the cyanide-laced Flav-r-ade distributed after word was received of the murders of U.S. Representative Leo Ryan and four other visitors at the airstrip. Clearly, over 200 children and an undetermined number of adults were murdered. Thought control and blind obedience to authority — brainwashing — surely account for some additional number of suicides. But the obvious cannot be ignored — that a substantial number of people, brainwashed or not, committed suicide. Since brainwashing occurs in other social organizations besides the Peoples Temple, it can only be a necessary but not a sufficient cause of the mass murder/suicide. The coercive persuasion involved in a totalistic construction of reality may explain in part *how* large numbers of people came to accept the course proposed by their leader, but it leaves unanswered the question of *why* the true believers among the inhabitants of Jonestown came to consider "revolutionary suicide" a plausible course of action.

In all the instant analysis of Jones' perversity, the threats posed by cults, and the victimization of people by brainwashing, there has been little attempt to account for Jonestown sociologically or as a religious phenomenon. The various facets of Jonestown remain as incongruous pieces of seemingly separate puzzles, and we need a close examination of the case itself in order to try to comprehend it.

In the following discussion, based on ideal-type analysis and *verstehende* sociology (Weber, 1977, pp. 4–22), I will suggest that the Peoples Temple Agricultural Project at Jonestown was an apocalyptic sect. Most apocalyptic sects gravitate toward one of three ideal typical possibilities—preapocalyptic Adventism, preapocalyptic war, or postapocalyptic other-worldly grace. Insofar as the Adventist group takes on a communal form, it comes to approximate the postapocalyptic tableau of other-worldly grace. Jonestown, I argue, was caught on the saddle of the apocalypse: it had its origins in the vaguely apocalyptic revivalist evangelism of the Peoples Temple in the United States, but the Guyanese communal settlement itself was an attempt to transcend the apocalypse by establishing a "heaven-on-earth." For various reasons this attempt was frustrated. The Jonestown group was drawn back into a preapocalyptic war with the forces of the established order, and thus "revolutionary suicide" came to be seen as a way of surmounting the frustration, of moving beyond the apocalypse to heaven, albeit not on earth.

In order to explore this idea, let us first consider the origins of Jonestown and the ways in which it subsequently came to approximate the ideal typical other-worldly sect. Then we can consider certain tensions within the Jonestown group with respect to its other-worldly existence in order to understand why similar groups did not (and are not likely to) encounter the same fate.

Jonestown as an Other-Worldly Sect

An other-worldly sect, as I have described it in *The Ways Out* (1978), is a utopian communal group that subscribes to a comprehensive set of beliefs based on an apocalyptic interpretation of current history. The world of society-at-large is seen as totally evil, in its last days, at the end of history as we know it. It is to be replaced by a community of the elect—those who live according to the revelation of God's will. The convert who embraces such a sect must, therefore, abandon any previous understanding of life's meaning and embrace the new world view, which itself is capable of subsuming and explaining the individual's previous life, the actions of the sect's opponents, and the demands that are placed on the convert by the leadership of the sect. The other-worldly sect typically establishes its existence on the "other" side of the apocalypse by withdrawing from "this" world into a timeless heaven-on-earth. In this millennial kingdom, those closest to God come to rule. Though democratic consensuality or the collegiality of elders may come into play, more typically a preeminent prophet or messiah, who is legitimated by charisma or tradition, calls the shots in a theocratic organization of God's chosen people.

The Peoples Temple had its roots in amorphous revivalistic evangelical religion, but in the transition to the Jonestown Agricultural Mission it came to resemble an other-worldly sect. The Temple grew out of the interracial congregation Jim Jones had founded in Indiana in 1953. By 1964 the Peoples Temple Full Gospel Church was federated with the Disciples of Christ (Kilduff and Javers, 1978, p. 20). Later, in 1966, Jones moved with 100 of his most devout followers to Redwood Valley, California. From there they expanded in the 1970s to San Francisco and Los Angeles, which were more promising locales for liberal, interracial evangelism. In these years before the move to Guyana, Jones largely engaged himself in the manifold craft of revivalism. He learned from others he observed — Father Divine in Philadelphia and David Martinus de Miranda in Brazil—and Jones himself became a purveyor of faked miracles and faith healings (*Newsweek,* December 4, 1978, pp. 55–56). By the time of the California years, the Peoples Temple was prospering financially from its somewhat shady tent meeting-style activities and from a variety of other money-making schemes. It was also gaining political clout through the deployment of its members for the benefit of various politicians and causes.

These early developments make one wonder why Jones did not establish a successful but relatively benign sect like the Jehovah's Witnesses, or, alternatively, why he did not move from a religious base directly into the realm of politics, as did the Reverend Adam Clayton Powell when he left his Harlem congregation to go to the U.S. House of Representatives. The answer seems twofold.

In the first place, Jim Jones appears to have had limitations both as an evangelist and as a politician. He simply did not succeed in fooling key California religious observers with his faked miracles. And for all his political support in California politics, Jones was not always able to draw on his good political "credit" when he needed it. A certain mark of political effectiveness is the ability to sustain power in the face of scandal. By this standard, Jones was not totally successful in either Indiana or California. There always seemed to be investigators and reporters on the trails of his various questionable financial and evangelical dealings (Kilduff and Javers, 1978, pp. 23–25, 35–38).

Quite aside from the limits of Jones' effectiveness, the very nature of his prophecy directed his religious movement along a different path from either worldly politics or sectarian Adventism. Keyed to the New Testament Book of Revelations, Adventist groups receive prophecy about the apocalyptic downfall of the present evil world order and the second coming of Christ to preside over a millennial period of divine grace on earth. For all such groups, the Advent itself makes irrelevant social action to reform the institutions of this world. Adventist groups differ from one another in their exact eschatology of the last days, but the groups that have survived, e.g., the Seventh Day Adventists and Jehovah's Witnesses, have juggled their doctrines that fix an exact date for Christ's appearance. They have thus moved away from any intense chiliastic expectation of an imminent appearance to engage in more mundane conversionist activities that are intended to pave the way for the Millennium (Clark, 1949, pp. 34–50; Lewy, 1974, p. 265).

Reverend Jones himself seems to have shared the pessimism of the Adventist sects about reforming social institutions in this world—for him, the capitalist world of the United States. It is true that he supported various progressive causes, but he did not put much stake in their success. Jones' prophecy was far more radical than those of contemporary Adventist groups: he focused on imminent apocalyptic disaster rather than on Christ's millennial salvation, and his eschatology therefore had to resolve a choice between preapocalyptic struggle with "the beast" or collective flight to establish a postapocalyptic kingdom of the elect. Up until the end, the Peoples Temple was directed toward the latter possibility.

Even in the Indiana years Jones had embraced an apocalyptic view. The move from Indiana to California was justified in part by his claim that Redwood Valley would survive nuclear holocaust (Krause, Stern, and Harwood, 1978, p. 29). In the California years the apocalyptic vision shifted to CIA persecution and Nazi-like extermination of blacks. In California also, the Peoples Temple gradually became communalistic in certain respects. It established a community of goods, pooled resources of elderly followers to provide communal housing for them, and drew on state funds to act as foster parents by establishing group homes for displaced youths.

In its apocalyptic and communal aspects, the Peoples Temple more and more came to exist as an ark of survival. Jonestown — the Agricultural Project in Guyana—was built, beginning in 1974, by an advance crew that by early 1977 still amounted to less than 60 people, most of them under 30. The mass exodus of the Peoples Temple to Jonestown really began in 1977 when the Peoples Temple was coming under increasing scrutiny in California.

In the move to Guyana, the group began to concertedly exhibit many dynamics of an other-worldly sect, although it differed in ways that were central to its fate. Until the end, Jonestown was similar in striking ways to contemporary sects like the Children of God and the Krishna Society (ISKCON, Inc.). Indeed, the Temple bears a more than casual, and somewhat uncomfortable, resemblance to the various Protestant sects that emigrated to the wilderness of

North America beginning in the seventeenth century. The Puritans, Moravians, Rappites, Shakers, Lutherans, and many others like them sought to escape religious persecution in Europe by setting up theocracies where they could live out their own visions of the earthly millennial community. So it was with Jonestown. In this light, neither disciplinary practices, the daily round of life, nor the community of goods at Jonestown seem so unusual.

The disciplinary practices of the Peoples Temple—as bizarre and grotesque as they may sound—are not uncommon aspects of other-worldly sects. These practices have been played up in the press in an attempt to demonstrate the perverse nature of the group, in order to "explain" the terrible climax to their life. But, as Erving Goffman has shown in *Asylums* (1961), sexual intimidation and general psychological terror occur in all kinds of total institutions, including mental hospitals, prisons, armies, and even nunneries. Indeed, Congressman Leo Ryan, just prior to his fateful visit to Jonestown, accepted the need for social control: ". . . . you can't put 1,200 people in the middle of a jungle without some damn tight discipline" (quoted in Krause, Stern, and Harwood, 1978, p. 21). Practices at Jonestown may well seem restrained in comparison to practices of, say, seventeenth-century American Puritans who, among other things, were willing to execute "witches" on the testimony of respected churchgoers or even children. Meg Greenfield observed in *Newsweek,* in reflecting on Jonestown, that "the jungle is only a few yards away" (December 4, 1978, p. 132). It seems important to recall that some revered origins of the United States lie in a remarkably similar "jungle."

Communal groups of all types, not just other-worldly sects, face problems of social control and commitment. Rosabeth Kanter (1972) has convincingly shown that successful communal groups in the nineteenth-century United States often drew on mechanisms of mutual criticism, mortification, modification of conventional dyadic sexual mores, and other devices in order to decrease the individual's ties to the outside or to personal relationships within the group and thus to increase the individual's commitment to the collectivity as a whole.

Such commitment mechanisms are employed most often in religious communal groups, especially those with charismatic leaders (Hall, 1978, pp. 225–26). Other-worldly communal groups, where a special attempt is being made to forge a wholly new interpretation of reality, where the demand for commitment is especially pronounced, in a word, where it is sectarian—these groups have tremendously high stakes in maintaining commitment. Such groups are likely to seek out the procedures that are the most effective in guaranteeing commitment. After all, defection from "the way" inevitably casts doubt on its sanctity, no matter how it is rationalized among the faithful. Thus, it is against such groups that the charges of brainwashing, chicanery, and mistreatment of members are leveled most often. Whatever their basis in fact, these are the likely charges of families and friends who see their loved ones abandon them in favor of committing material resources and persona to the religious hope of a new life. Much like other-worldly sects, families suffer a loss of legitimacy in the defection of one of their own.

The abyss that comes to exist between other-worldly sects and the world of society-at-large left behind simply cannot be bridged. There is no encompassing rational connection between the two realities, and therefore the interchange between the other-worldly sect and people beyond its boundaries becomes a struggle either between "infidels" and the "faithful" from the point of view of the sect, or between rationality and fanaticism from the point of view of outsiders. Every sectarian action has its benevolent interpretation and legitimation within the sect, and a converse interpretation is given from the outside. Thus, from inside the sect, various practices of "confession," "mutual criticism," or "catharsis sessions" seem necessary to prevent deviant world views from taking hold within the group.

In the Peoples Temple, such practices included occasional enforced isolation and drug regimens for "rehabilitation" that were like contemporary psychiatric treatment. From the outside, all this tends to be regarded as brainwashing, but insiders will turn the accusation outward, claiming that it is those in the society-at-large who are brainwashed. Though there really can be no resolution to this conflict of interpretations, the widespread incidence of similar patterns of "coercive persuasion" outside Jonestown suggests that its practice there was not so unusual, at least within the context of other-worldly sects, or total institutions in general for that matter.

What is unusual is the direction that coercive persuasion or brainwashing took. Jones worked to instill devotion in unusual ways—ways that fostered the acceptibility of "revolutionary suicide" among his followers. During "white nights" of emergency mobilization, he conducted rituals of proclaimed mass suicide, giving "poison" to all members, and saying they would die within the hour. According to one defector—Deborah Blakey—Jones "explained that the poison was not real and we had just been through a loyalty test. He warned us that the time was not far off when it would be necessary for us to die by our own hands" (cited in Krause, Stern, and Harwood, 1978, p. 193). This event initially left Blakey "indifferent" to whether she "lived or died." A true believer in the Peoples Temple was more emphatic. Disappointed by the string of false collective suicides, he said in a note to Jones that he hoped for "the real thing" so that they could all pass beyond the suffering of this world.[4]

Some people yielded to Jim Jones only because their will to resist was beaten down; others—including many "seniors," the elderly members of the Peoples Temple—felt they owed everything to Jim Jones, and they provided him with a strong core of unequivocal support. Jones apparently allowed open dissension at "town meetings" because, with the support of the seniors, he knew he could prevail. Thus, no matter what they wanted personally, people learned to leave their fates in the hands of Jim Jones and to accept what he demanded. The specific uses of coercive persuasion at Jonestown help to explain how (but why) the mass murder/suicide was implemented. But it is the special use, not the general nature, of brainwashing that distinguishes Jonestown from most other-worldly sects.

Aside from brainwashing, a second major kind of accusation about Jonestown, put forward most forcefully by Deborah Blakey, concerns the work discipline and diet there. Blakey swore in an affidavit that the work load was excessive and that the food served to the average residents of Jonestown was inadequate. She abhorred the contradiction between the conditions she reported and the privileged diet of Reverend Jones and his inner circle. Moreover, because she had dealt with the group's finances, she knew that money could have been directed to providing a more adequate diet for everyone.

Blakey's horal sensibilities notwithstanding, the disparity between the diet of the elite and that of the average Jonestowner should come as no surprise: it parallels Erving Goffman's (1961, p. 48ff.) description of widespread hierarchies of privilege in total institutions. Her concern about the average diet is more to the point. But here, other accounts differ from Blakey's report. Maria Katsaris, a consort of Reverend Jones, wrote her father a letter extolling the virtues of the Agricultural Project's "cutlass" beans that were used as a meat substitute (Kilduff and Javers, 1978, p. 109). And Paula Adams, who survived the Jonestown holocaust because she resided at the Peoples Temple house in Georgetown, expressed ambivalence about the Jonestown community in an interview after the tragedy. But she also remarked: "My daughter ate very well. She got eggs and milk everyday. How many black children in the ghetto eat that well?"[5]

The accounts of surviving members of Jones' personal staff and inner circle, like Katsaris and Adams, are suspect, of course, in exactly the opposite way to those of people like the "Concerned Relatives." But the inside accounts are corroborated by at least one outsider, *Washington Post* reporter Charles Krause. On his arrival at Jonestown in the company of U.S. Representative Leo Ryan, Krause noted that "contrary to what the Concerned Relatives had told us, nobody seemed to be starving. Indeed, everyone seemed quite healthy" (Krause, Stern, and Harwood, 1978, p. 41).

It is difficult to assess these conflicting views. Beginning early in the summer of 1977, Jones set in motion the mass exodus of some 800 Peoples Temple members from California. Though Jonestown could adequately house only about 500 people at that time, the population climbed quickly well beyond that mark. At the same time the population mushroomed beyond the agricultural potential of the settlement. The exodus also caused Jonestown to become top heavy with less productive seniors and children. Anything close to agricultural self-sufficiency thus became a more elusive and long-range goal.

As time wore on during the group's last year of existence, Jones himself became more and more fixated on the prospect of a mass emigration from Guyana, and in this light, any sort of long-range agricultural-development strategy seemed increasingly irrational. According to the *New York Times,* the former Jonestown farm manager, Jim Bogue, suggested that the agricultural program would have succeeded in the long run if it had been adhered to.[6] But with the emerging plans for emigration, it was not followed and thus became merely a charade for the benefit of the Guyanese Government.

This analysis would seem to have implications for the *internal* conflicts about goals at Jonestown. Jim Jones' only natural son, Stephan Jones, and several other young men in the Peoples Temple came to believe in Jonestown as a socialist agrarian community, not as an other-worldly sect headed up by Jim Jones. Reflecting about his father after the mass murder/suicide, Stephan Jones commented: "I don't mind discrediting him, but I'm still a socialist, and Jim Jones will be used to discredit socialism. People will use him to discredit what we built. Jonestown was not Jim Jones, although he believed it was."[7]

The seniors, who provided social security checks, gardened, and produced handicraft articles for sale in Georgetown in lieu of heavy physical labor, and the fate of agricultural productivity both reinforce the assessment that Jim Jones' vision of the Peoples Temple approximates the other-worldly sect as an ideal type. In such sects, as a rule, proponents seek to survive *not* on the basis of productive labor, as in more "worldly utopian" communal groups, but on the basis of patronage, petty financial schemes, and the building of a "community of goods" through prosyletization (Hall, 1978, p. 207). This was the case with Jonestown. The community of goods that Jones built up is valued at more than $12 million. As a basis for satisfying collective wants, any agricultural production at Jonestown would have paled in comparison to this amasssed wealth.

But even if the agricultural project itself became a charade, it is no easy task to create a plausible charade in the midst of relatively infertile soil reclaimed from dense jungle. This would have required the long hours of work that Peoples Temple defectors described. Such a charade could serve as yet another effective means of social control. In the first place, it gave a purposeful role to those who envisioned Jonestown as an experimental socialist agrarian community. Beyond this, it monopolized the waking hours of most of the populace in exhausting work, and it gave them a minimal—though probably adequate— diet on which to subsist. It is easy to imagine that many city people, or those with bourgeois sensibilities in general, would not find this their cup of tea in any case. But the demanding daily regimen, however abhorrent to the uninitiated, is widespread in other-worldly sects.

Various programs of fasting and work asceticism have long been regarded as signs of piety and routes to religious enlightenment or ecstasy. In the contemporary American Krishna groups, an alternation of nonsugar and high-sugar phases of the diet seems to create an almost addictive attachment to the food that is communally dispersed (Hall, 1978, p. 76; cf. Goffman, 1961, pp. 49–50). And we need look no later in history than to Saint Benedict's order to find a situation in which the personal time of participants was eliminated for all practical purposes, with procedures of mortification for offenders laid out by Saint Benedict in his *Rule* (1975; cf. Zerubavel, 1977). The concerns of Blakey and others about diet, work, and discipline may have some basis, but probably they have been exaggerated. In any case, they do not distinguish Jonestown from other-worldly sects in general.

One final public concern with the Peoples Temple deserves mention because it parallels so closely previous sectarian practices. The Reverend Jim Jones is accused of swindling people out of their livelihoods and life circumstances by tricking them into signing over their money and possessions to the Peoples Temple or to its inner circle of members. Of course Jones considered this a "community of goods," and he correctly pointed to a long tradition of such want satisfaction among other-worldly sects. In an interview just prior to the tragedy, Jones cited Jesus' call to hold all things in common.[8] There are good grounds to think that Reverend Jones carried this philosophy into the realm of a con game. Still it should be noted that in the suicidal end, Jones did not benefit from the wealth in the way a large number of other self-declared prophets and messiahs have.[9]

Like its disciplinary practices and its round of daily life, the community of goods in the Peoples Temple at Jonestown emphasizes its similarities to other-worldly sects — both the contemporary ones labelled cults by their detractors and historical examples that are often revered in retrospect by contemporary religious culture. The elaboration of these affinities is in no way intended to suggest that we can or should vindicate the duplicity, the bizarre sexual and psychological intimidation, and the hardships of daily life at Jonestown. But it must be recognized that the settlement was much less unusual that some of us might like to think. The practices that detractors find abhorrent in the life of the Peoples Temple at Jonestown prior to the final "white night" of murder and suicide are the core nature of other-worldly sects. Therefore, it should come as no surprise that practices like those at Jonestown are widespread, both in historical and contemporary other-worldly sects. Granted that the character of such sects — the theocratic basis of authority, the devices of mortification and social control, and the demanding regimen of everyday life— predisposes people in such groups to respond to the whims of their leaders, no matter what fanatic and zealous directions they may take. But given the widespread occurrence of other-worldly sects, the other-worldly features of Jonestown are insufficient in themselves to explain the bizarre fate of its participants. If we are to understand the unique turn of events at Jonestown, we must look to certain distinctive features of the Peoples Temple — traits that make it unusual among other-worldly sects— and we must try to comprehend the subjective meanings of these features for some of Jonestown's participants.

Persecution at Jonestown

If the Peoples Temple was distinctive among other-worldly sects, it is for two reasons. First, the group was more thoroughly integrated racially than any other such group today. Second, the Peoples Temple was distinctively protocommunist in ideology. Both of these conditions, together with certain personal fears of Jim Jones (mixed perhaps with organic disorders and assorted drugs), converged in his active mind to give a special twist to the apocalyptic quest of his flock. Let us consider these matters in turn.

In the Peoples Temple, Jim Jones had consistently sought to transcend racism in peace rather than in struggle. The origins of this approach, like most of Jones' early life, are by now shrouded in myth. But it is clear that Jones was committed to racial harmony in his Indiana ministry. In the 1950s his formation of an interracial congregation met with much resistance in Indianapolis, and this persecution was one impetus for the exodus to California (Kilduff and Javers, 1978, pp. 16–17, 19–20, 25).[10] There is room for debate on how far Jones' operation actually went toward achieving racial equality, or to what degree it simply perpetuated racism, albeit in a racially harmonious microcosm (Kilduff and Javers, 1978, pp. 86–7; Krause, Stern, and Harwood, 1978, p. 41). But the Peoples Temple fostered greater racial equality and harmony than that of the larger society, and in this respect it has few parallels in present-day communal groups.[11] It also achieved more racial harmony than is evidenced in mainstream religious congregations. The significance of this cannot be assayed easily, but one view of it has been captured in a letter from a 20-year-old Jonestown girl. She wrote to her mother in Evansville, Indiana that she could "walk down the street now without the fear of having little old white ladies call me nigger."[12]

Coupled with the commitment to racial integration and again in contrast to most other-worldly sects, the Peoples Temple moved strongly toward ideological communism. Most other-worldly sects practice religiously inspired communism—the "clerical" or "Christian" socialism that Marx and Engels railed against (1959, p. 31). But few if any to date have flirted with communism in the theories of Marx, Lenin, and Stalin. By contrast, it has become clear that, whatever the contradictions other socialists point to between Jones' messianism and socialism (Moberg, 1978), the Reverend Jim Jones and his staff considered themselves socialists. In his column, "Perspectives from Guyana," Jones (1978, p. 208) maintained that "neither my colleagues nor I are any longer caught up in the opiate of religion. . . ." (reprinted in Krause, Stern, and Harwood, 1978, p. 208). Though the practices of the group prior to the mass murder/suicide were not based on any doctrinaire Marxism, at least some of the recruits to the group were young radical intellectuals, and one of the group's members, Richard Tropp, gave evening classes on radical political theory.[13] In short, radical socialist currents were unmistakably present in the group.

It is perhaps more questionable whether the Peoples Temple was religious in any conventional sense of the term. Of course, all utopian communal groups are religious in that they draw true believers together who seek to live out a heretical or heterodox interpretation of the meaningfulness of social existence. In this sense, the Peoples Temple was a religious group, just as Frederick Engels (1964a; 1964b) once observed that socialist sects of the nineteenth century were similar in character to primitive Christian and Reformation sects. Jim Jones clearly was more self-consciously religious than were the leaders of the socialist sects. Though he preached atheism and did not believe in a God that answers prayer, he did embrace reincarnation. A surviving resident of Jonestown remembers him saying that "our religion is this—your highest service to God is service to your fellow man." On the other hand, it seems that the outward manifestations of conventional religious activity — revivals, sermons, faith healings—were, at least in Jim Jones' view, calculated devices to draw people into an organization that was something quite different. It is a telling point in this regard that Jones ceased the practice of faith healings and cut off other religious activities once he moved to Jonestown. Jones' wife, Marceline, once noted that Jim Jones considered himself a Marxist who "used religion to try to get some people out of the opiate of religion."[14] In a remarkable off-the-cuff interview with Richard and Harriet Tropp—the two Jonestown residents who were writing a book about the Peoples Temple—Jones reflected on the early years of his ministry, claiming: "What a hell of a battle that [integration] was— I thought 'I'll never make a revolution, I can't even get those fuckers to integrate, much less get them to any communist philosophy.' "[15]

In the same interview, Jones intimated that he had been a member of the U.S. Communist party in the early 1950s. Of course, with Jones' Nixonesque concern for his place in history, it is possible that his hindsight, even in talking with sympathetic biographers, did not convey his original motives. In the interview with the Tropps, Jones also hinted that the entire development of the Peoples Temple, down to the Jonestown Agricultural Project, derived from his communist beliefs. This interview and Marceline Jones' comment give strong evidence of Jim Jones' early communist orientation. Whenever this orientation began, the move to Jonestown was predicated on it.

The socialist government of Guyana was generally committed to supporting socialists seeking refuge from capitalist societies, and they apparently thought that Jones' flexible brand of Marxism fit well within the country's political matrix. By 1973 when negotiations with Guyana about an agricultural project were initiated, Jones and his aides were professing identification with the world historical communist movement.

The convergence of racial integration and crude communism gave a distinctly political character to what in many other respects was an other-worldly religious sect. The injection of radical politics gave a heightened sense of persecution to the Jonestown Agricultural Project. Jim Jones himself seems both to have fed this heightened sense of persecution to his followers and to have been devoured by it himself. He manipulated fears among his followers by controlling information and spreading false rumors about news events in the United States (Moberg, 1978, p. 14). With actual knowledge of certain adversaries and fed by his own premonitions, Jones spread these premonitions among his followers, thereby heightening their dedication. In the process, Jones disenchanted a few members who became Judas Iscariots and who in time brought the forces of legitimated external authority to "persecute" Jones and his true believers in their jungle theocracy.

The persecution complex is a stock-in-trade of other-worldly sects. It is naturally engendered by a radical separation from the world of society-at-large. An apocalyptic mission develops in suc w way that persecution from the world left behind is taken as a sign of the sanctity of the group's chosen path of salvation. Though racial and political persecution are not usually among the themes of other-worldly persecution, they do not totally break with the other-worldly way of interpreting experience. But the heightened sense of persecution at Jonestown did reduce the disconnection from society-at-large that is the signature of other-worldly sects.

Most blacks in the United States have already experienced persecution; and if Jim Jones gave his black followers some relief from a ghetto existence (which many seem to have felt he did), he also made a point of reminding those in his group that persecution still awaited them back in the ghettos and rural areas of the United States. In the California years, for example, the Peoples Temple would stage mock lynchings of blacks by the Ku Klux Klan as a form of political theater (Krause, Stern, and Harwood, 1978, p. 56). And, according to Deborah Blakey, Jones "convinced black Temple members that if they did not follow him to Guyana, they would be put into concentration camps and killed" (quoted in Krause, Stern, and Harwood, 1978, p. 188).

Similarly, white socialist intellectuals could easily become paranoid about their activities. As any participant in the New Left movement of the 1960s and early 1970s knows, paranoia was a sort of badge of honor to some people. Jones exacerbated this by telling whites that the CIA listed them as enemies of the state.

Jones probably impressed persecution upon his followers to increase their allegiance to him. But Jones himself was caught up in a web of persecution and betrayal. The falling-out between Jones and Grace and Tim Stoen seems of primary importance here. In conjunction with the imminent appearance of negative news articles, the fight over custody of John Victor Stoen (Grace's son whom both Jones and Tim Stoen claimed to have fathered) triggered Jones' 1977 decision to remove himself from the San Francisco Temple to Guyana (Krause, Stern, and Harwood, 1978, p. 57).[16]

We may never know what happened between the Stoens and Jones. According to Terri Buford, a former Jonestown insider, Tim Stoen left the Peoples

Temple shortly after it became known that in the 1960s he had gone on a Rotary-sponsored speaking tour denouncing communism.[17] Both sides have accused the other of being the progenitors of violence in the Peoples Temple.[18] To reporters who accompanied Representative Ryan, Jones charged that the Stoen couple had been government agents and provocateurs who had advocated bombing, burning, and terrorism.[19] This possibility could have been regarded as quite plausible by Jones and his staff because they possessed documents about similar alleged FBI moves against the Weather Underground and the Church of Scientology.[20] The struggle between Jones and the Stoens thus could easily have personified to Jones the quintessence of a conspiracy against him and his work. It certainly intensified negative media attention on the Temple.

For all his attempts to curry favor with the press, Jones failed in the crucial instance: the San Francisco investigative reporters gave much coverage to the horror stories about the Peoples Temple and Jones' custody battle. Jones may well have been correct in his suspicion that he was not being treated fairly in the press. After the mass murder/suicide, the managing editor of the *San Francisco Examiner* proudly asserted in a January 15, 1979 letter to the *Wall Street Journal* that his paper had not been "morally neutral" in its coverage of the Peoples Temple.[21]

The published horror stories were based on the allegations by defectors—the Stoens and Deborah Blakey being foremost among them. We do not know how true, widespread, exaggerated, or isolated the incidents reported were. Certainly they were generalized in the press to the point of creating an image of Jones as a total ogre. The defectors also initiated legal proceedings against the Temple, and the news articles began to stir the interest of government authorities in the operation. These developments were not lost on Jim Jones. In fact, the custody battle with the Stoens seems to have precipitated Jones' mass suicide threat to the Guyanese government. Not coincidentially, according to Jim Jones' only natural son, Stephan, the first "white night" drills for mass suicide were held at this point. Stephan Jones connects these events with the appearance of several negative news articles.[22]

With these sorts of events in mind, it is not hard to see how it happened that Jim Jones felt betrayed by the Stoens and the other defectors, and persecuted by those who appeared to side with them—the press and the government foremost among them. In September 1978 Jones went so far as to retain the well-known conspiracy theorist and lawyer, Mark Lane, to investigate the possibility of a plot against the Peoples Temple. In the days immediately following, Mark Lane —perhaps self-servingly—reported in a memorandum to Jones that "even a cursory examination" of the available evidence "reveals that there has been a coordinated campaign to destroy the Peoples Temple and to impugn the reputation of its leader." Those involved were said to include the U.S. Customs Bureau, the Federal Communications Commission, the Central Intelligence Agency, the Federal Bureau of Investigation, and the Internal Revenue Service.[23] Lane's assertions probably had little basis in fact. Although several of these agencies had looked into certain Temple activities independently, none of them had taken any direct action against the Temple, even though they may have had some cause for so doing. The actual state of affairs notwithstanding, with Lane's assertions Jones had substantiation of his sense of persecution from a widely touted conspiracy theorist.

The sense of persecution that gradually developed in the Peoples Temple from its beginning and increased markedly at Jonestown must have come to a head with the visit of U.S. Representative Leo Ryan. The U.S. State Department has revealed that Jones had agreed to a visit by Ryan, but that he withdrew permission when it became known that a contingent of Concerned Relatives as well as certain members of the press would accompany Ryan to Guyana.[24] Among the Concerned Relatives who came with Ryan was the Stoen couple; in fact, Tim Stoen was known as a leader of the Concerned Relatives group.[25] Reporters with Ryan included two from the *San Francisco Chronicle,* a paper that had already pursued investigative reporting on the Peoples Temple, as well as Gordon Lindsay, an independent newsman who had written a negative story on the Peoples Temple for publication in the *National Enquirer* (This article was never published) (Krause, Stern, and Harwood, 1978, p. 40). This entourage could hardly have been regarded as objective or unbiased by Jones and his closer supporters. Instead, it identified Ryan with the forces of persecution, personified by the Stoens and the investigative press, and it set the stage for the mass murder/suicide that had already been threatened in conjunction with the custody fight.

The ways in which the Peoples Temple came to differ from more typical other-worldly sects are more a matter of degree than of kind, but the differences profoundly altered the character of the scene at Jonestown. Though the avowed radicalism, the interracial living, and the defector-media-government "conspiracy" are structurally distinct from one another, Jim Jones incorporated them into a tableau of conspiracy that was intended to increase his followers' attachment to him but ironically brought his legitimacy as a messiah into question, undermined the other-worldly possibilities of the Peoples Temple Agricultural Project, and placed the group on the stage of history in a distinctive relationship to the apocalypse.

Jonestown and the Apocalypse

Other-worldly sects by their very nature are permeated with apocalyptic ideas. The sense of a decaying social order is personally experienced by the religious seeker in a life held to be untenable, meaningless, or both. This interpretation of life is collectively affirmed and transcended in other-worldly sects that purport to offer heaven-on-earth beyond the apocalypse. Such sects promise the grace of a theocracy in which followers can sometimes really escape the "living hell" of society-at-large. Many of the Reverend Jones' followers seem to have joined the Peoples Temple with this in mind. But the predominance of blacks, the radical ideology of the Temple, the persistent struggle against the defectors, and the "conspiracy" that formed around them in the minds of the faithful gave the true believers' sense of persecution a more immediate and pressing aura, rather than an other-worldly one.

Jones used these elements to heighten his followers' sense of persecution from the outside, but this device itself may have drawn into question the ability of the supposed charismatic leader to provide an other-worldly sanctuary. By the middle of October 1978, a month before Representative Ryan's trip in November, Jones' position of preeminent leadership was beginning to be questioned not only by disappointed religious followers, but also by previously devoted seniors, who were growing tired of the endless meetings and the increasingly untenable character of everyday life, and by key proponents of collective life, who felt Jones was responsible for their growing inability to deal successfully with Jonestown's material operations.

Once these dissatisfied individuals circumvented Jones' intelligence network of informers and began to establish solidarity with one another, the conspiracy can be said truly to have taken hold within Jonestown itself. If the times were apocalyptic, Reverend Jones was like the revolutionary millenarians described by Norman Cohn (1970) and Gunther Lewy (1974). Rather than successfully proclaiming the postapocalyptic sanctuary, Jones was reduced to declaiming the web of "evil" powers in which he was ensnared and to searching with chiliastic expectation for the imminent cataclysm that would announce the beginning of the kingdom of righteousness.

Usually other-worldly sects have a sense of the eternal about them—having escaped this world, they adopt the temporal trappings of heaven, which amounts to a timeless bliss of immortality (Hall, 1978, pp. 72–79). But Jim Jones had not really established a postapocalyptic heavenly plateau. Even if he had promised this to his followers, it was only just being built in the form of the Agricultural Project. And it was not even clear that Jonestown itself was the promised land. Jones did not entirely trust the Guyanese government, and he was considering seeking final asylum in Cuba or the Soviet Union. Whereas other-worldly sects typically assert that heaven is at hand, Jones could only hold it out as a future goal—one that became more and more elusive as the forces of persecution tracked him to Guyana. Thus, Jones and his followers were still within the throes of the Apocalypse as they conceived it—the forces of good fighting against the evil and conspiratorial world that could not tolerate a living example of a racially integrated American socialist utopia.

In the struggle against evil, Jones and his true believers took on the character of what I have termed a "warring sect," fighting a decisive Manichean struggle with the forces of evil (Hall, 1978, pp. 206–207). Such a struggle seems almost inevitable when political rather than religious themes of apocalypse are stressed. And it is clear that Jones and his staff acted at times within this militant frame of reference. For example, they maintained armed guards around the settlement, held "white night" emergency drills, and even staged mock CIA attacks on Jonestown. By so doing, they undermined the plausibility of an other-worldly existence. The struggle of a warring sect takes place in historical time, where one action builds on another and decisive outcomes of previous events shape future possibilities. The contradiction between this earthly struggle and the heaven-on-earth Jones would have liked to proclaim (e.g., in "Perspectives from Guyana") gave Jonestown many of its strange juxtapositions—of heaven and hell, of suffering and bliss, of love and coercion. Perhaps even Jones himself, for all his megalomaniacal ability to transcend the contradictions that others saw in him, and that caused him to be labeled an "opportunist," could not endure the struggle for his own immortality. If he were indeed a messianic incarnation of God, as he sometimes claimed, presumably Jones could have either won the struggle of the warring sect against its evil persecutors or delivered his people to the bliss of another world.

In effect, Jones had brought his flock to the point of straddling the two sides of the apocalypse. Had he established his colony beyond the unsympathetic purview of defectors, Concerned Relatives, investigative reporters, and government agencies, the other-worldly tableau perhaps could have been sustained with less repressive methods of social control. As it was, Jones and the colony experienced the three interconnected limitations of group totalism that Robert Jay Lifton (1968, p. 129) described with respect to the Chinese Communist Revolution — diminishing conversions, inner antagonism of disillusioned participants to the suffocation of individuality, and increasing penetration of the "idea-tight milieu control" by outside forces.[26] As Lifton noted, revolutionaries are engaged in a quest for immortality. Other-worldly sectarians short-circuit this quest in a way by the fiat of *asserting* their immortality—positing the timeless heavenly plateau that exists *beyond* history as the basis of their everyday life. But under the persistent eyes of external critics and because Jones himself exploited such "persecution" to increase his social control, he could not sustain the illusion of other-worldly immortality.

On the other hand, the Peoples Temple could not achieve the sort of political victory that would have been the goal of a warring sect. Since revolutionary war involves a struggle with an established political order in unfolding historical time, revolutionaries can only attain immortality in the widescape victory of the revolution over the "forces of reaction." Ironically, as Lifton pointed out, even the initial political and military victory of the revolutionary forces does not end the search for immortality. Even in victory, revolution can be sustained only through diffusion of its principles and goals. But, as Max Weber (1977, p. 1121) observed, in the long run it seems impossible to maintain the charismatic enthusiasm of revolution; more pragmatic concerns come to the fore, and as the ultimate ends of revolution are faced off against everyday life and its demands, the question for immortality fades, and the immortality of the revolutionary moment is replaced by the myth of a grand revolutionary past.

The Peoples Temple could not begin to achieve revolutionary immortality in historical time because it could not even pretend to achieve any victory against its enemies. If it had come to a pitched battle, the Jonestown defenders—like the Symbionese Liberation Army against the Los Angeles Police Department S.W.A.T. Team—would have been wiped out.

But the Peoples Temple could create a kind of immortality that is not really a possibility for political revolutionaries. They could abandon apocalyptic hell by the act of mass suicide. This would shut out the opponents of the Temple. They could not be the undoing of what was already undone, and there could be no recriminations against the dead. It could also achieve the other-worldly salvation Jones had promised his more religious followers. Mass suicide bridged the divergent public threads of meaningful existence at Jonestown— those of political revolution and religious salvation. It was an awesome vehicle for a powerful statement of collective solidarity by the true believers among the people of Jonestown—that they would rather die together than have their lives together subjected to gradual decimation and dishonor at the hands of authorities regarded as illegitimate.

Most warring sects reach a grisly end. Occasionally they achieve martyrdom, but if they lack a constituency, their extermination is used by the state as proof of its monopoly on the legitimate use of force. Revolutionary suicide is a victory by comparison. The event can be drawn upon for moral didactics, but this cannot erase the stigma that Jonestown implicitly places on the world that its members left behind. Nor can the state punish the dead who are guilty, among other things, of murdering a United States Congressman, three newsmen, a Concerned Relative, and those many Jonestown residents who did not willingly commit suicide.[27]

Though they paid the total price of death for their ultimate commitment and though they achieved little except perhaps sustenance of their own collective sense of honor, those who won this hollow victory still cannot have it taken away from them. In the absence of retribution, the state search for the guilty who have remained alive and the widespread outcry against cults take on the character of scapegoating.[28] Those most responsible are beyond the reach of the law. Unable to escape the hell of their own lives by creating an other-worldly existence on earth, they instead sought their immortality in death, and left it to others to ponder the apocalypse that they have unveiled.

Notes

1. *Louisville Courier–Journal,* 23 December 1978, p. B1.
2. Fallding does not want to "plunge into relativism," so he tries to retrieve the term "cultism" for sociological use by defining it as ascribing sacred status to anything

in the profane, actualized world. But this just displaces the problem of "false religion" onto the definition of "profane," which itself can only be defined within a religious perspective!

3. Even the constitutional guarantee is under fire. Prior to the Jonestown events, the U.S. Justice Department (texts in Krause, Stern, and Harwood, 1978, pp. 171–85) had carefully examined the legal issues involved in investigating religious sects, and determined against such action. But since Jonestown, there have been suggestions, for example by William Randolph Hearst, in the *San Francisco Examiner* (10 December 1978, p. 28), and a law professor, Richard Delgado, in the *New York Times* (27 December 1978, p. A23), that totalitarianism in the name of religion should not qualify for constitutional protection. Also, the *Washington Post* (16 December 1978, p. 3) reports that mainline churches have been reexamining their stands on freedom of religion in light of the Jonestown events.

4. *San Francisco Examiner,* 6 December 1978, p. 10.

5. *San Francisco Examiner,* 10 December 1978, p. 9.

6. *New York Times,* 24 December 1978, pp. 1, 20.

7. *San Francisco Examiner,* 10 December 1978, p. 9.

8. *San Francisco Examiner,* 3 December 1978, p. 16.

9. The list of these religious swindlers, if it is kept by God's angels someplace, must be a long one indeed! Some would want to suggest that even in the end, Jim Jones plotted to make off with the loot. One theory holds that he planned to escape with his personal nurse at the conclusion of the cyanide poisonings. But this theory seems far-fetched to the *New York Times* (25 December 1978, p. 15) reporter who attended the Guyanese coroner's inquest where it was proposed. It did not account either for the bequeathing of Temple assets to the Communist party of the Soviet Union or for the suicidal "lost hope" that Jones expressed in the taped portion of the mass murder/suicide episode.

10. *Time,* December 4, 1978, p. 22.

11. Only one contemporary, explicitly interracial communal group immediately comes to mind — Koinonia Farm in Georgia, a Christian group founded in the 1940s.

12. *Louisville Courier-Journal,* 23 December 1978, p. B1.

13. *San Francisco Examiner,* 8 December 1978, p. 1.

14. *New York Times,* 26 November 1978, p. 20.

15. *San Francisco Examiner,* 8 December 1978, p. 16.

16. Kilduff and Javers (1978, pp. 77–78) cite the imminent appearance of negative news articles as a cause of Jones' departure.

17. *New York Times,* 1 January 1979, p. 35.

18. *San Francisco Examiner,* 6 December 1978, p. 1; *Louisville Courier-Journal,* 22 December 1978, p. 5.

19. *San Francisco Examiner,* 3 December 1978, p. 14.

20. *New York Times,* 6 December 1979, p. 16; *Columbia (Mo.) Tribune,* 6 January 1979, p. 6.

21. "Letter to the Editor," *Wall Street Journal,* 5 January 1979, p. 21.

22. *San Francisco Examiner,* 17 December 1978, p. 5.

23. *New York Times,* 4 February 1979, pp. 1, 42.

24. *San Francisco Examiner,* 16 December 1978, p. 1.

25. *New York Times,* 1 January 1979, p. 35.

26. The Peoples Temple perhaps had already begun to undergo the third of Lifton's limitations — the "law of diminishing conversions" — before the move from San Francisco to Guyana.

27. On the trip into Jonestown with Ryan, Peoples Temple lawyer Mark Lane told reporter Charles Krause (1978, p. 37) that perhaps ten percent of Jonestown

residents would leave if given a chance but "90 percent . . . will fight to the death to remain." The U.S. State Department originally suppressed the tape recording of the mass murder/suicide, but I have listened to a pirated copy of it, and the event clearly involved a freewheeling discussion of alternatives, with vocal support as well as pointed resistance voiced for the proposed "taking of the potion." (*New York Times*, 10 December 1978, p. A28; 25 December 1978, p. A16).

28. *Washington Post*, 16 December 1978, p. 3; *New York Times*, 27 December 1978, p. A23.

29. In addition to the references cited in this article, it is based on personal interviews by the author conducted in Georgetown, Guyana, and in California during the summer of 1979.

References

Benedictus, Saint, 1975 (orig. written c. 525 ?)
Clark, Elmer, T., 1949
Cohn, Norman, 1970, 1st ed., 1957
Engels, Frederick, 1964a (orig. 1850), 1964b (orig. 1883)
Fallding, Harold, 1974
Goffman, Erving, 1961
Greenfield, Meg, 1978
Hall, John R., 1978
Jones, Jim, 1978
Kanter, Rosabeth, 1972
Kilduff, Marshall, and Ron Javers, 1978
Krause, Charles, Lawrence M. Stern, and Richard Harwood, 1978
Lewy, Gunther, 1974
Lifton, Robert Jay, 1968
Marx, Karl, and Frederick Engels, 1959 (orig. 1848)
Moberg, David, 1978
Weber, Max, 1977 (orig. 1922)
Zerubavel, Eviatar, 1978

Getting Straight with Meher Baba:
A Study of Mysticism, Drug Rehabilitation and Postadolescent Role Conflict

Thomas Robbins and Dick Anthony

The Sociological Analysis of Youth Culture and Youth Movements

Recently, a sociologist has noted that "youth culture is located at the point of conflict between the bureaucratic ethos and the ethos of modern childhood" (Berger, 1970:34). The separation of family and childhood from the productive process, the shrinkage in family size, and the diminishing likelihood of death during childhood have converged to produce a contemporary middle class childhood which "is vastly more humane than it was before" and which "brings forth more humane individuals" (Berger, 1970:35). Continuity is disturbed, however, because the humanistic and personalistic values fostered by the milieu of modern childhood cannot be carried over into the instrumental processes of the adult occupational milieu. The bureaucratic aspect of many post-childhood occupational and educational milieu is in some ways the antithesis of the "humanistic" patterns of childhood.

191

Modern childhood is marked by values and by a consciousness that are emphatically personalistic. Modern bureaucracy, by contrast, has an ethos of emphatic impersonality. Put simply, an individual shaped by modern childhood is most likely to feel oppressed by modern bureaucracy. Indeed, he is likely to have a very low "oppression threshold" when it comes to the impersonal processes of bureaucracy. Thus people today feel oppressed, "alienated" or even "exploited" simply by being subjected to bureaucratic processes . . . that a generation ago would have seemed pragmatic necessities (Berger, 1970:37).

A number of empirical studies have documented the increasingly "humanistic" character of middle class familial milieux (Flacks, 1967; 1970a), particularly with regard to the background of "alienated" youthful respondents. These studies and the analysis above recall S.N. Eisenstadt's earlier classical analyses of generational discontinuity in industrial society (Eisenstadt, 1956; 1961) as a consequence of the increasing differentiation of the family from the occupational structure. As the family increasingly specializes in the function of providing emotional gratification for its members, it tends to stress roles and relationships which are diffuse, affective, particularistic, and quality-oriented. These attributes define expressive or personalistic relationships which have terminal rather than instrumental value for participants.[1]

In contrast, the adult occupational structure (including preparatory higher educational institutions) increasingly stresses roles which are functionally specific, affectively neutral, universalistic and performance-oriented, in short, "bureaucratic" and "impersonal" instrumental relations (Eisenstadt, 1956). The transaction between the familial milieu and the adult instrumental milieu thus becomes increasingly difficult and young people experience sharp role conflict. Within the terms of this analysis, youth movements, although they may have explicit "anti-establishment" overtones, can often be seen as devices to ease the tension of the familial-occupational transition. They do this by constructing value orientations and normative frameworks which combine elements of both familial and bureaucratic role systems (e.g., bureaucratic universalism and familial diffuseness). Through youth movements, adolescents and postadolescents work out roles and relationships consistent with selected aspects of both "childish" and "adult" milieux.

Eisenstadt's analysis is relevant to discussions of the clash of the late 1960s "counterculture" with "technocracy" (Roszak, 1969; Reich, 1970).[2] It should be noted, moreover, that Eisenstadt and Berger interpret youthful "alienation" as essentially a problem of *community*.[3] There is a dearth of gratifying expressive-communal relationships and roles available for young people in the adult instrumental milieu. Such people face the prospect of being "love-starved." The formations of the counterculture will necessarily cater to these longings (Slater, 1970), and, moreover, can be expected on the basis of Eisenstadt's analysis to manifest an *integrative dimension* facilitating the working out of satisfying expressive patterns within the context of the larger society.

A number of scholars have called attention to an upsurge of mysticism and unconventional religiosity among American youth (Greeley, 1969, 1970; Needleman, 1970; Gustaitis, 1969; Robbins, 1969). Some of the scholarly and journalistic discussions of this phenomenon have focused on the status of youth-oriented mysticism as a "post-drug" phenomenon. These analyses contend that this "movement" recruits from persons who have been involved in "drug abuse" and facilitates the termination of involvement with hallucinogens, amphetamines, and/or opiates (Crenshaw, 1968; Dunn, 1968; Robbins, 1969; Gustaitis, 1969; Vachon, 1971). A study of the Meher Baba movement analyzed its capacity to resocialize deviant drug users and to resolve the tension between conventional and "hippie" values (Robbins, 1969).[4] This study was designed as a more comprehensive follow-up of the original study, with the aim of integrating an explanation of the consequences of involvement in the movement (e.g., "resocialization," termination of drug abuse) with an analysis of its continuing growth and appeal of the cult.

Methodology

This study was conducted during the summer of 1970. The first author spent most of that summer at the Meher Spiritual Center in Myrtle Beach, South Carolina. The study utilizes a participant observation or "anthropological" approach, which emphasizes living within a culture until one assimilates its meaning system (Bruyn, 1966). The meaning system is presumed to have been acquired when the investigator can participate in the symbolism, ritual, and patterned interaction patterns of the culture in a way that is deemed acceptable or correct by its members.

This general procedure was supplemented by detailed recording of prototypical interaction sequences, and by the tape-recording of interviews with people who appeared to be representative of types active within the movement. These interviews were generally informal and involved the respondent's description of his life from his initial involvement with drugs until his drugless present. The interviewer asked questions clarifying various points or seeking responses which would enable him to compare features of the respondent's history to that of other devotees. The respondents were aware of the interviewer's role as researcher, but tended to perceive him primarily as a fellow participant in the movement.[5] In addition, we taped various informal talks given by a group member for other group members in the Saroja Library at the Meher Center.

The generality of the conclusions drawn from the observation and interview data collected at the Meher Center was checked against the impressions arising from periodic attendance by both authors at Meher Baba meetings in Chapel Hill, North Carolina, Berkeley, California, and New York City over a period of three years.

The purpose of this study was to generate rather than verify theory through participant observation. This approach may be contrasted with one which seeks to verify deductive consequences of an abstract formal model (Glazer and Strauss, 1967). It was anticipated, however, that initial understanding of movement phenomena in terms of empathy or *Verstehen* (Bruyn, 1966) might subsequently be translated into categories of formal theories and models operative in the sociology of religion, the sociology of youth, or the sociology of deviance. The authors were, of course, familiar at the beginning of the study with various models and perspectives, which directed their observations somewhat. The study was, nevertheless, in its initial phase primarily inductive. Some of these models, as well as others suggested during the course of the research, eventually proved useful in conceptualizing our observations. Sections I and V present the formal concepts and theories which proved useful in this respect.

An Expressive Community of Believers

Meher Baba is a deceased Indian spiritual master who claimed to be the most recent manifestation of the avataric tradition. According to Baba, Zoroaster, Rama, Krishna, Buddha, Christ and Mohammed were all human manifestations of the same divine being whose appearances on earth have punctuated humanity's movement through an "avataric cycle." Baba is the most recent manifestation of this being, and His advent closes the cycle.

Meher Baba has hundreds of thousands of followers in India. His American following remained small and predominantly adult until the middle sixties, when an interest in Meher Baba developed among young people, including (but not exclusively) drug users and "hippies" (Robbins, 1969). Prominent in His "message" is a doctrine of metaphysical unity among all persons, summarized in the phrase "We are all one" (Meher Baba, 1967). He also became well known for his opposition to the use of psychedelic drugs (Meher Baba, 1966).

The Meher Spiritual Center in Myrtle Beach was founded at Meher Baba's direction by Western disciples.[6] Situated on 500 acres of virgin forest and fronting on about a mile of ocean beach, it is intertwined with paths. There is a random grouping of 15 to 20 residential cabins and communal buildings of one sort or another near the center of the property. Because Baba spent much time there, His "presence" is generally considered by Baba followers to pervade the area. In addition, the two western disciples who manage the Center spent much time in India as His intimate companions. Their advice and counseling is much sought after by young converts. A visit to the Center is frequently, therefore, a formative influence in the emergent life-style of neophyte Baba followers. Young converts come there from all over the United States, and it has been the experience of the author is that styles of interaction inculcated at the Center reinforce and give authority to emergent expressive patterns in small groups of believers around the country.

These patterns seem to be a basis for "expressive community" within these groups, and seem to alleviate the "love-starvation" mentioned earlier. For this reason we shall list briefly characteristics of interaction at the Center which seem relevant to the expressive quality of these nascent "communities."

1. Organizational procedures at the Center are mostly informal and "personal." Group activities are more or less spontaneously arranged by the people who happen to be there at the time. For instance, dining takes place in communal kitchens, all cooking is done by visitors themselves, and whether this shall be done individually or by groups is left up to the individuals concerned. Resident supervisory personnel live at the edge of the Center, not in the central visitors' area, and are usually seen only by appointment. There are a few rules posted on the cabin walls, but most of these have to do with the exigencies of living in the woods, e.g., carrying a flashlight at night as protection from snakes. A significant exception is a rule against possession of illicit drugs.

2. There is a deemphasis on formal proselytising. The only entrance criterion is some interest in Baba or the "spiritual path." Formal or intellectual belief is not emphasized.[7] Baba is quoted as saying "I came not to teach but to awaken." An interest in Baba is not considered inconsistent with other religious or worldly interests. Insofar as there is anything approaching worship services at the Center, they take the form of casually arranged get-togethers, e.g., to hear an older follower relate anecdotes of his experiences with Baba, to listen to music or song, or to watch movies of the Master.

3. Interpersonal style at the Center is markedly familial and intimate. Hugs and kisses are customary greetings, occasionally between people just being introduced. This sort of affectionate physical contact is common between people of the same as well as opposite sexes, and is not treated as primarily sexual in nature. There are no shibboleths of membership, and there is a lack of defensiveness toward newcomers. Intimate personal information is openly exchanged between relative strangers, and these exchanges cut across normal affinity boundaries, e.g., class, sex, age. People smile ecstatically at each other for no apparent reason. Occasionally someone cries without embarrassment. Although many converts come from "intellectual" backgrounds, most conversation is simple, concrete, and personal.

The impact that this environment can make on a newcomer can be seen in an excerpt from one of our interviewers.

> I had my doubts. But as the people started coming in for breakfast and cooking their food, I started getting to talk with them more and more and I just started loving them and it just really sparked something in me to want to find out about Baba, seeing what Baba had done to these people . . . I sensed a peace in them all. All their eyes sparked and their faces seemed to have light in them. They were just so warm. No separateness, really . . . It was just such a loving environment and they had such a love for Baba.

The Meher Center plays a central role in establishing the informal and expressive character of the movement. Followers from all over the country meet and lay the groundwork for longterm friendships. The researchers have observed new acquaintances at the Center eagerly writing down each others' addresses and making plans to visit each other. Thus one follower came to the Center for the first time this summer and subsequently traveled north with two other followers from Miami (whom he had met at the Center) and visited other followers in Boston and Yonkers (whom he had also met that summer in Myrtle Beach). The Meher Center takes on something of the aspect of a *social clearing house*. The nature of the Myrtle Beach Center plus the existence of Baba communities in a number of cities means that a follower who has visited the Center is likely to have friends and acquaintances in various places in which, were it not for his spiritual involvement, he would not know anyone. The authors have observed over the last three years that geographically mobile followers tend to resettle in places in which there are Baba communities.

It has been the authors' experience that social patterns observed at the Center tend to be mirrored within these communities. Like the Center, these groups, while having rather permeable boundaries and no formal membership criteria, seem to supply an expressive social cohesiveness which their members have formerly been unable to find.

Below, a respondent describes a weekly meeting of one of these groups in Atlanta.

> They're very free and open meetings and very pleasant to attend. There's little routine. We read a little, you know, everybody brings a little something to read, maybe five or six people bring in something to read. We do a few songs together and discuss this and that. After the meeting a bunch of us will just stick around and just chant things. Several times we stayed until four or five in the morning. We've gone over to our house and had tea and cakes that Price made and just really had a good time.

In a later section we will analyze the role of the movement's meaning system and of Meher Baba as a "love" symbol in providing the expressive basis for a community of believers. At this point, it will be briefly noted that the representation of Meher Baba within the communities we've visited is consistent with the overtly affectionate styles of interaction among his followers. In the stories told about Baba, and in movies shown of him, He is generally depicted as relating affectively, diffusely and particularistically to others. Baba is portrayed as jolly, playful, and "loving." He appears to function as a *model* for relationships within the community. Thus the Baba movement can be seen as a vehicle for establishing an expressive basis for community for adults outside of conventional technocratic channels. This community provides continuity with the expressive nature of modern childhood and eases the transition to adulthood by alleviating the "love starvation" felt in bureaucratic vocational milieux.

Failure of a Prior Expressive Lifestyle

The analysis of the Baba movement in the previous section, while adequate as far as it goes, requires further elaboration to explain certain features of the group's success.

One such feature: Most of our respondents had been involved in other counterculture expressive milieux prior to involvement with the group. And such involvement, while it alleviated certain problems, created others of even greater scope. Our interviews revealed that some degree of disillusionment with these milieux generally preceded spiritual involvement. It will be useful, then, in refining our analysis, to compare the Baba movement to the followers' prior drug-oriented drop-out expressive milieux; understanding why these involvements failed may help us to understand why the Baba movement works.

After an initial period of feeling pleasure in their release from bureaucratic educational or vocational milieux, many of our respondents began to feel that these drop-out milieux were not appropriate as permanent life situations for adults. These respondents had internalized residues of a middle-class work ethic such that prolonged dropping out ultimately engendered feelings of anomie. This development is illustrated by the case of one respondent who left school and joined a "clique of long-haired freaks" who filled their days with drugs and sex.

> We had an idea of finding some paradise in the woods or some tropical island and just staying in this paradise forever eating acid [LSD] and smoking grass . . . We thought that just doing what we were doing, taking acid, making love, making music and just trying to be happy all the time was really the free life, and we didn't want to get imprisoned in the life our parents were leading.

But the respondent was never entirely at ease in his psychedelic paradise. His gratifying expressive relations seemed somehow illegitimate because they were not linked to instrumental behavior from which the expressive gratifications could be seen to arise as a reward. The respondent felt guilty and parasitic.

> *Respondent:* I was a parasite. You see, I always felt guilty because I'd say all these things and yet I knew I was a parasite. I knew I was just sucking what I could out of it without doing anything for it. It gave me a few guilty feelings.
>
> *Interviewer:* So you got a feeling that somehow it couldn't be right to just sit around and trip and ball?
>
> *Respondent:* Yes. Exactly. Exactly. I think all through this trip that I knew deep down that it wasn't for me and I always had a hidden feeling that, you know, this is short lived. It's not going to last. But I just blinded myself, just to get away from the thought of ever having to face work and just getting involved in the whole [routinized, work-oriented] lifestyle.

The respondent's precultic history resembled that of another respondent who, prior to becoming a follower of Meher Baba, had become friendly with Charles Manson (alleged mastermind of the Sharon Tate murders), and spent some time at his California commune. The respondent was initially fascinated and awed by the uninhibited spontaneity which characterized group relationships: "Everyone was real free . . . These people are all stoned out on acid and really loose . . . and I thought their freeness, their looseness or uninhibited selves was a kind of trip, so I hung around for a while." Subsequently, the respondent became disillusioned and saw the commune members as "sad" and their existence as really "drab" because "They did nothing . . . they'd sit around all day long . . . they'd either ball or eat or take dope." Unable to succumb to the charismatic mystique of Manson, the respondent ultimately perceived the totally noninstrumental communal lifestyle as devoid of meaning.

The cases presented above indicate that a totally expressive drop-out lifestyle may be perceived as conflicting with a conventional adult role-identity. Many otherwise alienated persons have internalized such identities to a degree that simply dropping out is not psychologically viable for them in the long run. For such people, dropping out *requires a special legitimating rationale*. What we will refer to as "psychedelic utopianism" appeared to be a common legitimating mystique or premovement meaning system among our respondents. The inherent contradictions and ultimate failure of psychedelic utopianism as a legitimating mystique constitutes a second dimension of the failure of these respondents' prior expressive milieux.

Formulated by Timothy Leary, among others, psychedelic utopianism stressed the attainment of vital personal growth and expressive community through psychedelic drugs (Leary, 1968). Later "hippie" versions of psychedelic utopianism stressed the role of drugs and a drug-oriented life-style in operationalizing Universal Love (Yablonsky, 1968). One difficulty with psychedelic utopianism for our respondents was that there are intrinsic potentialities in drug use which are inconsistent with the utopian rationales which they utilized to rationalize drug-oriented life-styles. These problems can be illustrated by the case of two individuals who related to one of the authors how they had at one time been very much involved in a sort of utopian mystique centering around the concept of "love." This "love thing" was conceived as a new "way to live, a philosophy to live by." The respondents had some difficulty verbalizing the precise content of the new philosophy-life-style, i.e., how "loving" people and a "loving" life-style differed from conventional patterns. On the other hand, it was generally agreed that one clear difference between loving and nonloving people was that the former used psychedelic drugs while the latter did not. Drugs, however, were not, at least initially, the essence of the "love" scene; drugs were "not really it, *love* was the message." Gradually, however, the respondents perceived that drugs were beginning to overshadow the other elements of the scene. Drugs were becoming the very essence of the scene, and if the respondents ceased to use psychedelic drugs, users would not associate with them and would perceive them as having deserted the scene. The interviewer inquired why, in the respondents' opinion, many of their friends eventually "began to be very attached to drugs and that became their main thing although it was originally just incidental to a loving philosophy." One respondent commented:

> With drugs the pleasure is so intense that all the senses seem to be dulled while not on drugs, and so that becomes the most important aspect. The other things are *intangibles,* like "unity" is intangible but getting stoned and feeling stoned is a very tangible thing.

Drug use thus tends to become an end in itself rather than a device to accentuate a "loving" milieu. As such it takes on "nonloving" aspects. Much interview data could be presented to illuminate each "antiutopiate" aspect of heavy drug use. To conserve space this will not be done here. Below we will merely summarize some of the points of tension between drug use and utopiate mystiques.

1. Drug dependency often involves the proliferation of highly instrumental relationships with peers, which are treated not as ends in themselves but as means for obtaining drugs. Involvement in these instrumental relationships

conflicts with the legitimating mystique of spontaneous, expressive, personalist relationships.

2. The contradiction is particularly sharp when the need for drugs instigates dishonesty — people are "burned" (sold bad drugs) and "ripped off" (stolen from or otherwise cheated) — all of which falls short of "love."

3. The illegal status of drug use tends to breed "paranoia" over the everpresent threat of a "bust." Harassment of drug users also elicits negative stereotypes and vehemently hostile attitudes toward authorities, parents, "straight" nonusers, etc. Many utopiate drug users become aware that these orientations are "unloving" or "separative" and contravene the mystiques of universal love, unity and oneness which legitimate deviant patterns.[8]

The decline of psychedelic utopianism was probably a consequence of the problems we have discussed above. Drug use continues to be a major social problem and a central feature of adolescence and youth. However, it has been observed by several writers that since the middle sixties youthful middle-class drug abuse has been "secularized" (Robbins, 1970) in the sense that "it is no longer claimed that recreational drugs have extraordinary value for achieving higher social goals" (Schaps and Sanders, 1970). Hence "psychedelic drugs do not now have the spiritual and mystical aura they had formerly (Robbins, 1969).[9] The "secularization" of drug use was the original sociocultural context of the growth of movements such as Meher Baba's. As drugs lost their potency as symbols embodying utopian "love" mystiques, other movements, which became increasingly dissociated from drugs, arose to perform their expressive and communal functions.[10] The Meher Baba movement is one such source of expressive symbolism.

The Legitimacy Dimension of Expressive Youth Communities

The preceding section has suggested the importance of meaning or *legitimacy* in rendering an expressive milieu viable for its members. This section attempts to conceptualize the legitimacy factor, utilizing current theory from the sociology of religion to elaborate our initial formulation of the role-conflict dimension of youthful alienation.

People do not feel comfortable in their roles without some rationale which legitimates or confers meaning on their experiences. The absence or inadequacy of such a legitimating framework of meaning engenders anomie (Berger, 1967). In *The Sacred Canopy* (1967) Berger discusses the role of religions in legitimating actual social patterns by "locating" them in a "sacred cosmos," i.e., interpreting them as derivative from the inherent nature of things. Assuming the secularization of institutional Christianity, Berger (1965) and Luckmann (1967) have discussed various sexual, familist or psychoanalytic mystiques which are currently employed to legitimate social experiences and individual life-styles. As these legitimating mystiques are notably "privatized" (Luckmann, 1967), they are often inadequate to legitimate *communal* relationships.

Deviant roles and life-styles stand in particular need of special legitimating mystiques. Because the dominant ideology of a society often cannot be utilized to legitimate deviant patterns, there is frequently a liaison between deviant roles and deviant ideologies or religiosity (Peacock, 1969).

The problem of legitimacy is particularly aggravated among contemporary American youth. Eisenstadt's analysis of the growing discontinuity between familial-expressive and adult-instrumental milieux implies an increasingly sharp segregation between roles and relationships viewed as appropriate for an "adult" and relational patterns perceived as pertaining exclusively to "childhood." Extra-familial affective, ascriptive, diffuse and particularistic relationships among adults are thus inadequately legitimated. Postadolescents who drop out of conventional instrumental routines and revert to such "childish" patterns will sense the illegitimacy of their behavior and will feel uneasy until an effective legitimating rationale can be developed.

In this connection, both Berger and Weber (from whom Berger derives his concept of legitimacy) tend to discuss legitimacy primarily in terms of *rationalizing suffering*—the "problem of theodicy" which Weber (1956) and Berger (1967) discuss at length. But gratifying or ecstatic experiences also require a legitimating mystique, as a follower of Meher Baba has recently pointed out in a confessional essay.

> When you begin to realize that your own suffering has a purpose, you can bear it with dignity and poise, admit defeat or admit that you were wrong, without feeling that your life is worthless. Just as human suffering can be borne without too much trouble, so can human ecstasy (Townshend, 1970).

Meher Baba as a Universal Expressive Symbol

In previous sections we argued that expressive role patterns rendered most meaningful by modern childhood will be perceived as inappropriate for adults unless an adequate legitimating rationale is constructed. Given the current fragmentation of expressive and instrumental role systems, an effective strategy for legitimating postadolescent expressive roles is to *universalize* them. Such universalizing is essential to the transmutation of specific values into a "sacred cosmos" (Berger, 1967). Moreover, universalized expressive values combine the universalism associated with "adult" modernist instrumental roles with the diffuse solidarity of familial expressive milieux. This combination is a frequent characteristic of youth movements (Eisenstadt, 1956).

Meher Baba is perceived by his followers as a *Universal Saviour*. He is the "Avatar of the Age" and "The Highest of the High." He is a Messiah who incarnates on earth at crucial periods "when the earth is sunk in materialism and chaos as it is now"[11] and who comes to inspire humanity and lead mankind to a higher level of consciousness (Needleman, 1970; Robbins, 1969). We shall see later that Meher Baba is "universal" in a particular sense involving his immanence in all persons.

The essence of Meher Baba's universal message is "love," which, in its purest form "arises in the heart . . . in response to the descent of grace from the Master" (Meher Baba, 1967). Meher Baba descends to impart this grace and awaken love in humanity. In Baba's case, "the medium is the message" in the sense that He is viewed by his disciples as a quintessentially "loving" Master. One follower commented to a researcher: "You can look at Baba's picture and know that He loves you and that He'll never leave you." Baba is thus viewed as a personification of universalized expressivity. Below, a respondent discusses his perception of Baba as an infinitely loving master, the very essence and embodiment of affectivity.

> To me Baba *was* love and with God and love and all, it just seemed a really groovy thing and why didn't somebody tell me about Him before? . . . I remember reading, well, like He says "I can love you more than you can love yourself." Well, I know a little bit about self-love, hassling with it, and like that really seemed incredible to me . . . That I was into a love thing and here it was.

Another respondent comments:

> Love *is* God and *love* is Baba. Baba is love. Baba is God, it's like each one of us—we've got it within us. It's just finding it and finding it through Baba is the best way.

Meher Baba's status as the personified embodiment of love is expressed through His relationships with His followers. These role-orientations appear to follow the dimensions of expressivity articulated by Parsons and referred to by Eisenstadt (1956). They are: affective, quality-oriented, diffuse and particularistic. Baba's "loving" relationships to people are depicted in movies of Baba shown regularly at the Meher Center. One such movie shows Baba tenderly washing lepers, whom Baba is said to have called "beautiful birds in ugly cages." Baba is thus perceived as responding *qualitatively* to persons rather than in terms of their apparent circumstances or attainments.

Although He is the universal saviour, Baba is viewed as relating particularistically to persons. Followers tend to perceive their relationships with Meher Baba as idiosyncratic in the sense that Baba is perceived as deliberately manipulating their experiences, challenges or opportunities. Followers frequently declare that they obtained their jobs through Baba's intervention. Below, a respondent relates how he feels Baba has subtly manipulated his experiences to help him overcome a neurotic inability to communicate with others.

> . . . it seemed like Baba was putting me in situations where I had to confront this fear of mine, and in confronting it He sort of made me aware, that like it wasn't a big thing. It was always a little bit at a time sort of thing so I gradually in a large sense worked out of it.

Thus Baba is perceived as intervening in the unique and particular details of each follower's life-history. He is seen as ministering to each person's distinctive spiritual needs and as aiding in the development of his human potential. This produces a master-follower relationship which is not only idiosyncratic but diffuse: Baba, while loving everyone equally and infinitely, is perceived as treating each person differently according to his own distinctive spiritual needs; He is also perceived as controlling and pervading all aspects of one's existence.[12]

The relationship of the "Baba Lover" to the "Divine Beloved" also has a basic *ascriptive* dimension which derives from the *immanence* of Meher Baba within each lover as his "real" or "higher" self. Meher Baba is conceived as the personal embodiment of everyone's latent identity. Meher Baba's universal love is thus grounded in His universal identity; He loves everyone as He recognizes Himself in everyone. A Baba Lover has recently written:

> Baba loved all kinds of people. He could see God in each and every one of them, the criminal, the prostitute, the beggar, the false saint, the vainly rich, the indulgent westerner, the poet, the drug addict, the pusher, the soldier, the Christian, the Mohammedan, the middle road rock star (Townshend, 1970).

Meher Baba's immanence and His universal identity converts His "loving" role-orientations into universal and archetypal patterns. As such they hold the key to overcoming the segregation and age-specificity of expressive role patterns, which we discussed earlier. Meher Baba's relationship to His followers becomes the basis for interpersonal relationships involving Baba Lovers.

The interview excerpt below expresses the premise accepted by Baba Lovers that loving interpersonal relationships among themselves are derived from loving relationships to Baba.

Interviewer: Why was it you felt good when you were at the Center?

Respondent: Just because of the feelings. Just because of what people were expressing. I could feel Baba coming through these people. I even felt myself expressing these things which I never thought I would.

Thus, "loving" roles in the Baba community, "loving" relationships among Baba Lovers and "loving" attributes or "vibrations" of a Baba Lover are seen as emanations of Baba immanent within the lovers. In the passage below, the derivation of positive expressive qualities and expressive relationships from inner liaisons with Meher Baba is stated clearly.

I don't see Charlie as Charlie. Really, I see Charlie as—I see Baba in Charlie. I see Baba in the people in the Center. I see Baba in you. I see Baba in so many of the people in the Center. And it's not the individual Charlie; no, I think it's Baba in Charlie.

Summarizing this section, we have seen that Meher Baba is perceived as having conspicuous expressive role-orientations which, by virtue of Baba's status as universal saviour and immanent divinity, become archetypal and universal. Baba's love is viewed as diffusing through loving relationships among Baba Lovers, which are viewed as derivative from the participants' inner expressive liaison with the Divine Beloved. Expressive and affective relationships among followers are thus universalized and achieve a transcendental legitimization.

The Problem of Work Roles

This paper has undertaken a functional analysis of the Meher Baba movement, which we have viewed in its integrative aspect as embodying an effective strategy for coping with alienation. This analysis is still incomplete. Considering youthful alienation in Parsons-Eisenstadt role-conflict terms, no resolution of alienation is complete without resolution of the perceived tension between instrumental "Establishment" work roles (including preparatory educational roles) and expressive needs which allegedly cannot be satisfied by these roles.

The fact of the integrative consequences of involvement in the Baba movement has been cited earlier and is also discussed in an earlier paper by one of the authors (Robbins, 1969). Numerous Baba Lovers have been led to give up illegal drug use (Robbins, 1969; Dunn, 1968; Needleman, 1970; Townshend, 1970) *and* either resume educational career preparation or exchange casual and primarily menial "odd job" patterns for long-term career involvements. This change usually involves a concomitant upgrading of social respectability. Below a former "speed freak," college drop-out and convicted felon describes his return to college in Chapel Hill after an extended stay at the Meher Center.

The following year I went back to school. Give it one more try. When I left Chapel Hill, I had been thrown out. Like everybody was just trying to do me in—the administration, the police. They took me down to a cellar, you know, interrogating me. It was really something . . . So I went back up there, and I talked to the dean, who a year before had made very serious efforts to have me put in prison. He was shaking my hand, saying "Oh, it's so good you're back, you're just the kind of boy we need." That was an experience! He did everything but give me a scholarship.

It is the authors' belief that this transition from social alienation to social integration is accomplished through the particular form of universalized expressivity utilized by the Baba movement, i.e., expressive immanence. As explicated in the preceding section, an expressive community of believers is legitimated by this means. As a result, its members no longer suffer from "love starvation," and thus no longer feel a need to rebel against the impersonal institutions of the larger society. In addition, the logic of Meher Baba being the "real" universal self of all people compels a certain tolerance for people who are not members of the movement. The writer below is describing some of his acquaintances.

Even without knowing about Baba they live and breathe his love, as does everyone, I suppose, but in them it is a fairy tale of color and good vibes (Townshend, 1970).

Below, a respondent manifests this tolerance with distinct prosocial overtones.

I get along with people more. It used to be, I'd go into the street and I'd see some white-collar cat walk down the street and right away he's the enemy. I wouldn't go so far as ask him what he thought, he just *looked* like that and I didn't want to have anything to do with him. Or some cat would drive down the street in a Cadillac or something. There'd be no way in the world . . . I didn't want to meet him. But now like I want to talk to people. Even people like that, especially. Go out and tell them about Baba.

It has been argued in this paper that the Baba movement legitimates gratifying expressive relations by building them into a sacred cosmos defined in terms of an immanent divinity (Meher Baba) and His universal prototypical role-orientations. A sacred cosmos operates to legitimate or confer meaning on social experiences (Berger, 1967), but it must itself be validated by confirming social experiences. Unless it can be seen to be somehow socially *relevant,* its definitive premise of universality is imperiled.

The *affective* quality of the universal archetypal role-orientation of the "Baba Lover" implies that the worldly activities and relations through which one works out one's unique relationship with Baba and acts out, reaffirms, and ultimately validates one's meaning system must above all, be "loving." Thus one demonstrates the social relevance and universality of the Sacred Cosmos by *acting lovingly in the world.*

The next excerpt shows that gratifying relationships between Baba Lovers and non-Baba Lovers are frequently interpreted as manifestations of one of the participants' loving relationship with Baba. The respondent is describing hitchhiking home from the Meher Center.

> Normally, when I'm hitchhiking, I just talk drab with people, but I was so turned on I was really seeing Baba's form everywhere. And I was so full of His love, I was passing it on. You know, Baba says love is self-communicating. It normally would be rare to find a truck driver and a longhair really getting along. But this guy wanted to adopt me and wanted to know all about Baba. And then I got out of his truck and into another truck, and the same thing happened. And it happened all the way back!

Given that Baba followers regard others as manifestations of Baba as an immanent deity, and given Baba's prototypical affective role-orientations, it is hardly surprising that the ethic used to implement the universality of their "sacred cosmos" is one of "selfless service." This orientation, which discourages a drop-out life pattern, whether hedonistic or quasi-mystical, can be seen below in an excerpt from a television interview with Kitty Davy, cosupervisor of the Meher Center.

> The Avatar is God in human form. He comes again at the right moment, when the world is in chaos and materialism as it is now, to live again the way of life which is expressed in selfless service, because love means action. Baba says the material and the spiritual must go hand in hand. You cannot stay in a spiritual retreat for your whole life and find God. God must be found in the world, through service, through selfless action.

It has been the authors' observation that most Baba Lovers who remain committed to the movement for any length of time are eventually influenced by this ethnic (Robbins, 1969). Below, a follower discusses his return to an active routinized life-style.

> Without that [Baba's service ethic] it would have been very easy not to do anything. I still don't feel inclined to work, like I'm not in production. So without Baba's saying do something, I would have probably not done anything positive—I probably wouldn't have gone back to school, since I

didn't think school was the answer to my problem or was going to save me in any sense.

In a later segment of the interview, the respondent discussed Baba's modified work ethic. Baba maintains that action in the world is important for spiritual advancement, but to be really beneficial, i.e., to avoid enhancing the individual's sense of separateness from God, which most worldly endeavor reinforces, the spiritual aspirants must cultivate a sense of *inner detachment* from the results of his activity. He must dedicate and surrender his activity to "the Master" and in so doing he "liberates" himself from his own action and from the consequences of his actions, which are no longer his concern (Robbins, 1969; Meher Baba, 1967). A rationale of inner detachment from the results of one's work makes the impersonality of technocratic vocational routines less oppressive.[13]

Below, the respondent previously quoted discusses how this ethic of inner detachment mitigated the traumas associated with reentering school in his confused, post-LSD state of mind.

Anyhow, the idea of being in it but not of it, was of utmost importance because if I'd tried to go back into it and gotten into it, I really can't imagine being able to come out of my difficulties with as much ease and speed as it happened. Like I think I was in a state of mind that the school would have even reinforced some of that.

It can be seen how Baba's ethic of inner detachment, in conjunction with the expressive context of the "loving" Baba community, enables alienated individuals to accept work roles which are not in themselves perceived as intrinsically gratifying or expressive. Moreover, the ethos of "selfless service" actually appears to provide a basis for a limited renewal of personal involvement in interesting and exacting work roles. Some indications of this tendency can be seen in the interview exerpt below.

The relationship any job brings to spirituality is simply to use what I've been given as selflessly as possible. That is to say, I don't think it's right that if I happen to be a very intelligent person for me to spend my life stringing beads or washing dishes. It has to be put to use and it has to be lined up with the fulfilling of my own *karma*. . . . I don't think from the point of view of God-realization that it matters whether one were a dishwasher or a great scientist, except that if I could have been a great scientist, then maybe I wasn't fulfilling my karma and that's the reason I won't wash dishes any more.

Thus, the "selfless service" ethos can eventually become a basis for renewed motivation and career orientation. A sort of mutual validation occurs between the emergent work roles of Baba Lovers and their meaning system. The ethos of "selfless service" facilitates the crystallization of career involvements, which, in turn, act out the movement's "love" orientation and make it appear socially relevant. Baba Lovers thus strive to articulate their emergent work roles with their sacred cosmos.[14]

Conclusion

In the first section of this paper, we outlined arguments from Berger and Eisenstadt. Berger indicated that children raised in a modern technocratic setting would perceive themselves as love-starved when attempting to make the transition from the familial expressive milieu to the adult bureaucratic instrumental milieu. Eisenstadt has argued that *youth movements which seem to be attempting to perpetuate this expressive milieu in adult life often actually function to integrate the expressive and instrumental systems of role orientation.*[15]

In this paper we have argued that the Meher Baba movement has chosen one of the pattern variables from the instrumental system, viz., universalism and integrated it with role-orientations from the expressive system. In this way the movement has *legitimated expressive role orientations for adults.* Universalism seems to be a particularly useful orientation for legitimating expressivity, as it allows the elaboration of expressive role-orientations into a "sacred cosmos." This sacred cosmos, which presents itself as reflecting the nature and purpose of the universe, naturally supersedes all merely conventional institutions if their mandates should happen to conflict. It is thus an effective device for legitimating structural change, such as those arising from the fragmentation of modern society into a bureaucratic instrumental system and an expressive familial system.

The traditional work ethic, which rationalized the old small entrepreneurial instrumental-expressive synthesis of role orientations, derived expressive values from instrumental ones.[16] The "sacred cosmos" of Baba followers supersedes that ethic, by deriving instrumental values from expressive ones. It thus reduces the tension between conditions of modern childhood and the instrumental roles rationalized by the old ethic.

Other modern youth movements can also be seen as attempting to legitimate expressive role-orientations as a basis for community in adults by universalizing them. Thus we described the hippies' attempt to universalize their drop-out drug-oriented expressive life-style into an ethic of psychedelic utopianism. We saw that this attempt failed, at least for certain of our respondents, for two reasons: (1) the ethic led to behavior which was inconsistent with itself, e.g., use of drugs led to unloving behavior, and (2) it failed to include enough of the instrumental role-orientations in its synthesis, and thus never seemed quite legitimate to many of our respondents.

The Baba movement seems to have escaped these problems in that (1) its ethic does not produce consequences which are obviously inconsistent with it, and (2) it ameliorates the problem of "loveless" work roles in adult instrumental milieux by endowing instrumental role orientations with expressive meaning, not by trying to eliminate them entirely. It could be argued that insofar as a modern youth movement violates the second requirement, it will inevitably violate the former. That is, certain instrumental functions are necessary for the perpetuation of a total culture. If a subculture attempts to legitimate expressive functions by universalizing them, without including vital instrumental functions, it cannot maintain itself except as a specialized subsystem of the larger society. It must then, by its own logic of legitimation, convince the larger society to support it, because its expressive values rather than the larger society's instrumental values are the truly "universal" ones. But if the larger society were to accept this logic, it would adopt the purely expressive values of the subculture, and instrumental functions necessary to its maintenance would disappear. Thus, in order to maintain itself, the adult society rejects the love ethic of the hippies, and an escalating conflict between hippies and "straight" society appears. Hippies thus become Yippies, love-ins evolve into hostile confrontations with "Amerika," and the love ethic has become inconsistent with itself.

The particular form of universalism the Baba movement has chosen to legitimate its expressive values — expressive immanence — seems to have allowed it to escape these problems. This doctrine, which presents the same loving self as the "real" self of all, obviates "seeming" conflicts of opinion and belief. If one "self" is present in all, and that "self" is loving,[17] then people who have "realized" this must act in a way consistent with this awareness. They must attempt to act "lovingly" toward others, whether those others consciously accept their ethic or not.

In order to remain self-consistent, this form of universal expressivity is elaborated into a service ethic, which synthesizes expressive and instrumental role-orientations. The Meher Baba movement's ethic incorporates the instrumental values which allow it to perpetuate itself within the larger society, while maintaining the expressive emphasis which gave it birth.

Notes

1. Our analysis of these phenomena relies heavily upon a distinction between *expressive* roles and relationships and *instrumental* roles and relationships as defined by Parsons (1951: 58-67). Expressive or "personalistic" relationships are those which are (1) terminal values or ends-in-themselves, (2) diffuse, i.e., spilling over into many different sectors of the participant's life-space, (3) particularistic or idiosyncratic, and (4) effective or emotional. In contrast, "instrumental" or

"impersonal" roles and relationships are (1) means to ends, (2) functionally specific, (3) performance or achievement oriented, (4) universalistic, or capable of application without exception, and (5) unemotional or "affectively neutral."

2. Aspects of Eisenstadt's formulation were applied to hippies by Yablonsky (1968) and Von Hoffman (1968), who noted the childhood-familial elements in the hippie "tribal" mystique. Eisenstadt's analysis was also applied to student radicalism by Flacks (1970b), who suggested modifications and criticisms. Eisenstadt's role-conflict analysis has been an influential and distinctly sociological perspective on youth movements.

3. An unfulfilled need for community has often been identified as the general curse of modern society — or modern American society (Nisbet, 1956; Slater, 1970). Eisenstadt, Berger and others feel this problem is particularly acute for postadolescents of the present generation. Slater (1970) argues that the youthful counterculture necessarily serves those needs which are repressed by the dominant sociocultural pattern. He maintains that contemporary American culture systematically frustrates basic human needs for community. This frustration is least tolerable among modern middle-class youth whose environment is more differentiated, organized and bureaucratized than that of previous generations, and whose evident security and affluence undermines the scarcity premise which legitimates the dominant anticommunal ethos of competitive individualism (Slater, 1970).

4. Chapel Hill, North Carolina, the small college town in which the authors once lived, for several years featured a conspicuously deviant youth subculture. In the spring and summer of 1967 some prominent role-models of this culture began to promulgate a new religion centered about the person of Meher Baba, the "Avatar of the Age." Robbins (1969) has described the effect of the Meher Baba movement in facilitating the termination of drug use among the initial Chapel Hill converts. He also described some tendency toward reentry into conventional career and educational patterns. The integrative impact of the new faith on the deviant subculture of Chapel Hill was widely noted at the time by concerned authorities and the local media. (*Winston-Salem Journal Sentinal,* Oct. 22-26, 1967; *Chapel Hill Weekly,* Nov. 5, 1967; University of North Carolina *Daily Tar Heel,* Nov. 7, 1968).

5. The Meher Baba movement has no formal boundaries, membership certificates or criteria. The researchers, who have been interested in the movement for some time, do consider themselves committed to some degree to the meaning system, and thus are participants in the Baba subculture (hence there was minimal pretense involved in the interviews or participant observation). For purposes of sociological analysis of the data, the researchers have operated from a premise of what Robert Bellah (1970) has called "consequential reductionism" in which the truth or validity of the meaning system is viewed as irrelevant to sociological analysis. The details and attributes of the meaning system are thus viewed in terms of the functions they appear to serve for participants. Bellah may be correct in arguing that consequential reductionism cannot capture the real essence or full inner meaning of religious beliefs, but it has led to many sociologically significant insights.

6. The Meher Center in Myrtle Beach, South Carolina, established at the order of Meher Baba, is a place for "rest and renewal of the spiritual life." It is the only resident Baba center in the United States. Followers of Baba come from all over the country to visit the Center. See Dunn (1968) for a vivid description of the interpersonal atmosphere of the Center.

7. In this connection the evolution of the Monday night Baba meetings in Chapel Hill is instructive. Initial meetings in the summer and fall of 1967 were highly theoretical in tone and were characterized by intense discussions of Meher Baba's

cosmology and eschatology. Current meetings in Chapel Hill seem to have a much more relaxed atmosphere and increasingly take on the appearance of a social gathering with refreshments and gossip. The spiritual symbols and belief system of the movement are still objects of deep attachment, but they have become an implicit rather than an overt dimension of collective gatherings and social interaction involving followers. A shared spiritual meaning system operates as an underlying premise of movement-related social phenomena, but is often not the explicit focus of the gatherings. In the opinion of the authors, this does not imply "secularization" in the sense of diminished attachment to movement symbols and perspectives. It is, however, indicative of the growing sociocommunal dimension of movement involvement.

8. Yablonsky (1968) describes hippies cultivating drug-induced sensations of oceanic unity and oneness with everything. He goes on to criticize the hypocrisy of this utopianism which is belied by nonloving behavior (e.g., violence) within hippie communities. Countercriticism of Yablonsky as writing from an irrelevant "Establishment-Liberal" standpoint (Berger, 1969) is misleading, because hippies were themselves aware of these inconsistencies and experience and reacted to the resulting cognitive dissonance — or so our research would seem to indicate.

9. The secularization of the drug scene gave rise to a number of movements and ideologies which seek to operationalize a mystique of *universal love* which will legitimate expressive roles and relationships among postadolescents in a manner which evades the contradictions inherent in psychedelic utopianism. This tendency can be seen in the proliferation of postpsychedelic youthful "Jesus Freaks" or "street Christians." Vachon (1971) quotes one postpsychedelic convert to Jesus as commenting that in his prior drug-oriented period "we called ourselves love children, but we sure didn't love cops; now we love everybody."

10. There are a number of other intrinsic difficulties with a distinctly psychedelic approach to gemeinschaft. Hallucinogenic drugs are often used to enhance sensations of interpersonal communion and expressive spontaneity; however the aftermath of a "bad trip" can leave a user feeling utterly isolated and unable to relate to others (Keniston, 1968). A number of respondents reported traumatic experiences of this nature.

There is also an intrinsic problem of meaning associated with drugs. Drug-induced sensations tend to be perceived as ego-alien. They cannot easily be identified with. A follower of Meher Baba has recently described this problem in a confessional article in *Rolling Stone*:

> On the surface, then, it seemed I owed a lot to dope. It gave me beautiful girls, it gave me R & B. What it didn't give me was the feeling that any of the above were really *mine*. They were all thanks to dope. That's where the paranoia came in. If I hadn't been stoned that solo would have been a bummer. If I hadn't been stoned that chick wouldn't have wanted to know [me]. If I hadn't been stoned the sun wouldn't have come up (Townshend, 1970).

11. Quoted from a radio interview of Kitty Davy, co-manager of the Meher Spiritual Center.

12. The normative ideal of a follower's love and devotion to Baba parallels the fundamental expressive role-orientations ascribed to Meher Baba. The fervent affectivity of the ideal devotional orientation is expressed in followers' designation of themselves as "Baba Lovers." The diffuse nature of the ideal role-orientation of the "Baba Lover" is expressed in the statement of the respondent below, who is describing his spiritual awakening.

I understood why I was alive, why I had been born. I was born to love Him. That's the only reason I'm here. My life had no other purpose. That's the way I feel. He's my master.

The idiosyncratic nature of the role of Baba Lover is evident in the absence of *standardized* operations (e.g., a special chant or ritual, etc.) defined as *the* mode of acting out and further developing one's love for God.

13. The "detached" resolution of the problem of alienation from work roles is congruent with the increasing tendency of middle-class employees to segregate their personal identity from their occupational roles which has been noticed by a number of sociologists (Berger, 1965; Luckmann, 1967).

14. A somewhat disillusioned former Baba follower commented in an interview:

"Oh, Baba found me this job," like people say, "Oh, it's because of Baba I found this house, oh He directed me to . . ." That's what people do, say it's Baba. People have a way of fooling themselves . . . whenever they're going to do something, they say they're doing it for Baba. You know, I'm saving humanity . . . Baba has helped me to do this. Because of Baba I found this service. But if you really want something, it's there. You can say, "Well, Baba has helped me find it," or Jesus or anything.

The respondent's comments indicate the degree to which Baba Lovers continually strive to relate all their worldly activities to their cultic involvement in such a way that the former is viewed as inspired by and derivative of the latter. A process of mutual or reciprocal validation appears to take place whereby the meaning system legitimates worldly roles which in turn reinforce the meaning system.

15. We consider Eisenstadt's analysis of the function of modern youth movements to be most valuable as a formulation of the conditions which a successful youth movement must fulfill, rather than a causal explanation of all youth movements. It is not then "reductionistic." It provides a principle of "natural selection" defining successful youth movements, rather than positing some mysterious *élan vital* intelligently but unconsciously directing all youth movements. It is simply a descriptive language identifying dimensions and functions of self-regulating social systems, and thus defines the nature of adaptive solutions to change and stress.

16. Parsons (1937), paraphrasing Weber, has pointed out that Calvinism viewed man as an instrument for enhancing God's glory. This instrumental concept of man legitimated the assimilation of one's identity to a specialized instrumental work role.

17. It is not our intention to explain Baba's "worldly" service ethic and its integrative and resocializing consequences solely on the basis of Baba's immanence. The usual consequences of immanentist doctrines are "retreatist," as they imply the possibility of making direct contact with God through intense spiritual endeavor (e.g., meditation) which usually involves social withdrawal. In the case of the Meher Baba movement, the key factor is the emphasis on "love," and Baba's archetypal "loving" role-orientations. In the context of this theme, immanence operates to facilitate social reintegration. One must love Baba and this involves loving others in whom Baba is immanent. In consequence, one best validates and operationalizes the meaning system by acting lovingly in the world, which precludes retreatism.

References

Bellah, Robert N., 1970a
Berger, Bennett, 1969
Berger, Peter, 1965, 1967
Berger, Peter, and Richard Neuhaus, 1970
Bruyn, Severyn, 1966
Crenshaw, Richard, 1968
Dunn, J.A.C., 1968
Eisenstadt, S.N., 1956, 1961
Flacks, Richard, 1967, 1970a, 1970b
Glaser, Barney G., and Anselm L. Strauss, 1968
Greeley, Andrew M., 1969, 1970
Gustaitis, Rasa, 1969
Keniston, Kenneth, 1968
Leary, Timothy, 1968
Luckmann, Thomas, 1967
Meher, Baba, 1966, 1967
Needleman, Jacob, 1970
Nisbet, Robert, 1970
Peacock, James L., 1968
Parsons, Talcott, 1937, 1951
Reich, Charles A., 1970
Robbins, Thomas, 1969, 1970
Roszak, Theodore, 1969
Schaps, Eric, and Clinton R. Sanders, 1970
Slater, Philip, 1970
Townshend, Peter, 1970
Vachon, Brian, 1971
Von Hoffman, Nicholas, 1968
Weber, Max, 1964
Yablonsky, Lewis, 1968

Social Consciousness in the
Human Potential Movement

Donald Stone

Self-awareness has become the new panacea, according to a growing number of critics of the personal growth groups and self-realization trainings that are part of a more general Human Potential movement. They fear that activities such as gestalt, encounter, *est,* Zen, Aikido, Transactional Analysis, and Transcendental Meditation will invite preoccupation with self and sensation, and that they will dilute already weak feelings of social responsibility. Books and articles bearing titles like *The Awareness Trap: Self-Absorption Instead of Social Change* (Schur, 1976), *"The New Narcissism"* (Marin, 1975), *"The Me Decade and the Third Great Awakening"* (Wolfe, 1976), and *Social Amnesia* (Jacoby, 1976) have brought the controversy into national focus.

Since the early 1960s, more than seven million Americans have been exposed to some sort of encounter group, body discipline, or personal growth program. The more recent developments include "transpersonal disciplines" that emphasize "self-realization" and "enlightenment." 200,000 *est* graduates have "gotten it" in a rigorous 60-hour training. T.M. has initiated more than one million meditators. Meditation has become sufficiently fashionable that a recent Gallup poll reports six million Americans claim to have done it.

The influence of this movement expands as people in the helping professions apply human-potential techniques and assumptions in education, medicine, prison reform, humanistic psychology, psychotherapy, and business. Even the U.S. Army has taken notice by sending a drug rehabilitation unit to be trained at California's Esalen Institute, the mother church of the Human Potential movement.

Personal testimony of dramatic changes — the principal recruiting mechanism of this movement — has given way to almost millenarian claims about its social significance. Carl Rogers has declared that the encounter group is the most important social invention of the century. TM's Maharishi Mahesh Yogi has proclaimed a world plan "to eliminate the age-old problem of crime and all behavior that brings unhappiness to the family of man." Werner Erhard, founder of *est* (Erhard Seminars Training), has committed himself to the worldwide elimination of death by starvation within 20 years.

Every successful movement, particularly those making expansive claims, has its opposition. The psychiatric establishment was the first to scrutinize awareness trainings. Faulting the lack of clinical professionalism has given way more recently to social scientists claiming that far from heralding a new age, this middle class revival movement reinforces the American cult of individualism.

The most extended analysis of Human Potential ideology and its predicted social consequences is Edwin Schur's *The Awareness Trap: Self-Absorption Instead of Social Change*. Schur writes (1976) that "Americans are frantically trying to 'get in touch' with themselves, to learn how to 'relate' better, and to stave off outer turmoil by achieving inner peace. . . . With the premise that we should all accept responsibility for ourselves, the latent political implication seems equally apparent: complacency for those who succeed; resignation or self-blame for those who have not."

All human potential trainings emphasize that people are responsible for their lives and for their experience of living. Some *est* graduates go as far as to say that "you are responsible for all your experience; you create it." Critics predict that this ethic of individual responsibility will legitimatize the status of the wealthy, reinforce the self-doubt and self-blame of the disadvantaged, and discourage collective organization needed to redistribute power and wealth.

The possibility that such a pervasive movement contributes to social isolation by converting public issues into private failings warrants careful consideration. To date, no systematic evidence has been presented to document the social consciousness of participants. Predictions of social unconsciousness have been based mainly on selected statements made by leaders and participants. The behavior of participants especially has gone unexamined. Using survey and interview data gathered over five years from participants in a variety of awareness groups, a preliminary profile of the social consciousness of participants can now be made. Many of the examples are drawn from my research on *est*, the discipline I researched most thoroughly.

Survey of Attitudes About Poverty and Failure

Some evidence is provided by a survey interview of values, world views, and political orientations of 1,000 randomly selected residents from five San Francisco Bay Area counties. The interviews were conducted as part of the New Religious Consciousness Project at the Survey Research Center at the University of California at Berkeley. 173 people (17.3 percent) reported that they "had taken part in an encounter group, similar kind of training such as sensory awareness, sensitivity training, a 'T' group or growth group." These respondents were engaged in a wide range of awareness activities, ranging from *est* to Esalen-style encounter marathons to group dynamics labs required of college psychology majors.

The interviews included questions about the reasons for suffering in general and for poverty in particular. Compared with the other 827 respondents, the growth group participants offered social structural explanations more frequently, and they assigned blame less often. Growth group participants agreed more often than nonparticipants with the statement that "the poor are poor because the American way of life doesn't give all people an equal chance," and that "the wealthy and powerful keep them poor." Along with the other respondents, they disagreed with the statement that "the poor simply aren't willing to work hard."

TABLE 12.1

	Growth Group Participants (173)	Non-Participants (827)	
The poor are poor because the American way of life doesn't give all people an equal chance.	68	55	+ 13
The poor are poor because the wealthy and powerful keep them poor.	69	57	+ 12
The poor simply aren't willing to work hard.	24	27	− 3
More jobs should be provided and the country should also guarantee a minimum income for everyone.	46	34	+ 12

In response to specific questions about success and failure, participants were slightly less likely to agree with the following statements:

> Whenever I fail I have no one to blame but myself.
> If one works hard enough, he can do anything he wants to.
> If someone does not succeed in life, you can be pretty sure it's his own fault.

In terms of social policy, awareness group participants were more in favor of a guaranteed minimum income and laws limiting personal wealth. Twice as many favored affirmative action for hiring black persons in public jobs, and more gave "great importance to helping women get equal rights." In general, growth group participants held liberal political views, with one-half considering themselves "radical" or "very liberal."

The 173 growth group participants may be more liberal because they are younger and more educated than the other Bay Area residents, and because liberalism is generally associated with more education and younger age. The more liberal hue of the participants held up under further analysis that controlled for education and age. In particular, the older and less educated participants were just as liberal as the younger and more educated individuals.

The survey did not support the hypothesis that those who are involved more extensively become more conservative. The survey found that people who reported being involved "many times" in groups held views as liberal or more liberal than those participating only once. These findings should be considered as tentative ones — there was no measurement of attitudes previous to group exposure. It may be that particularly liberal persons are attracted to groups in the first place, and that they become less liberal subsequent to exposure.

These survey findings appear to apply to more than just the exotic culture of the San Francisco Bay Area. Similar results were found in a nationwide survey of 40,000 *Psychology Today* readers that asked similar questions about political attitudes and participation in growth groups.

Attitudes of *est* Respondents

The unexpected survey findings that group participants tend to be politically liberal and use social-structural explanatory modes were explored further in extended interviews with 40 *est* graduates. One-half were chosen through snowball sampling, and one-half were chosen randomly. These 40 men and women had participated in a two weekend training, the purpose of which was to "transform your experience of living so that the situations you have been trying to change or have been putting up with clear up in the process of life itself." The key to the training is "getting that you are responsible," which is an experience facilitated by 60 hours of didactic lectures, intense awareness exercises, and sharing among participants. Critics of awareness groups suspect that *est* teaches an ethic of personal responsibility that is a form of extreme solipsism. Accordingly, *est* graduates should be particularly insensitive to social forces and to any sense of involvement or implication in the lives of the disadvantaged.

When questioned about how they structured their reality and how they assigned responsibility, almost all agreed that "I'm the one responsible." Yet they were more reluctant to say that poor people created their own circumstances. This reverse double standard was probed further by asking the respondents why an *est* trainer could tell them to take responsibility, but why they were unwilling to tell the same thing to a poor person. When confronted with this apparent inconsistency, some agreed that the poor were responsible, but most were bewildered and had no ready explanation. One individual felt that an advantaged person like herself had no business telling poor people how to run their lives. Another person felt that people cannot be told they are responsible until they are ready to hear it. Apparently, people who are willing to pay $300 and to sit through hours of discomfort are more ready. Regarding people outside the training situation, Erhard says he sees little value in telling them they are responsible, and that he observes "when people come from the point of view of responsibility, their lives work."

Again and again, the term "responsibility" was being used in a very special and elusive way. A clue to its special meaning came with a respondent bridging the apparent contradiction by saying that "I am responsible for my experience of people being poor, and my experience of people creating their poverty does not mean I am any less responsible or less involved in the situation."

This use of responsibility is quite different from the usual meaning of individual responsibility. Because a person is responsible for his own success, this does not mean they are not responsible for the situation of others. People are "coresponsible" where their being 100 percent responsible does not lessen the fact that others are 100 percent responsible as well. Another difference is that there is not a sense of judgment or blame implied in the word. Because people are poor or rich does not mean they deserve it.

An official *est* definition goes into more detail:

> Responsibility starts with the willingness to acknowledge that you are cause in a matter. It starts with the willingness to deal with a situation from and with the point of view, *whether at the moment realized or not,* that you are the source of what you are, what you do and what you have. This point of view extends to include even what is done to you and ultimately what another does to another. Responsibility is not fault, blame, shame or guilt. All these include judgments and evaluations of good and bad, right and wrong, or better and worse. They are not responsible as they are all beyond a simple acknowledgment that you are cause in your own experience.

est interprets personal responsibility as including responsibility for having created a social world peopled with groups and institutions. The *est* definition even includes responsibility for what "another does to another," although few graduates report they have an immediate experience of this.

Total responsibility is considered a matter of awareness, rather than of determination or proof. *est* trainers say: "Who you are is responsible. It's not an issue of whether you are responsible. It's whether you are going to recognize it or not."

These kinds of statements about responsibility are confusing because of the variety of ways the term is used by participants, and because responsibility is considered a *context* or *place to come from* rather than a verbal formulation. Graduates who have not had a direct experience of this metaresponsibility tend to be baffled in trying to explain it. Yet some are willing to adopt it as a heuristic assumption, willing to suspend the belief that they do not create all their experience.

One payoff in taking this point of view is the sense of control it gives. A graduate noted: "If we consider ourselves responsible for everything that happens, then at least there is the possibility that we can change things. . . . If it turns out in fact, we aren't responsible, it doesn't make any difference."

Adopting this sense of total responsibility may catalyze action. A respondent noted that "the more responsibility that I accept the more action I'll take to control it. If I don't consider myself entirely responsible, the chance is that my efforts will be half-hearted." In principle, this ethic of responsibility leaves no way out but to act as if there is nothing external that will improve a situation. People are considered responsible even for setting up a system that leaves them no way out. They are told that is a choice they already made.

The final payoff of this point of view is a sense of satisfaction with a strangely nonmaterialistic twist. A Berkeley graduate student turned plumber writes that "satisfaction cannot come from having material stuff, position, status and so forth; satisfaction comes from 'getting' that you are responsible for the world, from getting that you created it."

The combination of emphasis on individual responsibility without the harsh edge of blame or fault is characteristic of the style of Jimmy Carter. Of twenty *est* graduates asked about how they voted in the last presidential election, three did not vote, four voted for Ford, and the rest voted for Carter.

Just as there was no pronounced tendency for the advantaged *est* participants to blame the disadvantaged for being poor, there was no evidence that disadvantaged people taking *est* had negative self-images reinforced. This would not be the expected outcome, according to such studies as Sennett and Cobb's *The Hidden Injuries of Class* and Lillian Rubin's *Worlds of Pain*. These studies show that working-class people with few opportunities for success tend to internalize their powerlessness in the form of self-doubt and low self-esteem. Recruits from urban gangs, ghetto schools, and federal prisons who have taken *est* appear to gain a sense of the personal empowerment that often follows conversion to the Black Muslims or initiation into the Delancey Street half-way house in San Francisco.

To specify the relative importance of personal and structural change, *est* respondents were asked if they would give priority to changing people as individuals, or changing the rules and institutions of society. Most felt individuals should be changed first. Supposedly, when enough individuals are changed, society will naturally follow. The implicit model for this is that if everyone took *est* training, the world would be transformed. Many did not grasp that it might be as difficult to find substantial numbers willing to go through *est* as to change the institutions in the first place. The more politically active graduates were more likely to say institutional change must accompany personal change. They tended to foresee the influence of *est* through a "critical mass" of graduates, particularly ones in positions of public influence. Erhard's view differs from that of most of the graduates interviewed in holding that social transformation must be accomplished at the institutional level, not just by aggregates of individuals.

Political Activism

The Bay Area survey asked about participation in political activities such as writing to public officials, attending political meetings, and marching in demonstrations. Growth group participants were much more likely than other Bay Area residents to have done these things, although the survey did not ask whether there was any increase following their group activities.

TABLE 12.2

	Growth Group Participants (173)	Non-Participants (827)	% DIFFERENCE
Has written a letter to a public official.	63	37	+ 26
Has attended political meetings, speeches or rallies.	77	45	+ 32
Has taken part in demonstrations or marches, not just watching.	44	12	+ 32

Source: 1973 Berkeley Religious Consciousness Project, "Perspectives on Life in America Today," Survey Research Center, U.C. Berkeley. Interview schedule and survey are reported in Robert Wuthnow, The Consciousness Revolution, Univ. of California Press, Berkeley 1976.

The in-depth interviews with *est* participants probed for changes in activism subsequent to the training. No clear pattern of political participation after *est* emerged. Several examples illustrate the range of political involvement. An *est* graduate who was a former antiwar activist said he would not get involved again until participating in politics would nurture him. He characterized his previous involvement as motivated in large part by guilt and anger. He claimed he had been more interested in justifying himself to his peers and thumbing his nose at authority than in changing anything. A student who was approached to work for a presidential candidate responded to the invitation by saying that "ordinarily I would say 'no' but Werner says you get more out of life when you participate, so I'll do it."

Many *est* graduates who had been politically inactive before the training did not expect that this would change in the future. Some continued their activism after *est* because they enjoyed it, and they felt their awareness training made them more effective in their organizing. One veteran of both the antiwar and Human Potential movement said: "I'll be out there doing social action for the simple reason that I'm that kind of person."

If there is no clear trend toward political activism, there is a shift toward self-conscious involvement in family life, friendships, and for many, in more human potential trainings. Respondents report taking more initiative in creating a supportive working environment by speaking up in meetings and seeking support from coworkers. These self-reported changes were substantially confirmed through brief interviews with friends, family, and coworkers of the *est* respondents.

Political Activism in Human Potential Organizations

The patterns of political involvement of organizations that sponsor awareness trainings are easier to characterize than the patterns of their trainees. Most ignore politics and community affairs. A few are slowly moving in the direction of discussing and acting on public issues. This recent interest is in part a defensive reaction to being so roundly criticized, and as such, it is good evidence that the critics have hit a vulnerable spot.

The professional and research arm of the Human Potential movement is the Association for Humanistic Psychology. At the 1977 annual meetings, at which 2,000 of the 6,000 members were present, about 20 percent of the workshops and presentations were devoted to politics, power, and social action. There was considerably more emphasis on social action than at the American Psychological Association meetings a week later. The theme for the 1979 AHP meeting at Princeton was: "Evolutionary Ethics: Humanistic Psychology and Social Change." The gradual shift toward social agendas stems in part from the growing awareness that personal growth is constantly undercut by environmental influences such as social competition and pollution. Some concern may also be attributed to both genuine compassion and to guilty conscience.

Many political dropouts from the 1960s are showing an increased interest in applying human potential awareness in the current political scene. An organizational manifestation of this is "Self-Determination: A Personal/Political Network." The purpose of this network is "to change ourselves *and* society . . . to promote expanded political expression of total human value through greater personal participation in social issues." The publications of this network have a New Left flavor in their analysis of how American society is dehumanizing. They differ in focusing more on legislative politics and less on indepth economic analysis. The style of groups influenced by awareness trainings is similar to that of the ecology movement. They are more likely to hold a benefit to save the whales than to support the Black Panthers. They tend to stress creative solutions based on cooperation and synergy rather than confrontation based on class interest.

Social Outreach in *est*

est has become increasingly involved in community projects, beginning with Erhard donating to educational organizations such as KQED (San Francisco's educational TV station), and Paolo Friere's grass-roots literacy and *consciencazicao* (consciousness-raising) project in Guinea-Bisseau. Encouraged by the initiative of *est* graduates to organize a holiday hospital project — in which 11,000 donated gifts and 6,000 delivered presents to patients in 207 hospitals — Erhard is inviting graduates and their friends to join him in supporting the Hunger Project to eliminate worldwide starvation within 20 years.

He sees this project to end death by starvation not as a specific program but as an alignment of intentions and commitments "to create a context to actualize an idea whose time has come." He encourages contributions not out of charity or guilty conscience, but as an opportunity to solve a problem whose persistence he considers self-demeaning and a living testament to the impotence of both the hungry and the well-fed. He also predicts that in ending starvation, people will be able "to discover the principles that are necessary to have the world work."

Such a noble undertaking is undoubtedly functional to the *est* organization. It maintains the interest of *est* alumni, involves their friends, and provides good copy for public relations. Yet there appears to be more involved than an audacious publicity gimmick. In the first year of the project, Erhard addressed 40,000 graduates and their friends, informing them about basic facts on hunger and confronting them with their own willingness to support its end. Erhard approaches consciousness-raising in an unusual way that merits careful attention. By providing a climate of excitement and positive anticipation rather than desperation or heavy obligation, many persons are attracted to the gatherings who might not otherwise pay much attention to hunger. As they learn how a number of countries have already ended starvation, using a variety of technological innovations and land reforms, they find it harder to be complacent about the inevitability of hunger.

Perhaps what is most striking is the relatively nonjudgmental atmosphere in which these sessions are conducted. Erhard avoids appealing to pity or to guilt. It appears that one of the outcomes of providing a setting that is less emotionally loaded and guilt-provoking is that participants become less defensive and more open to the ways that they may be part of the problem. Thus, some participants reported that they noticed they had prejudged the inevitability of hunger and it was not easy to give up their position on the matter. Several said they realized they would rather be right about their analysis of the problem than to have the problem solved by means that did not flow from their analysis. One graduate said he found it hard to admit that he would rather see Erhard fail than have starvation ended. But when he was willing to accept these feelings, he began to see that what he really wanted was to take part in solving the problem by using any means that worked.

As of May 1979, 350,000 pledges of personal commitment to witness the end of starvation had been gathered. A million dollars had been raised to underwrite the Hunger Project publicity and dissemination of facts on hunger and ways to become personally involved. Most of these signatures were not from *est* graduates, though most were obtained by graduates.

Some critics have debunked the Hunger Project as a ploy for favorable publicity for *est*. Others have pointed to it as evidence that *est* has a compassionate social conscience. While this hunger project cannot be simply dismissed as a public relations stunt, neither can it be celebrated as an example of magnanimous altruism. There is little dramatic sacrifice like Albert Schweitzer's or Che Guevara's to certify the purity of motive and righteousness of action. Participants in the Hunger Project talk about the satisfaction it gives them, rather than what they are doing for others. Feeling they can make a difference, they are attracted to the excitement of joining with thousands of others in ushering in an idea whose time has come. They are pleased to reclaim the energy that was previously lost in anesthetizing themselves against the knowledge of unnecessary suffering. Many claim that extending themselves to acknowledge and include others brings them a fuller sense of self. Social science lacks a concept for motives that produce service out of a sense of satisfaction.

Interpretation of Findings

In all, the survey and interview evidence does not indicate that awareness group participants are any less sensitive to social forces, less interested in improving the lot of disadvantaged people, or less individualistic than other people from similar backgrounds. Some *est* graduates seemed to have grown in social awareness, a development they attributed in part to taking the training. That the predicted self-preoccupation and social insensitivity was not supported by the evidence warrants further explanation.

In part, the predictions seem to be based on a general model of human nature and motivation that is very different from the one implied in Human Potential trainings. From the point of view of many of the critics, social responsibility is encouraged through the cultivation of "civic virtue." Civic virtue includes unselfishness, honesty, courage, sacrifice, and concern for community life. These are virtues not because they are God-given or legislated, but because they are needed to foster community and a coherent social order in which individual potential can emerge. Thus "selfish" and "socially useful" are the units of moral calculus.

Social life is seen as important for instilling these virtues. Shame and the "moral tension" of a guilty conscience are deemed necessary to motivate altruistic acts. Sacrifice is applauded. From this point of view the activities of the Human Potential movement simply reinforce self-indulgence that is already out of control in a capitalistic consumer society, and that survives by persuading people that accumulating more is better. The consumption of "experiences" becomes the successor to consumption of commodities. Awareness trainings are seen as reducing the moral tension of middle class liberals who might otherwise contribute to the common good.

Human potential culture is very different in its approach to providing for the common good. It downplays observing moral principles in favor of self-observation. Cardinal virtues are openness, awareness, and honesty rather than faith, hope, and charity. Awareness groups claim to train their participants in *enlightened self-interest*. As participants expand their notions of what supplies satisfaction and well being, their awareness of who they are is expected to expand as well. By becoming more conscious, participants are supposed to become aware of the way they present themselves socially and to experience who they "really" are underneath social roles. This true self is described as laying under the accumulation of social roles and learned responses. It is likened to a drama director who forgets who is in charge of the play and gets caught up in being an actor. While many of the experiences provided by growth groups are ego-strengthening, some of the self-centering disciplines assist in a person's identification with self rather than ego-process. As people become more aware of who they really are, it is assumed that they will experience themselves as being responsible and related to others. Participation and service then become satisfying experiences rather than moral obligations. Realizing the true or real self is the ultimate satisfaction.

Growth is considered developmental, involving both a return to the self and an outreach to others. It is assumed that as personal needs are attended to, more energy is available for participation with others. This is considered a natural process that is speeded up by awareness training. While there may be phases of inward-looking, this is not seen as promoting a narcissistic character structure, such as that described by Christopher Lasch in *The Culture of Narcissism* (1979). Abraham Maslow's theory of hierarchical needs is sometimes invoked to lend authority to the notion of an unfolding Self. But for the most part the authority for these assumptions lies not in appeals to science, but rather to the intense personal experiences that people have in the trainings.

The distinctiveness of human potential culture is especially clear in attitudes toward guilt, sacrifice, and change. A guilty conscience is considered an unreliable source of action. An action prompted by guilt is primarily intended to relieve bad feeling rather than to accomplish the deed. A guilty conscience becomes an easy alternative to facing up to what one wants and then taking the requisite action. Guilt becomes a means for social withdrawal.

Sacrifice is considered a form of manipulation rather than a gift freely given and received. The precept to sacrifice, like the admonition to love, is held to be a contradiction in terms. Sacrifice may contribute to the guilt of those who benefit, and to the resentment of those who do not feel their gift was sufficiently appreciated.

The Human Potential notion of change is perhaps even more foreign to Western ways of thinking. Change is thought to occur when striving ceases. Resistance is considered to strengthen and reify what is resisted. Paradoxically change is achieved:

- With becoming what one is, rather than trying to become what one is not.
- With blending with an opponent's energies and directing them as in karate or aikido.
- With synergy rather than with opposition or competition where someone loses.
- With avoiding moral accusations, which serve to strengthen an opponent's desire to fight.
- With being in touch with who one really is, rather than trying to help others from a sense of obligation.

These assumptions about change are derived from personal experiences in interpersonal interactions. Human Potential advocates insist that these are truths to be experienced rather than ideologies to guide action. Wanting to serve others is neither an altruistic or an egocentric ideological position: it is held to flow naturally from the experience of being in touch with one's essential self.

This perspective might be deemed "mystical." It is likely that some elements of the mystical vision, namely universality, interconnectedness, and moral relativity are shared by Human Potential participants. The Human Potential participants in the New Religious Consciousness survey reported a high incidence of peak experiences. Analyzing the same survey, Robert

Wuthnow found that people reporting mystical and peak experiences were less materialistic, less status-conscious, and more socially concerned. He found a moderately high correlation between mysticism and political activism scales. Moral relativism can be a lever for reforming a nonrelativistic status quo, and the experience of universal interconnectedness can be a template for bridging separation in the mundane world.

Mystics hold that their visions are not reducible to words, much less to ideologies. Likewise, Human Potential advocates insist that they are not creating alternative ideology, but rather new awareness. Yet participants often use the assumptions outlined here as ideological statements, and these are sometimes used to rationalize the status quo or to demonstrate superiority over the unenlightened.

Even if service naturally flows from knowing who one really is — and knowing this is no obvious matter — it is not clear that this service will be applied to transformation at the institutional and societal level. Whether the Human Potential movement will significantly contribute to creating a more humane society remains to be seen.

References

Earle, Mary, n.d.
Jacoby, Russell, 1976
Lasch, Christopher 1976, 1979
Lerner, Michael P., n.d.
Marin, Peter, 1975
Nord, Walter, 1977
Ogilvy, Jay, 1978
Rosen, R.D., 1977
Satin, Mark, 1978
Schur, Edwin, 1976
Stone, Donald, 1976, 1978
Wolfe, Tom, 1976
Wuthnow, Robert, 1976b, 1978b

Political Aspects of the Quietistic Revival

Robert Wuthnow

One of the assumptions in many popular discussions of the new religious movements is that they have "siphoned off" the political energies and interests of American young people. The religious experimentation of the 1970s, in contrast to the political activism of the 1960s, has been characterized as narcissistic, apathetic, irresponsible—as the most visible symptom of what has been called "the Me Generation." For example, the Harvard sociologist Daniel Bell, in describing the contributions of Norman O. Brown, R. D. Laing, and other spokesmen for what he calls the postmodern mood of the 1970s, stated:

> What is the meaning of all this? It is a program to erase all boundaries, to obliterate any distinction between the self and the external world, between man and woman, subject and object, mind and body. The boundary line between self and external world bears no relation to reality. . . . Separateness, then, is the fall—the fall into division, the original lie. . . .To give up boundaries is to give up the reality principle [which] is a false boundary, drawn between inside and outside, subject and object; real and imaginary; physical and mental (1977, p. 243).

Elsewhere, writing specifically of the new religions, he remarks that "the difficulty with the new cults is that while their impulses are religious, in that they seek for some new meaning of the sacred, their rites are still largely ones of release'' (1976, p. 170). Thus, the problem with the new religions is that they have championed the self and expression of its inner impulses to the expense of social responsibility and commitment to the public interest.

There is, of course, considerable precedent in the literature of social science for assuming what might be called a ''hydraulic'' relation between experiential religion and political commitment. Max Weber (1963) and his disciple, Ernst Troeltsch (1960), outlined a number of reasons for believing that the more mystical a person is, the less involved in political activity he is likely to be. For example, the mystic's chief concern — his avenue of salvation — is quiet contemplation. This stands in marked contrast to the dutiful this-worldly activity of the ascetic Calvinist. For another, the mystic, according to Weber, tends to be too idealistic and too universally loving to have his hands sullied by the practical affairs, compromises, and applications of force that are inherent in political life. Others have suggested that the mystic resigns himself to the status quo, regarding the world as tertiary and unworthy of efforts at improvement, or else he assumes such a completely antinomian posture that all activities aimed at reforming the body politic become disorganized and fall into disarray (see Adler, 1972).

For whatever reasons, it is probably safe to say that most contemporary social scientists have assumed that mystical religion reinforces withdrawal from political involvement and, thereby, promotes either tacit or avowed acceptance of social conditions as they are. And, with the religious movements of the 1970s following closely on the heels of the political activism of the 1960s, it has been easy to argue that this assumption has been vividly confirmed. Yet, it is not true that there has been confirmation of an empirical sort. Indeed, most of the speculation about the new religious movements has gone on in the absence of any systematic data.

The purpose of this paper is to summarize the findings of an empirical study that, among other things, sought to obtain data on mystical religious orientations and to examine the relations between these orientations and political attitudes. This paper (a) discusses the political attitudes and commitments of persons attracted to various new religious movements; (b) reviews evidence on some of the specific ideological links between mysticism and political action; (c) examines the hypothesis that political activists became absorbed by the new religions; and (d) speculates about some of the broader implications of these findings.

Data and Methods

The data on which this paper is based were collected in 1973 under the auspices of a grant from the Institute for Religion and Social Change to Charles Y. Glock and Robert N. Bellah at the University of California at Berkeley to study new religious consciousness. In addition to a series of ethnographic studies of particular religious groups, the grant called for a survey of the larger community to assess changes in religious consciousness that might be occurring among persons not involved in particular groups. Personal interviews were conducted with 1,000 randomly selected adult residents of the San Francisco-Oakland Standard Metropolitan Statistical Area (excluding Marin county). In order to better study those portions of the population in which changes in religious consciousness might be most concentrated, young people (ages 16 to 30) were oversampled at a ratio of approximately two to one, relative to their actual distribution in the population. For present purposes, a weighting factor has been applied to make the data representative of the actual Bay Area population. Further details on the sample and a copy of the interview schedule have been published in Wuthnow (1976a). For more details on the larger project, see Glock and Bellah (1976).

The San Francisco Bay Area was selected as the locus of the study, not because it was thought to be representative of any larger population, but because many of the new religious movements in which we were interested had either begun in the Bay Area or had gained substantial followings there. For example, the survey showed that one out of every four young people in the sample had taken part in at least one new religious movement (Wuthnow, 1976b). More generally, the Bay Area had been a leading center of the countercultural unrest of the late 1960s and early 1970s. Thus, it afforded an appropriate laboratory in which to examine social experimentation and change. Caution should be exercised, of course, in generalizing any of the present findings to other areas.

In addition to the Bay Area survey, some data are also drawn from a sample of students at the University of California at Berkeley. These data were collected as part of a larger study of the effects of alternative life styles on career orientations that was conducted by the Institute for Research in Social Behavior at Berkeley, and that was graciously made available by its principal investigators—Dean Manheimer, Glen Mellinger, and Robert Somers. Although these data contained only a few questions about religion, they are of special value for examining, at least in a crude sense, shifts in the direction of religious and political commitments because they were collected at two points in time. Nearly 1000 freshmen male students were interviewed in the fall of 1970 and then sent follow-up questionnaires in the spring of 1973. In addition, nearly 1000 male seniors were interviewed in the spring of 1971 and were later sent follow-up questionnaires in the fall of 1973. In combination, therefore, these data afford a glimpse at changes both among college students and college graduates during the critical period in the early 1970s when student activism was declining, and the new religious movements were gaining ascendancy. Again, it is impossible to generalize from these data. The fact that political and religious experimentation were especially prominent on the Berkeley campus, however, provides a fortuitous opportunity to examine the relations among these forms of experimentation. A preliminary report on these relations, based on the first wave of data, was presented in Wuthnow and Glock, 1973, and an examination of religious changes between the two time periods has been presented in Wuthnow and Mellinger, 1978.

Political Attitudes and Attraction to New Religious Movements

As part of our attempt to assess new forms of religious consciousness in the Bay Area, a battery of items was included in the Bay Area survey that asked respondents whether or not they had ever heard of and participated in a variety of new religious movements, and, for each movement they had heard of, whether they were attracted or "turned off" by the group. Among the movements asked about, four were of Asian origin (Transcendental Meditation, Zen Buddhism, Hare Krishna, and Yoga); two were of neo-Christian origin (Children of God and the Christian World Liberation Front of Berkeley); and two were quasi-religious movements of the "human-potential" kind (Scientology and Synanon).[1] In a random sample of this sort, too few people had actually taken part in any one of these groups to make feasible comparisons of their political orientations. As it turned out, however, enough people had heard of and were favorably disposed toward each group so that comparisons can be made of the larger constituencies of people attracted to these movements (for evidence on these frequencies, see Wuthnow, 1976b; and Glock and Wuthnow, 1979). Of course, these comparisons are limited because they are not based on actual participants, but in the absence of better data, they at least afford a crude means of examining the political orientations of people attracted to the new religions.

Judging from ethnographic comparisons of these religious movements and from other examinations of their constituencies in the Bay Area sample, we would judge that the groups of Asian origin are the most oriented toward mystical experiences and introspective values; that the neo-Christian groups are least oriented toward these kinds of experiences; and that the human potential groups fall in the middle of these two extremes (cf. Needleman, 1970; Glock and Bellah, 1976; Anthony and Robbins, 1979; Tipton, 1979; and Wuthnow, 1976b). If mysticism is incompatible with political action, we would, therefore, expect people attracted to the Asian groups to be less politically committed than people attracted to the other groups.

Table 13.1 shows the relations between attraction to each of the new religious movements surveyed and the main political items included in the Bay Area survey. The first row shows the percentages of those attracted to each group and of the total sample who said that "working for major changes in our society" was of "great importance" to them. The second row gives the percentages who indicated that "helping solve social problems such as poverty and air pollution" was of "great importance" to them. The third row shows the percentages who stated they had ever taken part in demonstrations or marches. The fourth row lists the percentages who indicated that we need either "a major overhaul in our form of government" or "a completely different system." The fifth row gives the percentages who agreed with a statement that suggested that "the poor are poor because the wealthy and powerful keep them poor." The sixth row shows the percentages who scored themselves as "liberal" or "radical" on a nine-point political continuum ranging from radical to very conservative. The seventh row lists the percentages who responded to a "story-type" question—about a revolutionary who was trying to overthrow the government but who hadn't broken any laws—that either "she should be treated like anyone else since she hasn't broken any laws" or "personally, I'm in favor of what she's trying to do, even if she does break a few laws." The eighth row shows the percentages who said that "helping women to get equal rights" was of "great importance" to them. And the last row indicates the percentages who responded to a question about what the country should do about poverty by saying that "more jobs should be provided and the country should also guarantee a minimum income for everyone." In combination, the items, therefore, illustrate various indications of how socially and politically-oriented—especially in liberal and radical directions, such as those characteristic of student activists of the late 1960s (e.g., Lipset, 1972)—people attracted to the various religious movements are.

What the data reveal is that people attracted to the more mystical religious movements are *not* less politically committed than other people in the Bay Area. Indeed, according to these measures, they tend to be more committed. People attracted to Transcendental Meditation (TM), for example, show higher percentages than in the total sample on all these items. On the average, the percentages are 15 points higher in the TM column than in the total-sample column. People attracted to Zen and to Yoga also show higher percentages than in the total sample (16 points and 10 points higher than the average, respectively).

On seven of the nine items, the percentages for people attracted to Hare Krishna are also higher than those for the total sample. As far as Scientology and Synanon are concerned, eight of the nine percentages in each case are again higher than in the total sample, although the differences are not as great as they are for TM, Zen, and Yoga. Only among the two neo-Christian groups, which were judged to be probably the least mystical of the groups, are the percentages approximately equivalent to those for the total sample: five of the figures for the Christian World Liberation Front (CWLF) are higher, two are the same, and two are lower. For the Children of God, two are higher, two are the same, and five are lower.

It is risky to infer very much from these figures because it isn't clear whether or not people who are attracted to these movements are actually committed to

TABLE 13.1
Political Items by Attraction to Religious Movements

	TM	Zen	Yoga	Hare Krishna	Scientology	Synanon	CWLF	Children of God	Total Sample
Value working for change	38%	39%	33%	30%	44%	32%	28%	25%	28%
Solve social problems	40%	41%	38%	30%	32%	39%	44%	33%	36%
Have demonstrated	43%	46%	32%	24%	24%	23%	18%	14%	17%
Overhaul government	64%	63%	58%	58%	62%	52%	47%	48%	48%
Powerful cause poverty	70%	64%	70%	69%	69%	57%	77%	63%	59%
Politically liberal	70%	63%	62%	48%	45%	48%	42%	29%	35%
Tolerate revolutionary	78%	78%	64%	69%	70%	67%	57%	56%	57%
Equal rights for women	26%	27%	20%	14%	20%	18%	11%	15%	15%
Guaranteed annual wage	50%	51%	43%	39%	38%	40%	55%	52%	36%
Number =	(99)	(90)	(170)	(41)	(42)	(49)	(24)	(28)	(1000)

what they teach in any significant way. Nor is it clear whether or not these political items are indicative of behavior or only of attitudes. Furthermore, there may be other differences, such as age or education, that would account for the seeming tendency of the more mystically inclined to be more politically committed. On the whole, however, the evidence in Table 13.1 seems to be more damaging than supportive to the idea that mysticism and politics are incompatible. It may be worth noting also that these findings are similar to those of several previous studies of new religious consciousness (Wuthnow, 1973; Wuthnow and Glock, 1974).

The Nexus Between Mysticism and Political Action

If there is some basis for assuming that mysticism and political action may have been positively related during the early 1970s, as the data in Table 13.1 suggest, then some consideration seems warranted about what the cognitive elements linking the two might be. It was not anticipated in our research design that there would be a positive relation between mysticism and political action. Accordingly, no attempt was made to build into the design a means for exploring this relation. On the basis of the questions that were asked, however, some exploration did become possible.

One of the things that was discovered in examining some of the literature on mysticism — in order to have a sense of what might make it conducive to political action, if indeed it was conducive—was that mysticism, perhaps like any religious belief system, appears to combine a number of attitudes and values that, at least on the surface, do not always seem consistent. For example, despite the fact that mysticism tends to be oriented toward the individual and his inward experiences, as Weber and Troeltsch stressed, it also seems to generate awareness of larger social conditions. One of the ways in which it does so is by "unmasking" ordinary social perceptions in the mystical experience. As Carlos Castaneda (1972) has characterized it, one "stops the world" and sees it in a different way. Also, mystics seem to have a relativistic or at least a tolerant view of the ways in which others pursue salvation, even though they themselves pursue it through contemplation. Or, as Anthony and Robbins (1979) have expressed it, mysticism tends to be "monistic," and this militates against dualistic distinctions between the saved and the damned. This orientation could conceivably affect the way mystics respond to political matters as well — perhaps making them more supportive of the rights of people to choose their own life styles. Or, to take still another example, even though mystics may feel apart from the world, they still have to live in it, as Weber recognized. They may feel inclined, as a result, to make improvements in the social world. In short, the point is simply that there may be elements within the mystical world view that have not been particularly emphasized in the social-science literature;

that indeed may appear contradictory to those that have been; but that could surface and have political implications if the conditions were right.

Two components of the mystical world view, in particular, of which the data did afford some exploration, were what I have referred to elsewhere (Wuthnow, 1978) as "moral relativism" and "liberalism." If mystics are indeed monistic and, therefore, relativistic with regard to moral distinctions between right and wrong, they may, given the proper occasion, feel compelled to speak out against bigotry, authoritarianism, discrimination, and other social conditions that fail to exemplify this relativistic spirit. And one of the ways in which they speak out may be through political activities. If mystics tend to be morally relativistic, and if they tend to be aware of the constricting nature of social reality—compared with their more idealistic conceptions of reality as mystically experienced—they may also be inclined toward liberal political views that would approve of measures aimed at changing or reforming the present political and social arrangements. Under the proper circumstances, they might feel compelled to act out these liberal inclinations by engaging in political action.

This, of course, is all conjecture. The reason for mentioning it, however, is that there does seem to be some support in the Bay Area data for these arguments. This evidence is reproduced in Fig. 13.1. All the variables shown are scales that were constructed through the use of factor analysis (see

FIGURE 13.1
Path Model for Mysticism, Moral Relativism, Liberalism, and Political Activism

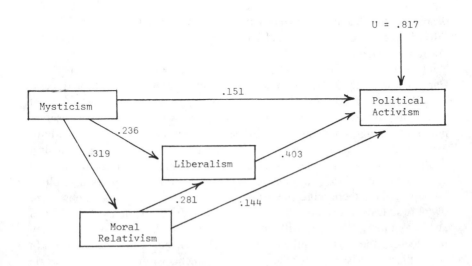

Source: Wuthnow (1978)

Wuthnow, 1978). The mysticism scale consists of items having to do with experiencing harmony with the universe, experiencing the beauty of nature, valuing getting to know the inner self, attraction to Asian religious movements, body awareness, and meditation. The items contributing most to the moral-relativism scale are ones that inquired about approval or disapproval of cohabitation, legalization of marijuana, homosexuality, and communal living. The main item on the liberalism scale is the nine-point political continuum question mentioned earlier. The chief items on the political-action scale are those that asked about attendance at political meetings and letters written to political officials. What the figure shows is that there are, in fact, positive relations between mysticism, moral relativism, liberalism, and political action. The causal ordering of the variables in the table is, of course, arbitrary, since the data are cross-sectional. The purpose of ordering the variables in this manner is to show what the effect is of hypothesizing that moral relativism and liberalism are intervening links between mysticism and political action. The effect is that about half of the overall relationship between mysticism and political action can be explained as a function of moral relativism and liberalism.

The other piece of evidence worth reproducing here is that which is shown in Table 13.2. We suggested earlier that the seemingly positive relation between mysticism and political items in the data might actually be spurious. This is especially true since other analysis has shown that mystically inclined people in the Bay Area tend to be younger, better educated, and from more liberal backgrounds than other respondents (Wuthnow, 1976a, 1976b). Table 13.2 shows the relations between the mysticism scale (as used in Figure 13.1) and the chief political items discussed thus far. It shows both the correlations, without any control variables applied, and the correlations with age, education, and father's political orientation controlled. In every instance except one, the correlations remain significant with these controls applied. In all cases they are positive correlations, ranging from .107 to .269.

This evidence on the whole is quite limited, of course, since the items used to construct the scales can be questioned. At least their validity must remain open to question because the data were collected at only one point in time. At a minimum, the data suggest that the positive relation observed in the foregoing section between attraction to mystical religious movements and political-activist attitudes is probably not spurious. It may also make sense in terms of some of the orientations that are inherent in the mystical world view itself, such as relativism and liberalism. The political climate of the late 1960s and early 1970s appears to have been conducive to the surfacing of these orientations, which allowed persons attracted to the new mystical religions to engage also in political activism. As such, the data seem to contradict the idea of a simple hydraulic relation between mysticism and politics. What these data fail to address, however, is the possibility that mysticism—although perhaps correlated with political activism at some point in the late 1960s or early 1970s—may

TABLE 13.2
Mysticism and Political Items
(Bay Area Data, N = 1,000)

	Correlations with mysticism scale	Correlations controlling for age, education and father's politics
Demonstrated	.297	.228
Written to officials	.150	.078*
Attended meetings	.255	.175
Radical or liberal	.274	.209
Support revolutionaries	.219	.168
Change government	.187	.167
Guaranteed wage	.135	.107
Value social change	.242	.209
Help solve social problems	.207	.183
Liberalism (Factor I)	.326	.269
Social concern (Factor II)	.224	.200
Activism (Factor III)	.332	.242

*Significance level = .01, all others = .001

Source: Wuthnow (1978)

indeed have siphoned off the energy of this political activism into more quietistic directions.

What Happened to the Student Activists?

The data that were collected from Berkeley students in 1970–71 and again in 1973 provide a means of determining how much of a shift there may have been away from political activism toward mystical religious movements in the early 1970s. The Berkeley campus had been a hotbed of political activism in the late 1960s and early 1970s. Thus, the data contained a sizable number of student activists whose religious orientations could be examined three years after the initial data were collected. It should be noted that when the first wave of data was collected, there was a positive relation between mysticism and political activism, just as we have seen in the Bay Area data. For example, among seniors who had grown up in Christian homes but who now identified themselves with one of the new Eastern or mystical religions, 81 percent listed their politics as "radical," and they said they had taken part in campus demonstrations. By comparison, only 23 percent of those who were still members of Christian denominations fell into this radical activist category (Wuthnow and Glock, 1973). The data do *not* suggest, however, that student activists turned to mystical religions in any sizable proportion between 1970–71 and 1973 (see Table 13.3). Of the 162 freshmen who said they had been in campus demonstrations when they were interviewed in 1970, only seven percent listed their religious beliefs as Eastern or mystical in 1973. Similarly, among the 331 seniors who indicated they approved of "nonviolent confrontations" in 1971, only 17 percent identified themselves as Eastern or mystical in 1973. By far, the largest proportion of both groups (78 percent and 67 percent, respectively) identified themselves in 1973 as having no religious beliefs. Strictly speaking, therefore, it would be inaccurate to assert that mysticism siphoned off student activism, at least in these data, because only a small minority of the student activists became actually identified with mysticism.

TABLE 13.3
Religious Preferences of Student Activists
(Berkeley Students)

	Students who had been in campus demonstrations as freshmen	Students who had approved of protests as seniors
Religious preference three years later:		
Mystical	7%	17%
Christian	15	16
Nonreligious	78	67
Number =	(162)	(331)

It should be noted that the percentages of student activists identifying themselves as Eastern or mystical in Table 13.3 are, in fact, larger than those in the total student samples: five percent of the total freshman cohort and four percent of the senior cohort listed their religious beliefs as Eastern or mystical in 1973 (Wuthnow and Mellinger, 1978). This is not surprising, because more of the student activists were already Eastern or mystically inclined when the first wave of data was collected. The important point is that there seems to be no evidence that mysticism came to serve as a substitute in any significant sense for political activities when the student activism of the early 1970s began to decline.

In summary, it seems highly likely that the political unrest of the late 1960s and early 1970s was conducive to defection from conventional religion and thus to experimentation with alternative forms of religion, including mystical religion (see Wuthnow, 1978). For a time, the two seem to have gone hand in hand. It has become evident also that many of the new religious movements that were born in the late 1960s and early 1970s have survived and prospered, even as political activism has virtually ceased. To assume that the new religions were responsible for sapping away the political energies of student activism does not appear to be a persuasive argument, however, in light of the fact that such small percentages of student activists—at least in the Berkeley samples—actually turned to mysticism. It would appear more accurate to assert simply that the new religions outlived the campus turmoil from which they initially grew.

Commentary

Caution should be exercised in generalizing from these results. In the early 1970s, when the Bay Area data were collected, confrontational politics lingered fresh in people's minds and, for many, in their experience as well. Cynicism and alienation were being fed by Watergate. In religion, it remained unclear how long defection from the churches would continue and to what extent experimentation with alternative religions would grow. Still, the picture one receives from these data gives pause to the conventional wisdom that has held that experiential religion and political involvement are necessarily contradictory. It may be useful, therefore, to comment briefly on several of the ways in which the relationship between mysticism and politics might be reconceptualized in future research.

Mysticism as shortcut to modernity. The correlates of mysticism that we have witnessed in the Bay Area—relativism, liberalism, political action—bear a striking resemblance to the traits that have been identified in other contexts as characteristics of modernity (e.g., Inkeles and Smith, 1974; Berger et al. 1973). This resemblance has been obscured by such a writer as Daniel Bell who has pictured mysticism as a profound threat to the ideals of modernity.[2] Yet the very fact that Bell and other thoroughgoing modernists have protested so loudly arouses suspicion. The possibility seems worth entertaining that mysticism, far from being contradictory to modernity, has become a shortcut to it. According to the testimony of many who have participated in some of the new religious movements, the experience of mystical or altered states of consciousness has elevated their sense of individual freedom and responsibility, heightened their awareness of the relativity of values, and evoked new social and political sensitivities (see especially Tipton, 1979). For young people who have found themselves suddenly incorporated into the mainstream of modern American culture, mysticism may have become a quick and relatively painless means of developing a new identity at the personal level that squares well with the larger values to which they are exposed through education and the marketplace. If this is the case—and the issue must await further research to be resolved—then perhaps the greatest irony of all is that the traditional religions of Asia have become one of the newest techniques for making Americans modern.

Mysticism as ritual release. Another clue to reconceptualizing the relationship between mysticism and politics comes in recognizing that the character of mystical commitment is markedly different now than it was in the societies in which Weber and others based their observations. Harvey Cox (1977, p. 65) has recently observed that meditation is like a "miniature Sabbath," a time-out that can be squeezed in amidst the complexity of everyday life. Thus, unlike its more demanding medieval counterparts, contemporary mysticism need be no more inimical to political action or other social involvements than the morning coffee break. It may be even functional to such involvements, insofar as it provides needed rest from the daily schedule. The specific effect of mysticism on politics, therefore, would probably vary from individual to individual.

Mysticism as antidote to narcissism. Since mysticism has been accused so frequently of narcissism (e.g., Malcolm, 1971), it is perhaps worth noting an argument to the contrary that probably has been articulated most clearly by Abraham Maslow (1962, 1970). According to Maslow, mystical or "peak" experiences overcome narcissism. They do so by instilling a sense of self-worth — contentment, confidence, esteem — that allows the individual to stop worrying about himself and to begin being concerned about the needs of other people. Some empirical evidence, in fact, tends to support Maslow's claim (see Wuthnow, 1978). As far as politics are concerned, therefore, mysticism may encourage political involvement as a means of helping other people.

Mysticism and inner direction. The nature of contemporary politics also affords an insight that needs to be taken into account in further studies of its relationship to experiential religion. The character of recent political campaigns indicates that party politics may gradually be declining relative to what some journalists have begun to call "issue politics." More generally, it appears that political issues fail increasingly to resolve themselves along clear ideological lines, but that they have to be decided on a case-by-case basis among a variety of conflicting alternatives. This, together with the growing popularity of plebescitary referenda, imposes strong ethical responsibilities on the average citizen. As in the occupational sphere, there is developing what might be termed "the professionalization of the citizen." Faced with ethical responsibilities of this sort, political actors require an increasing level of inner direction, an ability to make autonomous ethical judgments. To the extent that experiential religion provides a source of inner strength and resolve (what Nikos Kazanzakis once described as a "mystic whirling center"), it may, therefore, contribute valuably to the political process.[3]

The pillarization of mysticism. While it is true that much of the effect of mysticism on politics is likely to be determined by the manner in which the average citizen relates his religious experiences to his political convictions at a purely individual level, it is also true that mysticism has been the basis of new religious communities that are likely to continue as a feature of American life. It seems doubtful that these communities can attract more than a small fraction of the American population. There is evidence, however, that many of them have been undergoing a process—similar to what European sociologists of religion have called "pillarization" (e.g., Thung, 1976; Dobbelaere, 1977) — of solidifying their claims upon current members by encompassing greater areas of their lives. This move has been manifested by expansion into new areas of service, education, publishing, business, and even politics. Thus, the religious devotee can begin to live a kind of cradle-to-the-grave existence within the orbit of the religious community. Mysticism ceases to be a purely personal experience, and it functions as the basis of an institutionalized subculture or network of subcultures. And, although the political content of these subcultures varies widely, for example, from the anticommunism of the Unification church to the utopian socialism of some of the smaller communal sects, they become a potential political force, as have other religious subcultures in the past. As minority enclaves, they afford a voice through which political dissent can be expressed. Whether or not it is in fact expressed, depends, of course, on a variety of other social conditions. Still, the potential of mystical subcultures becoming such a voice should not be ignored in discussions about the political aspects of contemporary mysticism.

In conclusion, it bears repeating that these comments are intended only as suggestions about ways in which the study of mysticism, as it relates to the political sphere, might be advanced beyond the traditional stereotypes with which social scientists have tended to work. The research that has been made possible by the new religions of the 1970s has done much to challenge these stereotypes. With the spread of experiential emphases into other areas of religion, in the so-called "evangelical movement," for example, it seems safe to predict that new complexities in the nexus between religion and politics will continue to be observed.

Notes

1. Several other groups were also asked about, but they are omitted from the present discussion because they were not "new" religious movements of the kind under consideration here, or were not widely enough known to afford statistical comparisons.
2. The similarities between mysticism and modernity, of course, have been overlooked also by writers such as Theodore Roszak (1969) and R. D. Laing (1967) who have championed mysticism against modernity.
3. Much has been said, of course, in the popular press about this possibility with respect to both President Jimmy Carter and Governor Jerry Brown.

References

Adler, N., 1972
Anthony, D., and T. Robbins, unpublished paper, 1979
Bell, D., 1976, 1977
Berger, Peter, B. Berger, and H. Kellner, 1973
Castaneda, C., 1972
Cox, H., 1977
Dobbelaere, K., 1977
Glock, Charles Y., and Robert N. Bellah, 1976
Glock, Charles Y., and Robert Wuthnow, 1979
Inkeles, A., and D.H. Smith, 1974
Laing, R. D., 1967
Lipset, S. M., 1972
Malcolm, G., 1971
Maslow, A., 1962, 1970
Needleman, J., 1970
Roszak, T., 1969
Thung, M., 1976
Tipton, S., 1979
Troeltsch, E., 1960
Weber, M., 1963
Wuthnow, Robert, 1973, 1976a, 1976b, 1978a, 1978b
Wuthnow, Robert, and Charles Y. Glock, 1973, 1974
Wuthnow, Robert, and G. Mellinger, 1978

The Brainwashing Explanation

Witches, Moonies, and Accusations of Evil

Anson D. Shupe, Jr. and David G. Bromley[1]

As sociologist Andrew Greeley observed in his recent book, *Unsecular Man* (1972), and as others have since reaffirmed, the 1970s have not witnessed the continuation of the secularization process projected by observers during the 1960s. On the contrary, the current decade has been one of widespread religious ferment. Estimates given in the media of evangelical participation alone range as high as 30 to 40 million Americans. An NBC newscast recently reported, on the basis of a national opinion poll, that one out of every three Americans was "born again" and returning to fundamentalist Christianity. A number of public figures—from Charles Colson to Eldridge Cleaver to Larry Flynt—have been among the converts, and this has served to dramatize the influence of the movement.

Alongside this resurgence of conventional Judaeo-Christian religious activity, there has been a proliferation of marginal or "new" religious groups such as the Unification church, Children of God, Hare Krishna, Divine Light Mission, Scientology, and numerous other groups that are less well known. While these new, marginal religious groups include only a fraction of the number of Americans who are born-again Christians, such groups have commanded as much if not more public attention and concern. Much of this

247

negative publicity can be traced to the loosely organized but highly vocal members of a conservative countermovement that has been christened also the anticult or "deprogramming" movement. Deprogramming refers, in its coercive extreme, to the abduction and restraint of marginal religious group members for the purpose of pressuring them to recant their new faiths. The members of this countermovement — most of whom are disgruntled former members or relatives of members of these marginal religions—have charged that these groups gain converts through the use of coercive, manipulative mind-control techniques.

The spectacular charges of Svengalian brainwashing methods used by these groups create the impression that they constitute a rare social aberration. However, even a cursory examination of American history reveals that marginal religious groups have always existed in substantial numbers. For a variety of reasons, these groups sometimes become more visible and are regarded as threats to the conventional order. When the members of heterodox society perceive them to be a clear and present danger to cherished values, there follows a tendency to attach to them beliefs and powers that, in whatever the contemporary terms of the culture, constitute evil. From the perceived danger, therefore, has arisen a process of locating, identifying, and neutralizing that evil.

It is our contention that, irrespective of the era or culture in which it is undertaken, this process of locating, identifying, and neutralizing evil manifests remarkable continuities. The purpose of this paper is to describe some of the common properties of sprees of accusations of possession by evil forces, utilizing examples drawn from the contemporary American deprogramming movement and the British-American witchcraft prosecutions of the seventeenth century.

Evil and the Breach of Reciprocity

Outbreaks of accusations of evil possession tend to occur when there is a weakening in traditional norms of reciprocity. Evidence of such attenuations may be found both in parent-youth relationships in the 1970s and in interpersonal relationships among members of seventeenth-century colonial American communities. In the last five years, a small but visible minority of idealistic American young people have joined marginal religious groups. These groups pose, at least rhetorically, a direct threat to traditional cultural values. Their youthful converts openly condemn conventional religion as sterile and devoid of purpose, and they espouse values and lifestyles that, if institutionalized, would radically restructure American familial, religious, economic, and political institutions.

At a primary group level, the members' intense involvement and apparently permanent commitment to these religions constitute breaches of reciprocity between themselves and their families. Parents usually assume that their role in the nurturance and socialization of their children will ensure considerable intergenerational continuities in values and lifestyles. Indeed, parents often make substantial sacrifices in order to maximize educational and career opportunities for their children. As the need has increased for individuals to attain ever higher levels of education to ensure career mobility, so has the period in which parents feel obligated to offer various forms of support to their offspring. As this period of support-dependency has lengthened, the traditional transition points between adolescence and adulthood have become less clearly defined. Rights and responsibilities of both parents and their adult offspring have therefore become more difficult to define. As a result, when the children reject parental values, which renders such sacrifices meaningless and takes their children's lives in directions that they had never anticipated, feelings of shock, confusion, and eventually anger are produced. These feelings are followed soon by a suspicion that the cause of such abrupt discontinuities must be sought elsewhere.

The logical targets of their suspicions are the leaders of the marginal groups. Many outraged parents have concluded that the estrangement of their sons and daughters has unscrupulous, manipulative practices by designing cult leaders as its source. Members of the cults are thought to have knowledge about coercive psychological techniques that are variously called mind control or brainwashing. It is through the use of these little-understood processes that can have only destructive consequences for the individual that otherwise normal, healthy individuals are rendered psychological captives and become fanatical devotees.

Parents have received reinforcement from other guardians of traditional values for the view that cults have fundamentally evil purposes. For example, the National Council of Churches in New York City recently denied membership to Sun Myung Moon's Unification church. New York City officials refused permission to the Unification church to solicit funds within the city, and testimony, such as the following by Rabbi Maurice Davis to a national hearing chaired by Senator Robert Dole, has been widely reprinted:

> Senator Dole, the last time I ever witnessed a movement that was totally monolithic, that was replete with fanatical followers prepared to do anything, that hated everyone outside and fostered suspicions of parents —the last time I saw this was the Nazi youth movement, and I tell you, I'm scared (CEFM, 1976, Vol. 1, p. 40).

During the colonial period of the late seventeenth century, there was also a weakening of the traditional social order. As Joyce Bednarski, in "Salem Witch-scare Viewed Sociologically" (1970, p. 160), observed: "The men of the Bay had lost their purpose and, in doing so, had lost their way." The period was one of some instability because there was uncertainty about the Massachusetts Bay Colony's political autonomy in the 1690s due to vicissitudes in British home government, the expansion of suffrage to property-owning members of Christian sects other than Puritans, and secularization, following the colony's growth and victory over the hostile wilderness. These factors contributed to a loss of mission among the colonists. In general, the emerging cosmopolitan atmosphere of the successful eastern seaboard settlements became a threat to those who still adhered to the original sectarian perspectives of colonial community founders.

At the local community level, one consequence of the transition from folk societies to more impersonal, contract-oriented urban communities was that many community members found that traditional bases of reciprocity were no longer honored. What would seem to modern observers to be slights — job dismissal; refusal of refreshment upon request; denial of small loans of tools, money, or animals; or refusal to repay previously granted favors — were sufficient bases for accusations of witchcraft. Such interpersonal misunderstandings led to the imputation of ill will, and if one of the parties experienced unexplained misfortunes, such events were attributed to the witchcraft of the other. Individuals who were thought to be witches or warlocks were believed to have consorted with Lucifer—the personification of evil—in order to gain the powers they now utilized for their own vindictive purposes.

Data

In order to describe the principal characteristics of the process of accusation of evil possession, we have selected two examples in American history that are obviously remote in time and unrelated historically to one another—the current anticult movement in North America and the witchcraft prosecutions in the New England colonies (using also similar English data) in the late seventeenth century. Our data are drawn from a number of contemporary and historical sources. These include interviews and conversations conducted over the past 15 months with leaders and activists of the American anticult movement, their literature, and press reports of their activities—particularly those aimed against the Unification church—and historical accounts of the Salem witchcraft trials and those in Great Britain as related by both modern analysts and seventeenth-century observers, such as Cotton Mather.

Before presenting these parallels, we offer one caveat. While seventeenth-century interpretations of witchcraft trials seem amusingly archaic when viewed from the behavioral science framework of twentieth-century American culture, the claims of the current anticult movement have not been dismissed so easily. There is intense interest among many Americans about the validity of claims that many marginal religious groups brainwash recruits or use other subtle underhanded tactics to obtain members. Since much of the "evidence" comes from the testimony of apostates of these groups—prompted as they often have been to describe negative aspects of their experiences—or from observers who little appreciate the religious subcultural context of what they see, the "truth" or "falsity" of these claims cannot be substantiated. Moreover, truth and falsity are unimportant in one crucial sense. As is well known to students of symbolic interaction theory, what people perceive to be real will have real consequences for their behavior. Deprogramming is just as real a phenomenon in current American religion as witchcraft prosecutions once were, regardless of the validity of the evidence supporting the claims legitimating their use.

We shall discuss this process in terms of six dimensions: (1) the *location* or source of the evil; (2) the *vulnerability* of those individuals who become afflicted with the evil; (3) the *antisocial* purposes of those accused of promoting the evil; (4) the methods of *identifying* this evil as it appears in individuals; (5) how individuals become *transformed* by the evil; and (6) how the evil may be *neutralized*.

Location

When exchanges among persons inexplicably but unmistakably "go wrong," and when the problem occurs on a broad enough scale, there seems to emerge a need to account for these extraordinary breaches of conventional reciprocity. Frequently the search leads to postulating extraordinary causes, involving concepts of social good and social evil.

Every age possesses its own paradigm that incorporates ideas of evil. In the sectarian colonies of seventeenth-century America, the predominant paradigm was still characterized by other-worldly theological assumptions. Evil was ultimately located in Satan and other demonic forces. In modern American culture, social evil is interpreted within a this-worldly behavioral-science paradigm that does not directly refer to demons or infernal possession. Rather, behavior that is interpreted as pathological is attributed to breakdowns in social or personality structures.

In either case, individual persons may on rare occasions be afflicted by evil. Under the theological paradigm, individuals were believed to be literally and physically possessed by a demonic force that shaped their behavior to suit its purposes. Thereupon the individual was defined as a heretic. Using the behavioral-science paradigm, an analagous process has been claimed in which there is social and psychological manipulation of the individual that renders the person compliant to a manipulator. Such a condition is frequently referred to as mind-control, and the individual is regarded as a psychological captive.

Thus evil is allegedly introduced by some rarely encountered source in the routine of daily life. It is knowable but not commonly known or experienced. It is powerful, almost *preternatural* — not *of* the ordinary order of things but operating *within* that order.

For example, when modern individuals join marginal religious movements, spokespersons for the countermovement have charged that the conversions of these persons result not from true commitment but rather from coercive or deceptive mind-control techniques, as the following three representative newspaper quotations illustrate:

> I think I was hypnotized at first. Basically by the girl that met me because she kept staring into my eyes and I kept being attracted to her eyes. Then during the meal, it's very possible for some sort of a drug to make me more susceptible to the lecture. Then after that it was brainwashing because I was hooked. I wanted to stay there; I wanted to learn what they had to say. There was repetition all the time.

> Once they join the cult, these young people undergo a sophisticated form of mind control that alienates them from their families, their education, previous religious beliefs, this society and its value system, and ultimately from their country. During the process of deprogramming, the barriers of Moon's mind control are broken down, and eventually the young person regains his power to reason for himself.

> My mind was brainwashed, hypnotized, and under the control of Moon and the Church. I was in the process of becoming a totally obedient, non-thinking robot.[2]

When conventional behavior patterns were based in religion, religious change and defection were interpreted in diabolical terms. Thus, for example, Cotton Mather—in his apology for the Salem witch trials—stated (1974, pp. 67, 43):

> . . . . the very Devils are broke in upon us, to seduce the Souls, torment the Bodies, sully the Credits, and consume the Estates of our Neighbors, with Impressions both as real and as furious, as if the Invisible World were becoming incarnate, on purpose for the vexing of us.

> Most horrible whoes come to be inflicted upon Mankind, when the Devil does in great wrath, make a descent upon them. The Devil is a Do-evil, and wholly set upon mischief.

Possession

Vulnerability

As many observers of modern marginal religions have noted, these groups draw their memberships disproportionately from the cohort of young persons between the ages of 18 and 25. Likewise, Macfarlane (1970) and others, who have studied witch prosecutions, have commented that the majority of witch accusations were made against women. Thus, it appears that certain categories of individuals are believed to be unusually susceptible to possession because of some weakness or vulnerability. Such vulnerabilities are, of course, based on cultural beliefs. In colonial America, women were considered to be more likely to become possessed or to be seduced into pacts with Satan than men. In modern America, youthful instability and idealism are perceived as qualities that render young persons prey to unscrupulous exploitation.

Currently, in the United States activists in the anticult movement do not regard shifts of affiliation to marginal religions as "true" conversions. Instead, they assume what Hans Toch has referred to as "the seduction premise" (1965). That is, recruitment agenda for many marginal groups allegedly involve deliberate deceptions that exploit idealistic impulses coupled with nutritional and other sensory deprivations — and, at the extreme, sexual enticement/hypnosis/physical coercion—to weaken the critical rationality and will of individuals. It is the high, unfulfilled idealism of young adults, who are approached by marginal groups when they are at the cross-roads of their lives, that leaves them vulnerable to their appeals and unwary about their promises. Thus anticultists claim:

> The Unification Church attracts young people, Rabbi Davis says, because they're vulnerable. Their goodness makes them vulnerable. They're searching for a better world.

> The One World Crusade feeds upon our young, especially college freshmen who might be naive or bewildered or lonely or embittered. They feed upon our young, and we must be made aware (personal interviews).

Similarly, witches of the late seventeenth century were believed to have been seduced into pacts with infernal powers, although for less lofty reasons. A rich European lore of witchcraft, assembled in such treatises as Heinrich Kramer and James Sprenger's (two fifteenth-century Dominican friars) *Malleus Maleficarum* (*Witches' Hammer*) and in many smaller works by other demonologists, existed to provide a lengthy set of possible motives (1971). The natural "temperament" of women, for example, inclined them to be witches, it was believed. They were seen as inherently more carnal, deceptive, vindictive, and less intelligent than men:

> And indeed, just as through the first defect in their intelligence they are more prone to abjure the faith; so through their second defect of inordinate affections and passions they search for, brood over, and inflict various vengences. . . . Women also have weak memories; and it is a

natural vice in them not to be disciplined, but to follow their own impulses without any sense of what is due. . . . (Kramer and Sprenger, 1971, p. 45).

It was often claimed that demons visited persons of either sex by night in the form of either *incubi* (males) or *succubi* (females) to rape or beguile them. In exchange for promising their souls to the Devil, witches supposedly enjoyed material benefits, unlimited sexual license, and became embued with powers with which to afflict their enemies. Human weakness, rather than idealism, was the root cause of their seduction.

Purpose

Evil is antisocial. It makes no contribution to social order or to established institutions. Often, in fact, it operates to subvert them. Its goals and purposes thus come to be seen as parasitic, if not more overtly harmful. It should be recalled, however, that individuals who become defined as evil are themselves not evil's source but rather only its agents.

Members of marginal religions have been accused of such parasitism, acting as the agents of this evil. Much of their "missionary work" consists of fund-raising by means of street solicitations. The proceeds are not visibly returned to communities in the form of charitable operations or in any obvious enrichment of the citizens. At the same time, reported accounts of the wealth of leaders of groups lead many to conclude that these collections are simply used for the aggrandizement of a few:

> His "children" fill the streets selling peanuts or flowers, or begging for money to fight drug abuse or broken homes, or simply beginning. They have in fact no program for drug rehabilitation, and the money raised to fight the blight of broken homes is used to break up homes. They have in fact not one single program of social or human concern. Their only concern is to raise money for Moon.
>
> . . . he could admit that he told lies on Moon's behalf. Some of those lies were asking for donations for a drug abuse center when he knew the money would go to the Unification Church.
>
> . . . she began to realize that money Moon followers were raising by selling flowers and begging from strangers was only going to Rev. Moon's multimillion-dollar property holdings. . . . (personal interviews).

Likewise, the power allegedly possessed by witches was private and contributed nothing to the common good. Accusations during the Salem trials, as was the case in English trials during the same century, had their roots in perceived injuries to individuals. The motives imputed to suspected witches were malevolent and stemmed from interpersonal resentments. For example, reporting on the trial of Elizabeth How (later hung as a witch), Mather reported (1974, p. 123):

> Nehemiah Abbot testify'd, that unusual and mischievous Accidents would befal his cattle, whenever he had any Difference with this Prisoner. Once, particularly, she wished his Ox choaked; and within a little while that Ox was choaked with a Turnip in his throat. At another time, refusing to lend his horse, at the Request of her daughter, the Horse was in a preternatural manner abused.

The very notion of a pact with the Devil to edge out one's fellows in the competition of daily life was itself a heinous repudiation of customary social channels to success.

Identification

If there is a serious, threatening evil force that attacks the vulnerable and involves them in antisocial activities, some procedure for recognizing the evil and its agents will be established. When that evil can infiltrate or pass as normal society as it continues its pernicious work, then it becomes imperative to be able to identify evil.

Stigmata answer the seemingly recurrent question: How shall we know them? Stigmata are the tangible signs of evil—"the marks of the beast"—by which the followers of evil can be separated out from normal society. Stigmata constitute the elements of the stereotype used both to identify deviants and to justify actions against them.

For example, a survey of recent press articles, public statements by apostates of Sun Myung Moon's Unification church, and the literature circulated among anticult groups turned up 10 frequently repeated stigmata that allegedly characterize "Moonies":

1. linguistic changes (e.g., truncated vocabulary due to compulsive repetitions of group cliches)
2. monotonic, inflection-free voice level
3. fixed, permanent smile ("with the mouth only")
4. glassy eyes and dialated pupils
5. hunched frame
6. facial skin rash (due to vitamin A deficiency in diet)
7. body odor (due to neglect of daily hygiene)
8. ill-fitting, cheap out-of-style clothing
9. overall physical debilitation (gaunt facial appearance, hollow eyes)
10. hyperactivity, extreme nervousness

Typical press accounts link these characteristics to the behavior of the members:

> His parents noticed with alarm that he was becoming pale, withdrawn, nervous and acting almost as if he were in a trance. . . . "He was becoming a walking zombie and nothing at all like the son we had known."

> Richard was emaciated, thin, his eyes had a very blank stare. He was smiling all the time but all the kids were smiling all the time like they were really having some kind of ecstasy about being there.

> The minute I walked into that house, I told my husband, there has to be some kind of herb here that is a hypnotic because I have been in touch with those things before. My father was a pharmacist. The kids reeked of it. They all had this particular odor about them.[3]

Similar lists of stigmata that allegedly distinguished those possessed of evil can be found in the European folklore about witchcraft that was shared also by colonial Americans. For example, Reginald Scot, a sixteenth-century playwright-politician, wrote in *The Discoverie of Witches* (1973) that they were often "bleare-eied," toothless, hunchbacked, hollowed eyed, with pale wrinkled complexions, and "fowle" odors. A more systematic list of physical signs grew out of works like the *Malleus Malificarum*. The most widely adopted criteria for identifying witches were "Devil marks." According to folkore, the Devil sealed his pact with an individual by leaving a mark somewhere on the latter's body with either his pincers or hooves. These marks might "resemble" warts, scars, birthmarks, or any skin blemish, and they were accepted as evidence for the prosecution in witchcraft trials.

As prosecutions spread, however, the folklore evolved so that the Devil began disguising these marks, leaving them invisible in order to protect his followers. In response, witchcraft trials incorporated "pricking" the accused person with long needles until some spot that was insensitive to pain and that would not bleed could be found. Related to these marks was the alleged third teat, or "witches' mark" that the Devil gave witches so that they might suckle "familiars" — inferior demons left by the Devil to aid witches in their malevolent schemes.

Cotton Mather noted linguistic stigmata in accused persons that were also characteristic of Old World witches (1974, p. 150): "The Devil makes Witches unable to utter all the *Lord's Prayer,* or some such System of Religion, without some Deprevations [omissions] of it. . . ." Adversity to speaking the name of Jesus Christ and touching religious objects accompanied this tendency.

Such lists of stigmata do not merely make evil more easily recognizable. They also implicitly justify actions against its agents. In the case of the modern anticult movement, signs from the above list are frequently presented in the context of media atrocity stories. They serve as "evidence" for accusations of danger and exploitation by marginal group leaders.

Neutralization

The ultimate goal in identifying those who are "possessed" by evil is to neutralize, if not the ultimate source of evil itself, then at least its hold on victims. It is at this point that the analogy between brainwashing/possession and witchcraft prosecution becomes weaker. The deprogramming movement seems to have drawn more on early Christian traditions of exorcism. It attempts to both liberate young persons from the influence of marginal religions and to restore their autonomy, and thus does not resemble the inquisition prosecutions of witchcraft.

The rush to identify extraordinary evil can produce an interesting phenomenon of occupational innovation: the profession of either identifying and interpreting stigmata, or of neutralizing the evil. In both cases, a group of persons without formal credentials spontaneously arose to perform these tasks. Because group affiliation with modern marginal religions readily identifies the "possessed," the deprogramming occupation emphasizes neutralization of evil rather than identification of its agents. Through stigmata, identification has already been confirmed. In the case of witchcraft prosecutions, this profession concentrated on identifying and confirming the agents of evil, using stigmata as proof. Then they handed these agents over to authorized legal institutions for neutralization or sentencing. The extralegal nature of deprogramming contrasts with the legal processes of neutralization of witches.

Deprogrammers such as Ted Patrick and Joe Alexander have no special qualifications in psychology or psychiatry. Their "calling" appears to have flowed more from inspiration and, some have alleged, from the short-run profitability of deprogramming. At the same time, such pseudoprofessionals claim a monopoly on the skills of understanding and neutralizing evil. For example, in their recent book *Let Our Children Go!*, Ted Patrick and Tom Dulack immodestly assessed his abilities to a parent before a deprogramming in this way (1976, p. 82): "Please try to understand this: I haven't found a psychiatrist, or any attorney, or a doctor or anyone else who knows anything about brainwashing and mind control."

Similar to early and medieval Christianity, when previously exorcized persons were utilized at exorcisms because of their intimate familiarity with satanic evil, deprogrammed apostates also figure largely in deprogrammings. As one ex-Unification church member said of two such apostates-turned-deprogrammers:

People like Dick Brewster and Shelly Turner are the only ones who can get us out, because they have been through it. They know what has been done to us and what's in our minds. They know how to refute the cults' arguments and force us to accept facts and use our minds independently. Parents and friends and people like ministers or doctors or psychologists can't do it, because we had been programmed to handle them.[4]

Likewise, Matthew Hopkins, the most notorious witchfinder, built a fast reputation and lucrative, though brief, business during the Essex witchcraft outbreak in mid–seventeenth-century England by conducting "diagnostic" examinations on a commission basis (Haining, 1974, pp. 205-15). Like Patrick, Hopkins was an innovator. In his case, he used such techniques of identifying and explaining stigmata as "pricking" the bodies of accused persons with long needles in search of "Devil's marks."

The process of neutralization typically involves confrontation between the "possessed" and "truth"; the "possessed" person's initial extreme resistance; and his or her gradual transformation.

Similar to classical exorcism, forced exposure to Bible citations and scripturally based invectives against particular marginal religious beliefs are an integral part of the deprogramming process. For example, in one of several publicized accounts of a deprogramming, it was reported that

> every time Janis shouted out a memorized passage from the *Divine Principle,* the Unification Bible which outlined such principles as the Cain and Abel parable, Patrick disputed it with a reference from the Holy Bible. . . .[5]

Such confrontations with "truth" often precipitate violent resistance that is later followed by a marked transformation when the individual reassumes his former identity:

> And he fought it all the way, blocking his ears so he couldn't hear what they were saying, hypnotizing himself. Chanting these things over and over. He wouldn't listen to any suggestions. . . . When I came back I saw a change. He was beginning to be a little more receptive. That was after about five hours. We were in that room 14 hours. All that time nothing to eat or anything. Just constant, constant, constant fighting fire with fire. [Richard recalled]: "I ripped the mike out of their tape recorder and ripped out the phone because they wouldn't let me call Berkeley." After five hours Mrs. Greenwald said, "You could see the change like night and day. There was this smile, a genuine smile. And his eyes cleared up. There was a definite physical change in his face. . . . It's like two different people. You cannot believe the physical change in that kid's face."[6]

The final stage of neutralization—public confession—moves our analogy closer to witchcraft prosecutions. Deprogrammers prefer to have persons who have been deprogrammed make public statements, whether in newspaper articles or in formal affidavits, repudiating their participation in marginal religions. This act of confession serves to reaffirm the legitimacy of the originally abandoned values and lifestyle. It also severs any remaining link between the individual and the marginal group. Typical of such confessions is one issued by briefly famous apostate Ann Gordon:

> To Whom it May Concern,
>
> I, the undersigned, do hereby swear of my own free will that I have been the unconscious victim of a very powerful system of mind-control during the past two and a half years of my life. I wish to request that if anyone from the Unification Church [*sic*] — which is in fact a very dangerous subversive cult operating legitimately in the United States under the guise of a bona fide corporation—tries to take me, even by force or by any other form of persuasion, back to the cult and away from the protection of my parents, that they (those seeking to take me back to the Unification Church) will be forcibly restrained from doing so. I will not be under my own free will to accept or reject them if they come for me because of the mind-control devices in their power. If I ever return to the Unification Church or any of its subsidiary or branch organizations of same, it will not be of my own free will and mind and I hereby authorize [*sic*] my parents, Mr. and Mrs. James T. Gordon, to use this document in any way or form to effect my release from the above mentioned Church's control.
>
> I hereby release any claim against my parents, Mr. and Mrs. James T. Gordon, and any person or persons that they may hire to effect my release under this document.[7]

A parallel act expressing contrition was often required by witchcraft prosecutors in order to escape death (as in Salem) or further punishment. For example, Macfarlane (1970, p. 69) notes in *Witchcraft in Tudor and Stuart England* that when sufficient evidence of guilt had accumulated,

> the accused was ordered to do public penance—that is, to confess and promise amendment of life in front of the other villagers. This was usually on a Sunday in the parish church and the accused wore a white sheet and carried a white wand. For example, a woman was ordered to "penitentlie confesse that she is hartelie sorrie for that she hath geven vehement suspicion of wichecrafte and wicherie." Having asked for the forgiveness of God and of her neighbours, the accused was dismissed after payment of fees and production of a certificate of a completed penance.

Concluding Remarks

The objective of this paper has been to explore the recurrent process by which those who violate norms of reciprocity come to be viewed as possessed by evil. This process contains the following common elements: (1) congruent with the dominant cultural assumptions of the day, an ultimate source of evil is first located; (2) a rough theory of how evil possesses persons is constructed in terms of (a) a particular victim's vulnerability, (b) evil's ultimate purpose, and (c) how to identify the agent-victims of this evil; and (3) this evil is seen as capable of being neutralized by specialists who confront evil, overcome its resistance, and bring about a transformation or restoration to the original nonevil identity. The explanatory data presented here indicate that even in relatively disparate cultural and temporal contexts there are striking similarities in the accusatory process. If the continuities reported in our illustrative data can be found for other forms of deviance, as Szasz (1970) has attempted for mental illness, then these findings would indeed be an aid in understanding the mechanisms by which societies exert social control.

Finally, we have suggested that outbreaks of accusations of possession by evil tend to occur when there is a weakening in traditional norms of reciprocity, although our principal interest has been the location, identification, and neutralization of evil rather than its structural sources. When such breaches occur, human relationships lose much of their former predictability. Certain exchanges between persons become unrewarding and abrasive, undercutting the stability of those relationships. In the case of the deprogramming movement in modern America, the breaches of reciprocity involve a visible minority of young persons abandoning the lifestyles of their parents and rejecting parental expectations for careers, education, and the like. In the case of the Salem witchcraft prosecutions, the transition from a colonial folk community to a more cosmopolitan urban society generated tensions among persons used to values emphasizing an older form of cooperation.

Notes

1. The authors' names are ordered randomly.
2. These newspaper quotations and the articles in which they appeared are content analyzed in detail in Bromley, Shupe, and Ventimiglia (1980).
3. Ibid.
4. Ibid.
5. Ibid.
6. Ibid.
7. *Clear Lake Observer,* Clearlake Highlands, Calif., 10 October 1975.

References

Bednarski, Joyce, 1970
Bromley, David G., Anson D. Shupe, Jr., and Joseph C. Ventimiglia, forthcoming
Greeley, Andrew M., 1972
Haining, Peter, 1974
Holy Spirit Association for the Unification of World Christianity, 1973
Kramer, Heinrich, and James Sprenger, 1971 (orig. 1486, reprinted 1928)
Macfarlane, A.D.J., 1970
Mather, Cotton, 1974 (orig. 1692)
National Ad Hoc Committee Engaged in Freeing Minds (CEFM 1976)
Patrick, Ted, and Tom Dulack, 1976
Scot, Reginald, 1973 (orig. 1584)
Shupe, Jr., Anson D., Roger Spielmann, and Sam Stigall, 1977
Szasz, Thomas, 1970
Toch, Hans, 1965

New Religions, Families, and "Brainwashing"

Dick Anthony and Thomas Robbins

The religious wars of the seventies have involved accusations that new religious movements brainwash their converts. They are alleged to be using mind control in seducing young persons from conventional familial processes and career plans so as to psychologically imprison them in communes and monasteries. Increasingly the state is sanctioning the forcible abduction of adult converts for purposes of counterindoctrination or deprogramming. The involvement of the state in facilitating such reeducation programs has been both active and passive: passive through refusal of local courts to prosecute the perpetrators of extralegal abductions; active because of a more recent tendency of lower-court judges to issue thirty-day conservatorships to parents of allegedly incompetent religious converts. Parents who obtain conservatorships are then empowered to receive the assistance of police in forcibly seizing the converts and turning them over to deprogrammers.

Such conservatorships are frequently granted in ex parte "hearings" in the judge's chambers from which the potential conservatee and his legal representative are excluded. In such a closed hearing the proposed target of the conservatorship has no opportunity to challenge information which parents, deprogrammers, and apostate devotees may impart to a judge. Nor may the

263

religious converts present countertestimony regarding the impugned cult or their own mental state.

In addition to existing state laws facilitating these practices, several state legislatures have been asked to consider new legislation supporting the forcible removal of adults from cults. The Vermont senate, moreover, has recently passed a bill empowering judges to issue conservatorships in such cases without adversary hearings.

These procedures have raised serious questions with respect to the issues of due process of law and freedom of religion. Are there *any* circumstances under which the administrative processes of the state can properly be used to change a person's religious beliefs without jeopardizing the traditional separation of church and state? Should even incompetent persons be forcibly subjected to religious counterindoctrination?

Defenders of deprogramming argue that the true issue is not freedom of religion but freedom of thought. Such freedom is—given this interpretation—impossible while a convert is in the grips of the malevolent mind control which cults and pseudoreligions are accused of practicing on helpless young persons. As attorney Michael Trauscht stated at a well-publicized San Francisco hearing involving conservatorships over five followers of Reverend Sun Myung Moon: "Certainly the First Amendment guarantees freedom of religion, but necessary to each guaranteed freedom is freedom of thought." Since cultists allegedly do not possess this freedom of thought, their forcible seizure and physical restraint for purposes of deprogramming does not violate civil liberties. Such liberties are to pertain exclusively to rational and responsible persons who are not brainwashed.

Critics have noted an element of mystification in the controversy over alleged cultic brainwashing. Thomas Szasz argues: "Brainwashing is a metaphor. A person can no more wash another's brain with coercion or conversion than he can make him bleed with a cutting remark." Other psychiatrists might quarrel with the absolutist dictum that the concepts of brainwashing and coercive persuasion are inherently subjective and obscurantist. Nevertheless, most psychiatrists would probably be hesitant about transferring a concept developed in the study of P.O.W. camps to the context of formally voluntary spiritual movements. It seems far-fetched to equate movements such as Hare Krishna or the Unification church, which exhibit a rapid turnover and a high dropout rate (even without deprogramming), with P.O.W. camps.

As voluntary associations go, these movements *are* relatively authoritarian and totalistic. To the degree that they are, however, they are not really cults at all. The authoritarian movements to which this concept has been popularly applied by the anticult movement—the Children of God, the Unification church, or Hare Krishna—really correspond more to the sociological concept of sect than to the concept of cult, which generally denotes a relatively unstructured, loosely organized, and tolerant collectivity. (However, *sect* has a vaguely respectable connotation, while *cult* evokes occultism and the image of men wearing hoods and performing secret rituals in cellars. These unsavory associations to the term *cult* have been exploited at the expense of linguistic precision by the anticult movement.)

Nevertheless, even authoritarian sects such as the Unification church and Hare Krishna are not in the final analysis true total institutions in which the management has total control over movement to and from the premises. The psychological and peer group pressures which are mobilized to inhibit leaving cults should probably not be equated with armed guards and fences in their capacity to influence attitudes. Such nonphysical pressures are indeed frequently unavailing, since many converts do leave voluntarily. Moreover, a high percentage of those who attend initial meetings or workshops do not subsequently return for further indoctrination.

The metaphor of brainwashing can probably best be understood as a social weapon which provides a libertarian rationale for persecuting unpopular social movements and ideologies. There are three aspects of the current use of the metaphor which allow it to serve this purpose: its subjective status, a concealed concern with the content of others' beliefs, and an authoritarian denial that unpopular beliefs could be voluntarily chosen.

The Subjectivity of Brainwashing Notions

The subjectivity of *brainwashing, psychological kidnapping,* and *mind control* notions—as they are being used in the present controversy—suggests that these terms are being used as weapons of repression. It is easy to maintain that this or that monastery or commune interweaves dogma and ritual in such a way as to lock converts into rigid thought patterns. Why has it been mainly foreign Communists and domestic religious minorities who have been popularly believed to use mind control techniques (i.e., not parents, parochial schools, or marine boot camp)?

Edgar Schein (1961) has commented on this matter in *Coercive Persuasion*, a report on his research on Americans "brainwashed" by Chinese Communists. He argues that if the notion of coercive persuasion is to achieve objective status, it must be acknowledged as occurring in a variety of culturally valued contexts, e.g., religious orders, the army, fraternities, and mental hospitals. In his view the nature of the influence process is essentially the same in the Chinese and traditional American contexts. The Chinese case is distinguished from the others not by the techniques involved but rather by our general disapproval of the goal of the former process, namely the conversion of American citizens into Chinese patriots.

In his work Schein dealt with this issue with some subtlety. However, the present antagonists of cults have neglected to distinguish—as he did—between factual and evaluative claims about influence processes. They have capitalized upon the popular dislike of Chinese influence over American citizens by pointing out vague similarities in the influence process between the thought reform context and cultic conversion. Because the goal of the influence process, i.e., conversion to Chinese citizenship, was widely disapproved of in the Chinese case, they have argued that the goal of vaguely similar processes of influence, i.e., religious conversion, should be legitimately suppressed in the present instance. They have failed to acknowledge, as Schein did, that such influence processes are very common in traditional social institutions. The logic of their argument, then, would lead either to legal suppression of monasteries, fraternities, the Boy Scouts, and Alcoholics Anonymous, or to granting courts a discretionary authority in suppressing membership in voluntary associations, which is inconsistent with our legal traditions. While the former is not likely to occur, the granting of inherently subjective discretionary power to the courts in suppressing unpopular cults via the conservator laws has been noted above.

In spite of his own impeccable ideological neutrality, Schein has probably contributed somewhat to this subjective use of the brainwashing notion by downplaying the role of physical restraints (e.g., Chinese internment of American citizens) in coercive persuasion. In the absence of tangible physical restraint, what is the criterion for inferring a washed brain or an imprisoned will? Unless one focuses on explicit physical force—restraint over protest—it is impossible to prove or disprove the allegation that this or that program of heavy-handed sectarian indoctrination constitutes mind control which is inappropriate to a degree which justifies legal intervention. Brainwashing divorced from physical restraint is generally in the eye of the beholder.

Concealed Concern with Beliefs

The subjective use of the brainwashing metaphor in the manner noted above allows its proponents to argue that they are not really concerned with the content of beliefs and opinions but rather with the way in which these opinions are held or the manner in which they have been developed (i.e., through mind control). Parents and deprogrammers claim to be responding not so much to the specific insupportable beliefs, but to a general "brainwashed state of mind" manifested by young devotees. If this were so it might be anticipated that deprogramming would not necessarily alter beliefs but would enable devotees to hold their beliefs in a more flexible manner, i.e., a rigid Moonie might become a thinking Moonie. But the assault on specific beliefs is relentless. A frequent technique of deprogrammers in the Northeast is to guide their charges through hours of bible study to expose the allegedly false scriptural interpretations of Reverend Moon and other gurus. Byong-suh Kim (1979), a sociologist who studied deprogramming in New Hampshire, characterizes the process as an "attempt to remove that belief system which was perceived as a function of the 'mind-controlling.' '' Joe Alexander, senior deprogrammer at the Freedom of Thought Foundation at Tucson, Arizona, has acknowledged that he aims at convincing his charges that their involvement with Reverend Moon or Hare Krishna is not "of God."

Thus, candidates for deprogramming are actually viewed as brainwashed mainly by virtue of their affiliation with a certain religious group and their adherence to certain beliefs. More importantly, a deprogrammee is viewed as having been liberated from mind control and having regained mental competence only when he actually recants his beliefs. Pressure can thus be applied to religious or political movements and their members can be subjected to forcible confinement for purposes of counterindoctrination without the acknowledgement of any intention to suppress a point of view. In this connection it is noteworthy that deprogrammers are frequently foiled by dissimulation on the part of their captives.

According to the Los Angeles *Herald Examiner*, one deprogrammer has warned that "the therapist has to be astute because a cultee can try to fool him into thinking the deprogramming has been successful when it hasn't." Indeed there have been instances where persons earned release from captivity (or a lightening of physical restraint facilitating escape) by dissimulating, and subsequently returned to their cult. Obviously such therapists are highly vulnerable to dissimulation because they are using religious belief as an essential criterion of mental health. Additional criteria of mental health would render the therapist less dependent upon the deprogrammee's overt profession of belief or nonbelief. Deprogramming can thus be seen as an inquisition against heresy formulated in terms of mental health and freedom from brainwashing.

The "Involuntary" Nature of Unpopular Beliefs

The application of brainwashing and mind control metaphors to members of a social movement implies that they are not acting or thinking voluntarily and are not therefore entitled to the freedom of religion and freedom from physical restraint which applies to rational individuals. The primary "right" vouchsafed to "brainwashed" converts is the right to be "cured," the right to be forcibly liberated from psychoslavery. But are converts to authoritarian sects merely passive victims of conditioning? The latent assumption of those who support coercive deprogramming seems to be that no one would ever voluntarily surrender intellectual freedom and flexibility; hence those who submit to regimentation must have been coercively persuaded to do so. But people have been voluntarily joining totalistic movements for centuries, and much of the literature on Christianity in its first century of existence depicts the early Christians in totalistic and authoritarian terms.

Sectarian commitment might be alternatively conceptualized as an exchange relationship. This point has been made effectively by Mark Rasmussen (1977), who observed a Unification church indoctrination workshop. Although personally hostile to Moonism, Rasmussen concluded that "the desire to abandon reason for emotion had to be present before the person came to the workshop. No one was drugged or hypnotized or strapped to a chair. And the new identity which emerged from the workshop was an assertion of self that came from *submission*: submission to emotion, to the group, to a commitment to a new set of ideals. It was a willful submission." Rasmussen further comments: "I think the Moonies gave up a lot in their regimented devotion—they gave up the chance to think, to read, to confront—and the struggle for me was to recognize and respect the fact that they found in Moon something that was more important to them than certain things I value."

The Brainwashing Metaphor and the Decline of Familism

If the current use of the brainwashing metaphor is indeed best understood as a social weapon being used against forms of heresy, we might well ask, Heresy against what? What is the nature of the social reality being threatened by nontraditional religions, and who has a stake in protecting it? Members of the anticult movement have argued that the social reality which they are protecting is the integrity of the American family.

Part of the motivation for conversion to currently popular religious movements *is* the decline of American familism. However, the anticult movement not only fails to protect the family but may in some ways hasten its decline. (At best the movement may enable some of its members to conceal from themselves the reality and the causes of that decline.) The brainwashing metaphor and the style of argumentation within which it operates is a form of false consciousness which is itself a symptom of the social forces which it purports to explain.

The present use of the brainwashing concept involves an application of the medical model to religion. Certain religious beliefs are consigned to the realm of involuntary pathological symptoms. Despite growing criticism of the medical model by labeling theorists and antipsychiatrists, the importance of the model is likely to be enhanced in a society in moral flux in which authorities are hesitant to acknowledge a punitive intent and thus increasingly rely on social scientists to provide therapeutic legitimations for social control. (The suppression of heresy is thus reformulated as therapeutic deconditioning from induced mental pathology.)

The present revival of brainwashing mystiques is taking place in the context of a general backlash against forms of dissent and nonconformity which flourished in the late sixties and early seventies. Feminists, gay militants, and new religions are all experiencing retaliation for their stridency in the past decade (ironically, some guru groups and Jesus sects are antifeminist and socially conservative). Brainwashing, which failed as a rationale for exculpating a deviant (i.e., Patricia Hearst), has been having some success as a weapon *against* deviants. A backlashing "law and order" oriented public will not accept mind control as a means of absolving dissidents from responsibility for criminal acts, but it may accept such a notion as a persecutory rationale.

"Cults" like gay militants apparently are being used as scapegoats for the decline of American familism. "Brainwashing" is a convenient stick with which to beat totalistic sects which "break up families" and remove converts from conventional social processes. Countercult groups which are mushrooming across the nation thus generally dedicate themselves to "reuniting families" as well as "freeing minds." It is of course quite true that some of the more authoritarian sects such as The Children of God, Hare Krishna, or the Unification church of Reverend Sun Myung Moon have discouraged the maintenance of close family ties outside of the movement. It is worth noting, however, that there has been a recurrent tendency in the history of American sectarianism for new movements to exalt the spiritual "brethren" at the expense of the "fleshly" kindred. This is hardly a new development or a consequence of a new technology of mind control. What is new is the availability of a technodeterministic vocabulary (e.g., *programming, mind control*) with which frustrated relatives may express their anger and bewilderment.

Kenneth Keniston (1977) in *All Our Children: The American Family under Pressure* has shown that the integrity of the family has declined at least partly because other social institutions, e.g., schools, the medical profession, social welfare agencies, and psychotherapy, have taken over many of its functions. Such agencies have stripped the family of its legitimacy but have not been able to replace it as a context for supplying interpersonal warmth and commitment. Such trends seem relevant to the current controversy. Young people are at a stage in life when they are neither locked into the impersonal bureaucratic institutional structure nor the discredited traditional family structure. Therefore they are more likely than their parents to attempt to resolve the tension between the two realms by choosing a radical alternative to both.

It is not surprising that young people have turned to novel religions in seeking alternative social forms within which such tensions may be lessened. Traditional religion has normally served to legitimize the family's status as the arbiter of expressivity. Religion has in theory been the ultimate authority on affective issues but it has ceded practical authority to the family. (Remember the billboards dotting the countryside in the 1950s which proclaimed that "The family that prays together stays together. Attend church with your family this Sunday.") Psychiatrists and social welfare agencies have increasingly usurped these functions from the family—and from traditional religion as well. Understandably, young people have turned to nontraditional religions as a way of returning ultimate control over affective legitimacy to groups, i.e. cults, which resemble extended families.

An increasing consensus of informed commentators—most recently Harvey Cox (1977) in his book *Turning East*—have viewed the growing popularity of exotic sects and cults in these terms. Many such groups provide a reintegration of affective and instrumental functions into a coherent social unit in a way which the discredited family no longer can. The groups which attempt the most radical sectarian solution to this problem, e.g., Reverend Moon's Unification church and the Hare Krishna movement, tend to encourage withdrawal from normal worldly involvements—most explicitly from bureaucratic institutions which have compromised the integrity of the family.

As Keniston has argued, larger institutions have usurped the authority of the family but not its culpability. Parents continue to think of themselves as responsible for the way their children turn out because schools and psychotherapists blame them when things go wrong. It is not surprising that they react defensively when their children repudiate the social institutions with which they are identified. Nor is it surprising—although it is ironic—that they have chosen a metaphor, i.e., brainwashing, to account for such repudiation which originates from within social scientific rhetoric.

Social science is that part of the affective control apparatus of society which has stripped the family of its status as the ultimate arbiter of affective legitimacy. Parents of converts are caught in between their own allegiance to society and their children's repudiation of it. They thus tend to utilize metaphors and a style of argumentation characteristic of the institutions which have usurped their authority.

The anticult movement's use of brainwashing imagery represents the use of social science as a rhetoric of social control. By their acceptance of this metaphor, parents tend to mask the nature of the value conflict between themselves and their children. No one could disagree with the logic of bureaucratic social processes and be in his right mind, goes this line of reasoning. Our chlildren only *appear* to be repudiating our values because they have been driven crazy by evil men. In this way parents are able to absolve themselves of responsibility for their children's defection. Moreover, by using the social scientific style of explanation of deviant behavior, they hope to enlist the aid of those institutions to which they have ceded their authority, e.g., courts and psychiatrists, in subduing their children's desertion from themselves and their world.

There is a nice irony here. Many cults such as Scientology, *est*, Hare Krishna, or Nicheren Shoshu are responding to the pervasive sense of powerlessness which afflicts many Americans. These groups offer techniques which will enable the individual to "take power in his life" or "make his life work." Such themes are deceptively voluntaristic. Mastery and self-management are emphasized, but the latent premise is that in today's milieu no one is spontaneously masterful; only the person who meditates, chants, or is "trained" really has free will. Everyone outside of the movement is enmeshed in Karma or ensnared by Satan, etc. Deprogrammers merely reverse the scenario and view only those in cults as incapable of rational mastery. Only cultists are brainwashed, the rest of us are free—bureaucratic domination, media manipulation, and monopoly capitalism notwithstanding. Both cults and anticult groups thus benefit from the consequences of various sociocultural trends in undermining the subjective plausibility of traditional notions of personal autonomy and responsibility. The decline of traditional voluntaristic assumptions enhances the appeal of the medical model of deviance and the imputation of involuntary pathology to exotic or subversive orientations.

In our view, the upsurge of cults is indeed associated with trends undermining familial solidarity in America, but cultism is more a consequence than a cause of such trends. A study of J. Stillson Judah (1977) indicates that West Coast Moonies frequently become alienated from both parents and conventional routines *prior* to conversion to the Unification church. (Judah's study also reveals a rapid turnover among Bay Area Moon converts.) Research conducted by James T. Richardson (1978) suggests that conversion to a communal Jesus sect is not an isolated discrete event but is generally part of a broader sequence of spiritual seeking and experimentation with new lifestyles which Richardson terms a conversion "career." Available research is thus not consistent with a model of psychological kidnapping in which an otherwise dutiful and conformist young citizen is hypnotically overwhelmed and imprisoned in a deviant lifestyle which would otherwise be anathema.

Deprogrammers and their intellectual allies are essentially using the term *brainwashing* to refer to techniques of persuasion by means of tight information control. It is the relative totalism and milieu control exercised by totalistic sects such as The Children of God, Hare Krishna, or the Unification church which gives a surface plausibility to analyses in terms of mind control and coercive persuasion. Only a small percentage of the currently popular nontraditional religions exercise such tight information control. In the case of the more common loosely structured movements such as the Divine Light Mission of Guru Mahara-ji, mind control notions are deprived of even such surface plausibility. (Deprogrammers commonly fail to distinguish between loosely organized movements such as the Divine Light Mission or Transcendental Meditation and totalistic sects such as the Unification church.) However, the commitment of devotees in the more authoritarian groups *has* developed in a context of tight information control and continual social reinforcement for sectarian belief. These devotees *are* highly vulnerable to deprogramming techniques which not only separate them from social reinforcement for those beliefs but also coordinate milieu and information control to systematically assault the sectarian meaning system.

As Rasmussen and others have noted, there is a strong likelihood that such devotees have really *chosen* to enter an ordered utopiate environment and partake of the available rewards in terms of identity creation, interpersonal warmth, and a sense of service to mankind. In our view persons have a right to enter totalistic subcultures and have done so voluntarily for centuries, although more in certain periods than in others. What should be asked is why such people are choosing to eliminate ambiguity from their lives by committing themselves to dogmatic totalism. The hysterical overreaction of some parents, rationalized by their utilization of the brainwashing metaphor, seems to embody an attempt to resolve their own ambivalence about the contemporary technocratic situation. By denying that religious alternatives to contemporary social institutions could conceivably be voluntarily chosen, they betray their fear of examining their own involvement.

The Solution that Becomes the Problem

There is thus considerable mystification in the notion that deviant cults are breaking up families. The efforts of countercult groups often have the consequence of widening rather than healing the gulf between devotees and their parents. It is possible that parents might tolerate and try to relate to their children's commitments if the anticult movement did not encourage them to take drastic measures to rescue their child from brainwashing. Both cultic conversion and parental hostility to conversion are partially related to the family's loss of expressive authority to external agencies of social control which utilize the rhetoric of the social and behavioral sciences. Within this perspective, the use of the brainwashing metaphor is a symptom rather than an explanation of the conflict between the converts and their families. The use of such imagery tends to be seen by converts as an example of the denial of personal authenticity which they are seeking to escape in the first place. It is not surprising that the use of the brainwashing metaphor has amplified hostility between cults and their antagonists—and thus often between parents and children—and has further polarized the situation. It has encouraged parents to define their children's protests as the actions of dehumanized robots.

While deprogrammers generally induce their charges to read Robert Lifton's *Chinese Thought Reform and the Psychology of Totalism* (1961) to help them realize how they have been manipulated by mind control, Moon devotees on the West Coast are now being required by their leaders to study the same volume to prepare themselves against brainwashing at the hands of deprogrammers. Each side is convinced that their opponents are using insidious mind control techniques and mobilizing a legion of zombies against them.

Young persons who enter communal religious sects sometimes marry and raise children within the religious community. Parents who endeavor to remove their children from these sects are acting to break up their children's families (a situation like this recently developed in Arkansas where parents from New York and California attempted to gain custody of four members of The Alamo Christian Foundation, three of whom were married fathers). Thus the actual situation with regard to the allegation that cults are breaking up families is rather complex and it is by no means certain that prodeprogramming countercult groups such as Citizens Engaged in Reuniting Families (CERF) have reintegrated more families than they have further sundered apart.

Postscript

As of the present writing there are some indications that the tide of religious persecution is diminishing. The American Civil Liberties Union appears to have made progress towards discrediting religious deprogramming, or at least towards imbuing it with an aura of controversiality. As a result fewer judges are willing to grant conservatorships without open adversary hearings—or to grant them at all when religious issues are involved. A well publicized case in San Francisco involving followers of Sun Myung Moon ultimately resulted in a State Court of Appeals decision which declared that freedom of religion takes precedence over optimal mental health and that total incapacity to feed and clothe oneself must be established to justify a temporary conservatorship when religious issues are involved. The parents are appealing to the United States Supreme Court. Extralegal abductions for purposes of deprogramming still take place and are rarely prosecuted effectively; however, civil suits by unsuccessfully deprogrammed abductees are raising the costs of such operations and appear to have some deterrent value. There are indications that anticult groups are themselves undergoing a process of institutionalization which entails a rejection of controversial and violent methods such as forcible deprogramming. Such groups are increasingly relying on public relations techniques to accomplish their ends, e.g., the employment of a paid congressional lobbyist rather than forcible abduction and deprogramming.

An enlightened anticult perspective is becoming increasingly important in public discourse about cults. Such a perspective (typified by Stoner and Parke's *All God's Children: Salvation or Slavery* [1977]) expresses reservations about deprogramming but endorses the notion that certain contemporary religious movements use mind control on their converts. The continued use of the brainwashing metaphor, even within such an "enlightened" perspective, is unfortunate. This metaphor is inherently subjective and obscurantist. The use of this model is likely to continue to function as a smokescreen for discriminatory treatment of novel religious movements by our legal machinery.

It is conceivable that abuses exist in the fund-raising, proselytization, and political lobbying activities of some cults. Some regulation and control may be necessary. The danger is that such laws will be enacted and enforced as a way of continuing to persecute novel religious minorities. The anticult fight is likely to shift to issues such as religious tax exemptions, zoning regulations, rules regulating street solicitation, and the status of campus religious organizations. For instance, New York City wants to deny a tax exemption to the Unification church on the grounds that it is essentially a political movement. Reverend Moon's church may lose its tax exemption on the grounds of its political activities, while support of antiabortion lobbying by the Catholic hierarchy or the pro-Israel activism of Jewish rabbis is ignored. The selective enforcement of plausible rules regarding tax exemptions, campus proselytizing, and zoning may yet prove a convenient means of suppressing unorthodox religious groups.

The brainwashing metaphor, as it is used even in "enlightened" anticult literature, has the misleading implication that indoctrination and commitment processes within cults are qualitatively different from processes within respectable religious institutions such as evangelical summer camps, monastic orders, etc. The continued use of this metaphor is likely to enhance tendencies toward discriminatory regulation conducted largely in the interests of protecting the religious establishment and other conventional institutions from competion or critique by new movements. Mind control imagery is likely to continue to mask the legitimate dissatisfaction with conventional institutions which the current popularity of novel religious movements represents.

References

Collier, Peter, 1977
Cox, Harvey, 1977
Judah, J. Stillson, 1977
Kelley, Dean, 1977
Keniston, Kenneth, 1977
Kim, Byong Suh, 1979
Lifton, Robert, 1961
Rasmussen, Mark, 1977
Richardson, James T., 1978
Robbins, Thomas, 1977
Schein, Edgar, 1961
Stoner, Carroll, and Jo-Ann Parke, 1977

Integrating the "Moonie" Experience: A Survey of Ex-Members of the Unification Church

Trudy Solomon

Introduction

The rapid proliferation of new religious movements in America during the last two decades has not only unleashed a host of social scientists attempting to explain the phenomenon, but it has also entrapped many legal scholars in the concomitant constitutional crisis it has spawned. For, by their very existence, movements like the Unification church have called into question the meaning and application of one of our nation's most coveted guarantees, the First Amendment. Religious freedom, freedom of speech, and freedom of association—thought to be fundamental to the U.S. system of government—have been shown to be dependent, at least in part, upon the values and beliefs of those who interpret them. At issue is whether young people —the most frequent adherents to these new religions—will be free to participate and believe as they choose. Or will opposing parents and governmental agencies be permitted to intervene, and thereby limit individual participation in these groups and potentially their very existence.

Why should this kind of intervention be allowed in light of what appears to be a most flagrant violation of First Amendment rights? One answer, although a far from simple one, rests on an assumption made by the opponents of these new religions. They argue that freedom of thought, an even more fundamental right than those guaranteed by the First Amendment, has been taken away by these movements. Without this most basic human right, they argue, freedom of religion, speech, association, and other ancillary liberties are rendered meaningless. Both sides of this controversy are currently embroiled in what will prove surely to be a bitter and protracted battle whose outcome will be determined most probably through the courts.

At present, it is estimated that from one to three million Americans have joined one of the new religious movements that have proliferated in the past decade.[1] Yet it is not merely the increasing number of individuals involved that have caused a public outcry in the last few years. Nor is the criticism of religious groups new to the history of mankind or to that of America. What is new—and explosively controversial— is the attempt by critics of the new religions to characterize religious indoctrination as brainwashing or mind control (Clark, 1976; Singer, 1977). And the attempt by the new religions to criticize deprogramming as brainwashing is also new. Yet the question of who is brainwashing whom depends, in part, on which side you are on, and what you are prepared to call brainwashing (Sage, 1976).

The Brainwashing Controversy

Programming is the term that critics have applied to the process of change an individual undergoes as part of his or her indoctrination into one of the new religions. Proponents of deprogramming, then, claim to be fighting fire with fire. They obtain the involvement of subjects in their procedures either by taking the law into their own hands and kidnapping them, or by "legally" abducting members through conservatorship or guardianship actions in the courts. They believe that deprogramming is a process that enables individuals who have joined one of these movements to think for themselves. Autonomous thought, they argue, will invariably lead them to renounce their new beliefs.

The Unification church is the new religion that has received the most attention in the brainwashing controversy. Members are casually referred to as "Moonies" by the general public and sometimes by each other. Superficially, much of what transpires during conversion into and deprogramming out of the Unification church or Moon movement does follow some of the classic steps in the brainwashing process. Converts and deprogrammees alike are isolated from their customary environments, they are subjected to a variety of social influence techniques — including repetition, monopolization of input, and selective reinforcement—and they undergo some degree of pressure designed to prevent their leaving a tightly controlled environment.

Yet it is the *degree* with which these elements are applied, and not merely their presence or absence, that should be used as the criterion for whether brainwashing can be equated with either, both, or neither of the processes under discussion. It is crucial, therefore, to realize that brainwashing and its component parts are not "all-or-none" conditions. It is more accurate and useful to view them as a continuum of social influence, with such activities as mass-media advertising or child rearing at one endpoint, and the Korean or Vietnamese POW experience at the opposite. It is possible, then, to understand a myriad of influence processes, including brainwashing, as a question not of existence, but of degree.

It is no secret indeed that most religious groups (old and new) indoctrinate through a variety of subtle and often not so subtle social influence techniques. When both the indoctrination process and the religion using it are acceptable to society, it is called "religious training" or "religious instruction." When a sect, cult, or movement is new or unpopular, its proselytization activities are apt to be called "brainwashing or subversion." Even though some form of persuasion is practiced throughout society, how we feel about it and what we call it rests at least in part upon what goal that persuasion is applied toward, and whether it is viewed as desirable or destructive.

Perhaps the most damaging criticism of brainwashing as an explanation of either conversion or deprogramming processes is that it is a vague and empirically untestable concept (Solomon and Pines, 1977). The controversy over religious brainwashing has been called "an exercise in mystification." Brainwashing seems to be the perfect prosecutorial tool for both sides because it never can be proven false (Robbins, 1977; Robbins, Anthony, and McCarthy, 1980).

Clearly, removing both the conversion and deprogramming processes from the realm of brainwashing is a crucial first step in freeing them from the bonds of mysticism, and facilitating their entrance into the empirical world. Since I have previously characterized brainwashing as an extreme on a social influence continuum, it is natural to take the next step and begin to conceptualize the processes of conversion and deprogramming as less extreme points on that same hypothetical dimension.

Current Research

The present study was part of a much broader survey of former Unification church members. It sought to explore both conversion and subsequent contact with the anticult movement as social-influence processes that affect the individual's conceptualization of the Moonie experience. It hoped also to empirically examine the process of applying and perpetuating brainwashing explanations of Unification church membership among ex-members.

An individual's attitudes, values, and behavior are strongly influenced by the group with which he associates or wants to associate. The term — reference group—is commonly used to denote those groups to which individuals relate their attitudes and values. Kelley (1952) has described what he considers to be the two major functions of reference groups. The first he calls the "comparison function." A group functions as a comparison reference group for an individual to the extent that the behavior and attitudes of its members represent standards or comparison points that are used in making judgments and evaluations. This function is relevant primarily to social influences on an individual's perception and cognition, and it has been extensively studied by Sherif (1936), Chapman and Volkmann (1939), Festinger (1954), and Asch (1956).

Kelley terms the second function "normative." A group functions as a normative reference group for a person to the extent that its evaluations are based on an individual's degree of conformity to certain standards of behavior or attitudes—norms. This function is also affected by the degree to which the delivery of rewards and/or punishments is dependent upon these evaluations.

There is also evidence to suggest that the more strongly a person is oriented toward membership in a group, the more likely he or she is to refer attitudes to a particular group. Yet a person may be forced to remain in a group because others treat him as a member, because no other alternatives are available, or because of excessive costs incurred by withdrawal. However, such involuntary membership is not necessarily accompanied by aversion to the group. A collection of individuals who are forced to belong to the same group may develop a high degree of cohesiveness and pride in membership (Cartwright and Zander, 1968), and as cohesion of a group increases, so will a member's conformity to the norms of that group.

Most pertinent to the present study is a field experiment by Siegel and Siegel (1957) that was designed to study attitudinal changes taking place among female college students after a change of residence. In this study, a distinction was made between membership groups — those in which membership is maintained—and reference groups—those in which there is a desire to attain or maintain membership. The researchers not only found that attitude change over time is related to the influence of membership and reference groups. They found also that the *imposition* of a membership group has an effect on an individual's attitude and values, even when the imposed group is not accepted by the individual as his or her reference group. Moreover, these researchers discovered that if a person comes to accept the imposed group as a reference group, then the change in attitudes toward the level of the group norm is even more pronounced.

It can be seen readily that those groups, individuals, or organizations with whom ex-members associate on leaving should directly influence their conceptualization of the experience of being a Moonie and their attitudes toward the movement in general. This conceptualization should be indirectly influenced also by those groups or organizations with whom an ex-member's close friends and/or relatives associate either during or after the individual's membership in the Unification church. Furthermore, this influence will be as important whether or not ex-members freely chose such membership. Therefore, those who have been exposed to anti–Unification-church contacts should have a more negative conceptualization of the experience than those without such exposure. By extension, those who left the Unification church involuntarily—through deprogramming—should have more negative conceptualizations also than those who left without intervention because, in addition, they were quite obviously exposed to the anticult movement. Thus, conceptualization within this ex-member sample was predicted to be a function of: (1) method of exit — voluntary or involuntary, through deprogramming and/or rehabilitation––and (2) degree of contact with the anticult movement.

Method

Subjects

Subjects for this study were 100 ex-members of the Unification church who were primarily recruited for participation through the extensive nationwide anticult network of organizations and individuals who assist members, ex-members, and other concerned persons involved in a variety of "fringe" religious movements. In addition, each respondent to the study was asked to name other ex-members who could participate in the research. Participation was voluntary, and it was limited to adults of 18 years or older. Each study participant completed a mailed questionnaire packet. A cover letter identifying the researcher's interest in the area, the purposes of the study, the confidential nature of the data collected, and a request for the individual's cooperation accompanied each package. Questionnaires were identified by code number to insure complete anonymity.

Measures

The questionnaire was divided into two major parts. The first part gathered data on general background information such as sex, ethnicity, religious background, postexit activities, political perspective, perception of parental political perspective, perception of parental attitude toward discipline, social support networks, and satisfaction with school, work, life, and self. This portion also included an instrument designed to assess adjustment and the Texas Social Behavior Inventory (TSBI), Short Form A (Helmrich, Stapp, and Ervin 1974).

The second part concerned the subject's experiences both as a member and as an ex-member of the Unification church. This portion of the questionnaire included both short answer and open-ended questions designed for flexibility and ease in responding to questions focusing on necessarily complex issues. Thus, subjects were asked to rank-order factors that attracted them to the Unification church, provide information on initial contact and training within the church, the circumstances that led to their joining and leaving, and detailed questions concerning their voluntary and/or involuntary involvement and attitudes toward the treatment interventions of deprogramming, rehabilitation, and therapy. Subjects responded also to ten items designed to assess their amount of contact with present and former members of the church, anti-Unification church groups, and the deprogramming movement, as well as their friends and parents' involvement in such activities. Finally, subjects completed a 10-item measure designed to assess their conceptualization of the Moonie experience and two 5-point Likert-type ratings that assessed a subject's attitude toward his or her experiences as a Unification church member, and toward the church in general.

Results

Overview

Sample demographics. From an original mailing of 250 questionnaire packets, 108 were returned (over 43 percent), and 100 of these contained complete data and thus were used in subsequent analyses. Of these 100 respondents, 58 were male, and 42 were female. Subjects ranged in age from 19 to 33, with a mean age of 24. They had rather homogeneous educational, ethnic, and marital backgrounds—nearly 90 percent of the sample had attended college, 95 percent were Caucasian, and nearly all respondents were single. Most had had their initial contact with the movement in either the West or the Northeast, and they had joined the church within a month of that contact. Although training duration varied with geographical area and time of involvement (e.g., 1972 versus 1976), the majority of respondents received either 21 or 40-day training sessions near their areas of initial contact. Their time as members ranged from ten days to four years, with a mean of just over one year; their time since exit ranged from 150 days to four years, with a mean of 1.76 years.

Type of exit. Categorizing method of exit from the Unification church proved to be more complex than making a simple distinction between those who left voluntarily and those who left involuntarily through deprogramming. It had been assumed, on the basis of pretest interviews, that those who left on their own rarely received any formal help. It had been assumed also that rehabilitation and therapy were rarer forms of intervention that sometimes accompanied deprogramming as later, final stages of that process. This in fact was not the case. Sixty-five subjects had been deprogrammed; 76 subjects had received rehabilitation; and 38 subjects had had therapy. Only 7 subjects had received no formal help of any sort. Thus, it became clear, that at least within this sample, an exit rarely was successfully executed without some sort of intervention. Rehabilitation and therapy were far more prevalent than assumed, and they were employed separately as well as in conjunction with deprogramming. Because subjects could have received anywhere from none to all three of these "treatments," it was necessary, in categorizing the sample, to take all three possible interventions into account, rather than the mere voluntary/involuntary breakdown that was originally designed. This delineation resulted in a more complicated, yet more accurate depiction of the sample.

TABLE 16.1
Treatment Groups

Group	Intervention	N
1	None	7
2	Deprogramming	4
3	Rehabilitation	12
4	Therapy	3
5	Deprogramming and Rehabilitation	34
6	Deprogramming and Therapy	2
7	Rehabilitation and Therapy	4
8	Deprogramming, Rehabilitation and Therapy	25
Blank		9
	Total	100

The subjects' attitudes toward these interventions varied greatly. While the majority of those who had been deprogrammed felt "very negative" or "somewhat negative" about the process at the time of deprogramming, that negativity, in essence, reversed over time. At the time of sampling, the majority either felt somewhat positive or very positive about their own deprogramming. It is interesting to note that only a third of the deprogrammings were done under conservatorship, while the remaining two-thirds were executed without legal sanction. An average of three deprogrammers, almost always hired by the parents, were involved in each deprogramming—a process that took anywhere from one hour to 16 days, with a mean of 3.6 days. Time spent in rehabilitation and therapy showed much greater variation, and it ranged from three days to two years for rehabilitation, and from three days to three years for therapy.

Conceptualization and Contact

The prediction that an ex-member's conceptualization would be a function of method of exit and degree of contact with the anticult movement was strongly supported by the data. Conceptualization was measured by summing scores on the ten items of the Conceptualization scale (CONCEP) and two five-point Likert-type ratings—"very negative" to "very positive"—of attitudes toward a subject's experiences as a Unification church member (GENUC1) and toward the church in general (GENUC2). Conceptualization scores ranged from 11 to 46, out of a possible 1 to 50. The mean equalled 24.50, while the standard deviation was 6.495. Scores on the first general attitude question ranged from 1 to 5, with a mean of 3.11 and a standard deviation of 1.166. Scores also ranged from 1 to 5 on the second attitude question, while the mean was 1.54 and the standard deviation was .787. Unlike scores on Conceptualization and GENUC1 that focused on conceptualization of the experience and had fairly normal distributions, scores on GENUC2, and an item that measured subjects' attitudes toward the Unification church itself were quite skewed with nearly 90 percent of the sample using either the "very" or "somewhat negative" responses.

In analyses to determine the Conceptualization scale's reliability and validity, the scale was found to have an interitem consistency of .74, using

TABLE 16.2
Zero-Order Correlates of Conceptualization with
Theoretically Related Variables

Zero-Order Correlations of Conceptualization

with Theoretically Related Variables

	CONCEP	GENUC1	GENUC2
CONCEP	1.0000		
GENUC1	.7404***	1.0000	
GENUC2	.5264***	.2249*	1.0000

*p < .05

***p = .000

Cronbach's alpha, with the deletion of any one item causing a negligible drop in the alpha coefficient. The scale showed also a high degree of construct validity, correlating highly with theoretically related variables (see Table 16.2). The conceptualization score was also related to two questionnaire items sampling the level of postexit fulfillment (FULFILL) and the degree to which the subject would like to return to the Unification church (LIKERET). Subjects with higher scores, reflecting a more positive attitude toward the movement, tended to have needs that were once fulfilled by the Unification church, and that were as yet unfulfilled outside the church (r = $-.2797$; p = .003). They also expressed a desire to return to the church more often than those with lower scores (r = $-.3324$; p = .001). Thus the Conceptualization scale also achieved a degree of predictive validity, at least of behavioral intentions.

A factor analysis of the Conceptualization scale was also performed, yielding three substantive factors: (1) political aspects of conceptualization; (2) experiential aspects of conceptualization; and (3) religious aspects of conceptualization (see Table 16.3).

Three analyses of variance—Treatment Group × GENUCI, Treatment Group × GENUC2, and Treatment Group × Conceptualization—in conjunction with contrasts between appropriate group means were performed on the sample. Results showed significant differences between treatment groups and an individual's general attitude toward his or her experiences as a Unification church member (GENUC1) (F = 2.22; d.f. = 7/81; p = .04). Subjects who had received both deprogramming and rehabilitation had a more negative general attitude toward their experiences than those who had rehabilitation only (t = 2.07; p = .042). General attitudes toward the church (GENUC2) also differed significantly, according to treatment group (F = 2.60; d.f. = 7/76; p = .02). Subjects who had received no interventions had more positive attitudes than those who had been deprogrammed (t = 3.31; p = .001); those who had been deprogrammed and had had rehabilitation (t = 3.36; p = .001); those who had received only rehabilitation (t = 3.21; p = .002); or those who had received all three interventions (t = 3.50; p = .001). Conceptualization differed according to treatment group (F = 2.26; d.f. = 7/82; p = .04), showing a similar pattern of results. Those who received no interventions had more positive conceptualizations than those who had been deprogrammed (t = 2.08; p = .041); those who had been deprogrammed and had had rehabilitation (t = 3.43; p = .001); or those who had been deprogrammed and had had rehabilitation and therapy as well (t = 2.86; p = .005). An unexpected sex effect was also found. The women in the sample, regardless of treatment group, had more negative conceptualizations of the Moonie experience (r = $-.3619$; p = .001) and felt more negatively about their experience as a Unification church member (r = .1694; p = .047) than men.

Degree of subject contact with anti–Unification-church groups and/or present and former members was assessed by yes or no responses on 10 contact

TABLE 16.3
Item Loadings for Conceptualization Factor Analysis

Factor 1:   Political Aspects of Conceptualization

   Items: (3)   I was a victim of brainwashing and mind con-
                                    trol while a member of the Unification Church.

        (7)   I think it will be found that the Unification
                                    Church has ties to the Korean C.I.A.

        (8)   The Unification Church uses mind control to
                                    recruit and keep members.

        (9)   Unification Church members are simply young
                                    adults who are extremely committed to their
                                    work and their way of life.

      (10)   The Unification Church should not be a legal-
                                    ly recognized religion.

Factor 2:   Experiential Aspects of Conceptualization

   Items: (1)   Being a member of the Unification Church
                                    helped me to grow up and take responsibility
                                    for my own actions.

        (2)   I would just like to forget I was ever a mem-
                                    ber of the Unification Church.

        (4)   All in all, being a member of the Unification
                                    Church was a good experience for me.

        (6)   The training and instruction I received as a
                                    Unification Church member was valuable and
                                    rewarding.

Factor 3:   Religious Aspects of Conceptualization

   Item: (5)   Becoming a member of the Unification Church
                                    was a religious experience.

items and a question concerning the subject's involvement in deprogrammings (see Table 16.4).

Analyses on these items showed that contact with present members correlated with a more positive general attitude toward the Unification church (r = .1812; p = .039), while contact with ex-members correlated with a more

TABLE 16.4
Contact Items and Responses

Item (58)   Do you now have any contact with present members of
the Unification Church?

  Yes = 42   No = 55   Blank = 3

Item (59)   Do you now have any contact with ex-members of the
Unification Church?

  Yes = 76   No = 23   Blank = 1

Item (60)   Do you participate in Anti-Unification Church groups?

  Yes = 35   No = 62   Blank = 3

Item (61)   Do your parents participate in Anti-Unification
Church groups?

  Yes = 44   No = 53   Blank = 3

Item (62)   Did your parents participate in Anti-Unification
Church groups while you were a Unification Church
member?

  Yes = 44   No = 54   Blank = 2

Item (63)   Do your friends participate in Anti-Unification
Church groups?

  Yes = 77   No = 65   Blank = 3

Item (64)   Did your friends participate in Anti-Unification
Church groups while you were a Unification Church
member?

  Yes = 14   No = 84   Blank = 1

Item (65)   Are you now involved in getting others out of the
Unification Church?

  Yes = 33   No = 67   Blank = 0

Item (66)   Are your parents involved in getting others out of
the Unification Church?

  Yes = 27   No = 73   Blank = 0

Item (67)   Are your friends involved in getting others out of
the Unification Church?

  Yes = 29   No = 69   Blank = 2

Item (68)   Have you participated in any deprogramming?

  Yes = 61   No = 39   Blank = 0

negative conceptualization of the Moonie experience ($r = -.2456$; $p = .009$). Development of a more negative, general attitude toward the Unification church also correlated with a subject's participation in anti–Unification-church groups ($r = -.2558$; $p = .006$); participation in deprogrammings ($r = .1881$; $p = .031$); or friends' participation in anti–Unification-church groups ($r = -.1699$; $p = .047$).

Because it could be assumed that undergoing one of the three interventions—deprogramming, rehabilitation, and/or therapy—might influence the degree of contact a subject would have with various reference groups after exit had been accomplished, several analyses of variance (Treatment Group × Contact Item) in conjunction with contrasts between appropriate group means were performed to determine the effect of intervention on contact. Five of the ten contact items showed significant effects. Contact with ex-members was related to treatment group ($F = 2.26$; $d.f. = 7/82$; $p = .04$). Those who received none of the three interventions had significantly less contact with ex-members than those who had had rehabilitation ($t = -2.01$; $p = .048$); those who had had rehabilitation and had been deprogrammed ($t = -3.61$; $p = .001$); or those who had had both rehabilitation and therapy and also had been deprogrammed ($t = -3.01$; $p = .003$). Parental contact was also related to treatment group ($F = 2.38$; $d.f. = 7/80$; $p = .03$). Parents of those who had been deprogrammed and had had rehabilitation were presently more involved in anti–Unification-church groups than parents of ex-members who had no interventions ($t = -2.41$; $p = .018$). These parents were more involved also in these groups while their child was a member of the church ($t = -2.05$; $p = .044$). There were also significant differences between treatment groups with respect to whether parents were currently involved in getting others out of the church ($F.= 2.27$; $d.f. = 7/83$; $p. = .04$). In an individual was deprogrammed and had therapy, his or her parents were more likely to be involved currently in getting others out than those who had no interventions ($t = -2.62$; $p = .01$), or those who had only rehabilitation ($t = -2.65$; $p = .011$). If the ex-member had had rehabilitation only, his or her friends were less likely to be involved in getting others out than those who had had both deprogramming and rehabilitation ($t = -2.49$; $p = .015$), or deprogramming, rehabilitation, and therapy ($t = 2.06$; $p = .043$).

Whether or not an ex-member became personally involved in deprogramming others also varied by treatment group ($F = 4.41$; $d.f. = 7/83$; $p = .000$). Those who had been deprogrammed were themselves involved in deprogramming others more often than those who had had no interventions ($t = 2.67$; $p = .009$). Those who had deprogramming and rehabilitation were more involved also in deprogramming others than those who had no interventions ($t = 3.37$; $p = .001$). However, the individuals who had rehabilitation only or who had received all three interventions were less likely to deprogram others than were the deprogramming and rehabilitation group ($t = 2.67$; $p = .009$; $t = 2.51$; $p = .014$, respectively).

Since much of the negative conceptualization concerning the Unification church could come from associating with groups who focus on the political aspects of the movement, correlational analyses were performed to test this possible relationship with selected contact items and those items of the Conceptualization scale that comprised the political-aspect factor in the factor analysis discussed previously. Results show that ex-members who themselves either participate, or who have parents who actively participate in such groups, hold more negative attitudes on the political aspects of the church. They believe more strongly that the Unification church uses brainwashing and mind control; that it is tied to the Korean CIA; that it should not be a legally recognized religion; and that Unification church members are not simply young adults who are extremely committed to their work and way of life (see Table 16.5).

TABLE 16.5
Zero-Order Correlations of Political Aspect Items with Selected Contact Items

	Brainwashing Item	Korean CIA Linkage Item	Mind Control Item	Member Commitment Item	Legally Recognized Religion Item
Subject's participation in Anti-Unification Church groups	-.2596**	-.2329*	-.2434**	.0168	-.1832*
Parent's participation in Anti-Unification Church groups	-.2109*	-.1897	.0731	-.2078*	.0611

* p < .05
** p < .01

Discussion

Conceptualization and Contact

Conceptualization of the Moonie experience was found to vary as a function of method of exit and degree of contact with the anticult movement. Moreover, contact with this movement seemed to serve a reference group function, influencing an ex-member's attitudes and values, regardless of whether this group had been chosen by the subject or had been imposed, primarily through deprogramming and/or rehabilitation. Thus, contact and conceptualization were differentially distributed throughout the treatment groups in such a way that those who had received no interventions: (1) had less contact with the anticult movement, and (2) viewed their experiences as a Unification church member and the church in general more positively. These results are best exemplified by the subject's own written responses to the study questionnaire that are included below where they are appropriate.

This relationship can be understood readily by reading accounts of ex-members' experiences in rehabilitation and deprogramming because gaining the "proper" perspective on the experience is an important component of these two processes. It is commonly believed within the anticult movement that conceptualization of the experience and the desire to return to the Unification church are linked. These opinions were verified by the present study's results. The influence of continual contact with the anticult movement can readily be seen in the comments of two ex-members, the first describing deprogramming, the second rehabilitation.

> I felt a compulsion from deprogrammers, family and friends to categorize the Moon experience as bad, negative, what have you, even if unconsciously. I resented this and it made it more difficult to find a balance in my post-Moon thinking.

> I was in a miniature anti-Moon, anticult cult. I hardly heard anything else but news about groups.

The picture that emerges from the data points to an induction of a more negative conceptualization at the time of intervention—deprogramming and/or rehabilitation—and an amplification of that negativity through continued contact with the anticult movement after leaving.

Yet the foregoing discussion is not meant to imply that a negative conceptualization was necessarily linked to a less well-adjusted former member profile. In fact, there was some weak although inconsistent evidence in the data to support the opposite conclusion. For example, one ex-member who felt he had been aided by such contact put it this way:

> During my rehabilitation I toured the country helping deprogram others who had been deceived by Moon, and [was] strengthened by seeing that those who heard, understood their deception.

Results of the investigation into the relationship between conceptualization and contact tended to support also the thesis that contact with the anticult movement influences the degree to which one relies on explanations of brainwashing and mind control to account for attraction to and membership in the church. Thus, belief in such explanations increased if an ex-member was involved in anti–Unification-church groups and getting others out, or if his or her parents were so involved. Many who participated in the anticult movement counselled the present writer to read *Thought Reform and the Psychology of*

Totalism in order to understand the whys and hows of cult involvement. One deprogrammed ex-member described his own enlightenment on the subject in this way:

> When I met the deprogrammers they very calmly told me they thought I had been brainwashed and would I please read a description from a book about brainwashing in China. I am grateful to the deprogrammers for showing me the truth about the Moonies.

Another ex-member, however, saw the issue of brainwashing and the Unification church a bit differently:

> I was also a victim of mind control while a member of the Catholic religion just as everyone else who is brought up in a particular religion.

Contact with the anticult movement seemed also to increase the degree of belief in the other political-aspect items of the Conceptualization scale, including the feeling that the Unification church was tied to the KCIA, and that it should not be a legally recognized religion. Because the majority of evidence concerning the use of brainwashing and mind control within the church comes either from ex-members who have been deprogrammed and/or rehabilitated or from individuals involved in the anticult movement, these data begin to provide an explanation for how ex-members come to hold such notions, and how they in turn are perpetuated

The unexpected sex effect in the data — that females were more negative about their experiences as members than males — might be attributable to claims by ex-members of rampant sexism within the church. But it surely is a matter that requires further research, before such a conclusion can be reached. Nonetheless, claims of sexism were to be found among respondents' questionnaires. One female ex-member, who had been raped while fund-raising, explained the increased burden felt by women in the Unification church in this way:

> Many women are sent out fundraising alone, at night, in very seedy and dangerous areas to fundraise bars and all-night restaurants. Often no regard is given to their safety. The rationale is, ''God will protect you if your faith is pure.''

One of the most interesting findings in the data was that, while most ex-members were highly negative when questioned about their attitudes toward the Unification church in general, they were far more positive about their experiences as a church member. One ex-member explained this inconsistency as follows:

It may seem strange that I have said my experiences in the Unification church were extremely positive and yet my feelings about the organization itself is very negative. That is because I gained much insight personally about myself, others, and psychology that I could never gain in a university, to my knowledge, and certainly not from any book.

Yet even though many respondents wrote that their experiences as a church member had helped them to mature, be more aware and curious about people, question ideas, develop a more rewarding relationship with God, and gain strength as a person, few recommended it as a means to those ends. Typical of such responses was the following:

> I am very negative toward the Unification church now. But while there I had some good experiences, learned to live with others better and to be less selfish. . . . However, if I had it to do over again, I would not join the Unification church. And I would try to discourage anyone else from joining. There are better ways to learn and love.

Method of Exit

Since the impact of method of exit had in part been predicated on a simple dichotomy—voluntary versus involuntary—it was perplexing indeed to make sense of a sample where nothing was quite that simple. Some members were subjected to deprogramming but not rehabilitation and some left voluntarily and then requested deprogramming or rehabilitation. Others were talked out of belonging to the church by concerned parents, and they were subsequently placed in therapy. In short, all possible mutations of "voluntary" and "involuntary" were to be found within the sample. Thus, for the purposes of analysis, the sample had to be split into eight separate treatment groups, according to all the possible combinations of interventions each subject had received—deprogramming, rehabilitation, or therapy. After identifying each subject as a member of a specific treatment group, it was found that only seven of the original 100 subjects actually had accomplished their exit without any assistance whatsoever and even the members of this purely "voluntary" group most probably received support and assistance from someone. Yet this necessarily muddied classification scheme is itself a telling comment upon exit from the Unification church in that no simple distinctions can be made, whether they are researcher-imposed or defined by an ex-member.

The small number of voluntary exit subjects in the sample might be attributed to the common belief that it is impossible to leave the church without assistance. However, it seems equally plausible that, because there is such a ready supply of trained and untrained people anxious to be of assistance to members upon exit, services rendered are not so much sought out as given freely—though usually for a fee. In addition, the lack of purely voluntary subjects may be due to sampling bias because it is extremely difficult to successfully track down ex-members who left voluntarily and who have never been in contact with the ex-member network.

Attitudes Toward Interventions

The attitudes of ex-members who had undergone deprogramming varied from enthusiasm to disgust. While many considered it essential to break through a polarized state of mind, most, when questioned as to the necessity for postexit adjustment, responded that, while it could provide a genuine opportunity for self-awareness if executed properly, it was certainly not a necessity for everyone. In many cases, deprogramming merely provided a face-saving method of exit for members who had not quite resolved their own ambivalence about leaving. Two ex-members who had experienced deprogramming put it in these ways:

> It was the only way I personally could have left the church.

> I am glad that I am no longer with the organization but eventually would have "found" answers for myself. The deprogrammer made it easier to leave.

The extremes—between those who were grateful to their deprogrammers and their parents for having forced them to withstand the process, and those who greatly resented the use of force or felt humiliated and betrayed as a result of deprogramming—are difficult to reconcile. Ex-members who viewed the process positively tended to be those who felt they had been brainwashed while in the church, and that they never would have been able to be free of that mind-control without the help of deprogrammers. One former member stated:

> I know that I was brainwashed and the only way to correct this is deprogramming or reverse brainwashing. I did not enjoy being deprogrammed . . . but it is necessary.

Those who felt more negatively toward deprogramming tended to discount theories of brainwashing, and they based their own negative reactions largely on what they considered to be the unprofessional conduct of deprogrammers. Typical of this kind of criticism were the following statements:

> The damage done by very unprofessional "deprogrammers" took about six months to recover from. They accomplished their aim with mental brutality.

I feel that the precedent set by Ted Patrick is the wrong approach to the situation completely. I have more negative things to overcome in my personality and character resulting from the deprogramming than from being a member of the church.

Others who had negative reactions to the process often expressed displeasure at the fanaticism with which some deprogrammers performed the tricks of their trade—often calling deprogrammers "the ultimate cult" or the "anticult," and basing their negative judgments on a belief that the process of deprogramming manipulates people in many of the same ways as the Unification church.

Reactions toward rehabilitation by those who had received this intervention were less polarized. Though many felt rehabilitation was unnecessary, few saw it as inherently harmful. In fact, descriptions of the process sounded more like a summer vacation than anything "therapeutic," and they seemed to give ex-members merely some "space" between their exits and their entrances back into mainstream society. In many ways, rehabilitation was depicted as being analogous to a halfway-house situation. Those who did express negative reactions to rehabilitation either criticized its "anticult bias" or its "exploitation" and its use of newly deprogrammed members undergoing rehabilitation to deprogram others. Most simply saw it as a time to readjust to living in the real world once again.

Ex-members who had undergone therapy were more inclined to place the blame for their involvement in the Unification church on themselves rather than on some sinister aspect of the "cult." As one ex-member put it:

I am learning in therapy now that I always try to escape and that I have to learn to keep my feet on the ground and also not to give people complete power over me.

This discrepancy in orientation is consistent with the differences between therapy and deprogramming because therapy takes a more person-centered approach to the problem while deprogramming, with its heavy reliance on brainwashing and mind control as the major reasons for cult involvement, takes a more situation-centered approach.

Conclusion

It can be seen readily that contact with the anticult movement, either at the point of exit or subsequent to that time, serves an important reference-group function for former members searching for a framework within which to view their experiences. It is also influential in defining postexit attitudes and values. It is indeed ironic that this function is in many ways similar to the role played by the church in providing recruits with a new world view in which to perceive their past and present lives. In or out of the Unification church, the results of the present study can be seen as a microcosm of the struggle many young adults currently face in searching for something to give meaning and purpose to their lives. In many ways, this struggle of the 1970s bears much resemblance to those of other decades, only the objects of attraction have evolved from interest in drugs and politics to interest in new religious movements. Decisions among today's youth to join groups like the Unification church can, in large measure, be explained by the intensification of feelings of alienation and isolation, coupled with a need to find all-embracing belief systems that will give meaning to one's existence. As one chronicler of these movements has said·

> The message of all these cults is that modern civilization is in a hopeless snarl, and that it can only be salvaged through total commitment to one or another among the many self-proclaimed unsnarlers to which a person may happen to be drawn (Perry, 1975, p. 183).

However, upon finding that the Unification church is not in fact the answer to their existential quest, individuals either exit on their own in search of a replacement, or they have that exit accomplished for them. Though it may seem from the outside that this exit has not been helpful to them, or has resulted even in a net-loss in their ultimate search for meaning, this is in fact not the case. For, not unlike a suicide attempt, they have now made their plight known to kin and clinician alike who hastily mobilize to fill the void.

Luckily, ex-members also have selected a poison—namely cult involvement —for which there is a newly discovered antidote, deprogramming, rehabilitation, therapy, or some combination of the three. Thus regardless of the particulars of the interventions applied, former members will often arise from the ashes with new-found friends (other ex-members), a rejuvenated parent-child relationship, perhaps a new avocation (deprogramming), and definitely a new reference group and cause celebré—the anticult movement. Others will simply use the time provided them, especially during the rehabilitation phase, to readjust to society and decide upon a concrete course of action that most often includes work, school, or both. Indeed, it is only those who do not embark upon such a future plan who simply reenter the search-for-meaning cycle and begin the process once again.

No amount of probing nor degree of statistical significance will ultimately explain why both conversion into and deprogramming out of the Unification church have been so successful, at least in terms of numbers. We are still a long way from knowing why such complete transformations are attractive to the youth of the 1970s. Hoffer (1951) has discussed these kinds of conversions as a chance for a new life, or failing that, at least a possible way of acquiring pride, confidence, hope, or a sense of purpose and worth by an identification with a cause. Frank (1961) sees the process as providing its participants with a new sense of identity, harmony, and the enhancement of self-worth. Life thus regains its meaning, or it becomes more meaningful, and the individual is able to function effectively again—at least for a time—as a significant member of a group that by its acceptance helps to consolidate and reinforce the changes the individual has undergone.

Regardless of the particular theory proposed, these kinds of radical role changes seem to provide individuals who were previously alienated from themselves, their environment, and/or their significant others with a method of acquiring a more meaningful perspective and a more productive behavioral repertoire. One can only hope that the 1980s will provide its youth with less drastic alternatives for meaningful lives.

Note

1. *U.S. News and World Report,* 14 June 1976, pp. 52-54.

References

Anthony, Dick; Thomas Robbins, and J. McCarthy, 1980
Asch, S.E., 1956
Cartwright, D., and A. Zander, 1968
Chapman, D.W., and J. Volkmann, 1939
Clark, J.G., 1976
Festinger, L., 1954
Frank, J.D., 1961
Helmreich, R., J. Stapp, and C. Ervin, 1974
Hoffer, E., 1951
Hyman, H.H., 1942
Kelley, H.H., 1952
Perry, W.N., 1975
Robbins, Thomas, 1977
Sage, W., 1976
Sherif, M., 1936
Siegel, A.E., and S. Siegel, 1957
Singer, M.T., 1977
Solomon, T., and A. Pines, 1977

New Religions and the Decline of Community

Kids in Cults

Irvin Doress and Jack Nusan Porter

Why do young people join cults? Our research indicates that it is mainly young adults of post-high school age who are attracted, and not older, established families with children and careers. This fact alone tells us a great deal about their reasons for joining.

To find a family. The Unification church constantly emphasizes the breakdown of the American family, corruption and immorality in American life (divorce, pornography, suicide, drugs, and scandal), and, by contrast the work of the church toward the "perfect family" in a "perfect world." The stress on the family is so pervasive that one cult calls itself "The Love Family," while others call themselves "The Family" or "Love Israel." Family life in America is beset by conflicts and problems. A great many families espouse a set of workably good values, but they live their lives by a contradictory value set. When the progeny of such families see such contradictions, they begin to search out and seek answers from their parents. If answers are not forthcoming, or are of poor quality, the children may start looking elsewhere. They may look to surrogate families to meet their needs. Recent research has shown that American parents do a great deal of psychological and physical violence to their children. Many youths may be improving themselves by joining cults/sects and moving from a negative, hurting environment to one characterized by ego support, nonbelligerence, and persuasion rather than force.

A spiritual search for answers. Children reared in mature, established religions are used to not getting answers to their questions. This can lead to a sense of incompleteness and dissatisfaction. When a cult comes along and offers definitive and complete answers, it is very tempting for the youngsters to be caught up in the lifestyles of the answer-givers. Early phases of religions tend to be fanatical and full of "perfect" answers. Often the religion of the parents is nonexistent, or so part-time that it is totally ineffectual. The children see through this meaninglessness, and therefore seek a religion that offers meaning, structure, and full-time commitment. They desire religion as a way of life, not as a sometime thing.

Security. Though we need more research to bear this out, a significant percentage of families in our society seems to be afflicted by marital discord, marital breakdown, intergenerational strife, gross immaturities, and child/ adolescent abuse, all of which can lead to a sense of insecurity. What does one do when one is insecure? A variety of things, one of which is to look for a replacement family. Cults/sects often act as such secure "homes," even more secure than the political and cultural groupings of the 1960s.

Differentiation. According to Gail Sheehy's seminal and original treatise *Passages*, young people crave differentiation from their parents. If this is so, then the form that such adolescent rebellion can take is association with cults. In our interviews with cult "devotees," we found that they tried to rebel in various ways (drugs, promiscuity, running away, etc.) before turning to the cults. Examples of differentiation offered by the cults include: a religion that is totally different; communal living vs. nuclear family; spirituality vs. materialism; austerity vs. extravagant spending; a different culture and subculture; a different set of customs and traditions; a different set of attitudes; a different set of clothing, hair styles, etc. All of these differences constitute what one may call the process of differentiation that marks the period of growing up. It is a way to detach oneself from parental values and develop a new and vastly different value set.

Adolescent rebellion. Closely aligned with differentiation, adolescent rebellion is a concomitant of advanced Western industrial society. It takes many forms: panty raids, rushing into the marines at fifteen, smoking marijuana, alcoholic binges, riding the rails, living like a hobo, wrecking the family car, taking off, and, finally, joining a cult. Being in a successful cult can be a great opportunity to look out of the corner of the eye and say about one's parents: "Look at what they are doing and look at what I'm into. I'm so mad at them and their foul-ups. While they are about to go over Niagara Falls in a barrel, I'm approaching my zenith." Although permissiveness is not the major culprit leading to the rebellion that certain political and religious groups rail about, we would speculate that some young people rebel against structurelessness or overpermissiveness, or what sociologists call "alientation" or "anomie." They find it anxiety provoking and therefore go off to find such structure in a cult. The cult will represent a rebellion against all they knew before. It will provide the structure and content they seek. Often there is a complete turnabout, for example, from promiscuity to celibacy or from lack of self-control to tight control.

Adventure. Ever since Huckleberry Finn and Tom Sawyer, boys and girls have longed for adventure. Whether it is going to the candy store or the movies without parental approval or running away from home at fourteen, there is something exciting about the risk. Adventure contains elements of both rebellion and differentiation. In addition, it may represent an escape from boredom, strict parents, or onerous duties at home. Also, a person who seems relatively unsuccessful at trying to emulate a father who is a factory worker in Lowell, Massachusetts, or Milwaukee, Wisconsin, could "take off" and join a cult. In this sense, cults may even be a form of upward mobility in an economically stagnant society.

Attention. One of the basic needs promulgated by sociologist W.I. Thomas is recognition. When we speak of the desire for attention we are speaking at least partly of recognition. The cults seem to be a short-cut method of achieving instant attention and recognition. In the Unification church devotees are even taught how to smile at people. All guests are warmly welcomed. In a harsh urban landscape, this can prove almost irresistible to newcomers. Furthermore, as a devotee, one is visible and differentiated. The response from the general public may be negative, but at least it is a response of some kind; such individuality is very satisfying to youth in cults seeking attention, recognition, and even notoriety. The saffron robes of the Hare Krishna and the rough cloth robes of the Children of God are attention getting. It is a way of saying: "Here I am, whether you like it or not. I exist. And you'd better listen, or the world will come to an end!"

Idealism. In one case we know, the daughter attempted to replicate in a generic way her father's idealism. He was quite active in civil rights and peace movements. For this she admired him, but she had to do things in her own way. Ultimately she joined the Hare Krishna group because one of the major goals of the Krishnas (and many other cults/sects) is to bring about world peace. Of course, the cult's approach to peace is to convert everyone to their way of thinking. This is similar to the Pax Americana which the late President Kennedy warned against, by which everything in the world is relentlessly converted to America, Americanism, and American culture. In any event, many people join cults for such idealistic reasons.

Underemployment and dead-end jobs. There are probably few things as depressing or frightening as losing one's job and entering the ranks of the unemployed. Panic may set in, and an individual may take precipitous steps. Some go into serious depression. At any rate, an unemployed young man or woman may opt to join a cult. At least, such people have a roof over their heads and free meals in return for begging in the streets twelve to fourteen hours a day. At best, they could move up the hierarchy of the cult into a position of responsibility and status.

Why Do They Stay?

Needs being met. Whatever needs brought them in (security, rebellion, recognition, idealism) will also make them stay. For example, if they go in to obtain security and find it, why should they leave? They may not leave, and it will take a very persuasive argument to convince them to do so. And whether we abhor cults or not, a number of them do in fact meet the needs of many of their followers.

Loving interpersonal relations. Whether people are in the navy, at home with parents, or in a cult, loving relationships will tend to sustain them and make them want to remain in the institution. This is one of the reasons that cults are difficult to fight—they are hard to replace in this crucial area of loving care. People will not leave unless the cult changes or they begin to see the true nature of it, i.e., that it is *not* so loving and caring after all.

A finer, purer physical and moral environment. In the face of the moral decay of a society characterized by alcoholism, drug abuse, promiscuity, and violence, the cults are in a position to offer an environment that is alcohol-free, drug-free, violence-free, and virtually sex-free. Although a small number of cults have been accused of using drugs as well as practicing promiscuity and sexual orgies (in America this has historically been a popular—and sometimes truthful—denuciation), we have found that the major cults (Moonies, Krishnas, Scientology, The Way) tend to be quite puritanical regarding affairs of the flesh. Sex is forbidden unless one is married, and then only for procreation. Drugs and alcohol are also strictly forbidden as harmful to the body. Furthermore, the physical environment of the church and *ashram* is closely guarded. The Krishna *ashram* is cleaned everyday and is spotless. Many cults have moved or hope to move to the country in order to find a purer environment. Many already have country retreats, but stay in the city because potential converts are there in great numbers. Most cults seek an environment that is clean internally (mind, soul, and body) and externally (home, air, water, and food).

Spiritual hunger. The thing that brings hundreds of American youth into the cults in the first place also tends to keep them involved. Once the spiritual need is filled, it becomes habit-forming. Spiritual "trips" are more addictive and powerful than most drugs. There is a great deal of pleasure derived from chanting, dancing, and speaking in tongues. We also suggest that to a certain extent it is sexual sublimation.

Fear of leaving. Cult leaders claim that their followers are free to leave at any time. This is both true and false. While not forcibly restrained, it has been our observation that many devotees are told that if they leave or deviate from the "party line," God will punish them or their parents, or they will be crippled for life, afflicted by a dread disease, cursed, or even die. They are sometimes told that their parents and friends are "devils" and that their only true salvation is to stay in the cult. Thus, physical restraint is unnecessary. "Spiritual" persuasion is a way of keeping subjects in the cult, and it is quite effective.

Security and ego support offered by the cult is hard to find on the outside. Devotees are often afraid to leave because they fear lack of these qualities in the outside world. They fear making a total readjustment to the world. We have found that a small but constant number of devotees have some form of mental illness. In some cases, the cult acts as a benign and supportive "mental hospital" for these youths better than many public institutions. The cult allows these young people to act out their psychosis in a spiritual way. This fascinating issue should be studied more. There are devotees who leave the cult but still believe in many of its teachings. Such believers become householders, living in an apartment nearby and attending functions at the cult center. This appears to be a compromise with the full-time demands of the cult.

Why Do They Leave?

Many parents have given up hope that their children will ever leave the cult. There are ways, whether by choice or by force, by which young people leave.

Disillusionment. We do not know the attrition rate from cults (it undoubtably varies), but inevitably some devotees become disillusioned by the gap between promise and reality within the cult. They feel that they will never achieve their goal of "saving the world." Some give up hope; others lose patience; still others find life in the cult too difficult to maintain. Also, youngsters may have a genuine change of heart and leave. There have been a few cases of poor nutrition, inadequate health precautions, and similar factors that have induced some to leave.

Completion of stage of development. Some young people go into cults like into the army, in order to fulfill certain developmental tasks. When these are accomplished and the child recognizes it, he or she may decide to leave. If there is no undue fear of leaving the cult, they will leave on their own. Most cult followers are young people. As they grow older they may find the cult/sect useful in their lives and remain, or they may learn from it and leave when they have completed this stage of development, taking with them some interesting experiences and valuable lessons.

Kidnap rescue. This seems the most unnatural and most dangerous way of leaving, but in a few cases it may be the only way for parents to regain their children. Some devotees "ask" their parents to remove them forcibly by various cues, doubletalk, or nonverbal expression. Subjects who have been taken out this way often go later to therapists for help. It is impossible to state whether they went to a psychologist or psychiatrist because of the nature of the release from the cult or due to earlier problems. It is more likely that being in a cult for any amount of time has its traumatic effects and, then again, the readjustment period to the outside world is also a factor. The kidnapping methods of Ted Partick and others can be expensive, illegal, and not always effective, despite their claims. Some young people do not want to return or cannot return home. They may even be homeess, "orphans" in a sense. The cult may then become their family and, if it falls apart, they may seek other cults. We could call these people "cult addicts," serving a protean function of experimentation and existential trial and error.

Every age of history has had religious movements that are born, mature, and pass. Our age is no exception. Cults are not new. They will persist. What can be done about them? What can we learn from them? Some experts suggest that a child must be removed from the cult as quickly as possible and as forcibly as necessary. Educating people about the nature of cults is very important. Education, some feel, may be the most effective method in combating cults. Others insist that we must offer young children "dramatic" and appealing alternatives. Parents and educators must come together in order to choose the techniques and alternatives that best fit the situation of their child, school, or community.

References

Cox, Harvey, 1977
Enroth, Ronald, 1977
Yamamoto, J. Isamu, 1977
Lifton, Robert J., 1961

Freedom, Love, and Community:
An Outline of a Theory

George A. Hillery, Jr.

The interplay of one's values and research is a topic more often talked about than demonstrated. The research to be discussed here is an example of such interplay. All research reflects the researcher's values, but in some instances the relationship is more obvious than in others. In the present case, the values guiding the research stemmed equally from a desire to solve a sociological problem concerning the nature of community and from a personal commitment to Jesus Christ. I do not apologize either for my science or my religion. Whatever is accomplished in each area must stand on its own merits. I wish to show the unfolding of a particular line of research as it has developed from scientific to other-than-scientific areas and back to science again (though the process cannot be delineated that sharply).

Of all fields of sociology, the study of community is one of the most basic to understanding the manner in which Christian groups can be adequately constituted. As a Christian, I have discovered some things of vital importance to my life, on which my science has never more than touched fleetingly. Foremost among these is love. In studying both community and love, it has become apparent that one of the basic contexts, even mechanisms, in which these phenomena operate is freedom. But to gain an adequate comprehension of these things, I have found that I needed both science and religion. It is the interplay of these systems which I want to discuss.

A theory is composed of many parts. There is the set of propositions showing the relation between variables in a formal sense. There are also the definitions of the variables. But as important as any portion of the theory are the assumptions on which it is based, particularly the assumption concerning the types of truths employed. In science this assumption is unstated because everyone is aware that only one type of truth is being employed—scientific truth, or truth based on data determined by objective presentation of physical evidence.

In his monumental study of social change, Pitirim Sorokin postulated other kinds of truths. In addition to scientific ("sensate") truth, there is the truth based on faith ("ideational" truth). He went on to propose a third type, one which integrated both of the others: integralist truth. This article will take Sorokin's ideas as a point of departure and attempt to demonstrate the necessity of employing more than one type of truth in the study of social behavior.

Types of Truths

The problem of exploring the nature of truth is both metaphysical and epistemological. The metaphysical problem involves the nature of the assumptions concerning reality. The scientist assumes that reality is based on physical data, whereas a mystic assumes further that there is a superphysical—i.e., a spiritual—reality. Regardless of one's assumptions about reality, there are different ways of experiencing or knowing that reality, in terms of the type of evidence one will accept as truth. The experience may be direct, such as hearing sounds, being inebriated, or (in the experience of some to be studied here) perceiving God. This is the experiential aspect. Such experience can only partly (if at all) be communicated to others. Some types of knowledge may be communicated precisely, such as the designation of sounds by means of musical notes, discerning the alcoholic content of blood, or describing the fact that Christians believe in a trinitarian God. This is the objective aspect.

The combination of the metaphysical and epistemological dimensions reveals four types of truths (no claim is made that these are the only types of truths): mystical, theological, sensory, and scientific. These are depicted in Figure 18.1. Most written discussions are objective, whether scientific or theological, in the sense in which *objective* is being used here. Seldom can writing be fully experiential, though poetry comes close, as do novels. This article will concern itself mainly with *indicating* certain experiential truths. It cannot duplicate them. In contrast, there is frequently a dependence of objective on experiential truth. Scientists will tend to be more satisfied when they have done an experiment themselves. The writing of theologians has been known to change drastically upon their undergoing a mystical experience. But the separation between the two truths is often quite discrete. An example from sensory truth will help show the distinction: one who has never been drunk may do a breath analysis and establish that someone else is drunk. He may understand this analysis sufficiently to cause the drunk to be placed in jail. But he will not experientially understand what it is to be drunk. The same can be said for mystical truth. The theologian may understand that Christians believe in a trinitarian God. He may have faith in such a God, himself, and may even be able to prescribe certain theological readings to help someone see his point. But that does not mean that he has "known" God in the sense of having had a mystical experience.

FIGURE 18.1
Types of Truth

Metaphysics: Type of reality that is assumed:	Epistemology: Method of Knowing: Experiential	Objective
Spiritual	Mystical truth	Theological truth
Physical	Sensory truth	Scientific truth

This discussion will be based on all four types of truths. Special emphasis is placed on the relation between mystical, sensory, and scientific truth. The experiential pole of the epistemological dimension was made possible through participant observation. The objective pole was reached mainly through questionnaires. One of the major purposes in presenting such a discussion is to help demarcate more precisely the boundaries of science. A major assumption of this article is that the world cannot be understood purely from the scientific point of view. The question then arises, What is the perspective that exists outside of science? Granted that some of the topics to be treated here are not considered to be *sociology* as the term is generally used. However, the thesis being advanced is that in order to understand social behavior, to properly study society (i.e., socio*logy*), the customary horizons of sociology must be extended.

Theory of Organizational Freedom

We begin with a theory of communal organizations (Hillery, 1968, 1971). Basic to the theory is a general taxonomy of human groups (Figure 18.2). A major point of the taxonomy is that it depicts changes in human behavior: when degree of institutionalization is held constant, as between communal and formal organizations, then a change in whether a group gives primacy to a specific goal means that differences will also occur in the behavior of the members of those groups. From this reasoning, three hypotheses are developed. The hypotheses are based on observation of differences in behavior among groups as one moves across the theoretical boundaries between communal and formal organizations.

FIGURE 18.2

A General Taxonomy of Human Groups

The system has primacy of orientation
to specific goals

		Yes	No
	High	**Formal Organizations** Businesses Prisons Boarding Schools	**Communal Organizations** Vills (villages & cities) Monasteries Communes
	Low	**Expressive Groups** Social Movements Crowds	**Informal Groups** Ethnic Groups Cliques

Degree of Institutionalization

1. If a group is primarily oriented to the attainment of a specific goal, then it excludes familial behavior — i.e., formal organizations exclude families.
2. The greater the deprivation of freedom among groups, the greater the antagonism of those deprived.
3. Only if a group is not primarily oriented to the attainment of a specific goal will it maximize the freedom of its members—i.e., communal organizations maximize freedom more than do formal organizations.

Definitions

Data have been gathered which permit the testing of these hypotheses developed in my earlier work (the test is based on 46 groups, see Table 18.1). This section is concerned with presenting operational definitions of the hypotheses. Five measures of freedom are used. The first four are based on perceived freedom (see Hillery et al., for the list of questions used in the freedom scales).

Deprivation of freedom is measured by a five-item scale. A multiple-group factor analysis indicates that the scale items are tapping a singular underlying factor. The remaining three types of freedom were also isolated by means of factor analysis. Two of the types had been identified through prior theoretical work (Hillery, 1971). They are labeled "ego freedom" (wherein one's freedom is defined as doing what one wishes to do) and "disciplined freedom" (defined as a freedom requiring sharing and sacrificing). Conditional freedom, the third type, is that in which one's freedom is limited (or conditioned) by other people or external circumstances. A fifth type of freedom is measured not by perception but by social structure; that is, it is defined in terms of the rules one encounters in moving over the space of the group. Five types are involved: (1) groups in which anyone may enter or leave, as in crowds; (2) groups which permit only members to enter, as in a college classroom; (3) groups requiring members to have permission to come and go, as in monasteries; (4) groups which prohibit members from leaving, as in prisons; and (5) groups restricting the internal movement of their members, as in solitary confinement. For convenience in measurement, the last three are classified together as those which place restrictions on entering and leaving, and the first two are combined as representing groups without such mobility restrictions.

Antagonism is defined as *conflict,* which in turn is defined by asking the members of the various groups to report their behavior over a given week and a year. Seven questions were asked, specifying that respondents record only situations in which they were actually involved, as for example speaking with at least one of the persons participating directly in the action: (1) a discussion in which some disagreement occurred; (2) a discussion in which some tension occurred; (3) a discussion in which some antagonism occurred; (4) a disagreement in which shouting occurred; (5) a situation in which some physical force was used on someone; (6) a situation in which some physical harm was done to someone; and (7) a situation in which weapons were used or where someone was killed. For the first 27 groups studied, the analysis suggests that the scale is measuring a single dimension of reported conflict behavior. (Coefficients of reproducibility are more than .930 and coefficients of scalability are more than .680.) From the replies to these questions, two basic measures of conflict are derived: disputes, or the percent of a group falling into the first three scale types; and violence, or the percentage falling into the last four scale types.

Formal organizations are defined as those groups which give primacy to specific goals. It is important to emphasize two words in this definition: *primacy* refers to the purpose for which a group is designed, apart from which it would have no meaning; *specific* refers to something measurable. *Communal organizations* are defined as groups which do not give primacy to specific goals. Communal organizations may have purposes, but their success or failure is not readily measurable. The specific goals and the purposes of the groups are given in Table 18.1.

TABLE 18.1
Groups Used in the Analysis

Name and Type	Population Total	Sample	Purpose or Specific Goal*
Confined Communal Organizations			Purpose
Monastery 1	68	50	Prayer
Monastery 2	16	15	"
Monastery 3	34	16	"
Monastery 4	24	9	"
Monastery 5	63	20	"
Monastery 6	14	10	"
Yoga Commune	14	13	Tantra yoga, social service
Caphas volunteers, 1970	varies	9	Christian witness, communal living
Caphas members, 1970	15	14	Christian witness
Caphas members, 1973	25	20	" "
Walden	36	31	To approximate B. F. Skinner's Walden Two
Kincade Housing Project	650	10	Residential, low cost housing
Carr Housing Project	700	9	" " " "
Transient Communal Organizations			
Yoga Training Group	14	11	Tantra yoga, social service
St. Samuel	11	11	Community involvement and Christian witness
Martin House	34	24	Alternative to dormatory living, Christian witness (ecumenical), to "experience community"
Co-op	12	11	Communal living, sharing expenses
Anark	9	9	" " " " anti establishment
Sorority 1	31	29	Sorority life
Sorority 2	60	42	" "
Sorority 3	9	9	" "
Fraternity 1	39	33	Fraternity life
Fraternity 2	21	21	" "
Fraternity 3	41	34	" "
Confined Formal Organizations			Specific Goal*
Quaker boarding school			
students	60	55	Students graduated
staff	20	14	" "
Farm boarding school			
students	21	18	" "
staff	12	12	" "

TABLE 18.1 (Continued)

Name and Type	Population Total	Sample	Purpose or Specific Goal*
Old Age Home 1	35	28	Old persons housed
Old Age Home 2	80	46	" " "
Old Age Home 3	120	25 **	" " "
Women's minimum security prisoners	68	40	Prisoners maintained in custody
Men's medium security prisoners	627	45**	" " " "
Staff (excluding guards)	210	82	" " " "
Military Medical Corps	10	10	Patients treated
Women's Army Corps	10	10	Clerical duties
University military cadet corps			
Women	42	29	Cadets graduated
Men	396	215	" "
University dormitories			
Women 1	75	33	Students housed
Women 2***	75	21	" "
Social Work Staff	35	13	Cases handled
Transient Formal Organizations			
Drug Rehabilitation Center	27	15	Addicts treated
Military Police	500	46	Deviants apprehended
University dormitories			
Women 3	147	41	Students housed
Men 1	42	37	" "
Women's minimum security prison staff	41	29	Prisoners maintained in custody

*In the case of formal organizations, only one goal is given. There may be others, but without at least the measureable goal being fulfilled, the system could not be called successful.

**Random sample.

***From same dormitory as Women 1, except that Women 2 answered the questionnaire in terms of their position *vis-a-vis* the University.

TABLE 18.2

Various Familial Relationships (Spouse, Parent-Child, Sibling) Present in Formal and Communal Organizations

	Organization		ϕ	p
	Communal	Formal		
Total Relatives				
present	8	17	.397	.01>p>.001
absent	16	5		

Testing the Hypotheses

The first hypothesis presents the most difficulties. Either the numbers are too small to permit any distinctions, or the data clearly are in opposition to the hypothesis (Table 18.2). Thus, about the same number of communal and formal organizations in this collection of data have spouses in the system and have parents and children together. However, siblings are present more often in formal than in communal organizations, a finding opposite from the prediction made by the hypothesis. In all cases, siblings in formal organizations were found either among staff, if the group was staff, or among inmates, if the group was one of inmates (or clients, students, etc.). In no case did an inmate (etc.) have a sibling relative among staff, or vice versa. The staff/inmate split, where there is one, is the barrier or prohibitor of familial relations and in this sense the formal organization tends to exclude families, since only among formal organizations is there a staff/inmate split.

Most of the communal organizations are organized in part to form new kinds of primary group contacts, such as monasteries, communes, cooperative boarding houses, and fraternities and sororities. Thus one would expect fewer ties with former kin relations, such as siblings. Since many of the groups are composed of young people or celibates, the spouse and parent-child relationships would not or could not be formed. These qualifications notwithstanding, the first hypothesis is not tenable in all situations.

The second hypothesis also shows the need for qualification but otherwise fares much better (Table 18.3). When all groups are considered, disputes are not significantly related to deprivation of freedom, but violence is. A further qualification is necessary. When groups are divided into those the members of which spend most of their time within the groups (designated here as confined

TABLE 18.3
Spearman Rank-Order Correlations Between Deprivation of Freedom and Conflict for Selected Populations

Population	Number of Groups	Conflict Disputes	Conflict Violence
All groups	33	.254	.497**
Transient	18	.408*	.160
Confined	15	.193	.575**
Transient Nonstaff	15	.299	.144
Confined Nonstaff	14	.306	.754***

*significant at .05

**significant at .01

***significant at .001

groups), versus those that do not (transient groups), we find that in transient groups there is no significant relation between deprivation of freedom and either disputes or violence. However, we find that in confined populations violence is associated with deprivation of freedom, whereas disputes are not. A final qualification appears when staff populations are removed. When this is done, the correlation for confined groups is even stronger, rising to 57 percent of the variance explained. Partial correlations controlling for age, education, size of group, and size of community of origin do not alter the findings.

Deprivation of freedom does not lead to conflict in general; it leads to violence more than it does to disputes. Deprivation of freedom leads to violence only when group members spend most of their time in the group (that is, when they are confined rather than transient) and when they are not staff members. In other words, if a person can and does leave the group frequently (if he can "get away") and if he is a staff member (if he has power), then deprivation of freedom does not lead to violence.

Testing the third hypothesis requires a different measure, since one of the variables — type of organization — is dichotomous. Phi, derived from chi square, is used for this purpose. (Gamma is also used to indicate direction more readily.) Table 18.4 shows that for each of the four measures of perceptual

TABLE 18.4

Differences in Freedom for Communal and Formal Organizations

| | Organization | | ϕ | p | γ |
	Communal	Formal			
Deprivation of freedom					
less than 27%	16	5	.441	.007	.744
27% and over	8	17			
Disciplined freedom					
less than 70%	9	17	.401	.02	-.700
70% and over	15	5			
Egoistic freedom					
less than 20%	6	14	.339	.02	-.680
Table 18.5 I over	18	8			
Conditional freedom					
less than 63%	5	15	.447	.003	-.781
63% and over	19	7			
Structural freedom					
Restrictions placed					
on entering or					
leaving					
yes	7	9	.164	.44	-.330
no	17	11			

Scores computed by obtaining the mean percentage agreement on all items in the given scale.

For groups comprising communal and formal organizations, see Table 1.

freedom, members of communal organizations feel more free than members of formal organizations. The importance of this finding is increased when it is noted that there is no significant difference among groups in their structural freedom. There is no inherent bias in the selection of these groups concerning their structural freedom which would explain the differences in perceived freedom.

The question still remains whether membership in communal or formal organizations makes any difference in behavior, as has been claimed. Table 18.5 offers partial confirmation. There is a clear difference in violence scores—communal organizations are less violent, to judge from the reports of the

TABLE 18.5
**Differences in Internal Violence Between Communal
and Formal Organizations**

	Organization				
	Communal	Formal	φ	p	γ
Disputes					
less than 60%	14	12	.038	.969	.007
60% and over	10	10			
Violence					
less than 10%	16	6	.394	.018	.684
10% and over	8	16			

For groups comprising communal and formal organizations, see Table 1.

members. Disputes show no discernible difference. To some extent the basic hypothesis is confirmed—there is a difference in behavior between communal and formal organizations; the difference, however, is only apparent in extreme (violent) behavior. There are also extensive and systematic differences in perceptions of freedom, but the dichotomy is not absolute.

In terms of that portion of the theory that has been examined here, we may conclude that (1) deprivation of freedom is associated with violence in confined and nonstaff groups; (2) members of communal organizations perceive themselves to be more free than members of formal organizations; and (3) there is little evidence that formal organizations exclude families, except for the lack of interaction across the staff/inmate split.

The findings indicate that the general classification of human groups has value in understanding why people behave as they do. Group structure appears to make some difference in human behavior (see Hillery et al.). But the theory only relates three variables: group goals, perceived freedom, and violence. The task now is to see if the meaning of this theory can be expanded, particularly by incorporating other types of truths. We will examine sensory, mystical, and theological truth. The data with which the discussion will be concerned revolve around the concept of love.

Ideal Types

To pursue this analysis, the technique of the ideal type will be employed. Such a technique requires that one construct a model that is both pure and simplified. The model represents the conditions that would exist if all unnecessary things were removed, if all contradictory or contaminating influences were eliminated. It is akin to the idea of the frictionless surface or the absolute zero of the physicist, or (in a very crude sense) it is something like the germ-free mice that have been raised in certain laboratories. These are not necessarily or usually "reality," but by studying them, or as close as we can come to them, we learn something about reality. Normally, the purpose of constructing ideal types is not to depict a morally ideal situation—nor an immorally ideal one. However, since we are dealing with spiritual truth, such will be the aims here. The ideal types to be constructed will represent extreme moral poles. In this sense, the ideal types will be ideal.

I shall build four ideal types: the family, the monastery, the business, and the prison. These types are to be developed in two stages. The first employs variables from the hypotheses examined in the previous section. Thus, ideal types of groups are to be built (1) for those with maximum and minimum freedom and (2) for those that give primacy to specific goals and those that do not. In other words, the ideal types will vary along the organizational and the freedom dimensions. The second stage consists of using variables related to freedom and goal attainment but heretofore unexamined: love and personal involvement.

The Family

We start with that relationship in which a man and a woman give of each other, to each other, as completely as possible. In this act, they raise to the highest point both their freedom of choice and of discipline. Each must become disciplined to the other, and in so doing, each has maximum access to the other, including, of course, freedom to the body of the other. (See I Corinthians 7:4.)

Even these freedoms are not complete. For example, there is no group in which everyone can be the leader. Someone must lead, and thus one type of choice becomes closed to the one who does not lead. Second, because our bodies are discrete entities, we cannot give of ourselves completely, simply because we are separate. Ogden Nash has put it best: "We'd free the incarcerate race of man/That such a doom endures/Could only you unlock my skull/Or I creep into yours."

From this giving, children arise. This introduction of new persons into the two-person group immediately limits freedom of choice: children are not sexually accessible to parents or to each other. Freedom of discipline is also limited: children cannot give to parents as much as parents can give to children or to each other. Finally, both freedoms become radically diminished or even terminated when children establish their own families.

As this relationship is extended beyond the family to the village community (or even the city), freedoms are further limited. This limitation applies particularly to the general decrease of freedom in bodily contact. However, except for the reduction of this bodily freedom, community members in the ideal type still give of each other and receive from each other to the fullest, relative to other groups. (See the Book of Acts, Chs. 2 and 4, for expressions of this ideal.)

The Monastery

The monastery is built of community relationships (in the sense of village or city community) that are otherwise exclusive of the family. No family relationships occur in the monastery we are building here. There are two additional features: the most successful monasteries have been limited to one sex; and the members dedicate themselves to their God. Since community relationships in the monastery prevail only apart from the family, and since the group is unisexual, sexual giving to their God is irrelevant (at the very least). With this exception, the monk gives himself as completely as possible to his God and his God reciprocates, to the extent that the monk's humanity will permit. This second limitation is comparable to that of the spouse relationship: complete giving (and receiving) is not possible because the monk is human.

In one sense, the monastery lacks some of the freedoms found in the family, especially bodily freedom, both sexual and parental. In another sense, the monks are more free, and here we must assume a spiritual reality: the monk gives and receives from his God without the complications arising from sexual relationships. In other words, the monk gives (disciplines) himself as completely as possible to his God and only to his God, and he is thus able to receive from his God in like manner. Although this freedom is necessary to understand the monastery, it cannot be understood on a scientific basis. We can say scientifically only that the monk believes this to be so and acts accordingly. From the viewpoint of scientific truth, the monastery has fewer freedoms than the family.

The Business

All familial relations are also excluded from the business relation. The businessman is in this sense a monk. Only those relations are permitted which are pertinent to the specific goal of the business. In this ideal type, regardless of whether the customer may be a wife or a child, this customer is treated as any other: "business is business." This means all other alternatives and all other disciplines are also removed. The freedoms are accordingly reduced.

The Prison

All significant choices are removed from a particular segment of this group, the inmates. Discipline in the ideal type is at its maximum, but it is not a discipline that arises from free choice; it is enforced. The goal is quite specific:

custody of the inmates. Still, the goal is not that of the inmates but of the controlling staff. Because the goal is external to the inmates, and because individuals are discrete entities, discipline cannot be complete, if only because the prison in this type does not have access to men's minds.

Up to this point, freedom has only been examined as it relates to discipline, but freedom requires more pointed attention. The marital pair developed two of the freedoms discussed in the earlier section: disciplined and conditional freedom. The necessity of disciplined freedom is obvious, insofar as both partners give up the right to themselves. Conditional freedom arises because the freedom is tied to that of one other person. The monastery has only disciplined freedom. In the ideal sense, the monk's freedom is influenced only by his relation to his God, not by other people. The business has only conditional freedom—the sharing and sacrifice are not important in themselves but are only important as things the business must do. Similarly, the egoistic freedom of the business is curtailed by the need for conditional freedom. In the ideal type of the prison, there are no freedoms at all.

These ideal types in turn suggest another set. The same groups are involved, only different variables are used. The variables here are relationships to persons and to society. In introducing these variables, we are also using experiential truth, especially in relation to personal relationships, since the two poles of this variable are love and indifference. A central premise of this discussion is that love cannot be understood unless it has been experienced.

Because of the nature of experiential truth, any verbal description is necessarily limited. We can *suggest* a definition and a typology of love, we cannot *give* one. Accordingly, love is that condition wherein one attempts to work for the best interests of the beloved. The word used by Paul and the earliest Christians to discuss love was *agape,* which meant love (as here defined) in its purest sense, i.e., self-giving love. An alternative was *eros,* which has come to denote what Renaissance poets called "profane" love. The original meaning was not limited to sexual love, but we shall emphasize that meaning here.

Two other types of love are designated as fraternal and parental, admitting that the terms are not completely adequate to describe either. (The corresponding Greek terms are *philos* and *storgos* — see Lewis.) Fraternal love is that between friends, whether they be siblings or initially strangers. Parental love refers to both love of parents for children and vice versa, though emphasis is on parents. One could provide additional types, but these will do for our purposes. These types of love may be related to two variables: physical contact and detachment (See Figure 18.3). Physical contact is essential to erotic and parental love but is not as important to fraternal or agapic love. Parental love demands that the parent be willing to relinquish certain rights to the child; that is, the parent should exhibit some degree of detachment. Normally one does not consider such a condition necessary to erotic love. ("Therefore a man leaves his father and his mother and cleaves to his wife, and they become one flesh."

FIGURE 18.3
Types of Love

Detachment

		no	yes
Physical contact	yes	erotic	parental
	no	fraternal	agapic

Genesis 2:24.) There is a certain element of possessiveness to both fraternal and erotic love. Agapic love also carries a sense of detachment; indeed, it reveals the maximum amount of detachment love can have, if we consider Jesus as the prototype. We shall emphasize the erotic and agapic forms of love.

The other variable to be considered is one's relationship to society. The two poles to this variable are involvement and isolation. Involvement requires the maximum amount of interaction, isolation the least. Considering the relation of these variables to our four ideal-typical groups, in terms of the typology of love it is apparent that erotic and parental love characterize the family, whereas fraternal and agapic love characterize the monastery (Figure 18.4).

The monastery may seem to be the most contradictory type of the four. How can one be in a loving relationship with others and yet be isolated? The solution lies in the concept of detached or agapic love. The monk, being human, is not

FIGURE 18.4
Ideal Types According to Relation to Society and to Persons

Relationship to Persons

		Love	Indifference
Relation to Society	Involvement	Family	Business
	Isolation	Monastery	Prison

characterized only by agape—real friendships develop among monks for each other, and though this was officially discouraged in the past, it still happened. Nevertheless, the goal toward which the monk strives is detached love, which he can achieve in at least seven ways. Four of these are in terms of his vows (those of the Trappist-Cistercian Order are being used): celibacy, obedience, poverty, and stability. The remaining expressions of detachment are implicitly contained in the vow of "conversion of life": asceticism, separation from the world, and the prayer of quiet.

Celibate love is a form of detached love. The purpose of the detachment is usually expressed in terms of the consequent ability to be open to a nonpossessive love for everyone. The detachment found in obedience is central to monastic — particularly Cistercian — life. The monk vows to live under the guidance of a rule and an abbot. The rule is *The Holy Rule* of St. Benedict. The abbot is his temporal lord, the one who represents Christ to him. In offering obedience to the abbot, the monk does not give up his independence. He may leave whenever he wishes. But he does practice obedience as a form of humility. The same may be said of poverty, which again is a form of detachment, this time from the cares and seductions of the material world. The vow of stability detaches the monk from any temptation to leave the monastery to try and find his salvation elsewhere.

Asceticism is a form of detachment from the material world, but the relation to love may not be as apparent. The most immediate connection of asceticism with love can be seen in its further relationship to humility. The monk deprives himself of food, sleep, speech, etc., first in obedience to his God, because of his love for his God. But there is a further dimension: in asceticism, the monk is saying in effect that he will leave to his God any provision of earthly or spiritual pleasures—he will seek none himself. Separation from the world is in itself a detachment from the world—the ultimate purpose is to permit the monk greater opportunity for undisturbed meditation and prayer—often, prayer for the world. The prayer of quiet is the most basic form of monastic prayer. It consists of a condition in which the monk thinks no thoughts but simply stands in love, physically and mentally silent before his God. The prayer is the ultimate form of the monk's expression of love for his God, and it is occasionally accompanied by an experience of union with God.

Detachment in monks is relatively easy to understand, if only because it is so pervasive in their lives. But there is an element of detachment in erotic love as well, because no one can be completely accessible to another. But there is a more important aspect to detachment. The definition of love used here suggests that one works for the best interests of the beloved. If it is in the best interests of the beloved for the lover to leave, then failure to comply will mean less love on the part of the lover. If the spouse is ill, for example, and it would be better for the other partner to leave the spouse alone, then love itself will demand the degree of detachment that would permit the spouse the needed isolation. Thus erotic love cannot be completely possessive. Even in the very act of commitment, when one member totally commits himself to the other, then to that extent he becomes detached from himself. There is another he must consider, even as he considers his very own self.

Shifting to the other two ideal types, we note that in the prison as well as the business, love is absent as far as the system is concerned. The opposite of love here is not hate or conflict but indifference. One does not hate that toward which he is indifferent, but he may hate or even murder the one he loves, as statistics will attest. The businessman does not necessarily love his business, but he must be involved with it. In the isolation of the prison, we thus come to the ultimate negation of the basic values of community: love and involvement.

From this analysis of both businesses and prisons, it is apparent that formal organizations are antithetical to the basic value of love. Formal organizations are systems we use to get things done, in the spirit of efficiency. The attempt to operate a community, a marriage, or a monastery along business lines is essentially immoral, since such a course of action denies the very moral basis on which the existence of communal organizations is predicated. For example, if one were to make a group such as a monastery primarily oriented to economic profit, the purpose of the monastery would be subverted. In terms of monastic ideals, the economic orientation would be immoral. Or, for a family to function strictly as a business would mean that the husband and wife would have to prostitute themselves to each other and the children would have to pay for their room, board, and education. Communal organizations are based on a principle which in the ultimate sense can (and does) attain unilateral sacrifice, and this is the principle of love.

Love and Commitment

The analysis now returns to the first hypothesis: if a group gives primacy to specific goals, it excludes the family. The problem with this hypothesis should now be clearer: the hypothesis is formulated too specifically. As stated, the hypothesis may be quite relevant for some kinds of groups in some situations, but it is not substantiated when applied to a large number of different groups. The hypothesis may now be reformulated in light of the preceding discussion to read: Formal organizations tend to exclude love relationships. The ideal-typical analysis has suggested that formal organizations are indifferent to love relationships — until, that is, the love relationships interfere with the primacy of the specific goal. The hypothesis cannot be scientifically verified as it is given, since love is not a scientific concept. A testable hypothesis may be deduced from it: Groups established on the basis of love should have members that are more committed than groups not so established. Communal organizations should have members that are more committed than members of formal organizations.

Commitment can be conceived as having at least two subtypes: involvement and cohesion. Involvement, may be measured, after Kanter, by means of three questions: (1) "How important is it to you personally to have this group meet regularly for meals?" (2) ". . . for religious services?" (3) ". . . for group discussion?" Cohesion was measured by a modification of Seashore's work cohesion scale. This scale asks whether respondents feel that they "are really part of this group or community," whether the respondent wants to move from the group, and how the respondent compares his group with others. As may be seen in Table 18.6, the communal organizations studied here are both more involved and more cohesive than the formal organizations. Partial gammas, controlling for age, group size, and education, do not alter the relationships, except that the gamma between involvement and group size is reduced somewhat (from $-.489$ to $-.255$). We may conclude that the commitment in communal organizations is what one would expect if, as the ideal-typical analysis indicates, these organizations are based on love relationships. A qualification may be in order. There is no intention of claiming that all communal organizations are more committed than all formal organizations. The data show an overlap. The main point is that the findings concerning commitment are in agreement with the hypothesis concerning organization and love.

TABLE 18.6
The Relation Between Commitment and Social Organization

| | Organization | | | | |
	Communal	Formal	ϕ	p	γ
Cohesion*:					
Less than 40%	5	14	.463	.008	$-.764$
40% and over	16	6			
Involvement					
Less than 55%	9	14	.261	.140	$-.489$
55% and over	15	8			

*Cohesion measures not available for all organizations

For groups comprising communal and formal organizations, see Table 1.

Freedom, Love, and Community

Ladislaus Boros has said that the proper name of freedom "in its deepest sense is, after all, love." In order for one to act in the best interest of the beloved, he must be free to do so. The more freedom (and the less coercion), the greater the extent to which love can be exercised. Since we have presented evidence to suggest that communal organization is the realization of freedom, then it follows that freedom, love, and community form a basic unity. We cannot conclude that this unity necessarily exists in all cases. There are communal organizations without love. But the unity is inherent in these concepts such that each attains its fullest realization only in union with the other two. Let us examine each of the relationships in turn.

Freedom has its greatest realization in communal organizations and it is greater in communal organizations than in informal groups. This is so because the fullest attainment of freedom is possible only with commitment, that is, with discipline. The reasoning behind such a statement is as follows: ego freedom lives on the basis of having unhindered choices. Once a choice is made, other choices are ruled out. Making a choice—that is, realizing freedom—means imposing a discipline in the sense of ruling out other choices. Making a choice requires commitment. It follows that one will be able to make deeper commitments and thus realize more freedom to the extent that one is disciplined, and discipline requires rules. Thus, groups with more rules will be potentially capable of more freedom than those with fewer rules, and thus communal organizations will be potentially more free than informal groups.

The relation between freedom and love has been analyzed in the ideal type of the family and the monastery. It will be recalled that the marital pair making the greatest commitment to each other (thus having the most love) also had the greatest freedom. The monk goes even further. In giving his life to his God, in forsaking not only all others but all things insofar as he is able, he also attains, theoretically, the greatest freedom. He is, to the extent that he is successful, free not only of the constraints of all others but also of all else, all things. If he reaches the stage of complete freedom—the Buddhist *satori* or the Christian divine union—nothing binds him. And yet paradoxically, everything binds him, because in his attainment of love, he submits to all others and all else in love. It is a detachment that brings involvement. But the detachment is only possible in freedom.

The relation between love and community has been little more than implicit and remains to be sketched now, if only briefly. First we should note that the relation has been recognized by community theorists ever since Tönnies, particularly in the form of community sentiment. The contribution to be offered here is in emphasizing the potential, not the necessity of the connection. Communal organization does not necessarily mean community sentiment. (See Schmalenbach.) But in the same sense as freedom is related to community, so is love. For example, in the joining of two or more people to one another purely because they love one another and for no specific (measurable) reason, we find an essence of community. The peak experience is not necessarily there. The people so bound (but free) may not emote or celebrate continually. In fact, we would not expect them to. But the basis of the celebration, of the peak experience, is there, not only in the bonds that have grown through daily living but in the freedom with which those bonds have been forged, and continue to be.

Freedom, love, and community do not necessarily come together. Note that the correlations traced earlier between freedom and community were not perfect. And so it is in human experience: Husbands murder wives, wives divorce husbands, communities engage in internecine feuds (reputedly the bloodiest kind), and communities of various sorts—families, villages, cities, nations—place stifling constraints on their members. This is to be expected, in the sense of a necessary evil. In order for freedom to be real, there must be nonfreedom.

Conclusions

The ideal types as a whole point out several important variables of communal organizations, variables seen as difficult or impossible to phrase in a scientific manner. Communal organizations are groups which can maximize freedom and to which love is essential. It is possible for a communal organization to do without either of these attributes for a while, but eventually any such deficiency, whether in the name of efficiency or expediency, will mean the death of the system. Loss of love in the ideal type will obviously mean the death of the marital unit; loss of freedom will obviously mean the death of the monastery. Even should such groups continue in outward form, the death would be apparent. For example, consider the married couple who constitute a business partnership and who are seeking a divorce (but not a dissolution of the partnership); consider the monastery becoming a prison. Though both groups may continue, they are dead or dying in their original state. But in a more subtle way, loss of freedom means the death of the marriage, just as loss of love means death for the monastery. Should either partner in a marriage force the other into any act, then love is to that extent gone, and so is the marriage. And the monk who can love neither his God nor other people is no longer a monk.

The discussion of ideal types also shows the importance of detachment in any form of love, from erotic to agapic. And it shows the essential inhumanity of formal organizations. That these considerations are not scientific is admitted. But they began with a scientific basis (as indicated in the empirical tests mentioned in the earlier section), and they proceed to encompass elements which we have tried to argue are indispensable to the survival of the system.

Extending scientific discussions into areas of truth that are not scientific forces us to raise questions and search for answers that are crucial to the existence of humanity, not to mention science itself.

Theological truth has been largely neglected in this discussion, but at least one observation in this area can be offered. Monks have developed disciplined freedom as much or more than any other group considered here. Of the twelve groups which had the highest scores on disciplined freedom, all but two had 100 percent of their members believing in God. (These groups included the monasteries, two urban communes, a corps of women cadets, the staff of a boarding school for delinquent children, and a drug rehabilitation center. The last two groups had 73.3 and 16.7 percent believing in God, respectively.)

A continuum of freedom may be proposed, beginning with egoistic freedom, which is purely self-centered and concentrated on the physical world. Conditional freedom is still oriented toward the physical world but is centered on other things and people. Disciplined freedom, like egoistic freedom, is oriented toward the self, but for an entirely different reason. The theme of disciplined freedom is sacrifice and sharing. Taking a cue from the extremely high scores for disciplined freedom achieved by monks (Hillery et al.), the proposition is advanced that true disciplined freedom is centered on spiritual truth, which for the monks studied here means Jesus Christ. The monk disciplines his self in order that he may attain the freedom that Christ offers.

We have now the ingredients for another contingency table (see Figure 18.5). One axis concerns orientation to self, the other concerns orientation toward the physical or spiritual world. The table reveals that disciplined freedom is but a means to an end — unconditional freedom: for the monks, that type which is oriented outward from the self and toward Christ in an ideal-typical sense. This is the freedom of which theologians and mystics speak when they say that he who has the mind of Christ can do as he pleases. (See for example Luther in Dewey and Gould; the common source is probably St. Augustine: "Love, and do what you will.")

FIGURE 18.5
Types of Freedom

Orientation to world:

		Physical	Spiritual
	Inward	Egoistic	Disciplined
Orientation to self			
	Outward	Conditional	Unconditional

The importance of love and freedom to communal organizations may be used to expand the ideas presented in terms of a general taxonomy of human groups. Assistance may be received here from the work of William J. Goode, who has proposed "four great social control systems in all societies" — force (or power), wealth, prestige, and love (see also Warren). The hypothesis has now been raised that considerations of love (and freedom) are not entirely relevant to formal organizations. Nevertheless, it follows, from the nature of the goals of formal organizations, that force, wealth, and prestige are *quite* pertinent mechanisms of social control for these kinds of groups. Two extreme systems of control may be postulated. At one extreme, systems are operated purely in terms of power, wealth, and prestige. At the other extreme, the systems are operated purely in terms of love and freedom. Most groups have a mixture of both forms, but there are differing emphases. Formal organizations tend toward the use of power, prestige, and wealth. Communal organizations tend toward the use of freedom and love. We are not saying that communal organizations are all sweetness and light. Love and freedom are conditions which communal organizations *tend* to use, whereas formal organizations *tend* to use the other types. One should never forget that conflict is endemic to human interaction— and probably some form of love.

One may argue, after Emile Durkheim, that a formal organization has its own moral code, as moral for its purposes as those of communal organizations. The formal organization seeks efficiency and justice, whereas the communal organization seeks love and mercy. There is no argument with this position. The argument is rather one of hegemony and dominance. We live in an age heavily controlled by formal organizations, and this means that efficiency and justice (which are impersonal) may often come before love and mercy. To the extent that such dominance prevails, humanity is in a precarious position.

Formal organizations, especially in their ideal-typical sense used here, are not conducive to the welfare of human beings, particularly if they are not mitigated by communal organizations. There is no way to "prove" this statement scientifically, because the word *welfare*—especially if based on love — is not a scientific term. Nevertheless, the depersonalization of formal organizations should now be evident. The only saving grace is that formal organizations are operated by humans, but as numerous scholars since Durkheim have indicated, the human group has an existence sui generis. Formal organizations, for all their seductive utility, can have the power to cause us to act impersonally toward one another, and impersonal behavior is not in the best interest of humanity.

References

Boros, Ladislaus, 1973
Dewey, Robert E., and James A. Gould, 1970
Goode, William J., 1972
Gould, Julius, and William L. Kolb, 1964
Hillery, George A., Jr., 1968, 1971
Hillery, George A., Jr., Charles J. Dudley, and Paula C. Morrow, 1977
Kanter, Rosabeth Moss, 1972
Lewis, C.S., 1960
Nash, Ogden, 1941
Schmalenbach, Herman, 1961
Seashore, Stanley E., 1954
Sorokin, Pitirim A., 1937-41
Warren, Roland L., 1971

Bibliography

Adams, Robert, and Fox, Robert. "Mainlining Jesus: The New Trip." *Society* 9 (February 1972): 50–56.

Adler, N. *The Underground Stream: New Life Styles and the Antinomian Personality.* New York: Harper and Row, 1972.

Anthony, Dick. "The Fact-Pattern Behind the Deprogramming Controversy." *Review of Law and Social Change* 9, in press.

Anthony, Dick, and Robbins, Thomas. "The Effect of Détente on the Growth of New Religions: Reverend Moon and the Unification Church." In *Understanding New Religions,* edited by J. Needleman and G. Baker. New York: Seabury, 1978.

Anthony, Dick; Robbins, Thomas; Doucas, Madeline; and Curtis, Thomas. "Patients and Pilgrims: Changing Attitudes Toward Psychotherapy of Converts to Eastern Mysticism." In *Conversion Careers: In and Out of the New Religions,* edited by J. T. Richardson, pp. 43–64. Beverly Hills, California: Sage, 1978.

Anthony, Dick, and Robbins, Thomas. "A Typology of Nontraditional Religious Movements in Contemporary America." Unpublished paper, 1979.

Anthony, Dick; Robbins, Thomas; and McCarthy, Jim. "Legitimating Repression." *Society* 17, 3 (March/April 1980): 39–42.

Asch, S.E. "Studies of Independence and Conformity: A Minority of One Against a Unanimous Majority." *Psychological Monographs* 70, 9 (1956).

Austin, Roy. "Empirical Adequacy of Lofland's Conversion Model." *Review of Religious Research* 18 (1977). 282–87.

Bednarski, Joyce. "The Salem-Witch Scare Viewed Sociologically." In *Witchcraft and Sorcery,* edited by Max Marwick, pp. 151–63. Baltimore: Penguin Books, 1970.

Bell, D. *The Cultural Contradictions of Capitalism.* New York: Basic Books, 1976.

Bell, D. "Beyond Modernism and Self." In *Art, Politics, and Will: Essays in Honor of Lionel Trilling,* edited by A. Anderson, S. Donadio, and S. Marcus, pp. 213–53. New York: Basic Books, 1977.

Bellah, Robert N. "Christianity and Symbolic Realism." *Journal for the Scientific Study of Religion* (Summer 1970a): 39–96.

Bellah, Robert N. *Beyond Belief: Essays on Religion in a Post-Traditional World.* New York: Harper and Row, 1970b.

Bellah, Robert N. *The Broken Covenant.* New York: Seabury, 1975.

Bellah, Robert N. "New Religious Consciousness and the Crisis in Modernity." In *The New Religious Consciousness,* edited by Charles Y. Glock and Robert N. Bellah, pp. 333–52. Berkeley and Los Angeles: University of California Press, 1976.

Benedictus, Saint. *The Rule of Saint Benedict.* New York: Doubleday Image, 1975. (Originally written c. 525?).

Berger, Bennett. "Review of *The Hippie Trip.*" *Society* 6, 4 (February 1969): 54–56.

Berger, Peter. "Towards a Sociological Understanding of Psychoanalysis." *Social Research* (Spring 1965): 26–41.

Berger, Peter. *The Sacred Canopy.* New York: Doubleday, 1967.

Berger, Peter; Berger, B.; and Kellner, H. *The Homeless Mind: Modernization and Consciousness.* New York: Vintage Books, 1973.

Berger, Peter, and Luckmann, Thomas. *The Social Construction of Reality.* New York: Doubleday, 1966.

Berger, Peter, and Neuhaus, Richard. *Movement and Revolution.* New York: Doubleday, 1970.

Boros, Ladislaus. *We Are Future.* Garden City, N.Y.: Doubleday, Image Books, 1973.

Bromley, David G.; Shupe, Jr., Anson D.; and Ventimiglia, Joseph C. "The Role of Anecdotal Atrocities in the Social Construction of Evil." In *The Deprogramming Controversy: Sociological, Psychological, Legal, and Historical Perspectives,* edited by James T. Richardson. New Brunswick, N.J.: Transaction Books, forthcoming.

Bruyn, Severyn. *The Human Perspective in Sociology.* Englewood Cliffs, N.J.: Prentice-Hall, 1966.

Caplovitz, David. *The Religious Dropouts: Apostasy Among College Graduates.* Beverly Hills: Sage Publications, 1977.

Caplovitz, David, and Sherrow, Fred. *The Religious Drop-Outs.* Beverly Hills: Sage Publications, 1977.

Carroll, Jerry, and Bauer, Bernard. "Suicide Training in the Moon Cult." *New West,* January 29, 1979.

Cartwright, D., and Zander, A. *Group Dynamics.* 3rd ed. New York: Harper and Row, 1968.

Castaneda, C. *Journey to Ixtlan: The Lessons of Don Juan.* New York: Simon & Schuster, 1972.

Chapman, D.W. and Volkmann, J. "A Social Determinant of the Level of Aspiration." *Journal of Abnormal and Social Psychology* 34 (1939): 225–38.

Clark, Elmer T. *The Small Sects in America.* 1st rev. ed. New York: Abingdon-Cokesbury Press, 1949.

Clark, J.G. "Investigating the Effects of Some Religious Cults on the Health and Welfare of their Converts." Statement made before the Vermont Legislative Committee, August 12, 1976.

Clark, W.H. *Chemical Ecstasy: Psychedelic Drugs and Religion.* New York: Sheed and Ward, 1969.

Cohn, Norman, *Pursuit of the Millennium.* 2d ed. New York: Oxford University Press, 1970. (Originally published 1957).

Coleman, John. "Civil Religion." *Sociological Analysis* 31, 2 (1970): 67–77.

Collier, Peter. "Bringing Home the Moonies." *New Times* 18, 12 (June 19, 1977): 25–42.

Cox, H. *Turning East: The Promise and Peril of the New Orientalism.* New York: Simon and Schuster, 1977.

Crenshaw, Richard. "The Hippies: Beyond Pot and Acid." In *Maharishi The Guru,* edited by Marton Ebon, pp. 99–108. New York: New American Library, 1968.

Demerath, Nicholas J. *Social Class in American Protestantism.* Chicago: Rand Mc-Nally, 1965.

Dewey, Robert E., and Gould, James A., eds. *Freedom: Its History, Nature, and Varieties.* New York: Macmillan, 1970.

Dobbelaere, K. "Secularization: A Multidimensional Concept." Mimeographed, 1977.

Doress, Irvin, and Porter, Jack Nusan. *Kids in Cults.* RC Associates, 1980. (Originally published 1977.)

Dunn, J.A.C. "Don't Worry, Be Happy — I Will Help You." *Red Clay Reader.* Charlotte, N.C.: Southern Review, 1968.

Earle, Mary. "A Shift in the Wind." *The Hunger Project Newspaper.* San Francisco, n.d.

Eisenstadt, S.N. *From Generation to Generation.* New York: Free Press, 1956.

Eisenstadt, S.N. "Archetypal Patterns of Youth." In *The Challenge of Youth,* edited by Erik Erikson, pp. 29–50. New York: Doubleday, 1961.

Engels, Frederick. "The Peasant War in Germany." In *Karl Marx and Frederick Engels on Religion*. Edited by Reinhold Niebuhr. New York: Shocken, 1964a. (Originally published 1850).

Engels, Frederick. "The Book of Revelation." In *Karl Marx and Frederick Engels on Religion*. Edited by Reinhold Niebuhr. New York: Shocken, 1964b. (Originally published 1883).

Enroth, Ronald. *Youth, Brainwashing, and the Extremist Cults*. Grand Rapids, Michigan: Zondervan Publishing House, 1977.

Fallding, Harold. *The Sociology of Religion*. Toronto: McGraw-Hill Ryerson, 1974.

Fenn, Richard K. "Toward a New Sociology of Religion." *Journal for the Scientific Study of Religion* 11 (March 1972): 16–32.

Fenn, Richard K. *Toward a Theory of Secularization*. Society for the Scientific Study of Religion. 1978.

Festinger, L. "A Theory of Social Comparison Processes." *Human Relations* 7 (1954): 117–40.

Flacks, Richard. "The Liberated Generation: An Exploration of the Roots of Student Protest." *Journal of Social Issues* (July 1967): 52–75.

Flacks, Richard. "Who Protests: The Social Bases of the Student Movement." In *Protest! Student Activism in America*, edited by Julian Foster and Durwood Long, pp. 134–57. New York: Morrow, 1970a.

Flacks, Richard. "Social and Cultural Meanings of Student Revolt: Some Informal and Comparative Observations." *Social Problems* (Winter 1970b): 340–57.

Frank, J.D. *Persuasion and Healing*. New York: Schocken Books, 1961.

Fromm, Erich. *Psychoanalysis and Religion*. New Haven: Yale University Press, 1950.

Gerlach, Luther, and Hine, Virginia. *People, Power, Change: Movements of Social Transformation*. Indianapolis: Bobbs-Merrill, 1970.

Glaser, Barney G., and Strauss, Anselm L. *The Discovery of Grounded Theory*. Chicago: Aldine, 1968.

Glock, Charles Y. "The Role of Deprivation in the Origin and Evolution of Religious Groups." In *Religion and Social Conflict*, edited by R. Lee and M. Marty, pp. 24–36, 1964.

Glock, Charles Y., and Bellah, Robert N., eds. *The New Religious Consciousness*. Berkeley and Los Angeles: University of California Press, 1976.

Glock, Charles Y., and Stark, Rodney. *Religion and Society in Tension*. Chicago: Rand McNally, 1965.

Glock, Charles Y., and Wuthnow, Robert. "Departures from Conventional Religion: The Nominally Religious, the Non-Religious, and the Alternatively Religious." In *The Religious Dimension: New Directions in the Quantitative Study of Religion*, edited by R. Wuthnow, pp. 47–68. New York: Academic Press, 1979.

Goffman, Erving. *Asylums: Essays on the Social Situations of Mental Patients and Other Inmates*. Garden City, N.Y.: Doubleday Anchor, 1961.

Goode, William J. "Presidential Address: The Place of Force in Human Society." *American Sociological Review* 37 (October 1972): 507–19.

Gordon, David. "The Jesus People: An Identity Snythesis." *Urban Life* 3 (1974): 159–178.

Gould, Julius, and Kolb, William L., eds. *A Dictionary of the Social Sciences*. New York: The Free Press, 1964.

Greeley, Andrew M. "There's a New Religion on Campus." *New York Times Magazine*, June 1, 1969.

Greeley, Andrew M. "Superstition, Ecstasy and Tribal Consciousness." *Social Research* (Summer 1970): 202–11.

Greeley, Andrew M. *Unsecular Man.* New York: Dell, 1972.
Greeley, Andrew M.; McCready, William C.; and McCourt, Kathleen. *Catholic Schools in a Declining Church.* Kansas City: Sheed and Ward, 1976.
Greeley, Andrew M. *Crisis in the Church: A Study of Religion in America.* Chicago: Thomas More Press, 1979.
Greenfield, Meg. "Heart of Darkness." *Newsweek,* December 4, 1978, p. 132.
Gustaitis, Rasa. *Turning On.* New York: Macmillan, 1969.
Habermas, Jurgen. *Legitimation Crisis.* Boston: Beacon, 1973.
Hadden, Jeffrey. *The Gathering Storm in the Churches.* New York: Doubleday, 1969.
Haining, Peter, ed. *The Witch-Craft Papers: Contemporary Records of the Witchcraft Hysteria in Essex 1560–1700.* Secaucus, N.J.: University Books, Inc., 1974.
Hall, John R. *The Ways Out: Utopian Communal Groups in an Age of Babylon.* Boston: Routledge and Keegan Paul, 1978.
Hatch, Nathan O. *The Sacred Cause of Liberty.* New Haven: Yale University Press, 1977.
Heenan, Edward. *Mystery, Magic and Miracle.* Englewood Cliffs, N.J.: Prentice-Hall, 1973.
Heilman, Samuel C. *Synagogue Life.* Chicago: University of Chicago Press, 1976.
Heilman, Samuel C. "Inner and Outer Identities: Sociological Ambivalence among Orthodox Jews." *Jewish Social Studies* 39 (Summer 1977): 227–40.
Helmreich, R.; Stapp, J.; and Ervin, C. The Texas Social Behavior Inventory (TSBI): An Objective Measure of Self-Esteem or Social Competence. *Journal Supplement, Abstract Service Catalog of Selected Documents in Psychology* 4 (1974):79.
Hillery, George A., Jr. *Communal Organizations.* Chicago: University of Chicago Press, 1968.
Hillery, George A., Jr. "Freedom and Social Organization: A Comparative Analysis." *American Sociological Review* 36 (February 1971): 51–65.
Hillery, George A., Jr.; Dudley, Charles J.; and Morrow, Paula C. "Towards a Sociology of Freedom." *Social Forces* 3 (March 1977): 685–700.
Hoffer, E. *The True Believer.* New York: Harper and Row, 1951.
Holy Spirit Association for the Unification of World Christianity. *Divine Principle.* New York: HSA–UNC, 1973.
Horowitz, Irving Louis. "Science, Sin and Scholarship." *The Atlantic* (March 1977).
Horowitz, Irving Louis, ed. *Science, Sin and Scholarship: The Politics of Reverend Moon and the Unification Church.* MIT Press, 1978.
Horowitz, Irving Louis. "Religion and the Rise of the Rev. Moon." *The Nation* 228, 13 (April 7, 1979): 365–67.
Hyman, H.H. "The Psychology of Status." *Archives of Psychology* 269 (1942).
Inkeles, A., and Smith, D.H. *Becoming Modern: Individual Change in Six Developing Countries.* Cambridge, Mass.: Harvard University Press, 1974.
Jacoby, Russell. *Social Amnesia: A Critique of Conformist Psychology from Adler to Laing.* Boston: Beacon Press, 1976.
Johnson, Benton. "The Protestant Elite as a Formative Influence on American Religion." Paper delivered to the Society for the Scientific Study of Religion, Milwaukee, 1975.
Johnson, Benton. "Esame critico della religione liberale negli Stati Uniti." in *Vecchi e Nuovi Dei,* edited by Rocco Caporale, Chapter 19. Torino: Editoriale Valention, 1976. (English title: "A Critical Look at Liberal Protestantism in the United States.")
Jones, Jim. "Perspectives from Guyana." *Peoples Forum,* January 1978. (Reprinted in Krause, Stern, and Harwood [1978, pp. 205–10]).

Judah, J. Stillson. "Programming and Deprogramming." Paper presented to a Conference on Religion, Toronto School of Theology, 1977.

Kanter, Rosabeth Moss. *Commitment and Community.* Cambridge, MA.: Harvard University Press, 1972.

Kaplan, Lawrence. "The Dilemma of Conservative Judaism." *Commentary* 62, 5 (November 1976): 44–47.

Kelley, Dean. "Deprogramming and Religious Liberty." *Civil Liberties Review* 4, 2 (Summer 1977a): 23–33.

Kelley, Dean. *Why the Conservative Churches are Growing.* New York: Harper and Row, 1977b.

Kelley, H.H. "Two Functions of Reference Groups." In *Readings in Social Psychology,* edited by G.E. Swanson, T.M. Newcomb, and E.L. Hartley, pp. 410–14. New York: Hart, 1952.

Keniston, Kenneth. "Heads and Seekers." *American Scholar* (Winter 1968): 97–113.

Keniston, Kenneth. *All Our Children: The American Family Under Pressure.* New York: Harcourt, Brace, and World. 1977.

Kilduff, Marshall, and Javers, Ron. *The Suicide Cult: The Inside Story of the People's Temple Sect and the Massacre in Guyana.* New York: Bantam, 1978.

Kim, Byong Suh. "Religious Deprogramming and Subjective Reality." *Sociological Analysis* 40, 3 (Fall 1979): 197–207.

Kotre, John. *View from the Border: A Social Psychological Study of Current Catholicism.* Chicago: Aldine, 1971.

Kramer, Heinrich, and Sprenger, James. *Malleus Maleficarem (Witches' Hammer).* Translated by Montague Summers. New York: Dover Publications, 1971 (Originally published in 1486 and reprinted in 1928.)

Krause, Charles, Stern, Lawrence M., and Harwood, Richard. *Guyana Massacre: The Eye Witness Account.* New York: Berkeley Books, 1978.

Laing, R.D. *The Politics of Experience.* New York: Ballantine Books, 1967.

Lasch, Christopher. "Collective Narcissism." *New York Review of Books,* October 12, 1976.

Lasch, Christopher. *The Culture of Narcissism.* New York: Norton, 1979.

Leary, Timothy. *The Politics of Ecstasy.* New York: Putnam, 1968.

Lerner, Michael P. "*est* and Powerlessness." *Radical Therapy* 3.

Lewis, C.S. *The Four Loves.* New York: Harcourt Brace Javanovich, 1960.

Lewy, Gunther. *Religion and Revolution.* New York: Oxford University Press, 1974.

Liebman, C. "Orthodoxy in American Jewish Life." *American Jewish Yearbook* 66 (1965): 21–92.

Lifton, Robert J. *Chinese Thought Reform and the Psychology of Totalism.* New York: Norton, 1961.

Lifton, Robert J. *Revolutionary Immortality: Mao Tse-Tung and the Chinese Cultural Revolution.* New York: Vintage, 1968.

Lipset, S.M. *Rebellion in the University.* Boston: Little, Brown, 1972.

Lofland, John, and Stark, Rodney. "Becoming a World-Saver." *American Sociological Review* 30 (1965): 862–74.

Lofland, John. *Doomsday Cult.* Rev. ed. New York: Irvington, 1978.

Luckmann, Thomas. *The Invisible Religion.* New York: Macmillan, 1967.

Lynn, Robert Wood. "Civil Catechetics in Mid-Victorian America: Some Notes about American Civil Religion, Past and Present." *Religious Education* 68, 1 (1973): 5–27.

Macfarlane, A.D.J. *Witchcraft in Tudor and Stuart England.* New York: Routledge and Kegan Paul, 1970.

Malcolm, G. *Generation of Narcissus*. Boston: Little, Brown & Co., 1971.

Marin, Peter. "The New Narcissism." *Harper's,* October 1975.

Marx, John, and Ellison, David. "Sensitivity Training and Communes: Contemporary Quests for Community." *Pacific Sociological Review* 18 (1965): 442–60.

Marx, Karl, and Engels, Friederick. "Manifesto of the Communist Party." In *Marx and Engels: Basic Writings on Politics and Philosophy*. Edited by Lewis S. Fewer. Garden City, N.Y.: Doubleday Anchor, 1959. (Originally published 1848).

Maslow, A. *Toward a Psychology of Being*. New York: D. Van Nostrand, 1962.

Maslow, A. *Religions, Values and Peak-Experiences*. New York: Viking, 1970.

Mather, Cotton. *On Witchcraft (Wonders of the Invisible World)*. New York: Bell Publishing Co., 1974. (Originally published in 1962).

McCready, William C., with Andrew M. Greeley. *The Ultimate Values of the American Population*. Beverly Hills, California: Sage Publications, 1976.

Mead, Sidney E. *The Nation with the Soul of a Church*. New York: Harper and Row, 1975.

Meher, Baba *God in a Pill?* San Francisco: Sufism Reoriented, 1966.

Meher, Baba. *Discourses*. 3 vols. Ahmedegar, India: Adi K. Irani, 1967.

Miller, Perry. *The Life of the Mind in America*. New York: Harcourt, Brace, and World, 1965.

Moberg, David. "Prison Camp of the Mind." *In These Times,* December 13, 1978, pp. 11–14.

Nash, Ogden. *The Face is Familiar*. Garden City, N.Y.: Garden City Publishing Company, 1941.

National Ad Hoc Committee Engaged in Freeing Minds (CEFM). *A Special Report on The Unification Church: Its Activities and Practices*. Vols. 1 and 2. Arlington, Texas: National Ad Hoc Committee, A Day of Affirmation and Protest, 1976.

Needleman, Jacob. *The New Religions*. Garden City, N.Y.: Doubleday, 1970.

Needleman, Jacob. *A Sense of the Cosmos*. New York: Doubleday, 1975.

Nisbet, Robert. *The Quest for Community*. New York: Oxford, 1953.

Nord, Walter. "A Marxist Critique of Humanistic Psychology." *Journal of Humanistic Psychology* 17 (Winter 1977).

Ogilvy, Jay. "Personalizing Politics: Politicizing the Self." *Journal of Humanistic Psychology* 1, 17 (Winter 1977).

Ornstein, Robert. *The Mind Field*. New York: Viking, 1976.

Parruci, D.J. "Religious Conversions: A Theory of Deviant Behavior." *Sociological Analysis* 29 (1968): 144–154.

Parsons, Talcott. *The Structure of Social Action*. New York: McGraw-Hill, 1937.

Parsons, Talcott. *The Social System*. Glencoe, Ill.: The Free Press, 1951.

Patrick, Ted, and Dulack, Tom. *Let Our Children Go!* New York: Ballantine Books, 1976.

Peacock, James L. "Mystics and Merchants in Fourteenth Century Germany." *Journal for the Scientific Study of Religion* (Spring 1968): 47–59.

Perry, W.N. "Cults of Unreason." *Studies in Comparative Religion* 9, 3 (Summer 1975): 183.

Rasmussen, Mark. "Promising People the Moon: A View From the Inside." *State and Mind* (November–December 1977): 11–15.

Reich, Charles A. *The Greening of America*. New York: Random House, 1970.

Richardson, James T. *Conversion Careers: In and Out of New Religions*. Beverly Hills: Sage, 1978.

Richardson, James T., and Simmonds, Robert. "Thought Reform and the Jesus Movement." *Youth and Society* 4 (1972): 185–200.

Richardson, James T.; Stewart, Mary W.; and Simmonds, Robert B. *Organized Miracles: A Study of a Contemporary, Youth, Communal, Fundamentalist Organization*. New Brunswick, N.J.: Transaction Books, 1979.

Rieff, Philip. "The Impossible Culture." *The Soul of Man Under Socialism*, by Oscar Wilde. New York: Harper and Row, 1970.

Robbins, Thomas. "Eastern Mysticism and the Resocialization of Drug Users." *Journal for the Scientific Study of Religion* (Fall 1969): 1308–17.

Robbins, Thomas. "Characteristics of Amphetamine Addicts." *International Journal of Addictions* (Summer 1970): 183–93.

Robbins, Thomas. "Even a Moonie Has Civil Rights." *The Nation*, February 26, 1977, pp. 233–42.

Robbins, Thomas, and Anthony, Dick. "Cults, Brainwashing and Counter-Subversion." *Annals of The American Academy of Political and Social Science* 446 (November 1979): 78–90.

Robbins, Thomas; Anthony, Dick; Doucas, Madeline; and Curtis, Thomas. "The Last Civil Religion: Reverend Moon and the Unification Church." *Sociological Analysis* 37 (Summer 1976): 111–25.

Robbins, Thomas; Anthony, Dick; and Richardson, James. "Theory and Research on Today's New Religions." *Sociological Analysis* 39, 2 (1978): 95–122.

Roof, W. Clark. *Community and Commitment: Religious Plausibility in a Liberal Protestant Church*. New York: Elsevier, 1978.

• Roof, W. Clark. "Traditional Religion and Contemporary Society." *American Sociological Review*. 41, 2 (April 1976): 195–208.

Rosen, R.D. *Psycho-Bable*. New York: Atheneum, 1977.

Roszak, T. *The Making of a Counter Culture*. Garden City, N.Y.: Doubleday, 1969.

Sage, W. "The War on the Cults." *Human Behavior* (October 1976): 40–49.

Satin, Mark. *New Age Politics: Healing Self and Society*. West Vancouver: Whitecap Books, 1978.

Schaps, Eric, and Sanders, Clinton R. "Purposes, Patterns and Protection in a Campus Drug-Using Community. *Journal of Health and Social Behavior* (June 1970): 134–45.

Schein, Edgar. *Coercive Persuasion*. New York: W.W. Norton, 1961.

Schmalenbach, Herman. "The Sociological Category of Communion." In *Theories of Society*, edited by Talcott Parsons et al., pp. 331–347. New York: The Free Press of Glencoe, 1961.

Schur, Edwin. *The Awareness Trap: Self-Absorption Instead of Social Change*. New York: McGraw-Hill, 1976.

Scott, Reginald. *The Discoverie of Witchcraft*. Yorkshire, England: Rowman and Littlefield, 1973. (Originally published in 1584).

Seashore, Stanley E. *Group Cohesiveness in the Industrial Work Group*. Ann Arbor: Survey Research Center, Institute for Social Research, University of Michigan, 1954.

Sennett, Richard. *The Fall of Public Man*. New York: Knopf, 1977.

Sherif, M. *The Psychology of Social Norms*. New York: Harper, 1936.

Shupe, Jr. Anson, D.; Spielmann, Roger; and Stigall, Sam. "Deprogramming: The New Exorcism." *American Behavioral Scientist* (July/August 1977): 441–56.

Shupe, Jr. Anson, D., Spielmann, Roger, and Stigall, Sam. "Cults of Anti-Cultism." *Society* 17, 3 (March/April 1980): 43–46.

Siegel, A.E., and Siegel, S. "Reference Groups, Membership Groups, and Attitude Change." *Journal of Abnormal and Social Psychology* 55 (1957): 360–64.

Singer, M.T. "Brainwashing 1977." Paper read at a symposium held at the John Muir Hospital in Walnut Creek, California, May 21, 1977.

Slater, Philip. *The Pursuit of Loneliness.* Boston: Beacon Press, 1970.

Sklar, Dusty. *Gods and Beasts: The Nazis and the Occult.* New York: Thomas Y. Crowell, Publishers, 1977.

Solomon, T., and Pines, A. "Brainwashing and Psychotherapy: The Case of Children in Residential Treatment." Paper presented at the meetings of the Western Psychological Association, Seattle, April 1977.

Sorokin, Pitirim A. *Social and Cultural Dynamics.* 4 vols. New York:American Book Company, 1937–41.

Stark, Rodney. "Class Radicalism and Religious Involvement in Great Britain." *American Sociological Review* 29 (1964): 698–706.

Stone, Donald. "The Human Potential Movement." In *The New Religious Consciousness,* edited by Charles Y. Glock and Robert N. Bellah, pp. 93–115. Berkeley and Los Angeles: University of California Press, 1976.

Stone, Donald. "New Religious Consciousness and Personal Religious Experience." *Sociological Analysis* 39 (1978): 123–34.

Stoner, Carroll, and Parke, Jo-Ann. *All God's Children: The Cult Experience, Salvation or Slavery?* Radnor, Pa.: Chilton, 1977.

Szasz, Thomas. *The Manufacture of Madness: A Comparative Study of the Inquisition and the Mental Health Movement.* New York: Harper and Row, 1970.

Tipton, S. *Getting Saved from the Sixties: The Transformation of Moral Meaning in American Culture by Alternative Religious Movements.* Berkeley and Los Angeles: University of California Press, 1979.

Toch, Hans. *The Social Psychology of Social Movements.* Indianapolis: Bobbs-Merrill, 1965.

Townshend, Peter. "Loving Meher Baba." *Rolling Stone* (November 1970): 24–27.

Thibaut, J.W., and Kelley, Harold. *The Social Psychology of Groups.* New York: Wiley, 1959.

Thung, M. *The Precarious Organization: Sociological Explorations of the Church's Mission and Structure.* The Hague: Mouton, 1976.

Troeltsch, E. *The Social Teaching of the Christian Churches.* New York: Harper and Row, 1960.

Trine, Ralph Waldo. *In Tune with the Infinite.* New York: Thomas Y. Crowell, Publishers, 1897.

Vachon, Brian. "The Jesus Movement Is upon Us." *Look* (February 1971): 15–21.

Veroff, Joseph. "Americans Seek Self-Development, Suffer Anxiety from Changing Roles." *Institute for Social Research Newsletter* 7, 1 (Winter 1979): 4–5.

Von Hoffman, Nicholas. *We Are the People Our Parents Warned Us Against.* Chicago: Quadrangle, 1968.

Warren, Roland L. *Truth, Love, and Social Change.* Chicago: Rand McNally, 1971.

Weber, Max. *The Sociology of Religion.* Boston: Beacon Press, 1964.

Weber, Max. *Economy and Society.* Edited by G. Roth and Claus Wittich. Berkeley and Los Angeles: University of California Press, 1977. (Originally published 1922).

White, Richard. "Toward a Theory of Religious Influence." *Pacific Sociological Review* 11 (1968): 23–28.

Wolfe, Tom. "The Me Decade and the Third Great Awakening." *New West,* August 30, 1976.

Wuthnow, Robert. "New Forms of Religion in the Seminary." In *Religion in Sociological Perspective: Essays in the Empirical Study of Religion,* edited by Charles Y. Glock, pp. 187–203. Belmont, California: Wadsworth, 1973.

Wuthnow, Robert. *The Consciousness Reformation*. Berkeley and Los Angeles: University of California Press, 1976a.

Wuthnow, Robert. "Recent Pattern of Secularization: A Problem of Generations?" *American Sociological Review* 41 (October 1976b): 850–67.

Wuthnow, Robert. *Experimentation in American Religion: The New Mysticisms and Their Implications for the Churches*. Berkeley and Los Angeles: University of California Press, 1978a.

Wuthnow, Robert. "Peak Experiences: Some Empirical Tests." *Journal of Humanistic Psychology* 18 (1978b): 59–75.

Wuthnow, Robert, and Glock, Charles Y. "Religious Loyalty, Defection, and Experimentation among College Youth." *Journal for the Scientific Study of Religion* 12 (1973): 157–80.

Wuthnow, Robert, and Glock, Charles Y. "The Shifting Focus of Faith: A Survey Report." *Psychology Today* 8 (1974): 131–36.

Wuthnow, Robert, and Mellinger, G. "Religious Loyalty, Defection, and Experimentation: A Longitudinal Analysis of University Men." *Review of Religious Research* 19 (1978): 234–45.

Yablonsky, Lewis. *The Hippie Trip*. New York: Pegasus, 1968.

Yamamoto, J. Isamu. *The Puppet Master: An Inquiry into Sun Myung Moon and the Unification Church*. Downers Grove, Illinois: Intervarsity Press, 1977.

Yankelovich, Daniel. *The New Morality: A Profile of American Youth in the Seventies*. New York: McGraw-Hill, 1974.

Zerubavel, Eviatar. "The Benedictine Ethic and the Spirit of Scheduling." Paper read at the meetings of the International Society for the Comparative Study of Civilizations, Milwaukee, Wisconsin, April 1978.

Contributors

Dick Anthony is a psychologist of religion who is research coordinator for the Program for the Study of New Religions at the Graduate Theological Union in Berkeley. He has published numerous articles on contemporary religion, and he is the coauthor (with Robert Bellah and Thomas Robbins) of a monograph, *On Religion and Social Science.* University of California Press, forthcoming.

Robert N. Bellah is Ford professor of sociology and comparative studies at the University of California at Berkeley. He is the author of *Beyond Belief* (1970), *Emile Durkheim on Morality and Society* (1973), *The Broken Covenant* (1975), and is coeditor (with Charles Y. Glock) of *The New Religious Consciousness* (1976). He is interested in the comparative sociology of religion with emphasis on Japan and the United States.

David G. Bromley is chairman of the sociology department at the University of Hartford. He is coauthor (with Anson D. Shupe, Jr.) of two related monographs — *The Moonies in America: Church, Sect and Cult*, and *The New Vigilantes: A Study of the Anti-Cult Movement.* His research interests include deviance, and political and urban sociology

Irvin Doress is an associate professor of educational counseling at Northeastern University in Boston and is a trained psychotherapist and family counselor. He is also the father of a child in the Hare Krishna society.

Charles Y. Glock is professor emeritus of sociology at the University of California at Berkeley. Professor Glock is presently researching the cognitive dimensions of race prejudice in American society. He is the author, with Rodney Stark, of *Religion and Society in Tension.*

Andrew M. Greeley is a professor of sociology at the University of Arizona and a study director at the National Opinion Research Center. Father Greeley is a sociologist, a journalist, and a Catholic priest. His syndicated column is read in more than 80 newspapers. His recent catechism, *The Great Mysteries,* has become a best-seller in the United States. Other of his recent books include *The Mary Myth: On the Femininity of God* and *The American Catholic: A Social Portrait.*

John R. Hall is an assistant professor of sociology at the University of Missouri at Columbia. He has done field research on a psychiatric therapeutic community, migrant farm workers, and on secular and religious communal groups. His theoretical interests include the relation between substantive Weberian sociological analysis and the social phenomenology of Alfred Schutz. Dr. Hall is the author of *The Ways Out: Utopian Communal Groups in an Age of Babylon.*

Samuel C. Heilman is associate professor of sociology at Queens College of the City University of New York. He is the author of *Synagogue Life: A Study in Symbolic Interaction* as well as of numerous articles on such wide-ranging topics as face-to-face almsgiving among Orthodox Jews, identity, and the social functions of gossip. He is currently at work on a book exploring the contemporary condition of modern American Jewish Orthodoxy.

George A. Hillery, Jr. is professor of sociology at Virginia Polytechnic Institute and State University. His major area of interest is community theory. He is the author of *Communal Organizations,* and at present he is working on a monograph, "Freedom and Community: A Sociological Study of Trappist Monks."

Irving Louis Horowitz is Hannah Arendt distinguished professor of sociology and political science at Rutgers University and editor-in-chief of *Society* magazine. His most recent writings include *Taking Lives: Genocide and State Power,* 3rd ed., and, with Seymour Martin Lipset, *Dialogues on American Politics.*

Benton Johnson is chairman of the sociology department at the University of Oregon and
president of the Society for the Scientific Study of Religion. He is former editor of
the *Journal for the Scientific Study of Religion*. Professor Johnson has published
numerous articles on sectarianism and secularization.

Thomas Piazza is a data analyst at the Survey Research Center of the University of
California at Berkeley. He is completing a doctoral dissertation in sociology at
Berkeley on the social sources of feminism.

Jack Nusan Porter is a Boston-based sociologist, writer, and editor. He has taught
Jewish theology at Boston College; Jewish history at Emerson College; and general
sociology courses at DePaul, SUNY-Cortland, and elsewhere. He is coeditor of
Jewish Radicalism and *The Sociology of American Jewry*.

James T. Richardson is professor of sociology at the University of Nevada at Reno. He is
coauthor (with Robert Simmonds and Mary White Stewart) of *Organized Miracles*
(Transaction Books, 1979), a longitudinal study of a communal Jesus movement
group. He has edited also two anthologies of papers on new religious movements—
Conversion Careers, and ''Brainwashing,'' *Society* (March/April 1980).

Thomas Robbins is a sociologist of religion who has taught at Queens College. He is a
postdoctoral fellow in the sociology department at Yale. Dr. Robbins has published
numerous articles on ''new religions,'' including several on the legal and civil-
liberties issues involved in the social control of deviant sects.

Wade Clark Roof is professor of sociology at the University of Massachusetts at
Amherst. He is the author of the book, *Community and Commitment: Religious
Plausibility in a Liberal Protestant Church*. Professor Roof is executive secretary
of the Society for the Scientific Study of Religion.

Anson D. Shupe, Jr. is an associate professor of sociology at the University of Texas at
Arlington. He is coauthor (with David Bromley) of two complementary monographs that deal with the growth of the Unification church in America and societal
response to it.

Robert B. Simmonds is an associate professor of sociology at the State University of New
York at Cortland. He is coauthor (with James T. Richardson and Mary White
Stewart) of *Organized Miracles: A Study of a Contemporary, Youth, Communal,
Fundamentalist Organization* (Transaction Books, 1979).

Trudy Solomon is a social psychologist who is currently a policy analyst for the Division
of Policy Research and Analysis of the National Science Foundation in
Washington, D.C. She has published a number of articles and chapters in books on
law and psychology.

Mary White Stewart is an associate professor of sociology at the University of Missouri
at Kansas City. She is coauthor (with James T. Richardson and Robert B.
Simmonds) of *Organized Miracles: A Study of a Contemporary, Youth, Communal, Fundamentalist Organization* (Transaction Books, 1979).

Donald Stone is a research associate in the Program for the Study of New Religions at the
Graduate Theological Union in Berkeley. He is completing his doctoral dissertation
in sociology on the human potential movement.

Robert Wuthnow is an associate professor of sociology and director of the Program in
Science in Human Affairs at Princeton University. He is the author of *Experimenta-
tion in American Religion* and is the editor of *The Religious Dimension: New
Directions in Quantitative Research*.

1129